Dalits Development and Change

An Empirical Study

Dalits Development and Change

An Empirical Study

By

Dr. R.P. Mohanty

Nabakrushna Choudhury,
for Development Studies
Orissa

D P H

DISCOVERY PUBLISHING HOUSE
NEW DELHI-110002

First Published-2003
Reprinted - 2014
ISBN 978-81-7141-696-7

Published by

DISCOVERY PUBLISHING HOUSE
4831/24, Ansari Road, Prahlad Street,
Darya Ganj, New Delhi-110002 (India)
Phone: 23279245 • Fax: 91-11-23253475
E-mail:dphtemp@indiatimes.com

Printed at: Dynamic Printers, Delhi

FOREWORD

Since time immemorial, social inequality has been the bane of Indian society. Often manifesting as a hydra-headed curse, this phenomenon has somehow been woven inextricably into the country's social fabric. The omnipresence of this multifaceted inequality in most human societies is indisputable; notwithstanding, one has to accept the harsh truism that in Indian society it is invariably rigid, and at times irreversible. It reflects innate differences in socio-cultural abilities, power, wealth and status among individuals, groups and communities. Indian society, being a plural one, intrinsically includes a vast multitude of communities, which occupy different strata in its social hierarchy. Despite these communities being fundamentally disparate, they are mutually interdependent and bound up functionally. One notices that both the factors of attraction and repulsion govern human society. It is common knowledge that during vedic times Indian society was more or less homogeneous and the caste system had not evolved. Later on the caste system evolved and engulfed the Indian society as a whole. Originally conceived as a loose demarcation of people, according to their pecuniary occupations, into the four fundamental varnas—Brahman, Kshatria, Vaishya and Shudra; the caste system soon burgeoned from its inchoate state to become a system with several obscure sub-divisions. However, the purportedly 'philistine' Scheduled Tribes were not initially accorded a place in the caste system, or for that matter, even in orthodox caste society. In due course of time, due to the constraints of functionality, these local exterior and external groups were appended to caste society, in order to render various services. These communities, often viewed as being alien to orthodox Hindu society, were referred to as '*Ashprushya*' or untouchables. However, over the years, they became integral, if peripheral, parts of the Hindu society.

The list of problems and dilemmas that are intrinsic to the problem of social inequality is seemingly interminable, and untouchability is just one of the afore-mentioned issues. These communities, effectively ostracized by the elite of Hindu society, were designated with the rather pejorative appellations of '*Ashprushya*' or '*Achhut*'. They were allotted very lowly and despicable occupations by the higher castes. On the basis of their occupations, they were differentiated into several sub-categories, which also practised relative discrimination amongst themselves. Therefore, there was, and there still is, the vital factor of social hierarchy and parochial discrimination amongst them. In other words, their hierarchical ranks in the social order of the Indian society are indicative of social and cultural bigotry. When the British occupied India and established their colonial rule, for political and strategic reasons they kept these communities as comprising a separate category of the Indian population. They pioneered the novel nomenclature "Scheduled Caste" with the desired effect of designating them as a distinct block of people, taking cognizance of their exploitation by the higher castes in India. As a challenge to this British policy, which was viewed inimically by the general population, Gandhiji made a very sensible attempt to wipe out the social stigma of untouchability. Following the Gujarati saint Narasiṃha Mehta, he considered the Dalits as the children of God or Hari, and thus gave them the epithet of Harijan (child of god).

The modern leaders of the Dalit communities today resent being designated as 'Harijans', and prefer to be referred to as Dalits, or the depressed categories of people. The Indian Constitution designates them as 'Scheduled Castes', and guarantees a number of protective measures in order to ensure justice; social, economic and political to these people. It also bestows on them liberty of thought, expression, belief, faith and worship; equality of status and opportunities. The protective measures have been provided to them in order to ameliorate their status, and bring them up to the level of advanced communities of Indian society, through socio-economic development. The government of India has enacted laws to eliminate the practice of untouchability in any form from the public life of Indian society. Since independence a number of welfare measures are being operated for their benefit. Consequently the government has sought to bring about changes in the social status and economy of these communities; however, the efficacy of these measures remains to be proven and it is only a minuscule minority who have been emancipated from the yoke of untouchability.

The present study has been carried out among the *Bhoi* or *Bauris*, a Scheduled Caste community in the Bhubaneswar sub-division of the Khurda district of Orissa. Traditionally this community comprised the agricultural labour of the landholding caste groups in their place of residence. The study has been carried out in two adjoining community development blocks of the Bhubaneswar sub-division. The *Bhois*, being destitute and penurious, have traditionally been forced to take recourse to consuming unholy food materials, such as oysters, frogs and snails etc. These organisms might be considered as gourmet delicacies in countries such as France, but the Brahmin community abhors them. The *Bhoi* enjoyed a relatively higher status among the various Scheduled Caste communities of Orissa, as their caste calling was ritually pure.

The study is a comparative one, where *Bhois* of two different blocks have been studied and compared from the viewpoint of progress and development. *Bhois* residing in multi-caste Hindu villages have been selected for the study. From the study, one can infer that the *Bhois* of the village that is proximal to Bhubaneswar city have registered faster development. Those that are relatively far away suffer from a tardy and indolent pace of development. The *Bhois* of the Bhubaneswar block have better awareness about the various development projects and are well informed about the procedures for deriving benefits. The *Bhois* residing in far off villages have a very limited knowledge about socio-economic development projects and thus have not been able to articulate their grievances, to the development agencies and the government, effectively. The study indicates that proximity to the city and exposure to an urban milieu have a great impact on the development process.

It is needless to dilate on the fact that the villages under study have certain constant features that are common, and several variable factors such as proximity, exposure, mass media and interaction with urban forces have contributed to the development process. The author of the study has appropriately designed the same, and has tested certain hypotheses. He concludes that the degree of exposure of the beneficiaries is directly linked to the level of amelioration that they are able to achieve. Moreover, exposure to an urban environment and its concomitant milieu facilitates better communication and articulation of the beneficiaries, with development agencies and facilitators.

This pellucid study is extremely impressive from the point of view of planned economic development. The book has attempted to explicate several extant abstruse conundrums in a limpid manner, as well as posing several critical questions of its own. I am sure that the book will be of immense help to the development planners, executives, academicians, researchers, implementers of welfare measures and providers of services to the downtrodden.

Prof. N.K. BEHURA
Professor Emeritus, and at present
Honorary Fellow in Social Anthropology,
NKC Centre for Development Studies
(ICSSR Research Institute)
Orissa, Bhubaneswar.

PREFACE

The Scheduled Castes who are otherwise known as Dalits are one of the most disadvantaged sections of the Indian population. They do not find any place in the varna order of caste Hindu social hierarchy. Traditionally they were being considered as the fifth-born or panchama and referred to as asprushya or untouchables and, therefore, they were very prone to social discrimination, cultural deprivation and economic exploitation by the larger mass of the Hindu communities.

After independence of India, their broader interests are protected through various constitutional legislations, safeguards and economic provisions and special care is taken by both the state and union governments to bring them into the mainstream at par with the caste Hindus. More specifically the Constitution of India laid down a protective action plan vide Article 46 under the Directive Principles of state policies in part iv of the Constitution that manifests that,... 'the state shall promote with special care the educational and economic interests of the weaker sections of the people, in particular the Scheduled Castes and Scheduled Tribes and shall protect them from social injustice and all forms of exploitation'. With a view to executing this, the President of India is empowered to appoint a commission to look after the conditions of the Scheduled Castes and the Scheduled Tribes and submit its report to him from time to time.

By this time India has gone through nine Five-Year Plans and a couple of annual plans and crores of rupees have been spent for their economic development. In order to find out the extent of impact of various government plans and programmes, especially the poverty alleviation programmes, two caste Hindu villages; one nearer to Bhubaneswar city, the state capital of Orissa, and the other one away from this city, have been studied. The Dalits, particularly the Bauri households of each village have been divided into two groups as beneficiary and non-beneficiary and comparison has been made between the beneficiary households and also between the non-beneficiary households of these two villages.

This book contains a total number of seven chapters. The first chapter provides a sound theoretical backdrop and explains the methodological part of the study. Specifically it explains about the occupational basis of caste, and the Dalits, status of the Dalits through ages, and the history of social movement, protective discrimination etc. The next chapter speaks about the social structure, inter-caste relationship between Dalits and caste Hindus and also between the Bauris and other Dalit communities, persistence of untouchability etc. The third chapter explains about the constitutional safeguards, process of development, planning for the welfare of the Dalits in general and the Bauris in particular. It deals with the poverty alleviation programmes, funding agencies, mechanism of fund sanctioned to the Bauri beneficiaries etc. The fourth chapter discusses about the educational changes, occupational mobility, income level, expenditure pattern, indebtedness and the status of asset acquisition among the Bauri households. The succeeding chapter focuses on the constitutional impact on various aspects that have occurred due to the development planning and forces of modernisation. The sixth chapter explains about the quality of life in relation to the settlement pattern, changing dietary habits, changing concept of health and hygiene, use of modern dress materials, changing food habits and development of ability for self management. The last or the concluding chapter summarizes the findings of the study.

During the course of conduction of this research work I have received a lot of help and co-operation from a number of persons at different stages of the study. However, first of all I would like to express my gratitude and indebtedness to my teacher Prof. N.K. Behura, who has rendered his valuable guidance, personal attention, wholehearted co-operation as and when required during the entire course of investigation and preparation of the draft of this book in spite of his many unavoidable professional and personal engagements.

I express my deep sense of gratitude to Dr. Prafulla Chakrabarty, Professor of Sociology, Sociological Research Unit, Indian Statistical Institute, Kolkata, for his noble guidance and suggestions in data processing, compilation and analysis under the programme of 'Guidance and Consultancy in Data Processing', a scheme of Indian Council of Social Science Research (ICSSR), New Delhi, at Indian Statistical Institute, Kolkata. I am also indebted to Shri P. Nayak, former lecturer in Social Statistics, N.C. Centre for Development Studies, Orissa, and at present Director, Marketing Research, Ministry of Textiles, Govt. of India, for his suggestions and help in statistical calculations.

I would like to render my thanks to the block and bank officials, without whose help this work would not have been completed in time.

Finally I feel highly elated to express my sincere thanks and indebtedness to the inhabitants of the study villages, especially Magu Behera, Jagannath Das, Batu Behera, Fakir Behera, Shanti Dei, Nakhi Dei etc. who, despite their daily busy routine, had helped me in many respects.

Lastly I am very grateful to Shri S.P. Mishra of ACE Business Communications for having composed the manuscript in computer and prepared the tables and the graphics.

I hope that this book will be very useful to the researchers, academicians, administrators, action planners, NGO activists, banking institutions and all those who are interested in development studies among the Dalits and other backward communities of the Indian states.

—RAMESH P. MOHANTY

CONTENTS

GLOSSARY

Aai	:	Mother's Mother
Achhuān	:	Untouchable Castes
Adivāsi	:	Scheduled Tribe
Ajā	:	Mother's Father
A-jāti	:	Non-*jāti* or caste which is not included in the *Jāti* organisation or one who has been outcasted or illegitimate for caste point of view.
A-nārya	:	Non-*Arya* or those who are not considered as *Arya* (the members of the fifth *Varna*).
Antyaja	:	Last-born or those who belong to the fifth *varna*.
Apā	:	Elder sister.
Asthaprahari	:	Ritual that concerns the Lord Krishna. It is observed for 8-*Prahars* or hours continuously.
A-Varna/A-Savarna	:	Non-*Varna* or those who are not included in *Chatur Varna* organisation or one who does not belong to the first four *varnas*.
Bāboo	:	Gentlemen
Bada-Osā	:	Great ritual fasting on the day before the full-moon day of the Hindu month of *Kārtic* (October-November).
Badhei	:	Carpenter
Bāuri	:	Conch Shell blower and agricultural labourer who belong to the fifth *Varna* and hence are treated as untouchable.
Bhāi	:	Brother
Bhandāri	:	Barber

Bhoodan	:	Voluntary donation of land
Bidi	:	An indigenous smoke i.e., tobacco rolled in *Kendu* (Diospyrosm tovoxylon) leaf.
Bindi	:	An indigenous decorative item used on forehead of girls.
Brahmā	:	One of the three important Hindu deities who is considered to have created the universe.
Brāhman	:	Priest/Member of the highest *Varna*/ caste
Brundābati	:	One of the important Hindu deities worshipped in the form of a sacred plant called *Tulasi* (basil) in a decorated earthen platform in front of the house or inside the inner courtyard of Hindu households
Chāhāli	:	Traditional non-formal educational institution in a village.
Chamār	:	Toddy brewer
Chāridesha (or Sāgar)	:	The traditional intra-caste or inter-caste political organisation at the regional level.
Chasā	:	Members of agricultural caste.
Chaurā	:	Decorated earthen platform in which the sacred plant, *Tulasi* (basil plant) is worshipped (synonymous to *Brundābati*).
Chausthi-Yogini Temple	:	Temple of sixty-four different forms of goddess *Durgā*.
Dalit	:	Ex-Untouchables (Scheduled Castes) of Indian Societies.
Dashaharā	:	Annual festive occasion of killing the notorious ten-headed idol-evilman called *Ravana* by goddess *Durgā*.
Dharma-bandhu	:	Ritual-relative/friend.
Dhobā	:	Washerman
Dhoti	:	An indigenous long white cloth worn by men.
Dhupa	:	Holy-fire which is offered to appease the deities.

Dola-Yatrā	:	Annual festive occasion of Lord Krishna in which this deity is carried with wooden palanquins in a procession and exhibited in a holy-ground for three or more days.
Dom	:	Drummer (Traditionally untouch-ables.)
Dwija	:	Twice-born (*Brāhman, Kshatriya, Vaishya, Shudra*)
Durgā	:	An important Hindu Goddess.
Durgā-Pujā	:	Annual festive occasion pertaining to appeasement of Goddess *Durgā* in the Hindu month of *Ashwina* (September-October).
Ekaja	:	Once born.
Esāna	:	Doubed earthen platform in the north-east corner of the kitchen where the souls/spirits of the fore-fathers are believed to be residing.
Gangā Mālā	:	Water-nymph.
Gamhā Purnimā	:	Full moon day of the month of Shravana (July-August).
Gauda	:	Milkman who traditionally breed cattle and subsists on milk and milk products.
Ghat	:	Places where people take bath.
Gini	:	Beating bells.
Golā	:	Traditional sheep-breeding caste.
Gomātā	:	Mother-Cow (Hindu belief)
Grāma Sabhā	:	Village Meeting.
Gudiā	:	Traditional confectioner caste.
Habisā	:	Ritual fasting in the Hindu month of *Kārtic* (Oct.-Nov.)
Hādi	:	A low ranking Scheduled Caste group who traditionally remove carcasses and collect hide.
Haliā	:	Those who are employed specifically for ploughing agricultural fields in addition to do some other agricul-tural activities on contract basis.

Harijan	:	Scheduled Castes who were untouchable in the traditional Hindu social order.
Hetā	:	A piece of agricultural field given to the annual contract labourers. *(Haliā Kathiā)* on contract basis.
Homa	:	Holy fire oblation.
Indirā Āwās Yojanā	:	A national level subsidised housing scheme for the Scheduled Caste and other such rural poors in the name of Mrs. Indira Gandhi, ex-Prime Minister of India.
Jala Charniya	:	Castes from whom *Brāhmans* ordinarily accept water.
Jamidār	:	Landlord.
Jāmu	:	Syzgion cumini.
Jāti	:	Caste.
Jyotisha (Nāhāka)	:	Astrologer who forecasts the future of human beings and prescribes the ways of salvation.
Kālasi	:	A ritual specialist who is possessed by specific spirits or female deities.
Kamāra	:	Blacksmith.
Kandarā	:	Village watchman.
Karana	:	Scribe
Karma	:	Past deed or action.
Kirānā	:	Grocery items.
Khanjani	:	A tiny percussion instrument, generally made with hide of the terrestrial reptiles.
Kendu	:	Diospyrosmtovoxylon.
Keuta	:	Fisherman caste.
Kochiā	:	An acquatic snake like creature.
Kshyatriya	:	Warrior class.
Kuchā Food	:	Food prepared without ghee or oil.
Landa	:	Human excreta.
Lekhani	:	Traditional writing stick made of iron.
Lungi	:	An indigenous Indian daily casual (lower limb) wear of men.
Maa	:	Mother/Mistress/Madam (used for addressing wife/daughter of the master/landlord).

Maheswar	:	Presiding god of destruction of the Hindu Trinity.
Māli	:	Traditional caste florist who maintains the garden of the village deities and supply flower to the temples.
Māmu	:	Mother's Brother.
Mausā	:	Mother's Sister's Husband.
Māusi	:	Mother's Sister.
Nichajana	:	People belonging to the lower strata of caste hierarchy.
Nichavarna	:	People belonging to the lower or fourth *varna.*
Pāduka	:	Consecrated basil leaf or flower.
Pālaka	:	Rearing of animal on the basis of share.
Pān	:	Betel leaf.
Pāna	:	Hider and drummer who removes carcasses from village or village sites.
Panā-Sankrānthi	:	The Hindu equivalent of March equinox.
Panchamā	:	Fifth-born or those who are not placed in the four-fold *Varna* hierarchy.
Panchyāt Samiti	:	Electoral administrative unit below the block administration.
Pāni-āchhuān	:	Castes from whom an orthodox *Brāhman* does not accept water.
Pāni-chhuān	:	Castes from whom an orthodox *Brāhman* ordinarily accepts water i.e., when they have taken the day's bath.
Pātrā	:	Petty trader of traditional cosmetics required for various indigenous festive and ritual occasions.
Pattā	:	Document relating to the 'Record of Right' on landed properties.
Potali Baniā	:	Dealer in indigenous medicines.
Prasād	:	Consecrated edible items which have been offered to Gods or Goddesses.
Puccā food	:	Food prepared with ghee or oil.
Raja	:	Fertility festival relating to mother-earth.

Ratha	:	'Temple Car' made of timber to carry deities on procession.
Rangani	:	Weaver of silk cloth.
Rāmābali	:	Traditional loin cloth worn by *Brāhmān* priests during priestly rites.
Sābala	:	A long round or torsted steel bar used for digging earth.
Sāhi	:	Ward of a village settlement.
Sāhukār/Mahājan	:	Moneylender.
Saliāpātni	:	A wild quandruped cat like animal that lives in trees.
Sanja	:	Offering of incense holy-fire every evening to the manes.
Sankha	:	Conch-shell which is blown on auspicious occasions.
Sankrānti	:	First day of Hindu month according to solar calendar.
Sānta	:	Master/Landlord.
Sānta-Muliā-Samparka	:	Master-Servant-relationship.
Sāntāni	:	Mistress/wife of the master/landlord.
Sarpanch	:	Elected president of a village Panchyat.
Saraswati Pujā	:	Annual festive occasion relating to propitiation of the presiding Goddess of learning that is, *Saraswati,* who symbolizes wisdom.
Savarna	:	With *Varna* or those castes who belong to any one of the *varna* viz., *Brāhman, Kshyatriya, Vaishya* or *Shudra.*
Sevaka	:	Servant.
Sidha	:	Uncooked edible ingredients.
Sudasā-brata	:	Propitiation of goddess Sudesa, the presiding goddess of good luck and longevity.
Shudra	:	Once-born or members of *Shudra Varna,* the fourth in the hierarchy. Normally they are artisan and ritual service groups.
Stotras	:	Devotional hymn.
Surya-bandhu	:	Ritual or ceremonial friend.
Tāla	:	Borassus flabellifer (Palm).

Tanti	:	Weaver of clothes (a caste nomenclature)
Telli	:	Oil-Crusher.
Trinath-Melā	:	Worshipping of three important Hindu deities viz., *Brahmā, Vishnu* and *Maheswar.*
Tulasi	:	Basil plant.
Uchajāna	:	People belonging to upper strata of caste hierarchy.
Varandā	:	Portico or external gallery with or without a roof along the outer walls of a house.
Vaishya	:	The trader or the third *Varna* in the four-fold *varna* organisation.
Veda	:	Hindu religious scriptures.
Vishnu	:	One of the important Hindu Trinity who presides over the universe.
Yama	:	A supernatural deity that prescribes punishment to the deads depending upon their past deeds during their life time on earth.
Yātrā Kharcha	:	Gifted token money on festive occasions.
Yogini	:	Different forms of idols of goddess *Durgā.*

Chapter I

INTRODUCTION

1.1 THE HINDU SOCIAL ORDER AND THE DALIT

The Hindu social organization is traditionally divided into two substrata, known respectively as *Dwija* and *Ekaja. The Dwija* comprise three higher *Varnas*—the *Brāhman,* the *Kshyatriya* and the *Vaishya* with their future sub-divisions into castes but the *Ekaja* or *Shudra* consist of the lower castes who are meant to serve the *Dwija* and are thus placed lower in the social order. The whole system is known as *chaturvarna vyavastha* or four-fold division of society in which a large chunk of people belonging to a number of other castes do not find their place within this schematic structure. They are, therefore, called as *Panchama* or *Chandala, Avarna, Antyaja* etc. (cf. Buhler, 1886: 14-24; Hocart, 1950: 127; Hutton, 1951: 64; Mayer, 1956: 136; Ghurye, 1960: 55-56; Srinivas, 1962: 63-69; Mathur, 1964: 66 and Dutta, 1968: 3).

These people were known after various euphemisms as *Svapacha, Mritapa, Apapatra, Asprishya, Dasa Naga,* etc. in different parts of India in the past. Ghurye, 1960: 306-18; Venkataswaralu; 1990: 1, Makwana, 1990: 1-30). But later on in the first half of the current century these people came to be known as *Namashudra, Unclean Castes, Depressed Castes, Exterior Castes, Out-castes, Protestant Hindus* or *Non-conformist Hindus, Untouchables, Harijans* etc. After the official removal of untouchability in 1955, they are referred to as ex-untouchables and finally they are now branded with an official appellation, called the 'Scheduled Castes' which is used for all official purposes (cf. Hutton, 1951 : 192-222, Ghurye, 1960 : 317-338; Chetty, 1991: 17-18). But nowadays they are normally referred to as '*Dalits*', meaning the depressed castes.

Jati, Occupational Basis of Caste and the Dalits

Although the Hindu society is divided into four broad social divisions, i.e. *Varna,* the actual functional units of Indian society are not *varnas* rather much smaller closed groups, locally called *Jati* or caste which is based on birth and heredity of a person (cf. Srinivas, 1962: 63-69, Mathur, 1964: 66; Lynch, 1974:74). The *Jatis* or castes play a vital role in the society within the ideal scheme of social values. One of the major factors of caste is that it is very commonly associated with a traditional occupation. It is sanctioned by religion and the society. In the past violation of practice of any such occupation used to cause punishment and subsequently severe harassment. So, the ancient law-giver's prescription of occupations for different castes or *varnas,* at the wider level, used to be strictly practised. While the *Brāhmans* were assigned divinity and six duties of studying, teaching, sacrificing, assisting others to sacrifice, receiving alms and receiving gifts to the end that the *Vedas* might be protected; the *Kshatriyas* were assigned strength and duties of studying, sacrificing, giving alms, using weapons, protecting treasure and life, to the end that good government should be assured; the *Vaishyas* were allotted the power of work and the duties of studying, sacrificing, giving alms, cultivating, trading, and lending cattle to the end that labour should be productive; and *Shudras* were given the duty of serving the three higher *varnas* (Buhler, 1979: 199 quoted in Hutton, 1969: 149). Thus, castes are normally distinguished by their traditional occupations as each caste practises its traditional callings and hence "enjoys certain degree of cultural, ritual and judicial autonomy" (Srinivas, 1954: 24). This indicates a clear-cut caste hierarchy and defines the position of castes through the base line notion of super-ordinate or sub-ordinate ritual sanctity of caste occupations and thus it has made some castes economically prosperous over some others.

But the *Panchama*, who came into being from mixed unions, were outside the *varna* organization, and the low-givers had no concern for them in specifying their caste occupations and hence they had to take up occupations that involved dealing with dirty and unclean jobs, like scavenging, doing leather work, removing dead cattle from the village, removing human excreta and so on and so forth. They were, therefore, looked down upon as a profane group coming in contact with whom was defiling. As a result they were to live in separate colonies outside the village ritual boundary and fulfilling their purposes among themselves and confirming their relations to themselves only (cf. Kuppuswamy, 1986: 224; Ghurya, 1969: 55). In no case they were allowed to take up the professions of *varna* orders. They were even debarred from attending and observing the religious ceremonies of the four *varnas,* for which they had to lead a life of their own that was several degrees away from being ritually pure and hence prestigious. Persons from *varna* orders considered it improper to deal with them and even to touch them as the idea of purity and pollution had been a major characteristic feature of untouchability since remote past in traditional caste system all over the rural India. (Hutton, 1963: 149-69; Kuppuswamy, 1969: 223-225).

In addition to the practice of unclean and polluting jobs, sustained maintenance of dirty and unclean food habit that included consumption of beef, that too carcasses or even meat of many low grade creatures, like snakes, rodents, birds, and various insects by such groups reduced their status to such a low level in the society. Thus, the Indian traditional caste norms, based on the concept of purity and pollution cause some people superior to others leading the latter being discriminated against by the former.

Status of Dalits Through Ages

In order to trace the traditional status of the so-called *Panchamās* or ex-untouchables, one has to turn over the pages of Indian history.

During the vedic period, the last *varna* i.e. *Shudra* was considered as untouchable (Ghurye, 1969: 53). They had no civil or religious rights in the society. The disabilities they faced during that time were handed down to the *Panchamas* in the subsequent period.

During this period "the *shudra* secured to be a class of domestic servants, approximating very nearly to the position of slaves" (*ibid*: 50). It was because of the fact that they had to serve the upper three *varnas* due to their origin from the feet of the creator, the *Brahmā*. In this context, the Rigvedic literatures express that they had no other way than to be servants of another, and washing feet of the superiors even if they were prosperous. Further, the milk to be used for fire oblation was not allowed to be milked by *shudra*. Even he was not allowed to be addressed by a person consecrated for a sacrifice. He was declared to be unfit for sacrifice and not allowed to be present in the hall where the sacrifice was being made. The ancient caste rules also stated that a *shudra* was to be supported, to be fed, to be clothed, with the remnants and castaways of food and raiment by the higher three *varna*. They are restricted to listen to the recitation of *Veda* and even not allowed to perform a penance (*ibid*: 50-59). In this context the law-givers have reprimanded that a *shudra* trying to here the recitation of *Vedic* texts shall have his ears filled with molten, tin or lac, if he recites the *Veda* his tongue shall be cut off, and if he remembers it, he shall be dismembered" (Āpastamba, quoted in *ibid*,

61-62). Further it is also mentioned that if a *shudra* commits adultery with a woman of first three *varnas,* he shall suffer from captive punishment, or shall be burnt alive tied up in straw (*ibid*).

This practice of untouchability and discrimination between the *Dwija* and *Ekaja* or *Shudra* later passed on to the people below the rank of *shudra* but with a higher degree of rigidity and intensity of untouchability as per the caste norms associated with purity and pollution. During the post-vedic period the *Panchamas* or *Chandalas* or those who came into being from mixed unions between the *varnas* had to lead a life of sub-human conditions or even a life equal to animals. During that time a householder was exhorted to throw some food for them after all the members of the household had taken meals and the outcastes were to eat along with the crows and dogs outside the house (cf. Vasistha, quoted in *ibid*, 52). And as such they had to bear upon with rigorous life discrimination and hence were not permitted to use public wells, enter into the Hindu temples and even to the villages inhabited by the caste Hindus with a fear that their appearance would cause pollution.

During the mediaeval period, these people were not free from almost the same disabilities. They are also not free from many of such disabilities in the present era that too during the post-independence period of India.

Hutton notes that "in 1930 the *Kallar* in Rammnad propounded eight prohibitions, the disregard of which led to the violence by the Kallar against the exterior castes, whose huts were fired, whose granaries and property were destroyed and whose livestock were looted. These eight prohibitions were as follows:

(i) that the Adi-Dravidas shall nor were ornaments of gold and silver;

(ii) that the males should not be allowed to wear their clothes below their knees or above the hips;

(iii) that their males should not wear coats or shirts or banayans;

(iv) that no Adi-Dravida shall be allowed to have his hair cropped;

(v) that the Adi-Dravida should not use other than earthen vessels in their homes;

(vi) that the women shall not be allowed to cover the upper portion of their bodies by clothes or *ravokuvais* or *thananes*;

(vii) that their women shall not be allowed to use flowers or saffron paste; and

(viii) that the men shall not use umbrellas for protection against sun and rain nor should they wear *Sardas*.

But in June, 1931 when these prohibitions were not satisfactorily observed by those castes, the Kallars met together again and framed eleven prohibition as follows:

(i) that the Adi-Dravidas and Devendrakula Velarrs should not wear clothes below their knees;
(ii) that the men and women of these castes should not wear gold jewelleries;
(iii) that their women should carry water only in mud pots and not in copper or brass vessels. They should use straw only to carry the water pots and no clothes should be used for that purpose;
(iv) that their children should not read and make themselves literate and educated;
(v) that their children should be asked only to tend the cattle of the Mirasdars (Landlords).
(vi) that their men and women should work as slaves of the *Mirasdars* in their respective *pannais* (fields);
(vii) that they should not cultivate the land either on *Waram* or lease from *Mirasdars;*
(viii) that they must sell away their own lands to *Mirasdars* of the village at very cheap rates, and if they do not do so, no water will be allowed to them to irrigate their lands. Even if something is grown by the help of rain water, the crops should be robbed away, when they are ripe or harvested;
(ix) that they must work as coolies from 7 AM to 6 PM under the *Mirasdars* and their wages shall be: for men Rs. 0.40 per day and for women Rs. 0.20 per day;
(x) that they should not use Indian music (Melam etc.) in their marriages and other celebrations, and
(xi) that they must stop their habit of going on a horse in procession before tying the *tuali* thread in marriage and they must use their house doors as a palanquin for the marriage procession and no vehicle should be used by them for any purpose (1946: 205-206).

In many other parts of India such castes were also similarly discriminated and were considered as pollutants. Hutton further notes that Iravans or Tiyans were restricted to maintain at least 325 ft. distance from the curtain wall of the temple of Guruvayur in Malabar (1963: 82). Āiyappan (1937) notes that the Nayādi while travelling had to avoid not only the people of other castes but also the dwellings, tanks, temples and even certain streams when people were bathing in them. (Quoted in Hutton, 1946: 80). He further says that "if a Nayadi touched the water in which man of higher castes were bathing, the water was losing its purificatory qualities so long as the *Nayadi* was in contact with it within the sight of the bathers" (*ibid*). Further Thurston notes that at Vilayur there was a *tintal para* or pollution rock, which marked the limit within which Nayadis must not approach the village (quoted in *ibid*).

There were also certain restrictions for many of such untouchable castes on the use of garments, ornaments etc. In south India and also in many parts of Eastern India wearing of clothes above the waist was prohibited for *Panchamas* and was open only for the people belonging to the upper four *Varnas*. Similar prohibition was also in operation for the use of gold and silver ornaments, umbrellas, shoes and many other objects.

In Orissa, the Bāuris on whom the present study is based were treated as a polluting caste and hence were segregated at the outskirts of caste Hindu settlements. As obtained from any old informants, during the British regime in India the Bāuris were prohibited from following the Hindu housing settlement pattern and to imitate the housing style. They had no burial ground earmarked for cremation of their dead and hence, they were forced to throw away the corpses around their settlements so that the village dogs could consume them. They were forbidden from using the caste Hindu village roads during day time as their shadow was supposed to pollute the caste Hindus, particularly the Brāhmans equally with the degree of pollution transmitted by direct physical touch. During other times, they were required to move around very carefully so that the air displaced through their movements was not felt by the caste Hindus which otherwise was polluting them and in that case, they had to undergo ritual purification by taking of bath. Some of other important restrictions which were imposed on them are as follows:

(i) that the Bāuris must not spit on the land of caste Hindus and they must carry a spittoon with them while moving on the land of the caste Hindus. (This restriction was even there just a couple of decades ago. The investigator had witnessed such an incident when his grandfather had compelled a Bāuri lady to remove her spittle from his land adjacent to the front gate in 1976).

(ii) that they must salute their patrons with folded hands at the first sight by bending forward upto their knee level;

(iii) that they must not talk loudly in the Hindu ritual month of *Kartic* (Oct.–Nov.) or appear before the Brāhman widows observing *Habisa* as their vocal sound or sight was considered polluting. And during this month, they were supposed to wear a bell around their waist or thigh as to alarm such persons about their movement;
(iv) that they must not address a caste Hindu by his/her name;
(v) that they must beg apology after they have had any talk with their patrons;
(vi) that they must not use the public wells and bathing ghats etc.;
(vii) that they must maintain a regular scale of distance from the ritual boundary at the village deity;
(viii) that they must not grow moustache in a fashionable way;
(ix) that they must not oil their hair and comb or decorate it;
(x) that they must not wear *dhoti* beyond their knees;
(xi) that they must not use luxurious articles like shoes, precious metals as ornaments, umbrellas, lantern, bi-cycle, radio, wristwatch, brass or bell-metal vessels etc.;
(xii) that the Bāuri children must not get educated along with the caste Hindu children etc.

Social Movements and the Dalits

In order to remove the age-old practice of untouchability and thereby improving the socio-economic status of the *Dalits,* over the periods many social movements have taken place in many parts of India by various social reformers. Amongst the earlier reformers, Chakradhar, Ramanuja, Kabir, Chaitanya, Eknath, Tukaram, Rohidas, Chakhamela etc. of medieaval period could be cited as notable activists. But the revolution and movements led by these people could not succeed in subduing the discrepancies persisted in Indian caste system.

The next phase of reform started with the Britishers during eighteenth century. They advocated a casteless culture, made education liberal and provided full scope of individual liberty with the principle of 'equality of all before law' (cf. Singh, 1987:3). It brought about a new social climate in India to do away with the restrictions prevailed in the caste system. More particularly the British Government introduced certain legislations like the Caste Disabilities Removal Act of 1850 which spelt out that a person does not forfeit his ordinary rights over property by change of religion or loss of caste. The British Government also introduced some other legislations relating to education of all children without any caste distinction and some other administrative reforms, like 'Morley-Minto Reforms of 1909, the Montagu-Chelmsford Reforms of 1910 and the Government of India Act of 1935 etc. These reforms more or less aimed at empowerment of political power of the *Dalits* and also providing educational opportunities for these people. But till then the impact of these implications was not satisfactory in bringing out the *Dalits* into the mainstream at par with the caste Hindus. This was because of the fact that the British Government did not like to interfere much in the caste affairs in India and neither took any major attempt at the reform movements nor protected the reformers who fought for the *Dalits*. For this, Ambedkar in 1930 at the first Round Table Conference had rightly remarked that "even 150 years of British Rule did not alter a little the position of the untouchables" (Kuppuswamy, 1986:229).

The attempts which were made by the above social reformers during 19th century turned into a greater revolutionary momentum in early 20th century when three notable personalities like Shri Narayan Guru (1854-1928), Mahatma Gandhi (1869-1948) and B.R. Ambedkar (1891-1956) came into the picture.

In Kerala, Shri Guru established a secular organisation called 'Shri Narayan Dharma Paripālana Yogam' (S.N.D.P.) and advocated that all human beings belong to one caste, one religion and one God. He kept two broad objectives before his followers. The first is upliftment of Ezhavas; a *Dalit* group of Kerala, through popularization of education among them and the second one is to bring about a social change among these people by sanskritic model. His organisation established a number of educational institutions including colleges for these people and also constructed a number of temples throughout the state. And surprisingly, by these two means, "Shri Guru was able to transfer the Ezhavas from an untouchable group in Kerala to a backward caste community with a short span of 30 years" (*ibid*: 225). Thus, Guru's movement was mainly concerned to a limited state. But in course of time, when Gandhi came into the picture, he fought with unprecedented zeal against every odds prevailed between the caste Hindus and the Dalits.

Gandhi advocated caste system as a functional division of labour, rather than as a system of social hierarchy based on unequal status. Soon after Gandhi returned from South Africa in 1915, he wanted to eradicate all evil practices of untouchability through Indian National Congress and in 1917, Congress accepted the resolution. "Urging the necessity of justice and righteousness of removing the disability imposed by customs on the untouchables" (*ibid*: 227). When Congress organised the Karachi session in March 1931, a resolution on the rights of the untouchables was passed by the Congress. Session 4 of the Congress declared that "all the citizens are equal before law irrespective of caste, creed or sex. Session 6 declared, "all citizens have equal rights and duties in regard to public wells, tanks, roads, schools and places of public resort maintained out of the state or local funds or donated by private persons for the use of the general public. Session 10 declared universal adult suffrage. Thus in March 1931, the Congress finally liquidated the social institution of 'untouchability' as far as it was concerned" (*ibid*: 230). Later on Gandhi founded an organisation called *'Harijan Sevak Sangha'* that devoted for the social upliftment of the *Dalits* from various viewpoints. Subsequently various temple entry movements were led by the social activists of the organisation and in 1938, Madras Legislature passed the removal of the 'Civil Disabilities Act' which provided that no *Harijan* shall be deprived from social or public amenities. In the same year, it also passed the 'Malabar Temple Entry' resolution. Next in July 1939, with active participation of the social workers of the *Harijan Sewak Sangha* and also the Congress leaders the temple at Madurai was opened to the *Harijans*. This event also helped opening of some other temples for the Dalits in Tamil Nadu (cf. *ibid*: 234-235).

Baba Saheb Bhim Rao Ambedkar who was born as a *Harijan* at Mhow, and died as a Neo-Buddhist, also attempted to bring the *Dalits* into the main front at par with the Caste Hindus through some temple entry movements during 1920-30 but after 1930 he concentrated his attention on educational improvement of these people by which he thought that the actual goal of his movement could be achieved.

Starting from 1929, the British Government arranged three Round Table Conferences to discuss various issues. One of such issues was to discuss the problems relating to the *Dalits*. Ambedkar was nominated as a representative of the *Dalits* to all these conferences. He considered that there was no possibility by which the untouchables would be either assimilated with the Hindu Community or be granted rights equal to those of upper caste Hindus (Zelliot, 1966: 198-99). So in the Second Round Table Conference (Aug., 1932) he demanded a separate electorate for such people but the members could not reach at any satisfactory solution of the problem. Finally British Government announced their decision, what is known as 'Communal Award'. According to this, the *Dalits* were granted separate seats assigned to them for a period of twenty years in the provisional assemblies and they were given the right of double vote in which they could elect their own representative and were also entitled to vote for general constituencies (ef. Lynch, 1969:133-34; Kuppuswamy, 1986: 231; Duskin, 1957: 64).

Independence of India, Protective Discrimination, Dalits and Their Present Status

In 1947, India became an independent nation and it created new hopes for the *Dalits.* Ambedkar became the Law Minister in the first central cabinet of free India and as such he adorned the seat of Chairmanship of the drafting committee for the Constitution of India. He guided the 'Draft Constitution' until November 26, 1956 and enforced various Articles including Article 17 that provided the *Dalits* the 'removal of untouchability' and thereby ensured same legal rights as in case of any other citizen in the country. In 1955, Untouchability Offence Act (OUA) was passed by the Government against practice of untouchability fixing penalties for infractions (Ghurye, 1969: 326). Under the enforcement of religious disabilities, such as non-access to places of worship etc. or of social disabilities, like non-access to shops, watering places etc. or of abatement of such is considered cognizable offence punishable with imprisonment and cash fine and also cancellation of suspension of licences and public grants. Further it also prescribed punishment for any indirect support of untouchability or social boycott or excommunication of persons who refuse to practise untouchability (cf. *ibid*: 329-30).

Thus after a long struggle by Gandhi on one hand and Ambedkar on the other, the legal disabilities of the *Dalits* were removed and equality of all before law was assured to them on par with the caste Hindus. But as the noble efforts of many social reformers to bring the *Dalits* economically at par with the caste Hindus through eradication of untouchability had been considerably unsuccessful over a long period, at the same time when Article 17 was introduced the Constitution of India also laid down a 'protective action plan' under Article 46 that reads as "....... that the State shall promote with special care the educational and economic interests of the weaker sections of the people, in particular of the Scheduled Castes and Scheduled Tribes and shall protect them from social injustice and all forms of exploitation". In order to execute this Article, Article 398 of the Constitution empowers the President of India to appoint a Commission to study the conditions of the Scheduled Castes and Scheduled Tribes and submit an annual report to the President. Similarly, Articles, like 14,

15, 16, 19, 23, 330, 335, 337, 340, 341, 366 etc. were formulated to protect and safeguard the common interest of the *Dalits*. Simultaneously sufficient importance was also given in subsequent Five-Year Plans (FYPs) to fulfil the requirements of Article 46 and thereby to bring them into the mainstream at par with the caste Hindus.

So far India has gone through Eight Five Year Plans and couple of annual plans in which the main thrust of the objective has been on educational development and improvement of economic status of these people through inducement of a special package of privileges what is called as 'protective discrimination'. Under this package, apart from the above safeguards, the *Dalits* are provided with various privileges like reservation of seats in educational institutions, exemption of tuition fee, special library facility, special scholarship facility, pre-examination training facility for appearing at competitive examinations and reservation of jobs in Government and corporate sector organisations, reservation of departmental seats for promotion of such officers from one to the next higher cadre etc. In addition to all these, planned efforts on rural employment through various anti-poverty programmes have been made in different Five Year Plan periods especially with much emphasis on Sixth and Seventh plans in which the *Dalits* below the poverty line were identified and assisted with financial help under various poverty alleviation programmes, like Integrated Rural Development Programme (IRDP), Economic Rehabilitation of Rural Poor (ERRP), Bonded Labour Rehabilitation Programme (BLRP) etc. in order to reduce the economic gap pertaining between them and the caste Hindus. But the success of these programmes depended on various factors which, however, vary from place to place depending upon the administration of the Government officials, and the intensity of involvement of the beneficiaries in the schemes and also even on the locality of the beneficiaries where they reside. As it is but natural that those who live in or around urban centres are much more exposed to different forces of modernization, like greater exposure to mass media, bureaucratic administration, formal education, easy communication facility etc. than those who live in rural areas, they would be thrashing out more on how to extract highest benefit out of the assistance received from the Government. The situation may also be different. So, now, it remains at one's end to assess the field reality or the effect of poverty alleviation programmes, if at all there is any between these two groups of people viz. people who reside in urban fringes on one hand and those who live in rural areas on the other.

The Bauris—A Dalit Community in Caste Contexts

In the traditional caste contexts, both the Bāuris, a *Dalit* community and the caste Hindus are economically inter-dependent. The caste Hindus require the labour force of the Bāuris for agriculture and these in turn are dependant on the caste Hindus for their livelihood. But, under this mutual reciprocity between these two, the Bāuris become losers and sufferers since, traditionally, in most of the cases they reside in the land of the caste Hindus and are socially suppressed and economically exploited by the way of being compelled to work for their respective landlords in much cheaper rates than the actual market rates. But with the enforcement of land rules,[1] constitutional safeguards and growing awareness among the Bāuris, this traditional monopoly of the caste Hindus has been considerably narrowed down but economic exploitation and social suppression of the Bāuris still continues in rural areas since in that case the helpless poor Bāuris do not find any opportunity to work outside as is available for the Bāuris who live in or around Urban Centres. What is more particularly conspicuous in the present context is that when after the establishment of the state capital in Bhubaneswar[2] in 1948 ample wage earning opportunities were available for the poor or the Bāuris of fringe villages in various organized and unorganized sectors and also when conditions were created for self-employment or opening up of individual entrepreneurship with the economic assistance from various poverty alleviation programmes of the Government, the equation of economic interdependence between the Bāuris and the local caste Hindus started changing very fast and finally it look a new turn in the fringe villages of the city. Specifically, in the changing context, in the village Hirāpur, a nearer village to Bhubaneswar, the bargaining power of the Bāuris has significantly increased and conversely the caste Hindus have now become more dependent on these people than they were previously. Circumstances now facilitate the upward mobility of the Bāuris of the village.

Since the shifting of the capital of the state of Orissa to Bhubaneswar, the Bāuris of Hirāpur have been demanding treatment at par with the local caste Hindus. This creates a sustained social tension between the two. Whenever there is one of the various practical implications of untouchability, caste Hindus do not allow the Bāuris to enter the main village to purchase their daily commodities from the village shops. Consequently the Bāuris are compelled to go either to Balakati, a nearer town or Bhubaneswar for procuring their daily provisions. In such a situation, the Bāuris convened a regional level meeting of their caste and declined to work in the fields of the caste Hindus and come over to Bhubaneswar city to work as daily wage labour, for which there is ample scope. The caste Hindus, on the other hand, failed to procure the required labour force either in their own locality or in nearby villages as there is no other Scheduled Caste community constituting a substantial population who could substitute the Bāuris as agricultural labourers. So, as the caste Hindus could not afford to lose their crops they waited for some time for passions to cool down and then went to the doors of the Bāuri leaders for negotiation. In that situation, the voice of the Bāuris prevailed. Hence, the Bāuris have rightly realised the nature of dependence of the caste Hindus on them and thus exploited the situation to their advantage. Surprisingly it has accelerated the process of Sanskritization among the Bāuris of Hirapur whereby the caste Hindus were opposed to this and resented the change. However, they could not do anything to stop it. On the other hand, the Bāuris of the village Āmbadiha, a distant village to Bhubaneshwar, are still bound through the age-old traditional practice of master-servant relationship with the caste Hindus of the village. Because, unlike the Bāuris of Hirāpur, they do not have any other scope of earning their daily bread outside their village than to be simply remain as servants to the caste Hindus. This compels them to obey their caste Hindu masters and hence they have very little scope to agitate against their masters even if they are socially discriminated and economically exploited by them. Thus, from these situations two different points come out into the fore as mentioned below:

(i) that the Bāuris of the village Hirāpur face less discrimination but generate more conflict with the local caste Hindus and
(ii) that the Bāuris of the village Āmbadiha face more discrimination but react to it less, and hence instances of conflicts and open confrontation with the local caste Hindus are few and far between.

The Bāuris of Hirāpur have realised the importance of the caste Hindu culture and social practices of the caste Hindus in which their own position is subordinate. They have, therefore, started giving up many of their traditional practices which relegated them to an inferior position in the social order. On the positive side they have adopted many of the practices of the local caste Hindus with the hope of acquiring a better social position. For instance, the Bāuris, now claim to have descended from the same source as that of the Brāhmans. Some of them have already started adopting some of the Brahminical rites such as wearing a sacred thread and using *Ramābali* which is traditionally worn by Brāhmans during *vedic* and religious rites during propitiation of the Hindu deities.

The Bāuris are no more burying their dead. Many of them now prefer to cremate their dead as is the practice among caste Hindus. Interestingly, the Bāuris of this village have tried to learn the Hindu ways of cremation very carefully. Normally, the Bāuris carry the firewood to the cremation ground for cremation of caste Hindu corpses. They minutely observe the procedure of the rite and try to learn the process. So, when a Bāuri corpse is to be cremated, a number of such experienced Bāuris gather at the cremation ground to try to follow the process of cremation as they have learnt from the caste Hindus. In one cause, when three of such persons gathered for cremation of a Bāuri corpse, they could not agree with one another regarding the modes of the cremation, it led to a sharp altercation among themselves. Finally, the body was cremated in accordance with the instructions of their own caste priests.

Another factor that has opened the scope for upward mobility among the Bāuris of Hirāpur is that nowadays the landholding castes of the village find it very difficult to cultivate their fields because of hike in daily wage and sharp increase in the cost of manures, fertilisers and other critical inputs. So, many landowners prefer to cultivate on a share-cropping basis with the Bāuri wage-earners. It is advantageous to the both. Again the people who are employed in one way or the other in Bhubaneswar city, like to be free from the agricultural activities because of lack of time. They lease out their fields to the Bāuris on the basis of share-cropping. The Bāuris who are mostly landless agricultural labourers consider it as an opportunity and cultivate the crops with utmost care and sincerity in order to extract maximum benefit out of it. Many of the Bāuri households get this opportunity and hence try to improve their economic status.

The changing pattern of interdependence between the Bāuris and the caste Hindus has also vastly reduced the friction between the two. The frequency and intensity of untouchability has sharply declined. The caste Hindus have increasingly realised the futility of invoking age-old customs against the established principles and policies of the state.

Thus, it seems that the Bāuris of the village Hirāpur who are 'more exposed' to the forces of modernization because of their proximal nexus to the Bhubaneswar city, try to improve their socio-economic status. Whereas the Bāuris of village Āmbadiha cannot do so because of their isolation in remote areas and are less exposed to the forces of modernization. In such a situation, it is required to assess as to what extent the Bāuris of these two villages have so far been privileged to come up into the mainstream through the coverage under various poverty alleviation programmes of the Government and how these people response to such programmes. It is also essential to find out the impact of these programmes on the Bāuris of these two localities, if there is any.

1.2 LITERATURE SURVEY AND THE SPECIALITY OF THE PRESENT RESEARCH

Studies relating to different *Dalit* communities in India were first started by the western scholars during the British period. Many of them were English intellectuals belonging to Indian Civil Service. But, the studies conducted by such scholars are mainly of ethnographic in nature, and while many of them have dealt with the age-old practice of untouchability and how these down-trodden and under-privileged have been alienated and discriminated by the caste Hindus, very few have focused on the changing aspects of these people.

But after the end of the British regime in India, concerted efforts were made through constitutional safeguards and different welfare measures to integrate the Scheduled Castes within the fold of Hinduism and to bring them into the mainstream. Then a number of Indian scholars along with some foreign intelligentsia took interest and came forward to study if there was any reduction in social disabilities and economic development taking place among these people under the impact of constitutional inputs in post-independence period. And when some scholars conclude that there has been a remarkable change in the socio-economic and political status of these people, some also say that they are in the process of transition. On the other hand, some other scholars maintain that there is no change rather things have further accentuated and deteriorated. The important studies which have been made on various aspects of these people are as follows:

Studies on Accrual of Constitutional Benefits and Consequential Change

Even though the constitutional provisions and development plans are intended to create conditions conducive for the establishment of equality between the *Dalits* and the caste Hindus, many studies reveal that these people are still the under-privileged and are discriminated in various forms.

Issacs (1965) finds in several cases that the children belonging to the Scheduled Caste communities are still discriminated in the educational institutions. Despite constitutional safeguards, they continue to suffer. Anant (1972) in his 'changing concept of caste in India' has found that there is still pernicious manifestation of untouchability in the day-to-day life of the Scheduled Castes and any deviation from the traditional set practices is not tolerated by the caste Hindus. Aiyappan (1955), Singh (1967), Gough (1970-73), Radhakrishnan and Kumar (1989) in their respective studies show that *Harijans* are more harassed and discriminated by the caste Hindus when they demand equality with them. The study made by Parvathanma (1984) mentions that in Andhra Pradesh the position of the *Harijans* has deteriorated more than what it was in the pre-independence period. She shows many instances of the *Harijans* being beaten up and harassed in the socio-economic front when they demand higher wage during the lean seasons and attempt to switch over from their traditional occupations to some non-traditional ones.

Harijan atrocities are also noticed by Desai and Damle (1954), Goyal (1958), Alexander (1968), Atal (1968), Beals (1969), Barry (1972), Ramu (1977), Ghosh (1980), Kamble (1982), Vakil (1985), Singh and Sundaram (1987) etc. and when a country-wide study, covering about 15 states, was conducted by ICSSR under Chitnis (1977), it was concluded that though the practice of caste discrimination was not so pronounced, the Scheduled Castes were not altogether free from the problem of untouchability. They were also still subjected to grim conditions of poverty and unemployment.

In 1955, Srinivas conducated a study on the master-servant relationship that existed between *Holeyā*, an untouchable community *Vokkāligā*, the peasant in the village *Rāmapuram* in the district of Mysore of Karnataka and concluded that this traditional relationship in the rural areas was so tight it did not facilitate occupational mobility among the Scheduled Castes even if there was scope.

Betelle (1966) when studied the Brāhmans, non-Brāhmans and the Scheduled Castes of the village Sripuram in Thanjavur district of Tamilnadu, found that the centre of power had shifted from the *Brāhmans* to the non-Brāhmans but the position of the Scheduled Caste people remained the same.

Govindakuttey (1975) studied the Scheduled Castes of Kerala and states that notwithstanding law abolishing untouchability the evil phenomena does not seem to have completely loosened its hold in the minds of the people. Those who have remained in downtrodden through ages, cannot just shed their sense of inferiority. He further notices that despite educational development and economic advancement they are not better off than what they were in the past and finally states that it is not rash to conclude that the influence of traditionalism on social attitudes is still strong enough.

Rayappa and Mutharayappa (1986) made a study on the Scheduled Castes of the Karnataka and found that these people are still in the lowest income-group and their situation in rural areas is very serious as most often they borrow loan from either their masters or from the local *Sahukārs* and hence always remain in deficit.

Parvathamna (1984) concentrates on the Scheduled Castes of the state of Karnataka and has found that even though systematic efforts have been made through the constitutional measures and policy formations, the living condition of these people in the rural areas is still of agony. Everyday 'struggling for existence' is a common phenomenon to them who still live in huts separately from the caste Hindus and their asset position is very low. More then 80 per cent of them are landless who earn their daily bread out of agricultural wage.

Singh (1987) studied the Scheduled Castes of eastern Uttar Pradesh taking Chamārs, Pāsis, Musāhars, Doms, Baheliyās, Kanjars, Nāts, etc. as reference groups and conclude that the Scheduled Castes are still lagging behind the caste Hindus in economic front. Similarly they are also educationally much behind the caste Hindus.

Selvanathan (1989) is of the opinion that as there is a close relationship between caste and occupation in the traditional set-up, Scheduled Castes residing in villages are not allowed to shift to more productive occupations as a result of which they are still below the poverty line and their monthly income is significantly lower (Rs. 482) as compared to the non-Scheduled Caste people (Rs. 760). Likewise the literacy rate of these people is also very low.

However, on the other hand, studies conducted by Patwardhan (1965, 1967, 1973), Beteille (1969), Lynch (1969), Duskin (1972), Srivastav (1973), Singh (1976), Shamkunwar (1985), Lapoint and Lapoint (1985), Singh (1987), Dahiwale (1989), Prakash (1989), Chetty (1991), Rao and Babu (1994), etc. show that as consequences of the legal actions provided to the Scheduled Castes there has been an upward change in the socio-political and economic status of these people.

Beteille (1969) has opined that in pursuance of the Government plans and policies there seems to have taken place a slow but a steady erosion in the legitimacy accorded to inequality between the Scheduled

Castes and the caste Hindus. Duskin (1972) also obtained the same result as he says that there is a slow but positive change taking place among these people because of the benefit of the constitutional policies. But Lynch (1969) says that the legal measures have developed high confidence among the Jatāus, an untouchable community of Agra who experience an allround improvement in their socio-political life both under the impact of development as well as due to change of religion. Srivastava (1973) finds that among the Rāigars of Kundapur village in the proximity of Jaipur city, about 93.8 per cent of workers have left their traditional work (shoe-making) and have taken to different non-traditional occupations.

Singh (1976) studied the pattern of occupational mobility among the Scheduled Castes and is of the opinion that the modern forces have accelerated the process of upward mobility but if very lag behind, the reason has been surely that they .were deprived of the socio-economic as well as religious and educational opportunities by the caste Hindus.

Shamkunwar (1985) is of the opinion that the Scheduled Castes are now made conscious of their privileges, rights etc., and some have drifted away from their hereditary occupations because of their educational advancement and they are now leading quite a different upgraded life-style than their forefathers. Lapoint and Lapoint (1985) also concluded that there is an upward mobility among the Scheduled Castes of Bangalore district.

Singh (1987) shows the changing socio-economic conditions of the Scheduled Castes. He finds that they have gradually realised their self-world and some of them have also given up the practice of eating beef and have already begum to identify themselves as *Kshatriya* and even Brāhman also.

Dahiwale (1989) finds that among the Mahar, Mang, Dhor, Chamār and Bhāngi, 13 per cent of people have become qualified and about 29 per cent have taken to modern jobs as against 42.5 per cent who have been able to raise a better economic standard under the development programmes.

Prakash (1989) finds that the Scheduled Castes who have entered into different Government services through the push back network of the Constitution, experience upward mobility to a greater extent but while the persons of the higher jobs, particularly in class I, enjoy a life style at par with the caste Hindus, the person in class IV are still lagging behind the caste Hindu people.

Chetty (1991) evaluated the impact of development on the Scheduled Castes in Andhra Pradesh and concludes that the programmes have played a vital role in providing for the increased output, increased net income, and improved asset position of these people. However, still they have to go a long way to come up into the mainstream of Indian national scenario. Likewise, Rao and Babu (1994) have studied the Scheduled Castes of about 80 villages in the state of Karnataka to examine how far the development schemes have been able to achieve the proclaimed objectives. They conclude that while a good number of these people have been benefited by the schemes, some are much behind the upper castes and are distinguished as a separate community in terns of their socio-economic status.

Similar findings are also obtained by Gupta (1958) Sinha and Sinha (1960), Bhatta (1975), Abbasayulu (1978), Mallik (1979), Khan (1980), Mehra and others (1984) etc.

Studies on Educational Development and Consequential Changes

After independence a large chunk of money has been spent on educational advancement of the *Dalit* and quite a good number of studies have also been conducted by various scholars to see as to what extent education has helped these people to overcome the social disabilities. Alexander (1968) has shown that the educational achievement has been as one of the determining factors for social mobility among the Pulāyā, an untouchable community of Kerala. The study of Nijhawan (1971) shows that education along with the constitutional safeguards causes occupational mobility among the Scheduled Caste people. Doshi (1980) opines that illiteracy causes Scheduled Castes to stick to traditional occupations, and thereby it becomes a hindrance for social mobility among them. Mehra and others (1984) point out that educational has been a major factor for occupational mobility among the Scheduled Castes. Similarly the studies conducted by Beteille (1966), Singh (1968), Jha (1973), Pimpley (1980), Radhakrishnan and Kumar (1989) show that educational achievement is one of the causes of the social mobility among different Scheduled Caste communities. They are of the opinion that development of educational status among such people has definitely contributed towards an upward mobility as a result of which the Scheduled Castes have gained greater economic independence and utility for political participation. However, some other scholars like Issacs (1965), Patwardhan (1965), Rao (1981), Kamble (1982), Parvathama (1984), Singh (1987), Singh and Sundaram (1987), Prakash (1989) are of the opinion that education, though, is a major factor for social mobility, it has so far caused a partial change in the socio-economic and political status of these people.

Studies on Religion and Change

Rao and Rao (1951) have found that conversion to Christianity has definitely brought an upward mobility among the Scheduled Castes as the Christian Missionaries wanted to raise the number of their followers in India by their own way of development of the downtrodden. Lynch (1969) shows how the Jātavs, an untouchable community of Agra, have switched over to Buddhism under the leadership of Ambedkar with a hope of achieving equality in the Hindu society. A study by Dahiwale (1989) reveals that about 23.5 per cent of Scheduled Caste converts to Christianity have been able to be self-employed through the Christian Missionaries.

Studies on Tradition, Aspiration on Change

Some studies have been conducted by Kuppuswamy (1956), Rangari (1984), Singh and Sundaram (1987), Prakash (1987) etc. on the attitudes of the Scheduled Castes and their aspiration to achieve better standard of living.

Kuppuswamy (1956) surveyed 591 college students in south India and has found that there has been a considerable change in their attitude, which helped them to bring about a positive change in them. Rangari (1984) has tried to study inter-group differences. Like Kuppuswamy, he also confined himself to the college students. He compared the self-concepts, inter-personal relationship, personality adjustment, intelligence and academic achievement between the Scheduled Caste and non-Scheduled Caste students and found that a sense of self-confidence is coming out among the *Dalit* elites. They confined their studies to those groups of Scheduled Caste people who are educated and employed because of the constitutional safeguards, and tried to find out: (i) how far do these people identify themselves with their own community; (ii) how they are able and willing to provide a kind of leadership for the advancement of their community? and (iii) whether there is any identity crisis among such *Dalit* elites as a result of higher education and consequential socio-economic change in them? They concluded that the educated and employed *Dalit* elites, who should provide leadership to their fellow members, hesitate to communicate with the uneducated mass of their own community and consequently try to break away their ties with them. But some of them, however, want to raise the standard of their fellow members by arranging socio-cultural activities. Prakash (1989) also found that the Scheduled Castes who are in class 1 jobs do not like to remain content with the living and working conditions in which their previous generations as well as their fellow members were found. In the process of upward mobility they have become alienated from their own people and associated with the caste Hindus. Likewise, Sachidananda (1980), Jha (1979), and Verma (1980), Singh (1984) have also observed similar facts, but concluded that the caste tensions are generated more by the *Dalit* elites rather than by non-Scheduled Caste subjects or elites, because the *Dalit* elites have developed a vested interest in maintaining a separate identity in order to take advantage of the constitutional safeguards.

Studies on Industrial and Urban Growth and Change

Some scholars like Epstein (1962), Parmer (1978), Lapoint and Lapoint (1985), Prasad and Rajnikanth (1991), etc. have also conducted studies to see if there is any impact of industrial development and urban growth on the Scheduled Castes or not.

Epstein (1962) conducted a study in two villages of Karnataka, namely Dalena and Wangala, and found that the people of Dalena have undergone socio-economic change to a considerable extent while the people of the Wangala still steeped in tradition because of their locational difference in suburban and rural areas respectively.

Parmer (1978) has shown that industrial growth has been a major factor in bringing out occupational and social mobility among the Madyavāushis. Likewise, Lapoint and Lapoint (1985) have focused that the industrial growth in and around Meerut and Delhi cities have brought about an occupational mobility among the Jātavs.

Prasad and Rajnikanth (1991) show a different kind of mobility taking place among the Chamārs of West Bengal, Rajasthan, Bihar and Gujarat. They say that the development of leather industries has considerably ceased the traditional occupation of the Chamārs of the above states because the people prefer more of foot-wear produced by the industrial entrepreneurs than shoes produced in the traditional household-leather industries. As a result the Chamārs have left their traditional callings and taken to non-traditional occupations.

Studies in the State of Orissa

The studies conducted on different Scheduled Caste communities of Orissa are very few as compared to the studies made on various Scheduled Tribe communities of the state. However, though no major work has yet been undertaken on them, the work of Lacey (1933), Patnaik (1953, 1960, 1989), Mohapatra (1958), Jena (1959), Bose (1960), Govt. of Orissa (1964, 1965), Das (1966), Devi (1966),

Mahapatra (1970), Mohapatra (1972, 1973), Moharana (1986), Dash and Das (1989) etc. which came mainly in the form of short papers, are worth mentioning.

Lacey (1933) has described the sub-human condition of the Scheduled Castes of Bihar and Orissa followed by Patnaik (1953) who made a study on socio-economic condition of the Chamārs of Barpali village and proposed an action plan for the upliftment of the Scheduled Castes in general and the Chamārs in particular. Mohapatra (1958) tried to show the changing status of *Harijans* of a village in Cuttack district and found that their change was on snail's pace because of the persistence of rigid traditional practices in the village. Jena (1959), worked on the Pānas in certain typical villages of Orissa. He found that their position did not improve. Bose (1960) focused on a bench-line study; rich in ethnographic data, on several Scheduled Caste communities of the state. In 1960, Patnaik made a study on the Dhobā of the Dimiriā village in Puri district and showed their low socio-economic condition in the caste Hindu society. In 1964, Tribal and Rural Welfare Department prepared a report on the problems of the Scheduled Castes and granted educational and economic as well as other special concessions for their development. In the following year Planning and Co-ordination Department undertook a study to evaluate their living conditions and reported their position as horrible. Similarly Das (1966) studied the changing aspects taking place among the Scheduled Castes and he concluded very limited mobility. In the same year (1966), Devi pointed out that the sweepers and scavengers of Bhubaneswar city had remained at much below the mainstream. Mahapatra (1970) highlighted persistence of the institution of untouch-ability in caste Hindu villages. In 1972, Mahapatra found the status of Kuli caste did not improve in the districts of Bolangir and Sambalpur. But in the next year, he found an elite group among the Scheduled Castes who established themselves out of the constitutional benefits. The work of Maharana (1986) in Phulbani and Balasore districts throws some light that even though the diversification of economic activities coupled with the spread of education has made a few caste Hindus to eat and drink with the Scheduled Castes, the institution of untouchability is still prevalent among themselves to a great extent.

Mahapatra and Chowdhury (1989) found the Sāpuākelā, a Scheduled Caste community being treated as polluting by the caste Hindus and suggested a welfare plan to be adopted by the Government for the upward mobility of these people.

Mishra (1992) while evaluating the status of *Harijans* in tribal and caste contexts, is of the opinion that the Scheduled Castes are still discriminated by the caste Hindus and are lagging behind the mainstream of the national scenario. They have yet to go a long way to come up at par with the caste Hindus.

Studies on the Bāuris

The most important study on the Bāuri community was first carried out by Freemam, the outcome of which came out in printing in 1979.

In this study the author has attempted to know what it is like to be at the bottom of Indian life and what happens when a person belonging to untouchable group, breaks up his traditional role in the Hindu society. He records the life history of Muli, a 40-year-old Bāuri man living in old Bhubaneswar city and concludes that despite more than a quarter century of development programmes implemented on them, most of the Scheduled Castes in general and the Bāuris in particular remain desperately hungry, illiterate and socio-economically deprived by the caste Hindus. They are subjected to very brutal and inhuman discrimination and there is no hope of their development unless they become literate and fled away from the exploiting grip of their masters.

In addition to this work, some minor studies on the Bāuris have also been undertaken by some other scholars like Praharaj (1986), Risley (1892), Thurston (1909), Patnaik (1960) Mohapatra (1964,1966,1973), Bhowmick (1968), Tripathy (1968) and Devi (1973) in different time phases.

Praharaj (1834) gives an identifying remark on the Bāuris in '*Ordia Bhasakosa'*, followed by Risley (1982) and Thurston (1909) who have also indentified their cultural affinity in their voluminous publication of 'Tribes and Castes of Bengal' and 'Castes and Tribes of Southern India' respectively. Likewise, Patnaik also established the Bāuris as a distinct major ethnic group belonging to Scheduled Castes in Orissa who remain at the bottom of the social hierarchy.

Mahapatra (1964) takes an attempt to show the changes that are taking place among the Bāuris residing inside the Bhubaneswar city, but observed little change in their food habit, occupation, religion etc. In 1966 he also focused the caste organisation among them. Bhowmick (1968) studied the process of sex imitation among the Dule Bāuris of West Bengal and concluded that use of slang among themselves, most frequently with reference of sex organs, is one of the factors of their low position in their society. In the same year,

Tripathy made a genetic survey among them. In 1973, Mahapatra focused on the changing voting behaviour and increasing awareness among the Bāuris of Bhubaneswar city. Similarly Devi (1973) studied how the Bāuris were working like slaves and were even beaten up by the Brāhmans for slight neglect of their duties, who are now fighting with their masters with a hope of increasing their economic status as well as moving up the social order of Hindu society.

Thus, from the above discussion it can be observed that since independence of India, various studies have been made on different *Dalit* communities on different branches of problem but no stress has yet been given by any one to assess the extent of change that has occurred as an impact of development planning between such people who live in urban fringes and those who reside in remote rural areas. So, this study is designed to show the changes which have occurred among Bāuri beneficiary people of such a community living at the outskirts of Bhubaneswar city, compared to their counterparts who live in remote areas. Similarly, here at attempt has also been made to show the changes occurred between the non-beneficiaries belonging to these two localities. Thus, this study is primarily a comparative study between 'more exposed' Bāuris with those who are deprived of such facilities. Hence, it would provide some new information in a different direction of a separate thrust of problem area.

1.3 OBJECTIVES OF THE STUDY

As in impact assessment study the main objectives of the present work are:

(i) to find out the extent of educational development between the beneficiary households and also between the non-beneficiary households of the village Hirāpur and Āmbadiha;

(ii) to ascertain occupational mobility and changes pertaining to their economic condition between the beneficiary households and also between the non-beneficiary households of the village Hirāpur and Aímbadiha, and

(iii) to ascertain consequential changes pertaining to political participation and political awareness, family planning, treatment of disease, ritual belief and practices, mode of utilization of leisure time, sanitation, dress pattern, food habit and development of ability for self management between the beneficiary households and also between the non-beneficiary households of the village Hirāpur and Āmbadiha.

1.4 HYPOTHESES TO BE TESTED

The hypotheses which are taken to work out the objectives are as follows:

(i) that economic development inputs, i.e. poverty alleviation programmes, cause educational advancement among the family members of beneficiaries living in proximal villages of urban centres,

(ii) that the economic development inputs, i.e. poverty alleviation programmes do not create occupational mobility among the beneficiaries who live in urban fringes, and

(iii) that the income level of the beneficiaries living at the outskirts of urban centres is same as their counterparts living in remote areas.

1.5 RESEARCH DESIGN

In order to avoid technical inconveniences, comparative approach has always been an important method in anthropological studies. The present study is also based on this approach and it is primarily an empirical work.

Keeping the theoretical background and methodological strategy of the study in mind, it is designed to make a comparison of the objectified variables between the Bāuris of two caste Hindu villages located in two different areas of Khurdha district. One village (Hirāpur) is located in proximity of the capital city of Bhubaneswar and the other one (Āmbadiha) away from it. Hence the Bāuris of the former village are 'more exposed' to the forces of the modernization than those of the latter one, who are 'less exposed' to such forces.

Moreover, the village Hirāpur is located near the Block Head-quarters and also it is nearer to higher educational institutions, public health centres, post offices, banking institutions etc. But on the contrary the village Āmbadiha is away from all these facilities. The facilities available in Hirāpur and the limiting of Āmbadiha are mentioned below:

Village Hirāpur	*Village Āmbadiha*
1. It is a large multi-ethnic caste Hindu village having sizeable Bāuri population.	1. It is a large multi-ethnic caste Hindu village having sizeable Bāuri population.
2. It is located near Bhubaneswar city at about 2 Km. away from its municipal boundary.	2. It is located away from Bhubaneswar city at about 40 Km. away from its municipal boundary.

3. It is nearer to the block head-quarters (situated at a distance of about 1 Km. distance).	3. It is away from the block head-quarters (situated at a distance of about 16 Km. distance).
4. It is having well developed communication system and transport facility.	4. It does not have well developed communication system and transport facility.
5. It is nearer to public bus terminal.	5. It is away from public bus terminal.
6. It is nearer to high school (Primary school located within the village).	6. It is away from high school (Primary school located within the village).
7. It is nearer to Colleges or other such academic institutions.	7. It is away from Colleges or other such academic institutions.
8. It is nearer to Public Health Centre (PHC).	8. It is away from Public Health Centre (PHC).
9. It is nearer to the Post Offices.	9. It is away from the Post Offices.
10. It is nearer to Banks and other such institutions.	10. It is away from Banks and other such institutions.

In the next stage of design the beneficiary and non-beneficiary Bāuri households of each village are kept separate and comparison is made between beneficiary households of the village Hirāpur with those of village Āmbadiha. Similarly comparison is also made between the non-beneficiary households of the former village with those of the latter one.

The socio-economic variables which are compared between the target units of the two study villages include educational status, occupation, income, expenditure and savings pattern, position of asset acquisition etc. As consequential impact of development planning and modernization, some other variables have also been selected for comparison. These are: political awareness and participation in democratic politics, food habit and dietary pattern, status of health and treatment of diseases, sanitary habit and house pattern, family planning, ritual belief pattern and practices, mode of use of leisure time, development of ability for self-management etc. The differences obtained have been statistically calculated with the application of 'z' test in order to find out the significance of the result.

This design is presented schematically in Chart 1.1 for visual observation and to have a quick and easy understanding of the whole methodological procedure of study.

Chart 1.1
Schematic presentation of the research design

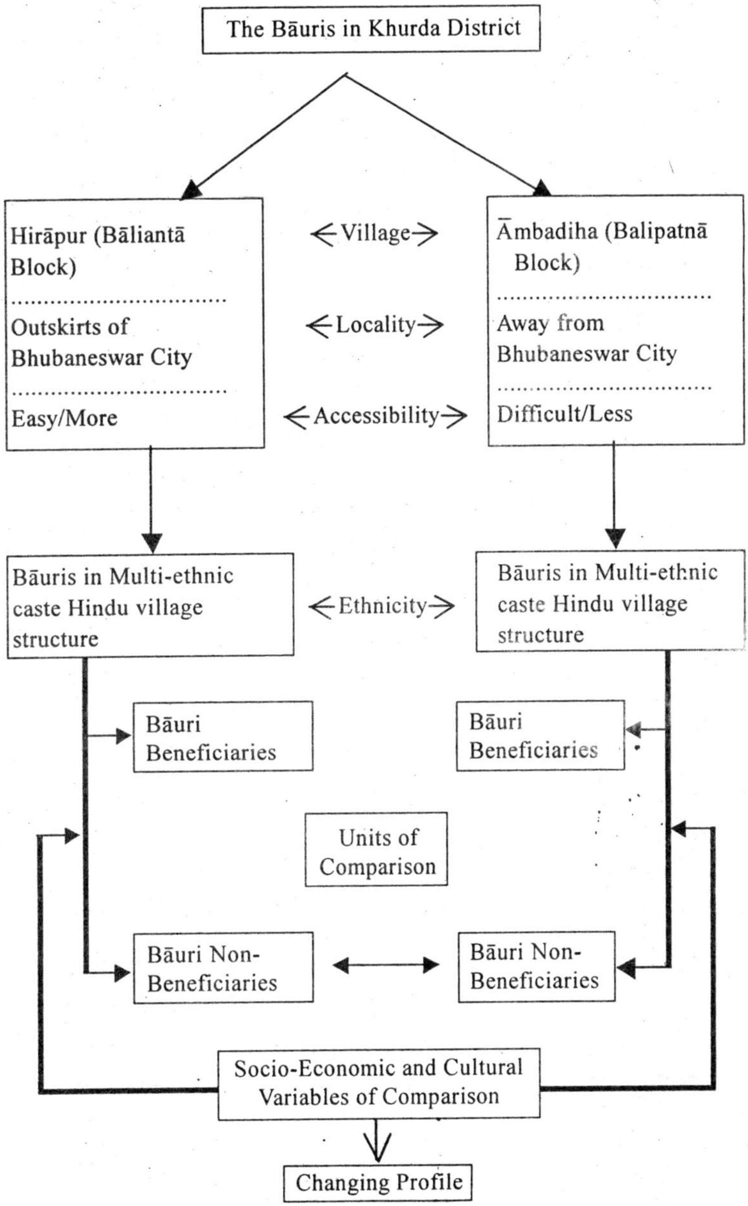

1.6 THE UNIVERSE-VILLAGE AND POPULATION

The universe of the study consists of all the Bāuri households of two caste Hindu villages namely Hirāpur and Āmbadiha of Khurdha district of Orissa. They account for a total number of 108 households with a 444 population in the former village as against 119 households with 560 population in the latter one. Hence, altogether the Bāuri population of both these villages account for 1004.

There are 55 (50.93%) beneficiary households in the village Hirāpur and the rest 53 (49.07%) are non-beneficiary households but respectively it is 50 (42.13%) and 69 (57.98%) households in case of the village Āmbadiha. The total population of the beneficiary households of the village Hirāpur comes to be 212 (47.75%) as against 232 (52.25%) of the non-beneficiary households. The corresponding figures are 240 (42.86%) and 268 (57.14%) for the village Āmbadiha.

The Bāuris are one of the 93 Scheduled Caste communities of the state of Orissa. They constitute a total number of 3,36,277 (1981)[3] population and account for 8.69 per cent of the total Scheduled Caste population of the state. Numerically they rank as the fifth largest Scheduled Caste community in Orissa. They are mostly concentrated in coastal districts of Puri[4] (28.71%), Ganjām (22.18%) and Cuttack (16.51%). The Bāliantā[5] and Bālipātnā block[6] of the undivided Puri district, they constitute significantly a large proportion and in each village of these two blocks they are found to be preponderant over other Scheduled Castes. So keeping these variables in mind, this caste has been considered for the present study as a representative caste of all the *Dalit* communities of the state as a whole.

1.7 CONCEPTS USED

The important concepts and terms which have been used in the body of the thesis are defined below:

Beneficiary/Non-Beneficiary

The beneficiaries are those who have received some kind of assistance either in cash, or kind or both for self-employment under various poverty alleviation programmes and persons who have not received any kind of similar help are considered as non-beneficiaries.

Caste Hindu

The caste Hindus are those who do not belong to any Scheduled Caste or Scheduled Tribe community and form the *Savarna* group of Indian Hindu social order or *varna* organization that includes *Brāhman, Kshatriya, Vaishya* and *Shudra*.

Dalit

This term is synonymous with 'Scheduled Castes' or 'Harijans'. But now the Scheduled Caste communities prefer to be referred to as *Dalit,* meaning the depressed castes.

Harijans

This term *Harijan* meaning children of Hari or God is used for the ex-untouchable castes in rural India. It is synonymous with the terms, like Scheduled Caste' and *Dalit.*

Sahi

Wards having households of a particular caste.

Scheduled Caste

This concept is the latest official appellation (used in the Constitution of India) used for the ex-untouchables or *Harijans.* It is synonymous with the above two concepts.

Unclean Food Habit

The food habit that includes eating of beef that too carcass, pork, some kind of snakes, frogs, earth-worm etc. which cause ritual pollution.

Unclean Occupation

Ritually polluting occupations, like removing night-soil or human excreta, sweeping, scavenging, removing carcass, working on hyde, beating of drums etc. are regarded as contemptuous and cause ritual pollution.

NOTES & REFERENCES

1. Under this rule, a person who stays in a particular piece of land continuously for a period of fifteen years, enjoys record of right over that land.
2. Bhubaneswar was a small town in 1921. Later on it became a class IV town and it continued the status until 1951. But in 1961 it was recognised as a Class III town and finally in 1971, it became Class-I depending upon its population strength and other urban characteristics (G.O.I., 1971:5).
3. Bauri population is not yet available in 1991 census reports.
4. Puri is divided into three districts namely Puri, Khurda & Nayagarh in 1993. So the Bāuri population of Khurda district is not available in 1991 census reports.

5 & 6. Blockwise data is not compiled in 1981 census reports and blockwise Bāuri population is not available in 1991 census.

Chapter II

SOCIO-ECONOMIC BACKGROUND OF THE VILLAGES

(Traditional social structure of the study villages and demographic composition of population)

2.1 GEO-PHYSICAL SETTING AND THE POPULATION PROFILE OF VILLAGE HIRĀPUR

The village Hirāpur is situated to the east of Bhubaneswar city at a distance of about two kilometres away from its municipal boundary on the bank of the river Bhargavi. The district main canal that runs in south-north direction along the river embankment, joins the village with Balakāti, the nearest town to its south. The pucca river embankment facilitates economic activities of the people by linking it with Bhubaneswar city and the outer world.

From the canal embankment, a *kutchā* road runs straight into the village. This road ends at the temple of the village deity, goddess *Mahāmāyee,* located in the north-east corner of the village. The whole village covers about two square kilometres, and is bordered by large tracts of agricultural fields to its south-east and north sides.

The village has mainly three distinct caste Hindu wards namely, Brāhman *Sāhi,* Karan *Sāhi* and Keuta *Sāhi.* The other caste groups are juxtaposed with one another irrespective of their social hierarchy. Very often they share a continuous roof. But the *Brāhman* and the Karan *Sāhis* which are situated to the south of the main village, are primarily nucleated and are arranged in one row. The Keuta *Sāhi* which is located to the south-east corner of the village, combines almost all the households with a continuous roof.

The caste Hindu communities of the village are mostly arranged in linear clusters leaving a straight street between two continuous rows of houses. However, many of the *Brāhman* households are situated in a separate *Sāhi.* But some of them share a continuous roof with the other backward caste Hindus.

Apart from these separate caste Hindu *Sāhis* the village has 7 *Harijan Sāhis* located on its outskirts which are detached from the main village and are surrounded by paddy fields. These *sāhis* are nucleated in nature. Of these 7 *Harijan sāhis,* the Bāuris are exclusively confined to 5 *sāhis* and the rest 2 belong separately to two different Scheduled Caste communities namely Kandarā and Pāna.

The five Bāuri wards namely Sāhābaj, Tala Bhoi *sāhi,* Hirapur Bhoi *sāhi,* Jagati and Sasan Bhoi *sāhi* constitute 32, 9, 23, 8 and 36 households respectively thereby representing a total number of 108 households. The former two hamlets are situated to the north and north-west corner of the village. But Hirāpur Bhoi *sāhi* and Jagati are located to the east side and the rest one i.e. Sāsan Bhoi *sāhi* is situated to south side. All these wards are sporadically located at the periphery of the main village.

The caste Hindus follow a norm whereby their houses face either north or south as these directions are considered auspicious, and afford good ventilation. But as the Bāuris were not allowed to follow this practice, their settlement pattern does not follow any particular order. While some of their houses face east or west, others face north or even south. Many of their houses are nucleated and are dispersed with space between the houses. This is because the land where the Bāuris have settled, belong to the local *zamindārs* with whom the Bāuris are traditionally attached. Land available for the purpose of constructing houses is limited. The Bāuris have to make do with whatever little land is given by the landlords who own most of the land. As a result of this all the Bāuri hamlets constitute as much as 51.96 per cent of nuclear houses. There are 33.33 per cent houses which are clustered having a continuous roof and a congested central courtyard as against 14.71 per cent linear clusters having a continuous roof without any courtyard.

The Bāuri houses are found clan-wise in clusters, shaped as a horseshoe and all the houses have a continuous roof. In this type of settlement, the houses are placed in two rows facing each other. The third row blocks the central courtyard facing the entrance of the settlement. The houses in this row may be a residential house, or a cowshed, or even a store for firewood. All these three rows are in many cases attached with a continuous roof. This type of clustered settlements are found to be in three numbers each in Sāhabāj and in Sasan Bhoi *sāhi,* two in Tala Bhoi *sāhi* and one each in Hārapur Bhoi *sāhi* and Jagati.

The houses in linear clusters share a continuous roof but do not have a common courtyard. The cluster includes houses of different clans.

Population Profile

The village Hirāpur is a multi-ethnic caste Hindu village. It constitutes as many as 19 caste groups and a total number of 275 households. The total population of the village is 1498 of which *Uchchajana* number 130, *Nichajana* 874, and the Scheduled Castes or *Harijan* number 540. These represent 8.68, 58.34 and 33.64 per cent of the total population of the village respectively. Although the village is substantially occupied by the *Harijans* comprising the Bāuri, Kandarā and Pāna people yet the other backward castes combinedly account for 133 (48.36%) households. The general castes consisting of Brāhman and Karana people though represent less than 10 per cent of the total households of the village. Socio-economically they are considered as the most advanced, and hence, are the dominant castes of the village. The voice of these people is highly respected by rest of the people of the village.

The size of an average Bāuri household is small, whereas it is largest among the Gudiās, possibly because of its solitary existence. The sex ratio of the village seems to be slightly low compared with that of the state as a whole, but there are certain castes like Rangani, Kamāra, Badhei etc. in which cases it is higher. The sex ratio is lowest among the Tanti (666) and it is highest, i.e. 1333 in case of both the Kamāra and Rangani people.

The Bāuris constitute a total number of 108 households and 444 population. This represents 39.27 per cent of the total households and 26.64 per cent of the total population of the village. The sex ratio of these people comes to be 842 as against the state average of 982 and the household size is seen to be the lowest among them. This is mainly because of their nuclear nature of most of the household (Table 2.1).

It may be observed from the Table 2.2 that the household size of the Bāuris varies from 1-9 and in a fairly large number of cases (26.85%), the household size is limited to 4 members only. Households with only two and three members account for 12.04 per cent each as in most cases, the Bāuris of this village get separated soon after their marriage.

It can be deduced from the Table 2.3 that the Bāuri population is concentrated more in the age groups of 0-5 to 16-20 years and highest per cent (15.99) of these people are found in the age group of 26-35. The number of males are significantly more than the females in the age group of 0-5, 6-10, 11-15 and 16-20 years and is more or less same in the subsequent age groups except the age group of 26.35. The unmarried people of the community are found to be 48.87 per

TABLE 2.1

Population profile of village Hirāpur by social category/castes

Social Category	Caste/Ethnic Group	Total HHs	Population			Sex ratio	Average HH size
			M	F	T		
(1)	(2)	(3)	(4)	(5)	(6)	(7)	(8)
General caste/ *Uchajana*	Brahman	14	42	37	79	815	5.64
	Karan	9	28	23	51	821	5.66
	Sub-Total	23 (8.36)	70 (4.67)	60 (4.01)	130 (8.68)	818	5.65
Other Backward Caste (OBC)/ *Nichajana*	Badhei	1	4	3	7	750	7.00
	Bhandāri	2	8	9	17	1125	8.05
	Gauda	10	33	36	69	1090	6.90
	Golā	6	21	22	43	1047	7.16
	Gudiā	1	5	4	9	800	9.00
	Jyotish	5	16	17	33	1062	6.60
	Kamāra	1	3	4	7	1333	7.00
	Kansāri	60	202	194	396	960	6.60
	Keuta	15	43	39	82	906	5.46
	Māli	4	10	8	18	800	4.50
	Pātrā	5	21	17	38	809	7.60
	Potali Baniā	1	4	2	6	500	6.00
	Rangani	3	9	12	21	1333	7.00
	Tanti	2	6	4	10	666	5.00
	Teli	17	58	50	108	862	6.35
	Sub-Total/ Average	133 (48.36)	447 (29.84)	427 (28.50)	874 (58.34)	950	6.94
Scheduled Castes/ *Harijana*	Bāuri	108 (39.27)	241 (16.09)	203 (13.55)	444 (29.64)	842	4.11
	Kandarā	5	15	12	27	800	5.40
	Pāna	6	18	15	33	833	4.67
	Sub-Total Average	119 (43.27)	274 (18.29)	230 (15.35)	504 (33.64)	839	4.24
	Total	275 (100.00)	787 (52.54)	711 (47.46)	1498 (100.00)	903	5.45

Note: (i) The Ethnic groups are alphabetically arranged
(ii) Figures in brackets represent %age.

cent as against 44.37 per cent of married and 6.76 per cent widow, divorced or separated people.

2.2 SOCIAL STRUCTURE OF THE VILLAGE HIRĀPUR

(i) Religiosity

The village Hirāpur is famous for its illustrious temple of sixty four *Yoginis,* (12th century B.C.). The temple is dedicated to the sixty

TABLE 2.2

Distribution of Bāuri households by no. of members (Hirāpur)

Household size (in Members)	Total HHs	%age	Total Population	%age
(1)	(2)	(3)	(4)	(5)
1	9	8.33	9	2.02
2	13	12.04	26	5.86
3	13	12.04	39	8.78
4	29	26.85	116	26.13
5	23	21.30	115	25.90
6	11	11.19	66	14.86
7	8	7.41	56	12.61
8	-1	0.93	-8	1.80
9	1	0.93	9	2.03
Total	108	100.00	444	100.00

four attendants of goddess Durgā. The *Yoginis* are also believed to represent different forms of Durgā. Since remote past this village has been a place of great historical importance as "it was a centre of Brāhminical tantric religion in 8th-9th century A.D. when this cult was predominant in Orissa", (Senapati, 1977: 673). Now the village also retains its religious and historic importance and has become an important tourist centre of the state of Orissa.

(ii) Caste Composition

All the existing 19 caste groups of this village are categorised into two broad divisions, such as *Savarna* and *Avarna*. The *Savarnas* are further divided into two groups, namely *Uchchavarna* and *Nichavarna*. The *Brāhmans* remain at the top of the hierarchy as *Uchchavarna* and the rest of the people come under *Nichavarna*. The people belonging to *Nichavarna* are separated into two sections as *Pānichhuān* and *Pāniachhuān* depending on whether water touched by them is or is not acceptable by the *Brāhmans* (Chart 2.1).

The Uchchavarna

The *Brāhman* of the village belong to this category who officiate in religious functions and in ceremonies associated with life cycle rituals of the caste Hindus. They also render their priestly services to the village deity and are also even required to attend or partake of mortuary feasts of caste Hindus. It is done for the salvation of the

TABLE 2.3

Age, sex and marital status of the Bāuris of Hirāpur

Age group	Marital Status								Grand Total
	Unmarried		Married		Widowed/ Div./Sep.		Total		
	M	F	M	F	M	F	M	F	
(1)	(2)	(3)	(4)	(5)	(6)	(7)	(8)	(9)	(10)
0-5	28	22	-	-	-	-	28	22	50 (11.26)
6-10	29	20	-	-	-	-	29	20	49 (11.03)
11-15	30	24	-	-	-	-	30	24	54 (12.16)
16-20	24	14	1	5	-	-	25	19	44 (9.91)
21-25	7	8	6	19	-	-	13	27	40 (9.01)
26-35	10	1	29	29	1	1	40	31	71 (15.99)
36-45	-	-	27	28	-	1	27	29	56 (12.61)
46-65	-	-	24	16	4	11	28	27	55 (12.39)
66+	-	-	4	9	6	6	10	15	25 (5.63)
Total	128 (28.83)	89 (20.05)	91 (20.05)	106 (23.87)	11 (2.48)	19 (4.28)	230 (51.80)	214 (48.20)	444 (100.00)
G. Total	217 (48.87)		197 (44.37)		30 (6.76)		444 (100)		

Note: Figures in brackets represents %age.

soul of the departed persons. Presently there are very few *Brāhmans* who have stuck to their traditional occupation, and hence there are many to be cared for by a few. Most of them have taken to white collar jobs in Bhubaneswar City and also in other places.

THE NICHAVARNA

PĀNI-CHHUĀN

The *Pāni-chhuān* castes are those from whom the *Brāhmans* may accept water only when they are physically pure, i.e. they have taken the day's bath. The Karana occupy the topmost position followed by the Māli, Gauda, Gudiā, Pātrā, Kamāra, Badhei, Potali Baniā, and Bhandāri.

Chart 2.1

Ritually hierarchical caste composition in the village Hirāpur

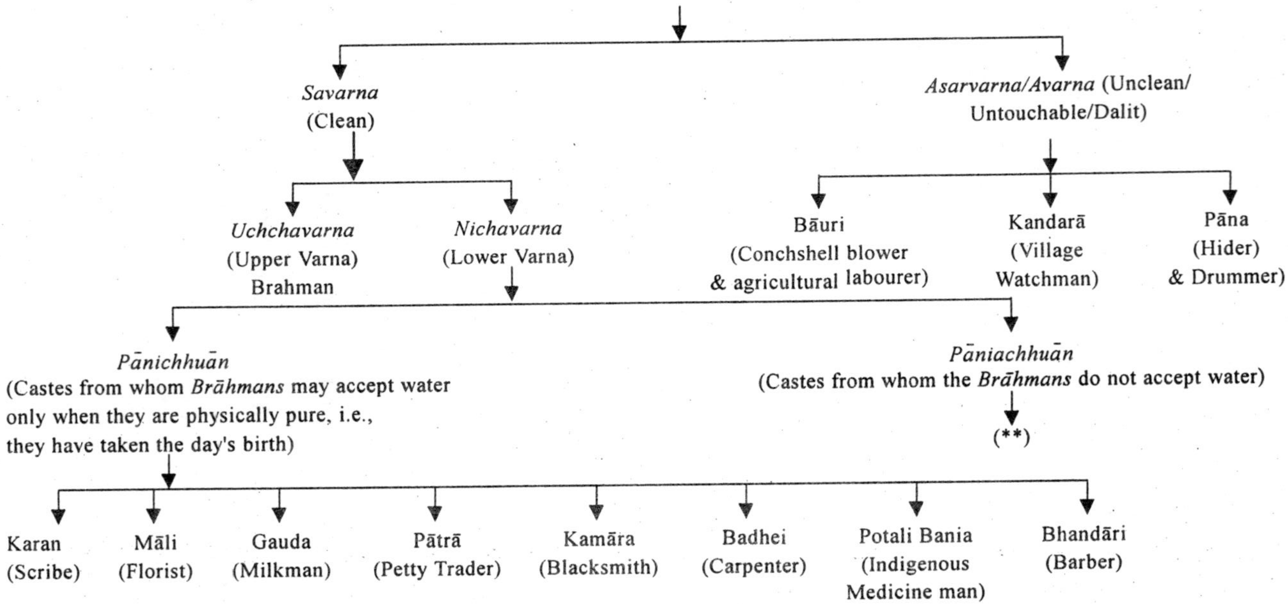

contd.

Chart 2.1 (contd.)

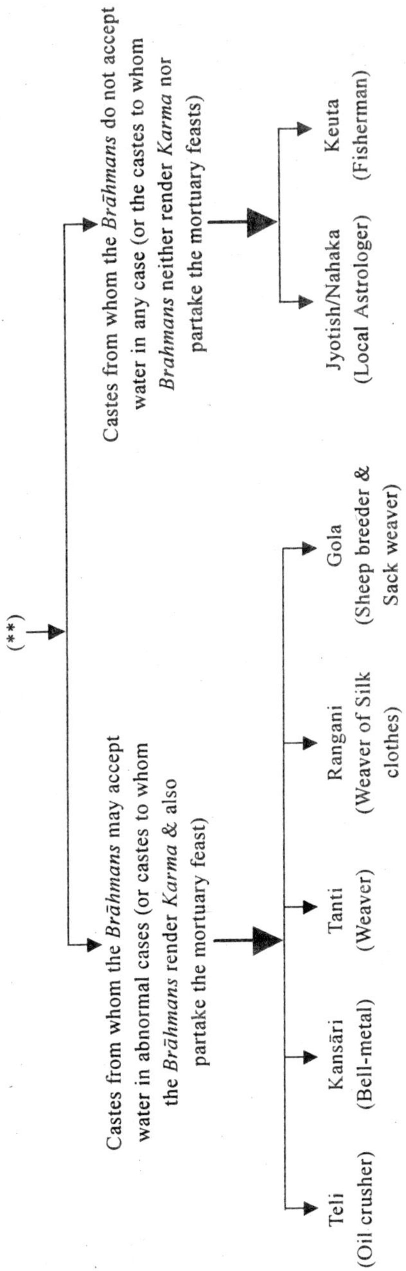

1. Karana

The Karanas are a writer caste who were engaged in maintaining official records during dynastic administration. Nowadays they have taken to various white collar jobs and also earn their bread out of agriculture. They claim *lekhani,* as their caste symbol and identity which is worshipped on the day of *Dusherā.*

2. Māli

The Mālis are a caste whose traditional calling is to maintain the garden of the village deity and to supply flower regularly to the village deity. They also render this service to the caste Hindus on different religious and ceremonial occasions. Economically they are poor. Still they depend on the same source of livelihood. These people enjoy a piece of agricultural land of the village deity, goddess *Mahāmāyee* as *heta* for rendering their service to the goddess.

3. Gauda

These people are professional cattle breeders who deal in milk and its various products such as cottage cheese, curd, butter, ghee. They supply their products to the village deity and also to the caste Hindus on different festive and ceremonial occasions. They worship lord Krishna and claim their origin from his dynasty. They carry the deity on decorative pedestal palanquins during *Dola* festival and also carry the palanquins of brides and bridegrooms during the marriage processions. But as nowadays this tradition has lost its importance, these people are no more doing this job.

4. Gudiā

The Gudiās are those who make various sweets on different occasions and are required to supply the same to the village deity as and when required. Some of them have now opened sweetmeat stalls in Bhubaneswar, and in nearby urban areas in order to raise their income.

5. Pātrā

These people trade in cotton and silk yarn, vermilion, sacred threads etc. meant for various rites and rituals. They are also required to supply these materials to the village deity and also to the caste Hindu people of the village on various ceremonial as well as religious occasions. They have stuck to their tradition. In addition to this they also practice some petty business both inside and outside the village.

6. Kamāra

The traditional occupation of these people is to manufacture farm implements required mainly for agricultural and domestic purpose. They also make such implements as required for the village deity.

7. Badhel

These people rank equally with the Kamāra, who work on wood. Generally, they prepare wooden articles for both agricultural as well as domestic purposes. They also make palanquins, chariots, and other wooden articles required for the ceremonial purpose of the village deity. They are to provide holy wooden flakes (*Bārasikātha*) required for performing monthly *homa* at the village deity.

8. Potali-Baniā

The Potali-Baniās are a sub-section of Baniā caste who deal in herbs and are required to supply herbs when the village deity ritually falls ill. They also render their service to the ordinary people of the village when they are ill. These days they mainly subsist on agriculture.

9. Bhandari

The Bhandāris assist the *Brāhman* priests on different ceremonial as well as religious and ritualistic occasions of the village deity and of the caste Hindus. Both the men and women of this caste group play a major role in life cycle rituals of the caste Hindu people. They assist in preparing marriage pandals and act as messengers for conveying auspicious news to relatives of the organising caste Hindu households and get remuneration, both in cash and kind from either parties.

PĀNI-ACHHUĀN

The Pāni-achhuān castes are those from whom the *Brāhmans* do not generally accept water. The caste groups falling under this category can be divided into two groups. The first group includes those castes from whom the *Brāhmans* can accept water in abnormal cases and to whom they render their priestly services (*karma*) and also partake mortuary feasts on the eleventh day of the death rites. The second group of castes constitute those from whom the *Brāhmans* do not accept water at all. Neither do they render their priestly services to these castes, nor attend the mortuary feasts. The castes which fall under the first groups are Teli, who occupy the topmost position in this category. They are followed by the Kansāri, Tanti, Rangani, and Golā. The castes of the second group include the Jyotish or Nahāk and the Keuta.

(a) CASTES FROM WHICH BRAíHMANS MAY ACCEPT WATER IN ABNORMAL SITUATIONS

1. Teli

The Teli are a caste who crush oil-seeds and provide oil to the village deity and also to the caste Hindus on ceremonial occasions, particularly on the day of *Jāgar* or *Siva Rātri.* Most of them are now doing different business in Bhubaneswar city.

2. Kansāri

The Kansāri people work on brass, bronze and bell-metal for manufacturing utensils and earning their livelihood. They are required to make the utensils as and when required for the village deity. Almost all these people have stuck to this occupation as it seems to be a profitable occupation even in the present times.

3. Tanti

These people weave clothes in their traditional looms and are required to supply the same to the village deity on various occasions. They also trade on their products.

4. Rangani

These people belong to the weaver caste who specialise themselves in weaving of silken yarn. Nowadays they mainly earn their livelihood out of petty business ventures in Bhubaneswar city.

5. Golā

The Golās are a specialised group. Traditionally they breed sheep. They also weave and stitch old sacks of the agricultural castes. The females of this caste accompany the brides of karan people when they go to their in-law's house after marriage.

The people of these five castes are treated as low caste Hindus. Because each of them use a piece of leather in one way or other in their traditional working instruments. While the Telis use a piece of leather in their crusher, the Kansāri people use it in the bellows for pumping air into their hearths used for softening metals. The Tantis and Ranganis use it in their traditional looms.

(b) CASTES FROM WHOM BRAíHMANS NEVER ACCEPT WATER

1. Jyotish/Nāhāk

These people are the local astrologer who prepare horoscope of the new born babies and forecast the auspicious moments for ceremonial and ritual purpose. They assist the *Brāhman* priests during marriage ceremonies, birth rites and other such occasions.

2. Keuta

Traditionally the keuta people subsist on fishing. But they are divided into various endogamous sub-groups and their traditional occupation varies accordingly. The keuta people of this village prepare flattened and puffed rice and supply these to the village deity on specific occasions and also to the caste Hindu people during various occasions and also in ordinary days.

THE ASAVARNA OR AVARNA

The *Asavarna* or *Avarna* people of the village include the Bāuri, the kandarā and the pāna. They are considered as *Achhuān* or *A-jāti* and are referred to as *Harijana*. The Bāuris occupy the top-most position among all these people because of the purity of their traditional caste occupation. Next to them, the Kandarā and the Pāna people occupy their hierarchical position depending on their traditional caste callings.

1. The Bāuri

The traditional occupation of the Bāuri people is to blow conch shell on different ceremonial and ritual occasions of the village deity. They also render this service to the caste Hindus. They clean up the village festival grounds where the wooden palanquins of the lord Krishna are exhibited and are worshipped for two or more days during annual *Dola* festival. They are also required to clean up the community ponds as well as the ponds of the village deity annually or whenever required and traditionally get some remuneration depending upon the nature of the job as specified by the caste Hindus. They get a share of the *prasad* collected from different households by the devotees of Lord Krishna during *Dola* festival. When they clean up the community village ponds, they enjoy a special share of the catch. Thus utilisation of their labour force had been traditionally accepted and it is inevitable for the smooth management of village festivals and other communal activities.

2. Kandaras

The kandarā people traditionally work as village watchmen. But nowadays, most of them earn their daily bread as agricultural labour.

3. Pāna

The Pāna people are required to remove carcass from the village and work on skin of it. They also beat drums on ceremonial occasions of the caste Hindu people and also during the rituals of the village deity. Some of them also beat drums in public as messenger of the *Panchāyat Samiti,* if at all they are appointed to do so.

2.3 GEO-PHYSICAL SETTING AND THE POPULATION PROFILE OF VILLAGE ĀMBADIHA

The village Āmbadiha is situated to the south-east corner of Bhubaneswar city at a distance of about 40 kilometres away from its municipal boundary, on the bank of the river Kushavadra. From the district sub-canal, that runs from south to north along the above river embankment, a *kucha* road forks off into the village. This village covers an area of about two square kilometres and is surrounded by paddy fields.

The village constitutes as many as 11 *sahis.* Of these 11 *sāhis,* the caste Hindus reside in 4 *sāhis* and the *harijan* people of the village reside in the rest 7 *sāhis.* The 4 caste Hindu *sāhis* are: Deula *sāhi,* Khandait *sāhi,* Gauda *sāhi* and Badhei *sāhi* and while in all these *sāhis* almost all the caste groups reside together, the Deula *sāhi* exclusively belongs to the *Brāhman* people. Some of these households are also found in the Khandāit *sāhi.* The Bāuris exclusively reside in 5 hamlets and the rest 2 hamlets of the untouchable communities belong separately to two different *Dalit* communities like the Kandarā and Dhobā people.

As when one enters into the village, he comes across the Khuntia Bhoi *sāhi* (34 households) and Bali Bhoi *sāhi* (3 households) at the canal side from which the road begins into this village. Then he comes across the Bādhei *sāhi.* The houses of this *sāhi* are situated along both sides of the village main-road. This *sāhi* includes people like Kamāra and Gauda who are juxtaposed with each other. Further along the road he reaches at the Tinghariā Bhoi *sāhi* which is located south-west of the Bādhei *sāhi.* It consists of 5 households. This hamlet follows the majhi Bhoi *sāhi.* It is located at about 100 metres away from Tingharia Bhoi *sāhi.* It consists of 38 Bāuri households. From this *sāhi,* the village main road forks off into two. One runs into north where the khandāit *sāhi* is located. The other one runs straight leading to the Deula *sāhi* where the *Brāhmans* live. The temple of the Lord Siva, the village deity, is located in this *sāhi.* This temple is almost centrally situated in the *sāhi.* The Bauris of Deula *sāhi* are settled just behind the *Brāhman sāhi* and it consists of 39 houses.

As in Hirāpur, the Bāuris of this village are also detached from the caste Hindu wards and hence are segregated. The settlement pattern of the Bāuris of this village also does not follow any particular order as in Hirāpur. Their houses are situated haphazardly without any particular order or arrangement. There are altogether 119 houses of which 69 (57.98%) are nucleated, 23 (19.33%) are clustered having central courtyards and 27 houses (22.69%) are linear clusters having a common roof but no central courtyard.

Population Profile

Like the village Hirāpur, this is also a multi-caste Hindu village but more populous than Hirāpur. Only 13 caste communities live here against 19 of Hirāpur. It contains 334 households with a total population of 2083. Of the total population, 117 belong to *Uchchavarna*, 12323 to *Nichavarna* and 643 to the *Harijans* or Dalits. Respectively they comprise 5.60, 63.51 and 30.87 per cent of the total population of the village (Table 2.4).

Socio-economically this is a *Brāhman* dominated village even though numerically they form only 5.62 per cent, and the Khandāits constitute 21.46 per cent, the largest component of all the backward castes of the village. However, economically the Khandāits are the equals of the *Brāhmans*. The Khandāits occupy large tracts of agricultural fields and use the labour force of the local *Dalit* people, particularly of the Bāuris. Hence, in matters of common interest of the community the voice of both these castes are sought for and most often needed to.

The average size of the *Brāhman* household is 7.31, of the backward caste 7.11 and that of the *harijans* is 4.87, whereas the average household size of the village as a whole is 6.24. The household size of the Kandarā people is found to be lowest (4.0). It is highest (13.00) among the Keuta who are, however, represented by a single household in the village. The average household size of the whole village comes to 6.24 as against 5.45 of Hirāpur.

The Bāuris of Āmbadiha form 119 households with a total population of 560. These represent 35.63 per cent of the total households and 30.87 per cent of the total population of the village as against 39.27 and 29.64 per cent of households and population of Hirāpur respectively. The sex ratio of these people is 906 as against 842 of Hirāpur, and 982 of the state of Orissa respectively.

TABLE 2.4

Population profile of village Āmbadiha by social category/castes

Social Category	Caste/Ethnic Groups	Total HHs	Population			Sex ratio	Average HH size
			M	F	T		
(1)	(2)	(3)	(4)	(5)	(6)	(7)	(8)
General caste/ *Uchchajana*	Brāhman	16	63	54	117	857	7.31
	Sub-Total Average	16	63	54	117 (5.62)	857	7.31
Other Backward Caste (OBC)/ *Nichajana*	Badhei	20	63	55	118	873	5.9
	Bhandāri	3	9	6	15	667	4.00
	Chasā	43	141	149	290	1056	6.74
	Gauḍa	26	101	97	198	960	7.62
	Gudiā	3	22	14	36	636	12.00
	Golā	21	89	102	191	1146	9.10
	Kamāra	3	9	6	15	667	4.00
	Keuta	1	6	7	13	1167	13.00
	Khandāit	59	221	226	447	1023	7.58
	Sub-Total/ Average	186 (55.69)	661	662	1323 (63.51)	1002	7.11
Scheduled Castes/ *Harijana*	Bāuri	119 (35.63)	278	252	560 (26.88)	906	4.71
	Dhobā	10	40	31	71	756	7.1
	Kandarā	3	7	5	12	714	4.00
	Sub-Total Average	132 (39.52)	325	288	6113 (30.87)	886	4.87
	Total/Average	334 (100.00)	1067	1018	2083 (100.00)	954	6.24

Note: (i) The ethnic groups are alphabetically arranged

(ii) Figures in brackets represent %age.

Table 2.5 reveals the household size of the Bāuris of this village. It varies from 1-11 members. But in the case of many (27.73%) households, the size is limited to only four members. They are followed by households having 6 members (16.81%), 3 members (12.6%), 5 members (12.61%) and 2 members (10.92%). The rest households constitute less than 10 per cent of the total households.

So far as the age structure of the Bāuri people of this village is concerned, it is found that in all the age groups the Bāuris are evenly distributed excepting in the age groups of 21-25 and 65+ which represent 8.29 and 2.86 per cent of the total population of the

TABLE 2.5

Distribution of Bāuri households by no. of members (Āmbadiha)

Household size (In Members)	Total HHs	%age	Total Population	%age
(1)	(2)	(3)	(4)	(5)
1	4	3.36	4	0.71
2	13	10.92	26	4.64
3	15	12.61	45	8.04
4	33	27.73	132	23.57
5	15	12.61	745	13.39
6	20	16.81	120	21.43
7	6	5.04	42	7.50
8	6	5.04	48	8.57
9	4	3.36	36	6.43
10	1	0.84	10	1.79
11	2	1.68	22	3.93
Total	119	100.00	560	100.00

community respectively. More or less equal proportion of men and women are found in almost four age groups, viz. 0-5, 6-10, 21-25 and 26-35. While the proportion of men is higher in the last three age groups, viz 36-45, 46-65 and 66+, the proportion of the women is found to be higher in the age groups of 11-15 and 16-20. The unmarried population of the community constitute 44.46 per cent as against 52.14 per cent who are married. About 3.4 per cent are divorced, widowed or are separated (Table 2.6).

2.4 SOCIAL STRUCTURE OF THE VILLAGE ĀMBADIHA

(i) Religiosity

As like as the village of Hirāpur, Āmbadiha is also a multi-caste Hindu village. Locally this village is famous for its *Siva* temple (1200 A.D.) where large number of devotees of the neighbourhood gather during annual festive occasions associated with the deity.

(ii) Caste Composition

As mentioned earlier, there are 13 castes in the village Ambadiha. These castes are divided into different social categories as in Hirapur. All these caste groups are divided into two broad categories as *Savarna* and *Asavarna* or *Avarna*. The *savarnas* are further divided into two groups viz., *Uchchavarna* and *Nichavarna*. While as usual, the

TABLE 2.6

Age, sex and marital status of the Bāuris of Āmbadiha

Age group	Marital Status								Grand Total
	Unmarried		Married		Widowed/ Div./Sep.		Total		
	M	F	M	F	M	F	M	F	
(1)	(2)	(3)	(4)	(5)	(6)	(7)	(8)	(9)	(10)
0-5	45	47	-	-	-	-	45	47	92 (16.43)
6-10	38	37	-	-	-	-	38	37	75 (13.39)
11-15	26	25	-	7	-	-	26	32	58 (10.36)
16-20	20	4	9	35	-	-	29	39	68 (12.14)
21-25	5	1	19	22	-	-	24	23	47 (8.39)
26-35	1	-	42	44	-	-	43	44	87 (15.54)
36-45	-	-	35	22	-	1	35	23	58 (10.36)
46-65	-	-	37	17	2	3	39	20	59 (10.54)
66+	-	-	3	-	10	3	13	3	16 (2.86)
Total	135 (24.11)	114 (20.36)	145 (25.89)	147 (26.25)	12 (2.14)	7 (1.25)	292 (52.14)	268 (47.86)	560 (100.00)
G. Total	249 (44.46)		292 (52.14)		19 (3.39)		560 (100)		

Note: Figures in brackets represents %age.

Brāhmans represent *Uchchavarna,* the rest of the *savarnas* come under the *Nichavarna* section. The *Nichavarna* people are sub-divided into two, viz., *Pani-chhuan* and *Pani-achhuan,* as mentioned depending on whether the *Brahmans* accept or do not accept water from them (Chart 2.2).

The *Pani-chhuan* section constitutes 7 castes namely Khāndait, Chasā, Gudiā, Badhei, Kamāra, Gauda and Bhāndari from whom the *Brāhmans* may accept water only when these people are physically pure, i.e. they have taken the day's bath. There are only two caste groups who are not found in Hirāpur. These two castes are Khandāit and Chasā. Their traditional occupations and roles are mentioned hereinafter:

Chart 2.2

Ritually hierarchical caste composition in the village Āmbadiha

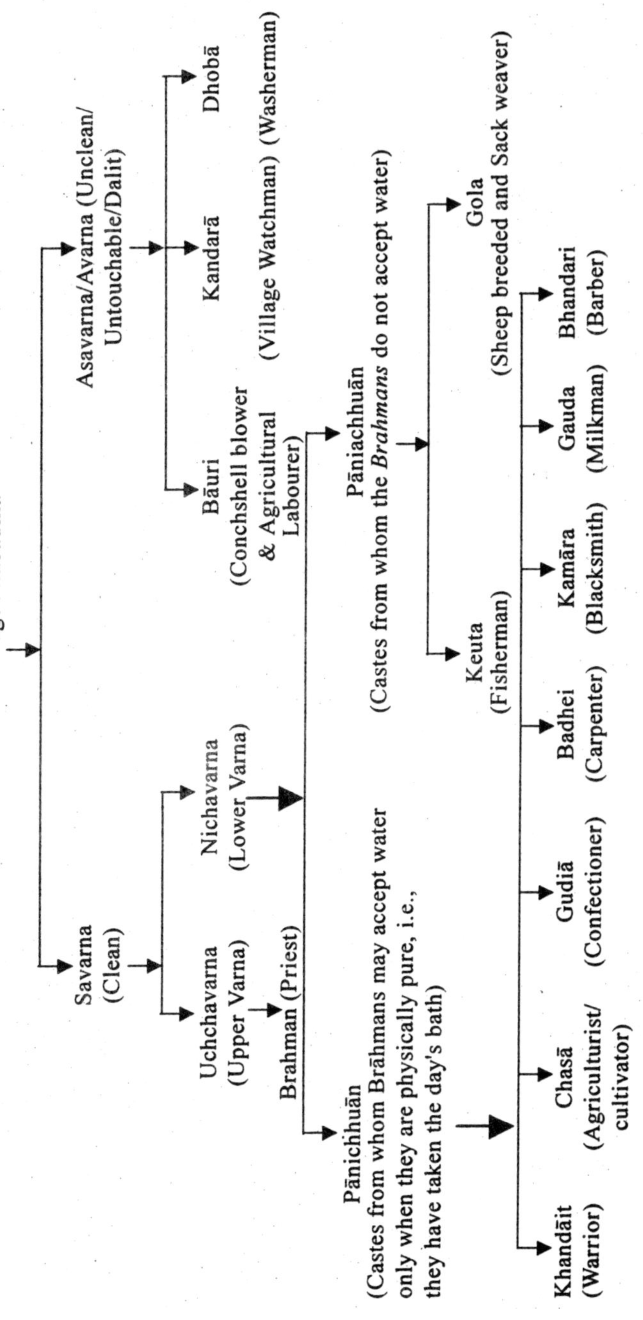

PANI-CHHUAN

(1) Khandait

The Khandaits belong to a class of peasant warriors who were the landed militia during the medieval period under feudatory administration. These people worked as soldiers during periods of war and were provided with large grants of land. This resulted in their becoming local *zamindars* in course of time. Nowadays these people primarily subsist on agriculture. They exhibit their martial skills during some annual festive occasions like *Dola* and *Dushera* etc. They worship their weapons on the day of *Durga Puja* as their caste symbol and identity.

(2) Chasā

The Chasā people are traditionally peasants or cultivators who generally possess land of their own, in some cases fairly large. Some of them also do share-cropping, while others earn or augment their income as agricultural labourers.

PĀNI-ACHHUAN

There are only two castes, viz. Golā and Keuta who come under this category. The Golās are the local sheep rearers and sack weavers. The keuta people are the local fishermen. Normally, they catch fish daily and sell it in the local markets. The *Brāhmans* never accept water from them and also do not render their priestly services to these people. They do not partake of the mortuary feasts in the houses of these people.

(iii) Asavarna/Avarna

As elsewhere the *Asavarna* or *Avarna* people of this village are called *Achhuan* or *Harijans.* This village has 3 such castes namely Bāuri, Kandarā and Dhobā. The Dhobas represent the lowest of the *Harijan* castes of the village. They wash polluted clothes of the caste Hindus during death and birth rites. They are also required to wash such clothes which are polluted during the monthly periods of the Hindu women.

2.5 TRADITIONAL INTER-CASTE RELATIONSHIP BETWEEN THE BAURI AND THE CASTE HINDUS AND BETWEEN THE BĀURI AND OTHER HARIJAN COMMUNITIES AND CHANGE

Man is a socio-cultural being and gregarious by nature. He lives in groups and associations to lead a regulated life style. He has created division of labour through caste system and each caste or group is a specialised section of the society having a particular assignment to render for the benefit of the society. The function of one caste was required by the rest, and hence, the human groups are all interrelated with one another within a society. Thus, the socio-economic and cultural reciprocity among themselves is inevitable for the smooth functioning of the society.

No caste can refuse to render its customary service in its selfish interest. Traditional society views the social set-up not merely as a contract of mutual convenience but as also being divinely ordained, the regulation of which has been vested in the hands of subsequent kings of ancient India and later in caste Panchayat (cf. Bose, 1972: 102). So, each caste group of a village or a society is required for the benefit of all the others and the breakage of the system is punishable under the oral laws of the caste Panchayats. Even the *Dalit* castes who have been treated as outcastes since time immemorial are also not excluded from the set practice as they are also an integral part of the society. However, the people of each caste group are not bound to extend their customary services to the *Harijans* because of the prevailing age-old social practices and existing superior-inferior complexity.

These traditional set practices are age-old. But these have almost come to an end, or have considerably weakened in the periphery of urban centres by the impact of modernity. Hence, the inter-caste relationship that exists between the backward people and the caste Hindus in the village Hirāpur is now more flexible than in the village Āmbadiha.

The interaction pattern between the Bāuris and the caste Hindus reflect the practice of pollution and maintenance of social distance between these two sections. But even though the practice of untouchability has been officially abolished and its practice in any form is treated punishable under law, the *Dalits* of these villages practise the strict rules of purity and pollution and maintain social distance even among themselves in the same pattern as they are treated by the caste Hindus. Thus, since the social distance is maintained between the Bāuris and the caste Hindus and also between the Bāuris and other *Dalit* castes, the interaction prevailing in both the situations are discussed below. But as it is found that there are three distinct classes, like *Brahmān, Pani-chhuan* and *Pani-achhuan* the interaction of the Bāuris with these classes are discussed below on the levels of socio-economic, political and religious stratifications. The prevailing interaction of the Bāuri people with the people of the other *Dalit* castes of the study villages are discussed later in this chapter.

(A) BETWEEN BĀURIS AND CASTE HINDUS

(i) Economic Interaction and Change

Earning one's daily bread in any form is the prime impulse behind establishment of relationship with one another. Thus the caste Hindus especially the *Brahmāns* and the Karans on one hand and the Bāuris on the other are very strongly tied upon with each other through the traditional master-servant tie. This relationship is locally known as *Sānta-muliā Samparka.*

Agricultural System

The *Brāhman* and Karan people had large tracts of agricultural fields but did not have sufficient manpower to cultivate the fields. So, they brought Bāuri labourers from distant villages and gave them small patches of land in their coconut orchards to settle under a mutual contract of enjoying the possession of land, as long as they served their masters.

The Bāuris had to watch the orchard as also to work as agricultural labourers in the field of their respective landlords. Remuneration for their services was being paid on the basis of an annual contract. Under this contract a Bāuri was getting much lower remuneration than that paid for the same work to those not provided with homestead land by the caste Hindus. Such Bāuris had no other way than to accept all the terms and conditions forced on them because of their helplessness and destitution.

Presently, the Bāuris who are assigned the duty to guard the coconut groves, receive one coconut as their remuneration, for every eighty coconuts plucked. The Bāuris engaged to look after mango groves, get one-fourth of the total collection of fruits provided that they themselves pluck the same. Otherwise they may get either cash or kind or both depending upon the terms of the contract made between the parties. There is no hard or fast rule for determining remuneration for this type of work.

It was customary for Bāuris who availed homestead lands from caste Hindus, to serve their respective landlords on a priority even if they get work elsewhere. They did not have the liberty to work anywhere else without the prior permission of their landlords. However, in spite of this rigid restriction, the Bāuris found it convenient to sustain their life under such a mutual contract.

Thus, the relationship of the Bāuris with the *Brāhmans* and Karans was mutually convenient and became so inter-dependent and so intense that it became very difficult on their part to remain away from each other. Even nowadays they cannot fully manage their affairs smoothly and earn their livelihood without each other's help and co-operation.

It is now found that 78.70 per cent Bāuri households in Hirāpur have homestead with record of right, as against only 47.06 per cent in the village Āmbadiha (Table 2.7). This is so because the Bāuri people of Hirāpur are more demanding and tactful than the Bāuris of Āmbadiha in claiming and securing their record of right over the homesteads where they have lived all their lives. They have also taken steps to see that they fulfil other legal requirements for the ownership of such land.

TABLE 2 7

Homestead landholding with record of right of the Bāuris in the study villages

Village	Bāuri Households with record of right of their homesteads	Bāuri Households without record of right of their homestead land	Total
(1)	(2)	(3)	(4)
Hirāpur	85 (78.70)	23 (21.30)	108 (100.00)
Āmbadiha	56 (47.06)	63 (52.94)	119 (100.00)

Note: Figures in brackets represent %age.

It is interesting to note here that the Bāuris who have got the homesteads recorded in their names and possess the records of right, do not feel obliged to their erstwhile landlords. After gaining freedom from the clutches of their landlords, the Bauris prefer to serve others and earn more wage at prevailing rates. Such Bāuris also exercise their freedom to cultivate the land of any person on a share-crop basis. In many cases, it is observed that even though the poor backward castes belonging to *Pāni-chhuān* and *Pāni-achhuān* castes request a share-cropping agreement with land-holding households they are not accepted in preference to Bāuris interested in share-cropping. This is because of the fact that Bāuris are skilled and seasoned agricultural labour. Thus, while on the one hand the traditional tie between the Bāuris and the caste Hindus has broken up because of the movement of the Bāuris to get the record of right over their homesteads, on the other hand a new equation based on mutuality of interests is growing between the two. All round inflation in general, and the high cost of inputs in particular has pushed up the cost of agricultural production to a level where the interests of both have converged. The capital required for the critical inputs is provided by the caste Hindus and the expertise and labour of the Bāuris has heralded a new spirit of help and co-operation between the two. This new spirit has removed much of the discrimination faced by the Bāuris earlier when they were staying on the land of the local landlords without record of right. The inevitability of change and modernism has overtaken both and compelled them into co-operation, often against their sentiments and will.

In Āmbadiha almost the same trend in the relationship between the Bāuris and the caste Hindus is noticeable. Today 47.06 per cent of Bāuri households (Table 2.7) have received the record of right over their homesteads, and hence, are free from the clutches of their landlords. Unfortunately, however, they do not get much opportunity of share-cropping as it is not very popular with the local people.

Normally the Bāuris render their services to their *Brāhman* and Karan patrons in the mortuary rites and ceremonial occasions free of cost. But in such cases, they get the leftovers of the feast on the following morning. Apart from this, they are also given some cash or kind or both depending upon the interest and ability of the patrons.

Each Bāuri household is traditionally attached to a caste Hindu household which acts as a patron. As a result, in no case the patrons can transfer the duties of the Bāuri family attached to it without their prior knowledge. Failing to this the concerned Bāuri may demand his dues even if no service has been rendered during any festive occasions. The Bāuri clients sometimes get *dhoti,* napkin, petty money etc. during special festive occasions. It is known as *yatra-Kharcha.*

(b) Transaction of Loan System

During the lean seasons, the Bāuris seek loans from their respective *Brāhman* and Karan patrons. In case of failure, they knock on the doors of the local moneylenders, mostly belonging to Teli and Kansāri castes. These are locally called as '*Sāhukār*' or *Mahājan.* The Bāuris usually mortgage their brass or bronze utensils at an interest rate as high as 60 per cent per annum. This in some cases goes up to 100 per cent also. Generally, a year is mutually fixed upon between the parties. Within this stipulated period of time the debtor has to repay the loan with the due interest and recover the assets otherwise he forfeits his right to the same. In such cases, the Bāuris are also exploited by the creditors. The debtors work in the fields of the creditors on a discounted wage; favourable to the creditor. If the creditor wants, he may return the mortgaged assets after the lapse of the contractual period. But as most of the Bāuri people fail to repay the loan and recover their assets within time, now two Karan and three *Brāhman* households have realised the profitability and have taken to lending money to the Bāuris at cent per cent interest per annum.

In Āmbadiha the Bāuris either go to Khandāits or *Brāhmans* or Chāsās for loans to meet urgent expenses. The rate of interest is 60 per cent per annum and the Bāuris are free to take back their mortgaged assets within five years from the date of contracting a loan.

(c) Renderance of Traditional Occupation

Although the Bāuris render their traditional services, i.e. blowing of conch shell in ceremonial occasions and in agricultural activities to almost all caste Hindus of Hirāpur, neither they prefer to blow conch shell nor to work for few castes belonging to *Pānichhuān* and *Pāniachhuān* category, whom they consider socially below themselves. It is amazing to note that the Bāuri people consider some of the Hindu castes like Jyotish, Kansāri, Teli, Pātrā, Tanti degraded and inferior to themselves. As a result, they are unwilling to work for them. The Bāuris consider the Jyotish people as the younger brother of *Yama,* who gather 'sin' (*Pāpa*) by meting punishment as atonement to people after death. They think that working for these people or even accepting water from them means accumulating 'sin' for self. Of late there is some relief to this cynical thinking and the situation has changed somewhat. Some of the Bāuris are found to render their traditional services to these people. But they never partake of *Kutchā* food from them. Some Bāuris are also participating in the marriage festivities of these people and blow conch shells, but even then they do not partake of *Kutchā* food unless it is cooked by *Brāhmans.* In such cases they take *Sidha* as their remuneration. Likewise, the Bāuris also do not like to render their services to the Kansāri, Teli and Tanti people as these people use pieces of hide as the part of their traditional work-tools; the leather bellows to air the hearth in case of the Kansari, the leather strap to yoke the bullock to the oil crusher in case of the oilman and a leather strap used in the traditional loom in case of the Tanti people. Contact with leather in any form was considered demeaning. The Pātrā people are also ranked equally with the Jyotish people.

They are thought to be a degraded caste by the Bāuri people as they worship an indigenous sweet material prepared out of various edible items but in a form that resembles human excreta called '*Landa*'. The younger Bāuris, however, consider all these to be superstitions and stand up for breaking these down and work as labourers in the house of Pātrā people.

In contrast, most of the caste Hindus do not render their traditional services to the Bāuris. But the carpenters (Badhei), blacksmiths (Kamāra), florists (Māli), the indigenous medicine man (Pātrā) and Astrologer (Jyotish) are found to render their respective customary services to the Bāuris. The carpenters are supposed to make the Idol (Khāi) of the village deity and other wooden agricultural implements of the Bāuris. The blacksmiths provide their services by making agricultural implements of iron or mild steel. The florists also render their traditional services to the Bāuris by supplying flower on some special occasions such as on the day of *Panā Sankrānti* and the medicine man is to prescribe as well as supply indigenous medicines to Bāuri clients. The Astrologers also render their traditional services to the Bāuri clients (Chart 2.3).

In Āmbadiha, though there is no Jyotish, Kansāri, Teli, Tanti or Pātrā inside the village, the Bāuri render their services to all these castes except the Jyotish people and pātrās of nearby villages. But, they never take any Kutchā food from any of these caste groups. (Chart 2.4).

(ii) Religious Interaction and Change

Religion has two inter-related constituents; religious beliefs and religious practices. Belief is the mode of conception and ritual is the mode of action. Religious rituals throw some light on social relations and the mode of interaction that express the structural arrangement of the society.

The Bāuris are required to blow conch shell on different ceremonial occasions of the caste Hindus and during the religious rites of the village deity, goddess *Mahāmāyee.* In return, they get *Pāduka* during the annual *Panā* festival. They collect the Pāduka from the temple priest and flower from the florists and also collect a small piece of napkin of the Goddess *Mahāmāyee* on the day of *Panā Sankrānti.*

On the occasion of *Panā-Sankrānti* the Bāuri *Kālasi* shaman makes a bridge in trance between the villages and the deities of the supreme world. On this day, the Bāuris including some other people

CHART 2.3

Interaction of Bāuris with different caste Hindus in Hirāpur

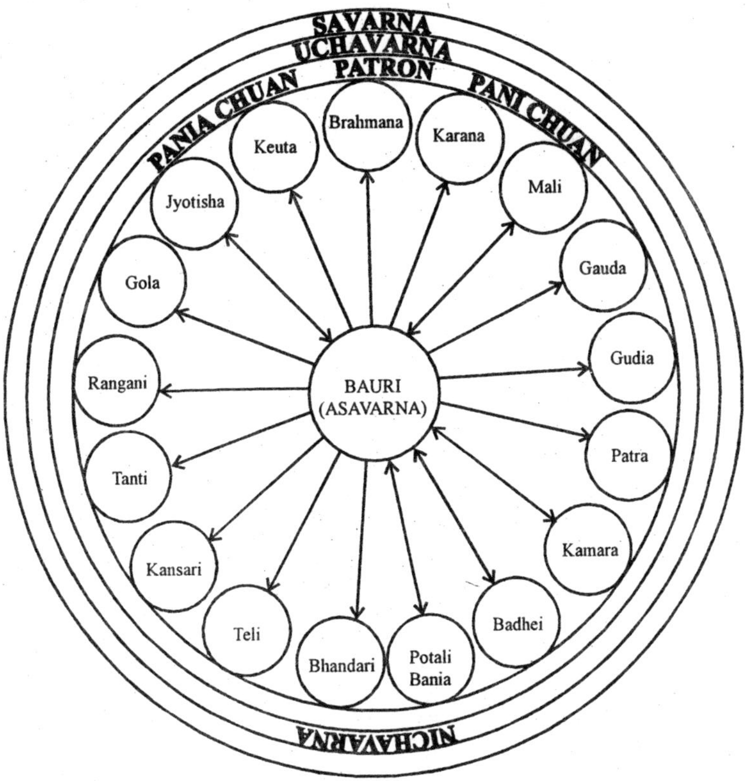

belonging to both the *Pāni-chhuān* and *Pāni-achhuān* castes prostrate themselves before the *Bāuri-Kālasi* to get divine oracles for one's self and family members. Traditionally, there is chanting of *stotras* and offerings of incense in the form of holy fire at the door of Karan and Keuta. However, many caste Hindus do not believe in Bāuri *Kālasi* and regard him as an ordinary person and even behave accordingly.

On this occasion, the Bāuri clients send message to their caste Hindu patron households whom they are supposed to pay ceremonial visits. The message is sent through a special messenger by sending betel-leaf and betel-nuts as a token of esteem (*sanmāna*). Nowadays this tradition is no longer observed as rigidly as in the past. The Bāuris

CHART 2.4

Interaction of Bāuris with different caste Hindus in Āmbadiha

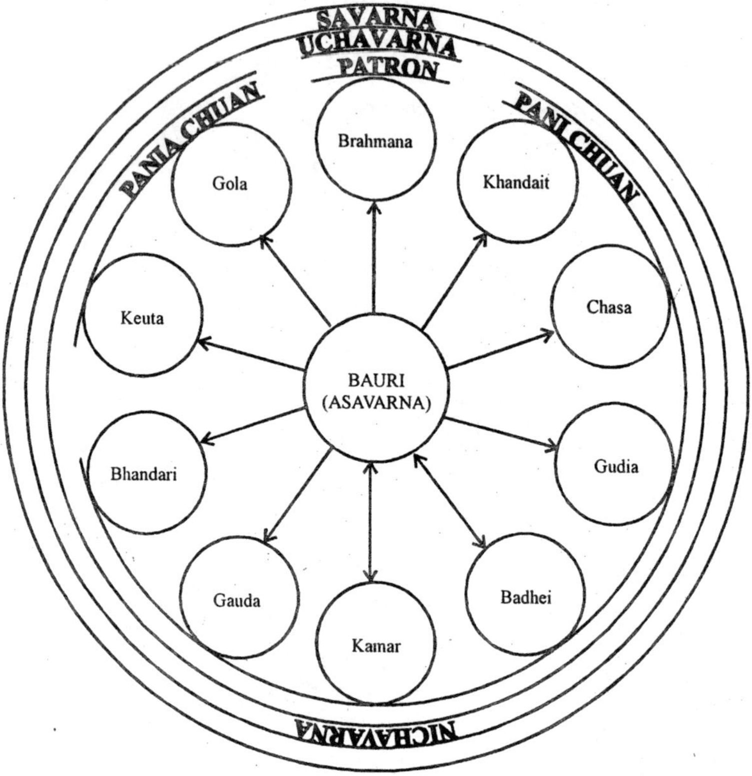

no longer bother to send the customary betel-leaf and nut to their caste Hindu patrons, but prefer to go to Bhubaneswar in a procession along with their deity and earn much more in the form of obeisance fees in a shorter time than what they could have made by doing the rounds in the village.

The carpenters make the idols of the deity of the Bāuris and palanquins to carry them. When the idol of their deity gets time-ravaged and worn out, the Bāuri priests have a new idol in accordance with their own traditional rites. The *Brāhman* priests do not interfere in this matter as the existence of this deity is accepted only by the Bāuris and worshipped only by them. But recently, when the Bāuris of Hirāpur wanted to install a new deity in their pantheon, they sought the help of *Brāhman* priests of the village. In 1987, during a post-tension period, when the caste Hindus had surrendered to the Bāuris, the Bāuris wanted to place a new idol in their pantheon and demanded the services of the *Brāhman* priests who had no option but to give in and oblige. The *Brāhman* priests who never render their priestly services to these people, went to their hamlet and placed the new deity ritually with all the elaborate rituals. However, *Brāhman* priests had to convene an inter-caste panchayat to take the permission and to render such a service to the Bāuri people. On the other hand in this matter, the Bāuris of Āmbadiha do not dare ask for the help of *Brāhman* priests as they think it is unprecedented and break with tradition may herald untold miseries.

The Bāuris clean the village ritual grounds during *Dola* festival. They also clean the ponds of the village deity. In return they get a share of the *prasād* and the catch from the pond, respectively. But of late, the Bāuris of Hirāpur neglect this duty and demand more remuneration than what they were getting a few years back whereas in Āmbadiha the Bāuris do not charge any remuneration for rendering this service. However, whenever a ceremonial function like *Ashta-prahari* is arranged for the well-doing of the villagers the Bāuris clean the grounds and make the pandal and its roof without any remuneration.

(iii) Political Interaction and Change

Since time immemorial man has been living in groups for reasons of security and protection. Culturally, the people in a village community may be different from one another, but so far as politics is concerned they are tied with one another as specific entities of a wider political world.

Whenever an inter-caste conflict arises in the village, a meeting called '*chāri-desha*' or *sāgar* is convened under the Chairmanship of the village head, who is a *Brāhman*. All the caste heads including the Bāuris are notified to attend the meeting. If someone is held responsible for the flare-up, he is declared a culprit and his family is excommunicated. The Bāuris, as a part of the village community, are informed not to render any service to the excommunicated household.

In such meetings, the Bāuris generally sit on the ground maintaining a respectable distance between them and the caste Hindus but whenever an inter-caste meeting is convened and they are required to attend such a meeting, they demand equal seating facilities, failing which they never come to attend such meetings. In the prevailing changed scenario the Bāuri leaders of the village Hirapur have become very adamant and prestige conscious. If the leaders feel in any way inconvenienced in one meeting, they do not attend the succeeding meetings and send representatives on their behalf. Presently, not only they participate in such meetings but also freely give their judgement, even against caste Hindu culprit, no matter, even if it goes against the known or stated opinion of caste Hindu leaders.

In Āmbadiha, the Bāuris are invited to attend such meetings but are still not provided separate seats or they are not permitted to exercise the right of judgement against any caste Hindu culprit. Even if they are asked to give their opinion, they refrain from doing so and usually agree with the decision taken by the caste Hindu leaders.

(iv) Social Interaction and Change:

(a) Mode of Address

Ordinarily the *Brāhman* and Karan patrons irrespective of age and sex address the Bāuris by name. But the Bāuris normally honour their Brāhman and Karan patrons by addressing them as *Sā̃nta* and the Teli and Kansāri moneylenders as "*Sahukār*" or *Mahājan.* They address the Nāhākas as "*Abadhan*". But presently, most of the Bāuris of Hirāpur, address *Brāhman* and Karan patrons by their names suffixing the word 'baboo' meaning gentleman. However, those Bāuris who are related with the caste Hindus by ritual kinship or friendship, use various terms for addressing one another. For instance in this relationship even the *Brāhman* address Bāuri clients as *Mausā, Māmu* etc. The Bāuris in turn also follow the same norms. In ordinary cases, the Bāuris address womenfolk of caste Hindu patrons as *Sā̃ntā̃ni* or *Maa.*

So far as the mode of address is concerned between Bāuri and the caste Hindus in the village Āmbadiha no noticeable change is observed. Traditionally the Bāuri clients call their *Brāhman* and Khāndait patrons as *sā̃nta* and ladies as *Sā̃ntā̃ni* or Maa. They also address their patrons using different kinship terms if, however, they are particularly close.

(b) Treatment of Diseases

When someone, either from among the Bāuris or from amongst caste Hindus falls sick, the witch doctor of any community is consulted. A Bāuri witch doctor may simply go into the courtyard or the outer room of a caste Hindu patient and is free to touch unmarried patients. Any type of dry medicines from the Bāuri witch doctors is acceptable by a caste Hindu patient. If any Bāuri patient needs the service of a caste Hindu witch doctor, he goes to his door but in exceptional cases the caste Hindu witch doctor may go to the door of the Bāuri patient but he may claim more fee in that case. But, the Golā and Rangani witch doctors belonging to *Pāni-achhuān* castes, most frequently go to the door of Bāuri patients in order to fetch more money. The same tradition is also found in the village but normally the caste Hindu witch doctors hesitate to go to the door of the Bāuri patients.

(c) Midwifery

Bāuri midwives are most often consulted by the Keuta people during labour pain and delivery. They are also employed to watch expectant mothers. Bāuri midwives normally tender advice but are not allowed to touch expectant mothers. In Āmbadiha Bāuri midwives are never employed by any of the caste Hindu people for this purpose.

(d) Commensality

In the village of Hirāpur, previously the Bāuris were just casually informed through their caste heads to attend the ceremonial feasts given by the caste Hindu patrons on the concerned day. The Bāuris had to wait at the dining ground; usually arranged outdoors, till such time as all the caste Hindus have had their food. The Bāuris were also supposed to clean up the ground after having partaken of the food. But, now as they have become conscious of their prestige, they do not attend the feasts unless they are invited in the same manner as caste Hindu invitees are invited. Under the present scenario, they are first informed at their doorsteps; at least three days before and again they are required to be called at their individual doors just before dinner time. No more are they willing to wait at the dining ground till the caste Hindus have had their food as in the past.

The Bāuris of Āmbadiha have also become prestige conscious and do not like to wait at the dining ground. But their caste head is just informed about the date and time of feast and he collects all his fellow members to attend the same. They do not demand that the caste Hindus should go to their doors to invite them and repeat the process again on the day of the feast. Ordinarily they come spontaneously and join the feast at the appointed time.

Self Identity and Conceptual change among Bāuris of the village Hirāpur and Āmbadiha

To know the self-perception and changing conceptual views of the Bāuris, both the younger (15-40) and older (40+) Bāuris were asked different questions relating to caste system and the practice of untouchability, which is more or less directly associated with their low socio-economic status in the society.

It is revealed from Table 2.8 that most of the younger persons constituting 83.75 per cent of the village Āmbadiha as against only 56.25 per cent of the village Hirapur opine that the caste system is divinely ordained, and that they must obey its tenets, while the others differ with this view. However, even though most of the people of both the villages say that they must follow the rules and regulations of the caste system, a total number of 119 and 94 constituting 74.78 and 58.75 per cent of Hirāpur and Āmbadiha respectively, claim that it is a matter of great injustice that people engaged in most useful

TABLE 2.8

Believers in caste system as divinely ordained with obligation to follow its rules and regulations

Village	Age Group of the Bāuri Respondents				Total	
	15-40 (Group-I)		41+ (Group-II)		N=160 (per village)	
	N=80					
	Yes	No	Yes	No		
(1)	(2)	(3)	(4)	(5)	(6)	(7)
Hirāpur	45 (56.25)	35 (43.75)	73 (91.25)	7 (8.75)	118 (73.73)	42 (26.25)
Āmbadiha	67 (83.75)	13 (16.25)	78 (97.50)	2 (2.50)	145 (90.63)	15 (9.38)

Note: (i) N is 80 for each group & 160 for each village.
(ii) Figures in brackets represent %age.

services to society are placed at the bottom and are discriminated in various forms by the caste Hindus (Table 2.9). However, in both the villages the younger Bāuris hold opinions contrary to their elders, and say that birth in a particular caste does not depend on one's *karma* of the previous life. Hence while a total number of 104 persons of the village Hirāpur constituting 65 per cent do not agree that the caste Hindus should be their masters and they should obey them, there are as many as 110 persons or 68.25 per cent in the village Ambadiha who agree with the statement (Table 2.10).

Further, it is interesting to note that as many as 55 of the younger Bāuris constituting 68.75 per cent of Hirāpur as against only 39 persons (48.75%) of the village Āmbadiha, think that the intelligence of their people is no less than that of caste Hindus while a total number of 72 and 79 persons constituting 45.00 and 49.38 per cent of the total population of the villages Hirāpur and Āmbadiha respectively, do not

TABLE 2.9

It is a great injustice that the people who are engaged in the most useful services to society are placed at the bottom and are discriminated by the caste Hindus

Village	Age Group of the Bāuri Respondents 15-40 (Group-I)		41+ (Group-II) N=80		Total N=160 (per village)	
	Yes	No	Yes	No		
(1)	(2)	(3)	(4)	(5)	(6)	(7)
Hirāpur	72 (90.00)	8 (10.00)	47 (58.75)	33 (41.25)	119 (74.78)	41 (25.63)
Āmbadiha	64 (80.00)	16 (20.00)	30 (37.50)	50 (62.50)	94 (58.75)	66 (41.25)

Note: (i) N is 80 for each group & 160 for each village.
(ii) Figures in brackets represent %age.

TABLE 2.10

The upper caste Hindus should be our masters and we must obey them

Village	Age Group of the Bāuri Respondents 15-40 (Group-I)		41+ (Group-II) N=80		Total N=160 (per village)	
	Yes	No	Yes	No		
(1)	(2)	(3)	(4)	(5)	(6)	(7)
Hirāpur	18 (22.50)	62 (77.50)	38 (47.50)	42 (52.50)	56 (35.00)	104 (65.00)
Āmbadiha	43 (53.75)	37 (46.25)	67 (83.75)	13 (16.25)	110 (68.75)	50 (31.25)

Note: As per Table 2.8

agree with the statement (Table 2.11). However, as most of the younger Bāuris of Hirāpur think that their people are as intelligent as those of the caste Hindus, most of them constituting 76.25 per cent think that they could have acquired a status equal to that of the caste Hindus if they had been given equal facilities for higher education (Table 2.12). But on the other hand it is surprising that even though the younger Bāuris of Hirāpur village have greater self-confidence than those of Āmbadiha, the literacy of the Bāuris of the former village is much lower than that of the latter. This is because of various interrelated factors which will be discussed later on in the concerned chapter.

TABLE 2.11

The innate intelligence of the people of my caste is not less than those of the caste Hindus

Village	Age Group of the Bāuri Respondents				Total	
	15-40 (Group-I) N=80		41+ (Group-II)		N=160 (per village)	
	Yes	No	Yes	No		
(1)	(2)	(3)	(4)	(5)	(6)	(7)
Hirāpur	55 (68.75)	25 (43.75)	33 (41.25)	47 (58.75)	88 (55.00)	72 (45.00)
Āmbadiha	39 (48.75)	41 (51.25)	42 (52.50)	38 (47.50)	81 (50.63)	79 (49.38)

Note: (i) N is 80 for each group & 160 for each village.
(ii) Figures in brackets represent %age.

TABLE 2.12

Had I been given better facilities for higher education, I believe that I could have acquired a status equal to those of the caste Hindus

Village	Age Group of the Bāuri Respondents				Total	
	15-40 (Group-I) N=80		41+ (Group-II)		N=160 (per village)	
	Yes	No	Yes	No		
(1)	(2)	(3)	(4)	(5)	(6)	(7)
Hirāpur	61 (76.25)	19 (23.75)	32 (40.00)	48 (60.00)	93 (58.13)	67 (41.88)
Āmbadiha	27 (33.75)	53 (66.25)	12 (15.00)	68 (86.00)	39 (24.38)	121 (75.61)

Note: (i) N is 80 for each group & 160 for each village.
(ii) Figures in brackets represent %age.

Thus as may be seen most of the younger Bāuris of Hirāpur have become more conscious and self-reliant than their counterparts of the village Āmbadiha. They try to break set social practices now prevailing which go against them, and hence, are considered unfavourable even though now they are much less discriminated than the Bāuris of Āmbadiha, where the past continues with very little change. Again, as most of the Bāuris of the village Hirāpur opine that untouchability should be based on one's caste occupation and since they do not have any unclean caste occupation, and their traditional caste calling is as prestigious as that of the *Brāhmans,* they claim that they should not be treated as untouchables. Hence, nowadays the Bāuris revolt against any practice that hurts their sentiment. Thus, repeated protests and movement of the Bāuris of Hirāpur against narrow, parochialistic behaviour of caste Hindus has opened the gateway to a broader scope for their socio-economic upliftment than their counterparts in the village of Āmbadiha.

Untouchability

Untouchability, the by-product of Hindu caste system, is still practised in various forms even after half a century of independence of our country. According to Maffatt it may be understood from two angles: (i) the stigma attached to certain people because of the ceremonial pollution they allegedly convey and (ii) the set practices engaged in by the rest of the society to protect itself from the pollution conveyed by the untouchables. He further defines the untouchables as the persons of discrete set of low castes, excluded for the reason of their extreme collective impurity from particular relations with higher beings (both human and divine) (1975: 4).

Āiyapan says that the term untouchability denotes the socio-religious practice of which Hindus keep large number of lower castes from touching or coming near their persons, houses, temples, tanks and sometimes even public roads (1966: 37). He calls it contact taboo by which persons by reason of their birth or physiological or ritual state...... act as carriers of pollution and induce temporarily a similar state in others by their contact, either direct or with a prescribed distance, which impurity has to be removed by ritual means to restore those polluted to their original condition (*ibid*). In this context Āmbedkar says that "untouchables are treated worse than the slaves and untouchability underlines the notion of defilement, pollution and contamination and the ways and means of getting rid of that defilement (1945: 131).

Bailey notes that the untouchables who are otherwise known as 'outcastes', are not allowed to be within others in society and they tend to separate themselves from the rest of the village and try to order their relationship with their caste group in the village not in terms of the village structure, but with the framework of administration (1975: 227).

Vidhyarthi says that the disabilities on untouchable Hindu castes are felt in the religious, social and civil areas. They were refused access to temples, they were prohibited entry to schools, movement on roads and drawing water from wells used by the high castes. In certain parts of India they were shunned by higher caste (1977: 4). And Ambedkar has rightly said that "this type of untouchability among the Hindu stands in a class by itself..... There is nothing which can make the untouchables pure..... They are born impure, they were impure while they live, they have the death of impurity and they give birth to children who are born with the stigma of untouchability affixed to them" (Quoted in *ibid*).

However, even though untouchability is still practised in various forms in this modern world of 20th century, its intensity and gravity varies from place to place depending upon the locality and the awareness and consciousness of the people. The untouchables living in urban areas have become more conscious, and hence, are also less discriminated than their counterparts living in rural areas. Thus, the Bāuris of Āmbadiha still suffer from many socio-economic disabilities as persistence of untouchability is more pronounced here than in the village of Hirāpur.

In the village of Hirāpur, the Bāuris were once forbidden to use the village roads, common wells, bathing ghats, worship in temples, shops, hotels etc. and were also restrained from using items like umbrella, lantern, bicycle, radio, watch, foot-wear and gold and silver ornaments which were then considered luxurious. Nowadays, these restrictions no longer hold good and they are now allowed to use the road, but even now they are not permitted to carry their corpses on the village road. They are also not permitted to use the road for performing of the mortuary rites on the tenth-day rite.

The Bāuris of Hirāpur have not yet been sanctioned any cremation ground, but they are free to use the river bank for cremating their corpses. In no case, the Bāuris touch earthen cooking pots and pitchers of the caste Hindus of any of the villages as these are considered as the most pollutable items. They are also not permitted to enter into the village temple but they may enter its outer boundary. However, they are now quite free to get their children admitted into any public school located within or outside the village.

The Bāuris were once denied being served tea, either in cups or in glass tumblers, and had to be satisfied with coconut shells in roadside village tea-stalls. Now it is found that the Bāuris are served tea in common glasses used by one and all irrespective of caste, creed or economic status. The Bāuris of Hirāpur have now separate benches in the village tea stalls. These benches are not used by any caste Hindu people, even if there is a rush of caste Hindus in the stalls.

The sound and air that come from the Bāuris do not cause pollution any more to caste Hindus and there are no restrictions for them to dress as caste Hindus do, and move on the village road riding bicycles and holding flashlights or umbrellas. Surprisingly, some caste Hindus, belonging to *pāni-chhuān* section, do not hesitate in sharing a common pipe for smoking mari-juana (*ganjā*) with their Bauri friends and as the rigidity of caste system is becoming more flexible, the caste panchayat can hardly do anything to punish those caste Hindu members who openly share such pipes with Bāuris in public premises inside the village.

The old belief that physical contact with Bāuris is polluting is not subscribed to by many caste Hindus of Hirāpur. Most of the caste Hindus of *Pāni-chhuān* and *Pāni-acchuān* categories do not feel polluted when they come in contact physically with their Bāuri clients while the womenfolk are more conservative and strictly observe caste rules.

To quantify the persistence of untouchability, different questions concerning to the aspects on civil areas, commensality and on day-to-day affairs were put to caste Hindus belonging to all the three social categories of population viz. *Brāhman, Pani-chhuān* and *Pāni-achhuān* of both the villages.

(A) Persistence of Untouchability Between Bāuris and Caste Hindus

(a) Use of wells

In both the villages, the Bāuris are not permitted to touch or draw water from the wells of the caste Hindus which are lined with kiln-fired earthen rings. But in some cases they can draw water from wells lined with bricks and plastered with cement mortar. Table 2.13 shows that while not a single *Brāhman* of either villages allows any Bāuri to draw water from their wells; earthenware-lined or cement mortar lined, there are as many as 70.09 of the *pāni-chhuān* and 43.59 per cent of the *pāni-achhuān* people of Hirāpur who do not allow Bāuris to fetch water from their wells as against 91.45 and 84.62 per cent , respectively, of such people in the village Āmbadiha. Thus, while 90.14 per cent of the caste Hindus of Āmbadiha do not allow Bāuris, there are only 64.44 per cent of such people in Hirāpur who restrict Bāuris from doing so.

(b) Use of Public Bathing *Ghāt*

In allowing the use of public bathing ghats, the caste Hindus of Hirāpur are fairly liberal towards the Bāuris. But even though the Bauris are allowed to use the common bathing ghats, they are strictly

TABLE 2.13

Do you allow Bāuris to draw water from your well which is lined with concrete wall ?

Village	Social Category of Population						Total N=284	
	Brāhman N=50		Pānichhuān N=117		Pāni āchhuan N=117			
	Yes	No	Yes	No	Yes	No	Yes	No
(1)	(2)	(3)	(4)	(5)	(6)	(7)	(8)	(9)
Hirāpur	—	50 (100.00)	35 (29.91)	82 (70.09)	66 (56.41)	51 (43.59)	101 (35.56)	183 (64.44)
Āmbadiha	—	50 (100.00)	10 (8.54)	107 (91.45)	18 (15.38)	99 (84.62)	28 (9.86)	256 (90.14)

Note: Figures in brackets represent %age.

forbidden from bathing along with the caste Hindus. The Bāuris are either to wait till the caste Hindus have taken their bath or go to a separate ghat meant for them and other untouchables. But, sometimes the Bāuris try to bathe along with the caste Hindus intentionally, often resulting in quarrels and inter-caste tension in the village. But, in Āmbadiha, the Bāuris are neither allowed to take bath along with the caste Hindus nor permitted to use the *ghāt* even while not being used by caste Hindus. Hence, when about 17.18 per cent of caste Hindus of Hirāpur do not permit Bāuris to bathe with them in common bathing *ghāts,* there are as many as 85.92 per cent people in Āmbadiha who restrain Bāuris from doing so (Table 2.14).

TABLE 2.14

Do you allow Bāuris to take bath with you in a common bathing ghat ?

Village	Social Category of Population						Total N=284	
	Brāhman N=50		Pānichhuān N=117		Pāni āchhuan N=117			
	Yes	No	Yes	No	Yes	No	Yes	No
(1)	(2)	(3)	(4)	(5)	(6)	(7)	(8)	(9)
Hirāpur	12 (24.00)	38 (76.00)	47 (40.17)	70 (59.83)	91 (77.78)	26 (22.22)	150 (52.82)	134 (47.18)
Āmbadiha	—	50 (100.00)	18 (15.38)	99 (84.22)	22 (18.80)	95 (81.20)	40 (14.08)	244 (85.92)

Note: Figures in brackets represent %age.

(c) Admission in Educational Institutions

With regard to education in public schools (maintained with public funds), the Bāuri students are neither denied admission nor are they placed in back benches because of their caste, but they are not treated as equals of caste Hindu students. Some caste Hindu students do not like to sit beside Bāuri classmates as their parents object to their doing so. Thus, it is found from the Table 2.15 that there are still as many as 23.74 per cent of caste Hindu parents in Hirāpur as against 19.01 per cent of Āmbadiha who restrain their children from sitting beside Bāuri classmates.

TABLE 2.15

Do you object to your children sitting beside the Bāuri classmates in the classroom ?

Village	Social Category of Population						Total N=284	
	Brāhman N=50		Pānichhuān N=117		Pāni āchhuan N=117			
	Yes	No	Yes	No	Yes	No	Yes	No
(1)	(2)	(3)	(4)	(5)	(6)	(7)	(8)	(9)
Hirāpur	2 (4.00)	48 (96.00)	17 (14.53)	100 (85.47)	3 (2.56)	114 (97.44)	66 (23.24)	218 (76.77)
Āmbadiha	27 (54.00)	23 (46.00)	23 (46.00)	94 (30.34)	4 (3.42)	113 (96.58)	54 (19.99)	230 (80.99)

Note: Figures in brackets represent %age.

(d) Dress, Public Road and Use of Luxurious Materials

In the matter of dressing, as large a chunk as 86.22 per cent of caste Hindus of Hirāpur, against 77.82 per cent of those of Āmbadiha, who do not object to Bāuris dressing up as well as they do, and go riding bicycles on the village road. They have got accustomed to this changeover the years. However, they do not normally tolerate cheeky behaviour of some of the Bāuris who often cut jokes and pass comments on them. The caste Hindus feel rather helpless in doing anything against the Bāuris, for the fear of provoking caste conflict. But whenever a serious situation arises the caste Hindus ban the Bāuris from entering the village and preventing the purchase of provisions from the village grocery shops (Table 2.16).

TABLE 2.16

Do you tolerate if the Bāuris are dressed as well as you are while going along the village road riding a bicycle ?

Village	Social Category of Population						Total N=284	
	Brāhman N=50		Pānichhuān N=117		Pāni āchhuan N=117			
	Yes	No	Yes	No	Yes	No	Yes	No
(1)	(2)	(3)	(4)	(5)	(6)	(7)	(8)	(9)
Hirāpur	41 (82.00)	9 (18.00)	92 (78.63)	25 (21.37)	113 (96.58)	4 (3.42)	246 (86.62)	38 (13.38)
Āmbadiha	38 (76.00)	12 (24.00)	77 (65.81)	40 (30.34)	77 (65.81)	40 (34.19)	192 (67.61)	92 (32.39)

Note: Figures in brackets represent %age.

(e) Mode of Address

With regard to the mode of addressing caste Hindus, many of the younger Bāuris have been very haughty by addressing caste Hindus by their first names suffixed by the word '*bāboo*'. This behaviour of the Bāuri people is not easily tolerated by most caste Hindus of both the villages. But as the caste Hindus have hardly any scope to take any action against the Bāuris, about 46.83 per cent of caste Hindus of the village Hirāpur tolerate this behaviour of their Bāuri clients as against 42.96 per cent people of the village Āmbadiha (Table 2.17).

TABLE 2.17

Do you tolerate a Bāuri addressing you by your name with the suffix 'Baboo'?

Village	Social Category of Population						Total N=284	
	Brāhman N=50		Pānichhuān N=117		Pāni āchhuan N=117			
	Yes	No	Yes	No	Yes	No	Yes	No
(1)	(2)	(3)	(4)	(5)	(6)	(7)	(8)	(9)
Hirāpur	13 (26.00)	37 (74.00)	51 (43.59)	66 (56.41)	69 (58.97)	48 (71.03)	133 (46.83)	151 (53.17)
Āmbadiha	7 (14.00)	43 (36.00)	48 (41.03)	69 (58.97)	67 (57.26)	50 (42.74)	122 (42.96)	162 (57.04)

Note: Figures in brackets represent %age.

(f) Coming in Contact with Bāuris by Physical Touch

Coming in physical contact with Bāuris causes pollution is the old belief. But it is revealed from the Table 2.18 that there are still 55.99 per cent caste Hindus in Hirāpur, against 77.46 per cent in Āmbadiha, who consider the Bāuris as pollutants, and hence, purify

TABLE 2.18

Do you purify yourself if you come in physical contact with a Bāuri?

Village	Social Category of Population						Total N=284	
	Brāhman N=50		Pānichhuān N=117		Pāni āchhuan N=117			
	Yes	No	Yes	No	Yes	No	Yes	No
(1)	(2)	(3)	(4)	(5)	(6)	(7)	(8)	(9)
Hirāpur	39 (78.00)	11 (22.00)	87 (74.36)	30 (25.64)	33 (28.21)	84 (71.79)	159 (55.99)	125 (44.00)
Āmbadiha	50 (100.00)	-	103 (88.03)	14 (11.97)	67 (57.26)	50 (42.74)	220 (77.46)	64 (22.54)

Note: Figures in brackets represent %age.

themselves whenever they come in physical contact with these people. Table 2.19 reveals that while there are as many as 68.31 per cent people in Āmbadiha, and 13.38 per cent in Hirāpur who would not share common unpollutable mats with their Bāuri friends. This means that even though these people do not believe in untouchability as a practice in private, they do not like to demonstrate this in public for fear of offending public or peer opinion. A further cursory look at the same table shows that the caste Hindus of Āmbadiha are more prestige

TABLE 2.19

Would you share a common mat with a Bāuri ?

Village	Social Category of Population						Total N=284	
	Brāhman N=50		Pānichhuān N=117		Pāni āchhuan N=117			
	Yes	No	Yes	No	Yes	No	Yes	No
(1)	(2)	(3)	(4)	(5)	(6)	(7)	(8)	(9)
Hirāpur	–	50 (100.00)	41 (35.04)	26 (64.96)	49 (41.88)	68 (58.12)	194 (68.31)	90 (31.69)
Āmbadiha	–	50 (100.00)	18 (15.38)	99 (84.62)	20 (17.09)	97 (82.91)	38 (13.38)	246 (86.62)

Note: Figures in brackets represent %age.

conscious than those of Hirāpur, as a result of which, most of them do not like to share mats which are unpollutable.

However, as many as 63 per cent people of Āmbadiha as against 80 per cent of the village Hirāpur can allow their Bāuri friends to enter into their bedrooms but certainly not to sit on their beds or any wooden seats (Table 2.20).

TABLE 2.20

Would you allow your Bāuri friend to enter your bedroom and have his seat on the floor?

Village	Social Category of Population						Total N=284	
	Brāhman N=50		Pānichhuān N=117		Pāni āchhuan N=117			
	Yes	No	Yes	No	Yes	No	Yes	No
(1)	(2)	(3)	(4)	(5)	(6)	(7)	(8)	(9)
Hirāpur	17 (34.00)	33 (66.00)	101 (86.32)	16 (13.68)	111 (94.87)	6 (5.13)	229 (80.63)	55 (19.37)
Āmbadiha	2 (4.00)	48 (96.00)	66 (56.41)	51 (43.59)	111 (94.87)	6 (5.13)	179 (63.03)	105 (36.97)

Note: Figures in brackets represent %age.

(g) Acceptance of Water and Non-food Materials

It is important to note that where inter-dining is not at all possible between Bāuris and caste Hindus of both the villages, there are about 8.45 per cent of such people in the village Hirāpur, as against only 1.06 per cent in Āmbadiha, who can accept water from the Bāuri even if in ordinary situations (Table 2.21). On the other hand comparatively

TABLE 2.21

Would you accept a glass of water from a Bāuri when you are thirsty?

Village	Social Category of Population						Total N=284	
	Brāhman N=50		Pānichhuān N=117		Pāni āchhuan N=117			
	Yes	No	Yes	No	Yes	No	Yes	No
(1)	(2)	(3)	(4)	(5)	(6)	(7)	(8)	(9)
Hirāpur	–	50 (100.00)	13 (11.11)	104 (88.89)	11 (9.40)	106 (90.60)	24 (8.45)	260 (91.55)
Āmbadiha	–	50 (100.00)	–	117 (100.00)	3 (2.54)	114 (97.44)	3 (1.06)	281 (98.94)

Note: Figures in brackets represent %age.

a larger number of persons accounting for 61.27 per cent of the former village as against only 34.15 per cent people of the latter village opine that they can accept green coconuts opened by Bāuri coconut pluckers while the rest persons consider it polluted and hence do not permit the Bāuri coconut pluckers to open it in their hand and to serve the caste Hindus (Table 2.22). At the same time comparatively higher

TABLE 2.22

Would you accept a green coconut if it is opened by a Bāuri coconut plucker?

Village	Social Category of Population						Total N=284	
	Brāhman N=50		Pānichhuān N=117		Pāni āchhuan N=117			
	Yes	No	Yes	No	Yes	No	Yes	No
(1)	(2)	(3)	(4)	(5)	(6)	(7)	(8)	(9)
Hirāpur	6 (12.00)	44 (28.00)	69 (58.97)	48 (41.03)	99 (84.62)	18 (15.38)	174 (61.27)	110 (38.73)
Āmbadiha	2 (4.00)	48 (96.00)	27 (23.08)	90 (76.92)	68 (58.12)	49 (41.88)	97 (34.15)	187 (65.86)

Note: Figures in brackets represent %age.

percentage of people in both the villages, i.e. 41.55 per cent of people of Hirāpur as against 45.42 per cent of Āmbadiha consider *Pān* unclean if it is prepared by Bāuris, and hence they do not like to accept it from them (Table 2.23).

TABLE 2.23

Would you accept a Pān (*betel leaf*) from a Bāuri person?

Village	Social Category of Population						Total N=284	
	Brāhman N=50		Pānichhuān N=117		Pāni āchhuan N=117			
	Yes	No	Yes	No	Yes	No	Yes	No
(1)	(2)	(3)	(4)	(5)	(6)	(7)	(8)	(9)
Hirāpur	15 (30.00)	35 (70.00)	61 (52.14)	56 (47.86)	98 (76.92)	27 (23.08)	166 (58.45)	118 (41.55)
Āmbadiha	18 (36.00)	32 (64.00)	33 (28.21)	84 (71.79)	104 (88.89)	13 (11.11)	155 (54.58)	129 (45.42)

Note: Figures in brackets represent %age.

(h) Purchasing of Provisions from Bāuri Shop-Keepers

Further the people are also very hesitant to procure provisions from Bāuri grocery shop-keepers because of the stigma of untouchability attached to them. Table 2.24 shows that there are about 95 per cent people in the village Hirāpur who do not like to purchase any provision from Bāuri shop-keepers. About an equal percentage of people are also there in Āmbadiha who are reluctant to go to the Bāuri shop-keepers and purchase provisions from them.

TABLE 2.24

Do you purchase provisions from Bāuri grocery shops?

Village	Social Category of Population						Total	
	Brāhman N=50		Pānichhuān N=117		Pāni āchhuan N=117		N=284	
	Yes	No	Yes	No	Yes	No	Yes	No
(1)	(2)	(3)	(4)	(5)	(6)	(7)	(8)	(9)
Hirāpur	–	50 (100.00)	2 (1.71)	115 (98.29)	7 (5.98)	110 (94.02)	9 (3.17)	275 (96.83)
Āmbadiha	–	50 (100.00)	. (2.56)	114 (97.44)	8 (6.84)	109 (93.16)	11 (3.87)	273 (96.13)

Note: Figures in brackets represent %age.

Thus, from the above discussions it may be concluded that the persistence of untouchability is more pronounced among the villagers of Āmbadiha than those of Hirāpur as the caste Hindus of the latter village have become significantly liberal than their counterparts of the former village.

Further a cursory look at all the above tables reveals that maintenance of social distance between the Bāuris and Brāhman people is more that the distance maintained between the Bāuris and *pānichhuān* and *pāniachhuan* group of people.

(B) PERSISTENCE OF UNTOUCHABILITY BETWEEN BĀURIS AND OTHER HARIJAN COMMUNITIES

Social distance is not only maintained between caste Hindus and the *Dalits* but also among the Dalits themselves. As a factor, the Bāuris who normally occupy a higher social position in the caste hierarchy also discriminate against other *Dalit* castes whom they consider lower than themselves.

The Pāna, Kandarā and Dhobā people opine that the Bāuris are socially superior to all of them in the caste hierarchy. But they are unable to rank themselves as each of them claim socio-religious superiority over the others. While the Kandarās rank themselves next to the Bāuris and claim Dhobā as the lowest because of their unclean occupation, the latter do not agree with the ranking made by the Kandarā people and claim their superiority over both the Kandarā and Panā people. However, caste ranking among these four groups was made after personal interviews with 20 sample persons from each of these castes. The result indicates that the Bāuris occupy the top-most position amongst these four castes.

According to the Bāuris, the practice of untouchability should be there but it should be properly practised without any bias. They argue that the people who do not have any unclean caste occupation should not be treated as untouchables. Hence, as they claim that their caste occupation is as prestigious as that of the *Brāhmans,* they consider themselves on par with *Brāhmans* as 'touchable' and hence they also discriminate others who are engaged in menial occupations in the same manner as they are treated by the caste Hindus.

Bāuri-Panā

Depending upon the above criteria focused by the Bāuri people, they consider pāna as untouchable. Because the pāna work on hide, beat drum and consume beef. They do not allow the pāna to fetch water from their personal or community wells. But in no case the Bāuris accept drinking water from the hand of pāna people. During the festive occasions of the Bāuri people, the panas beat drums and collect alms from them. But the Bāuris neither render their customary services to the pānas nor take any type of alms from them.

Hence, the Bāuris consider themselves as *Jajmāns* or patron to the pānas. So they do not normally like to work as labourers in the fields of the pāna people.

Bāuri-Kandarā

The Kandāras are treated as the lowest category of untouchables by the Bāuris. These people have left their traditional occupation and taken to agricultural wage-earning as their primary source of livelihood. Bāuris consider them as their client and give a *dhoti* to the caste head of kāndaras as a token of esteem during matrimony of Bāuri bridegrooms.

The Bāuris neither take any type of *kutcha* food from these people nor they allow them to fetch water from their community wells. The Bāuris do not like to work in the fields of these people but most often they play cards together and share common mats while playing the game.

Bāuri-Dhobā

The Bāuris consider the Dhobās as pollutants but as the economic condition of Dhobā people is considerably better than any other *Harijan* castes, sometimes, the Bāuris work as *Haliā* or *Kothiā* in the household of these people. However, the Bāuri labourers never feed the cows of Dhobā people which is considered as very low and perform work and causes loss of prestige. They do not accept either water or any *kutchā* food from each other but in the village Hirāpur, it is observed that many times the Bāuri children beg for alms from the Dhobā womenfolk when they return through their hamlets with their collection of alms during Hindu festive occasions. The Bāuris of Āmbadiha neither beg for alms from Dhobā women nor permit them to use their village roads for returning with polluted clothes collected from the caste Hindu patrons.

Thus, from the above discussion, it can be concluded that the Bāuris of Hirāpur have become more conscious about their right and have also been very tactful than their counterparts of Āmbadiha and hence try to revolt against the caste Hindus whenever they are ill-treated and get the advantage of the situation to their credit for their socio-economic upliftment in the society.

Chapter III

DEVELOPMENT PROCESS AND THE DALITS—THE BAURIS

3.1 CONSTITUTIONAL SAFEGUARDS—NATIONAL AND STATE OBJECTIVES

With the dawn of independence, when the Constitution of India was formulated, the planners emphasized on the alleviation of poverty, the development of educational facilities and the social upliftment of weaker sections of society, particularly of the Scheduled Castes who had been suffering from various socio-economic disabilities since time immemorial. One of the most important objectives of Government policy has been to bring them into the mainstream of national life. Government of various states also followed the policies of the Union Government and laid due emphasis on development of these people.

On the twenty sixth day of November, 1949, India adopted, enacted and gave to itself a Constitution which declared India to be a sovereign, socialist, secular and democratic republic. The philosophical and ideological backbone of the Constitution is the pledge to secure for all its citizens justice, liberty, equality and fraternity. This is clearly stated in its Preamble which reads as follows:

> "We the people of India, having solemnly resolved to constitute India into a sovereign, socialist, secular democratic republic (substituted in Forty Second Amendment Act, 1976 for Sovereign, Democratic Republic, w.e.f. 3.1.1977) and to secure to all its citizens, Justice: Social, economic and political; Liberty of thought, expression, belief, faith and worship; Equality of status and opportunity; and to promote among them all; Fraternity assuring the dignity of the individual and the unity and integrity of the nation (substituted in *ibid*, Section 2 for unity of the nation, w.e.f. 3.1.1977).

Thus, the Preamble promises the noble principles of justice, liberty, equality and fraternity to each and every citizen of free India. The Constitution of India thereby equalises the Scheduled Castes, who had been deliberately deprived of their legitimate rights and privileges since remote past. But as it was not possible on the part of these people to join the mainstream of national life on their own, the Constitution provided a package of safeguards which aimed at helping these people to join it. Specific measures were spelt out for State Governments under the 'Directive Principles of State Policy' contained in Article 46 of the Constitution. The Ministry of Home Affairs of the Union Government had been given the overall responsibility of properly implementing the safeguards provided in the Constitution, for the betterment of the Scheduled Castes.

Article 14

This Article categorically asserts the equality of all in the eyes of law. The State shall not deny to any person equality before law or the equal protection of the laws within the territory of India. Hence the Scheduled Castes can invoke legal protection against any discrimination or exploitation.

Article 15

It prohibits discrimination on grounds of religion, race, caste, sex or place of birth.

1. The state shall not discriminate against any citizen on grounds only of religion, race, caste, sex, place of birth or any of them.
2. No citizen shall, on grounds only of religion, race, caste, with regard to sex, place of birth or any of them, be subject to any disability, restriction, or condition with
   (a) access to shops, public restaurants, hotels and places of public entertainment: or
   (b) the use of wells, tanks, bathing ghats, roads and places of public resort maintained wholly or partly out of state funds or dedicated to the use of general public.
3. Nothing in this Article shall prevent the state from making any special provision for women and children.
4. Nothing in this Article or in clause (2) of Article 29 shall prevent the State from making any socially and educationally backward classes of citizens or for the Scheduled Castes and the Scheduled Tribes (added by Constitution in the First Amendment Act, 1951, S.2).

Article 16

It attempts at ensuring equal opportunities in matters of public employment.

1. There shall be equality of opportunity for all citizens in matters relating to employment or appointment to any office under the state.
2. No citizen shall, on grounds only of religion, race, sex, caste, descent, place of birth, residence or any of them, be ineligible for or discriminated against in respect of any employment or office under the state.
3. Nothing in this Article shall prevent Parliament from making any law prescribing, in regard to a class or classes of employment or appointment to an office "under the Government or any local or other authority within a state or union territory, any requirement as to residence within that state or union territory" (subs. by *ibid* in Seventh Amendment Act, S, 29) and for any state specified in the first schedule or any local or other authority within its territory any requirement as to residence within that state) prior to such employment or appointment.
4. Nothing in this Article shall prevent the state from making any provision for reservation of appointment or posts in favour of any backward class or citizen which in the opinion of the state is not adequately represented in the services under the state.
5. Nothing in this Article shall affect the operation of any law which provides that the incumbent of an office in connection with the affairs of any religious or denominational institution or any member of their body thereof shall be a person professing a particular religion or belonging to a particular denomination.

Article 17

'Untouchability' is abolished and its practice in any form is forbidden. The enforcement of any disability arising out of untouchability, shall be an offence punishable in accordance with law.

Article 19

It protects certain rights relating to right of speech, occupation etc.

1. All citizens shall have the right to:
   (a) freedom of speech and expression;
   (b) assemble peacefully without arms;
   (c) form associations or unions;

(d) roam freely throughout the territory of India;
(e) reside and settle in any part of the territory of India;
(f) acquire, hold and dispose of property; and
(g) practice any profession or carry on any occupation, trade or business.

2. Nothing in sub-clause (a) of clause (1) shall affect the operation of any existing law or prevent the state from making any law, insofar as such law imposes reasonable restrictions on the exercise of the right conferred by the said sub-clause in the interests of the sovereignty and integrity of India, the security of the state, friendly relations with foreign states, public order, decency or morality or in relation to contempt of court, defamation or incitement to an offence.
3. Nothing in sub-clause (b) of the said clause shall affect the operation of any existing law insofar as it imposes or prevents the state from making any law imposing in the interest of the sovereignty and integrity of India or public order or morality, reasonable restrictions on the exercise of the right conferred by the said sub-clause.
4. Nothing in sub-clause (c) of the said clause shall affect the operation of any existing law, insofar as it imposes or prevents the state from making any law imposing in the interest of the sovereignty and integrity of India or public order or morality, reasonable restrictions on the exercise of the right conferred by the said clause.
5. Nothing in sub-clause (d), (e) and (f) of the said clause shall affect the operation of any existing law insofar as it imposes or prevents the state from making any law imposing reasonable restrictions on the exercise of any of the rights conferred by the said sub-clauses either in interest of the general public or for the protection of the interests of any Scheduled Tribe.
6. Nothing in sub-clause (g) of the said clause shall affect the operation of any existing law insofar as it imposes or prevents the state from making any law imposing, in the interests of the general public, reasonable restrictions on the exercise of the rights conferred by the said sub-clause and in particular, nothing in the said sub-clause shall affect the operation of any existing law in so far as it relates to, or prevents the state from making any law relating to;
   (i) the professional or technical qualifications necessary for practising any profession or carrying on any occupation, trade or business, or

(ii) the carrying on by the State, or by a corporation owned or controlled by the state, of any trade, business, industry or service, whether to the exclusion, complete or partial of citizens or otherwise.

Article 23

It prohibits the traffic in human beings and 'Beggar' and forced labour.

1. Traffic in human beings 'Beggar' and other similar forms of labour are prohibited and any contravention of this provision shall be an offence punishable in accordance with law.
2. Nothing in this Article shall prevent the state from imposing compulsory service for public purposes, and in imposing such services the state shall not make any discrimination on grounds only of religion, race, caste or class or any of them.

Article 25

It provides freedom of conscience and free profession, practice and propagation of religion.

1. Subject to public order, morality and health and to the other provisions of this part, all persons are equally entitled to freedom of conscience and the right freely to process, practice and propagate religion.
2. Nothing in this Article shall affect the operation of any existing law or prevent the state from making any law—
   (a) regulating and restricting any economic, financial, political, or other secular activity which may be associated with religious practice.
   (b) providing for social welfare and reform of the throwing open of Hindu religious institutions of a public character to all classes and sections of Hindus.

Explanation I

The wearing and carrying of kripans shall be deemed to be included in the profession of Sikh religion

Explanation II

In sub-clause (b) of clause (2), the reference to Hindus shall be construed as including a reference to persons professing the Sikh, Jaina, or Buddhist religion, and the reference to Hindu religious institutions shall be construed accordingly.

Article 29

It protects the interests of minorities.

1. Any section of citizens residing in the territory of India or any part thereof having a distinct language, script or culture of its own shall have the right to conserve the same.
2. No citizen shall be denied admission into any educational institution maintained by the State or receiving aid out of state funds on grounds only of religion, race, caste, language or any of them.

Article 30

It empowers minorities to establish and administer educational institutions.

1. All minorities, whether based on religion or language, shall have the right to establish and administer educational institutions of their choice.
2. The state shall not, in granting aid to educational institutions, discriminate against any educational institution, on the ground that it is under the management of a minority, whether based on religion or language.

Article 46

It speaks of the directive principles of state policy;

The state shall promote with special care the education and economic interest of the weaker sections of the people and in particular of the Scheduled Castes and shall protect them from social injustice and all forms of exploitation.

Article 164

It concerns provisions as to Ministers specially appointed to look after the interests of Scheduled Castes and Scheduled Tribes.

1. The Chief Minister shall be appointed by the Governor and other Ministers shall be appointed by the Governor on the advice of the Chief Minister and the Ministers shall hold office during the pleasure of the Governor, provided that the state of Bihar, Madhya Pradesh and Orissa, there shall be a Minister-in-charge of the welfare of the Scheduled Castes and Backward Classes who may in addition be in charge of any other work.

Article 330

It reserves seats for Scheduled Castes in the House of People.

1. Seats shall be reserved in the House of People for Scheduled Castes.
2. The number of seats reserved in any state (or union territory) (substituted by constitution in Fifty-first Amendment Act, 1984, S. 2 for sub-clause (b) w.e.f. 16.6.1986) for the Scheduled Castes under clause (1) shall bear, as nearly as may be, the same proportion to the total number of seats allowed to that state or union territory in the House of People as the population of Scheduled Castes in the state or union territory.... or part of the state or Union territory as the case may be, in respect of which seats are so reserved, bears to the total population of the state or union territory.

Article 332

It reserves seats for Scheduled Castes in the Legislative Assemblies of the state.

1. Seats shall be reserved for the Scheduled Castes.... in the Legislative Assembly of every state (The words and letters specified in Part A or Part B of the First Schedule omitted by the Constitution in the Seventh Amendment Act).
2. The number of seats reserved for the Scheduled Castes.... in the Legislative Assembly of any state under clause (1) shall bear, as nearly as may be, the same proportion to the total number of seats in the Assembly as the population of the Scheduled Castes in the State.

Article 334

It deals with reservation of seats and special reservation to cease after fifty years (substituted by *ibid* in Sixty-second Amendment Act, 1989, S. 2 for forty years w.e.f 20.12.1989).

(a) The reservation of seats for Scheduled Castes.... in the House of the People and in the Legislative Assemblies of the State.

(b) shall cease to have effect on the expiration of a period of fifty years from the commencement of this constitution:

Provided that nothing in this Article shall affect any reservation in the House of People or Legislative Assembly, as the case may be.

Article 335

It claims Scheduled Castes..... to services and posts.

The claims of the members of the Scheduled Castes...... shall be taken into consideration, consistently with the maintenance of efficiency of administration, in the making of appointments to services and posts in connection with the affairs of the union or of a state.

Article 338

It appoints special officers for Scheduled Castes.

1. There shall be a special officer for Scheduled Castes....to be appointed by the President.
2. It shall be the duty of the Special Officer to investigate all matters relating to the safeguards provided for the Scheduled Castes.....under this constitution and report to the President upon the working of these safeguards of such internals as the President may direct, and the President shall cause all such reports to be laid before each house of Parliament.
3. In this Article, reference to the Scheduled Castes.....shall be construed as including references to such other backward classes as the President may, on receipt of the report of a Commission appointed under clause (1) of Article 340.

Article 340

It provides for the creation of a commission to investigate the condition of backward classes:

1. The President may by order appoint a Commission consisting of such persons as he thinks fit to investigate the conditions of socially and educationally backward classes, within the territory of India and the difficulties under which they labour and to make recommendations as to the steps that should be taken by the union or any state to remove such difficulties and to improve their conditions and as to the grants that should be made for the purpose by the union or any state and the conditions subject to which such grants should be made, and the order appointing such commission shall define the procedure to be followed by the Commission.
2. The Commission so appointed shall investigate the matters referred to them and present to the President a report setting the facts as found by them and making such recommendations as they think proper.
3. The President shall cause a copy of the report so presented together with a memorandum explaining the action thereon to be laid before each house of Parliament.

Article 341

1. The President "may with respect to any state" (substituted by *ibid* in First Amendment Act, 1951, S. 10 for may after consultation with the Governor or Rajpramukh of a state)", or 'Union Territory', ins. by *ibid* in seventh amendment act, 1956, S. 29 and Schedule and "*where* it is a state", (the words and letters specified in part A or part B of the first schedule, omitted by S. 29 and schedule, *ibid*), after consultation with the *Governor* (The words or Rajpramukh omitted by S. 29 and Schedule, *ibid*) thereof public notification (of constitution Scheduled Castes, Order, 1950 (C.O. 19) the constitution (Scheduled Castes) Union Territory order, 1951, (C.O. 32).
2. The Parliament may by law include in or exclude from the list of Scheduled Castes specified in a notification issued under clause (1) any caste, race, or tribe or part of or group within any caste, race or tribe, but save as aforesaid a notification issued under the said clause shall not be varied by any subsequent notification.

WELFARE MEASURES FOR SCHEDULED CASTES

1. Central Level

The Constitution has not only provided the above safeguards but also implements different socio-economic welfare programmes to fulfil these aims and objectives. The main thrust of welfare programme taken up by the Government of India for the betterment of the Scheduled Castes in the economic, educational, political and social sectors are discussed below:

(a) Economic Programmes

The economic programmes meant for the development of the Scheduled Castes include various schemes relating to poverty alleviation, allocation of land and construction of houses, development of co-operatives and cottage and village industries, and reservation of posts and services in public and private sectors which are either partly or fully assisted by Central or State Government.

(i) Allotment of land and building of houses

The Scheduled Castes were mostly landless. They used to stay in the land of caste Hindu landlords and for whom they worked on a contract basis. In order to avoid this problem, Government provide land free of cost to the landless Scheduled Castes and those who are engaged in unclean occupations. The land which is provided to them is generally available from three sources:

(i) reclaimed wastelands, (ii) surplus land released through ceiling on agricultural holdings, and (iii) land made available through *Bhoodan* movement and allotment of cultivable wastelands after proper reclamation (G.O.I., 1969: 71). In addition to these provisions of allotment of house sites, Government also provide building materials free of cost and establish new settlements through *Indira Awas Yojana* and other related housing schemes. In many states 75 per cent of the cost of the house is provided by the Government and the rest 25 per cent is met by the beneficiary in the form of labour or other means.

(ii) Facilities on Co-operatives

Development of co-operatives is another programme meant primarily for the economic development of the Scheduled Castes. Some of the important co-operative societies meant for these people are "industrial co-operatives, and co-operative housing societies, poultry co-operative societies, co-operative societies for dairying schemes, co-operative farming societies, sweepers' co-operatives, leather workers' co-operatives, basket makers' co-operatives, rickshaw pullers' co-operatives etc. (Dube, 1973: 23-24).

(iii) Reservation in Employment

Article 16(4) provides reservation of posts for the Scheduled Castes. For them, 15 per cent of posts are reserved in case the recruitment is made directly by open competition on all-India basis and it is 16 2/3 if the requirement is made on an all-India basis or by open competition (cf. Upadhyay, 1991: 65).

Reservation is also made of 15 per cent of the vacancies for the Scheduled Castes.......in promotion on the result of the competitive examination limited to departmental candidates in group B, C and D and in promotion by selection in group B, C and D to the lowest range of group A in grades or services to which direct recruitment, if any, does not exceed 66 2/3 per cent . Reservation has also been provided for Scheduled Castes.......in promotions based on seniority, subject to fitness, in group A, B, C and D post in grades or services to which direct recruitment, if any, does not exceed 66 2/3 per cent (*ibid*).

To facilitate their representation in different jobs they are provided with various concessions like relaxation of age limits, relaxation in standards of educational suitability, relaxation of qualification regarding experience in the case of direct recruitment etc. The fee payable for selection to any service or post is also reduced for candidates belonging to this class.

Government has also taken much care to let the Scheduled Caste candidates know about the existing vacancies or posts, with notification to the employment exchange, the reserved posts are also advertised in newspapers and the posts are announced over the stations of All India Radio located in areas having high concentration of Scheduled Castes. Vacancies filled through the UPSC otherwise than through examination, are advertised on the first occasion as exclusively reserved for Scheduled Castes.....and are readvertised if the first advertisement is infructuous. After the second advertisement, other community candidates can be considered, if candidates belonging to Scheduled Castes are still not available. Reservation for Scheduled Castes......is subject to a ceiling of 50 per cent of the total number of vacancies. This scheme of reservation is not only confined to Government organizations but also opened to the public undertakings and NGOs who are in receipt of substantial grants-in-aid from Government. However, they are required to adopt certain specific features of the reservation policy (*ibid*: 66).

(b) Educational Programmes

Keeping the constitutional safeguards in view, special plan and programmes are framed for educational development of the Scheduled Castes. The educational programmes in the central sector include reservation of seats in educational and technical institutions, pre and post-matric scholarship, special book bank facility, construction of girls' hostel, overseas scholarship, pre-examination training facilities and running of 'Ashram Schools'.

Article 15(4) empowers State Governments to make reservation of seats of admission of Scheduled Castes in various educational and technical institutions. As per the rule, 20 per cent of seats are reserved for the Scheduled Caste candidates in educational and technical institutions with a distinct reservation of 15 per cent of Scheduled Castes and the rest 5 per cent for the Scheduled Tribe candidates. However, it is interchangeable, i.e. if sufficient Scheduled Tribe candidates are not available, the seats meant for them may be filled up by the Scheduled Caste candidates and vice versa. They also enjoy relaxation in age and the minimum qualifying marks to get admitted into the institutions.

The book bank facility for Scheduled Caste students was started in 1978-79 with a view to providing expensive books to these students studying in medical and engineering colleges. A set of books costing about Rs. 5,000 is meant for these students who share the books among themselves for a period of three years. (cf. Upadhyay, 1991: 175).

The hostel facilities are made available for both the Scheduled Caste girl and boy students. The hostels are constructed on a matching grant of 50:50 basis provided by the Union and State Governments. Special care is taken to ensure hostel facility for the Scheduled Caste girl students in middle, high school, higher secondary schools, colleges and even Universities.

As education and employment are of paramount importance in eradicating poverty, Government have taken care to provide not only necessary education but also adequate coaching and training facilities for students of Scheduled Castes to help gain entry into All-India services such as the I.A.S., I.P.S., and other allied central cadre positions. Similar coaching facility is also provided for entry into public services of state cadre and banking, insurance and defence services. Such pre-training centres are run by both the central and state Governments on a 50:50 per cent basis and the centres run through Universities are financed exclusively by the Union Government.

(c) Removal of Untouchability

In order to achieve social equality, the heinous practice of untouchability in any form is legally forbidden under Article 17 of the Constitution and the enforcement of any disability arising out of this is an offence punishable in accordance with the law. Further, Article 15 combined with Articles 16, 19, 23, 25 and 29 are also closely related with Article 17 in attempting to abolish various manifestations of untouchability.

In 1955, the Parliament passed the Untouchability (Offence) Act, known as UOA which allows no disabilities on the ground of untouchability in regard to, inter alia, entrance and worship at temple, access to shops and restaurants, practice of occupations and trades, use of water sources, places of public resort and accommodation, public conveyance, hospitals, educational institution, construction and occupation of residential premises, holding of religious ceremonies and processions, use of jewellery and finery. As per the law, the imposition of disabilities on these grounds is made a crime punishable by fine upto Rs. 1,000, imprisonment for upto two years, cancellation or suspension of licence and of public grants. The Untouchability Offence Act makes it an offence to molest, injure, array, obstruct or attempt to obstruct the exercise of any right occurring to a person by reason of Article 17 (cf. Galanter, 1969: 139-140, Kshirsagar 1991: 42-43 and Venkataswaralu 1991: 47).

However, even though the Constitution was adopted in 1950, the law providing punishment for offences relating to untouchability was passed by Parliament only in 1955. This act, originally known as the Untouchability Offence Act (UOA), was amended and renamed as Protection of Civil Rights Act, 1955. It came into force from the 19th November, 1976 (cf. Upadhyay, 1991: 71 and Kshirsagar, 1991: 43). Further, in pursuance of the provisions made under section 15 A of the Protection of Civil Rights Act, central assistance is given to State Governments and Union territories. Provisions for legal aid has been made for victims belonging to the Scheduled Castes for protection of their civil rights. Special courts/cells/squads have been created and special officers appointed by different states for initiating and supervising prosecutions for contravention of the provisions of the Protection of Civil Rights Act. A number of states have set up committees at various levels to periodically review problems of untouchability, and cases related to it, and suggest measures for effective implementation of the PCR Act (Vatsyayan, 1987: 314-315). Similarly, for implementation of the Scheduled Castes and Scheduled Tribes Prevention of Atrocities Act, 1989, various state Governments and union territory administrations have specified District and Session courts as special court for trial of offences under this act, and in most cases monetary relief, rehabilitation and assistance are rendered to victims of atrocities. Further to completely eradicate the practice of untouchability, various schemes have been drawn up to encourage inter-caste marriage and provide legal aid in the matter. Programmes are also under way to make the general public, particularly rural, aware of the evils of untouchability, and the legal implications thereof, through the media, in both the formal and non-formal sectors.

2. State Level

In addition to the above plan and programmes of the union government, the Government of Orissa is also taking a number of additional measures for the socio-economic advancement of the Scheduled Castes of the state. These are as follows:

(a) Provision of land to landless Scheduled Castes

The Government of Orissa has made a provision for the landless Scheduled Castes under the Orissa Land Reforms (Amendment) Act,

1973. According to the Act, 70 per cent of surplus land vested with Government shall be settled with persons belonging to the Scheduled Castes and Scheduled Tribes in proportion to their respective population in a village in which the lands are situated and the remaining lands shall be settled with persons not belonging to the aforesaid categories", (C.R.S., 1982: 88). Further, unlawful alienation of land belonging to Scheduled Castes....has been prohibited under the provision of ORL Act, 1960. Similarly, drastic amendments have been effected in the Orissa Money Lenders Act, 1967 to provide relief to the weaker sections including Scheduled Castes in the field of liquidation of their indebtedness (G.O.O, 1986-87: 5-6).

(b) Establishment of Human Welfare Advisory Board

The Government of Orissa has set up the *Harijan* Welfare Advisory Board at the state level which "generally advises the state Government on all matters pertaining to *Harijan* welfare, and in particular, assessment of the requirement of the *Harijan* and formulation of welfare schemes for them and review from time to time of the working of sanctioned schemes and appraisal and evaluation of the benefits derived thereform, with a view to suggesting improvements or change in the scheme where necessary. The Board consists of 15 members including the Chief Minister and the Minister in charge of Tribal Welfare who are set as the Chairman and Deputy Chairman of the Board respectively. At least 10 members of the Board are taken from amongst the members of the State Legislature. Eight out of the entire are from the *Harijan* Community who are either members of the Legislature or from outside" (C.R.S., 1982: 77-78).

(c) Establishment of Scheduled Caste Finance Corporation

With a view to economically rehabilitating the poorest of the poor among the Scheduled Castes, the Government of Orissa have established a state level Corporation called Orissa State Scheduled Castes & Scheduled Tribes Development Finance Cooperative Ltd., during the year 1979-80. This is to act as a catalyst in channelling bank credits to the eligible and deserving Scheduled Caste families living below the poverty line by providing the required financial inputs to enable them to loans towards creation of durable assets for generating additional income. The financial input is provided in the shape of Margin Money loan @ 25 per cent of the unit cost at concessional rate of interest of only 4 per cent per annum chargeable from the second year (G.O.O, 1986: 2). However, even though the Corporation works for the betterment of the Scheduled Castes of the state as per the guidelines, it raises its fund both from the Central as well as State Government in the ratio of 49:51 (C.R.S., 1982: 77-78).

(d) Education and Employment Programme

The concessions and facilities provided to the Scheduled Caste students include mainly pre- and post-matric scholarship, reading and writing materials including nationalised and other textbooks and garments for students studying at the primary level free of cost. Special book bank facility is opened for them in the engineering and medical colleges of the state.

For imparting education to the students belonging to Scheduled Caste and Scheduled Tribe communities, Government have so far established 180 High Schools, including 42 for Girls, 104 Ashram schools including 31 for girls, 103 residential and 1,004 non-residential sevashrams. Besides, 1,411 primary school hostels in ITDA (Integrated Tribal Development Agencies) areas, and 8 special *Adivasi* hostels are running in different districts and ITDA areas of the state. Students residing in the hostels are provided with free boarding facility and stipend of Rs. 150 per boy and Rs. 155 per girl per month (G.O.O., 1994: 1).

In order to maintain good health of the boarders, the Government have introduced health card facility on the basis of which proper medical treatment is provided to each of these students free of cost.

To increase the interest of Scheduled Caste students in education and to facilitate easy entry into various technical and non-technical courses, Government have made reservation of seats in different educational institutions for admission of these students. The proportion of seats reserved for them is as follows:

1. 10 per cent in schools, colleges and hostels under the Education and Youth Service Department.
2. 8 per cent in institutions under the Orissa University of Agriculture and Technology.
3. 20 per cent for both Scheduled Caste and Scheduled Tribe students in medical colleges under Health and Family Welfare Department.
4. 15 per cent and 5 per cent in Regional Engineering College, Rourkela and University Engineering College, Burla, respectively.
5. 16 per cent in the Industrial Training Institutes and Orissa School of Engineering under Industries Department.

6. 16 per cent in the School of Printing and Allied Trades under Commerce Department.
7. 16 per cent in the training of Sanitary Inspectors, Para Medical Workers, ANMs under the Health and Family Welfare Department, and
8. 20 per cent in the Stockman Training Centres under the F.F. and A & H Department.

Reservation of Posts and Services

Keeping in view the constitutional provisions laid down in Article 16(4) and Article 335, the legislature of the Government of Orissa enacted a legislation called the Orissa Reservation of Vacancies (ORV) in posts and services (for SCs and STs) Act, 1975, with effect from 1st July, 1976. The Act has been amended from time to time to make it more effective and fine tune to the changing needs. In making the Act and Rules as provided under the Constitution of India to safeguard the interests of the Scheduled Castes and making the facility of reservation in posts and services, Orissa has become one of the pioneer states in the country.

The ORV Act, as amended upto 1992, bears the following salient features:

1. Size of Reservation

Section 4(2) of the ORV Act, 1975 provides that the percentage of reservation of vacancies in posts and services for Scheduled Castes shall in no case be less than the percentage these people form of the total population of the state. Hence, the present percentage of reservation has been fixed at 15 on the basis of the population according to the 1981 census.

2. Applicability of the Act

The act is not only applicable to the initial appointments but also to the promotional appointments to posts and services under the state or in other authorities under the central or state Government.

3. Promotional Benefits

The Act has provision for promotion of Scheduled Caste officers on the basis of seniority subject to fitness. According to the Act, the Scheduled Castes officers shall be promoted to the next higher posts or grades against reserved vacancies irrespective of their seniority provided they possess the minimum qualification and experience required for such promotion under section 10 of the Act. Likewise, in case of promotion on the basis of selection, i.e. merit-cum-ability with due regard to seniority to Class III and within Class III posts. Separate zone of consideration numbering seven times of the reserved vacancies is applicable and Scheduled Caste candidates can be promoted against reserved vacancies subject to the candidate satisfying the minimum prescribed standard as per the provisions under rules 7(b) of the ORV rules.

Promotion to Class II within Class II and Class I (Jr.) on the basis of selection against reserved vacancies is to be made applying seven times common zone of consideration to the estimated number of vacancies. The Scheduled Caste candidates who are in zone of consideration can be promoted against reserved vacancies irrespective of merit but found fit for promotion, under rule 7(9) (ii) of the ORV Rules.

4. *Maintenance of Roster*

To ensure that the prescribed reservation has been effected, Section 5 of the Act prescribes a model roster of 100 points both in respect of initial recruitment and promotion which indicates the serial number of vacancies to be reserved for the Scheduled Castes. The roster is to be maintained in the form of a running account year by year and all the appointing authorities are required to maintain prescribed roster registers for filling up the vacancies separately for each grade in each recruitment year.

5. *Submission of Annual Report for Appointment*

It is further specified under section 13 of the Act and Rule 8 of the ORV Rules, 1976, every appointing authority is to furnish a report annually in the prescribed form to the Tribal Welfare Department, through their administrative department by 31st October of each calendar year.

6. *Inspection of Roster Register*

As per provision U/S 13(2) of the ORV Act, 1975 officers at the district level like ADM, P.A., ITDA, Sub-Collector, D.W.O., Employment Officer, ADWO, as well as, the officers at the state level starting with Director, all Deputy Secretaries, Deputy Directors, Special Officers, and S.O.-cum-U.S. of Tribal Welfare Department have been authorised to conduct inspections. The DWO has been made responsible for drawing up annual inspection programme for all the Officers and get it approved by the Collector at the district level. Similarly at the state level inspecting programme is drawn up by the

Tribal Welfare Department. Besides, the Joint Directors at the divisional level have also been asked to undertake such inspections and review the inspection reports of the district level officers under their respective jurisdiction and submit the review reports to Government. Monthly review of inspection reports received is also being made at Government level.

In addition to the above, the liaison officers of the respective departments have been authorised under section 14(d) of the ORV Act to inspect the roster register of appointing authorities under the administrative control.

7. *Appointment of department-wise officers to check violation of the Act*

For ensuring proper inspection of the Act, an officer of the rank of under Secretary or above in each department has been empowered to act as a liaison officer u/s 14 of the Act. He is responsible for checking any violation of the provisions of the Act.

8. *Punishment to the authorities violating the Act*

According to the provision under section 12(A) of the Act, if any appointment is made in contravention to the provisions of the Act and Rules, it shall be treated as voidable with effect from 1.6.82. Moreover, any authority which makes an appointment in violation of the provision of the Act and Rules shall on conviction be punished with a fine upto one thousand rupees. The Government may also draw up disciplinary proceedings against the authority concerned, and the punishment so imposed shall be recorded in the confidential character roll as provided in section 12(B) of the Act with effect from 19.12.1987. Section 19 of the Act has an overriding effect on all other acts, rules, resolutions, orders, etc.

9. *Formulating of a State Level Committee to review the implementation of the Act*

Under section 15 of the Act, a provision has been made to form a state level committee under the Chairmanship of Minister, H & TW (Harijan & Tribal Welfare referring to the Scheduled Castes & Scheduled Tribes) and five members of the Orissa Legislative Assembly, the Chief Secretary, the Secretary of the Home Department as members, and Secretary, H & TW department as Member-Secretary to review the implementation and to suggest measures for improvement in the implementation of the Act.

SPECIAL EMPLOYMENT EXCHANGE FOR SCHEDULED CASTE JOB SEEKERS

The Government of Orissa have established a Special Employment Exchange in the State Headquarters at Bhubaneswar in November, 1979, to provide better employment facilities to the educated Scheduled Caste candidates. The main objectives as envisaged in the scheme are as follows:

(a) To maintain duplicate cards of the educated registrants who have registered their names in Exchange at different levels.

(b) If an exchange in the State is not able to find out Scheduled Caste...... candidates in the area, it should send requisitions to the Special Employment Exchange which will submit candidates.

(c) The Special Employment Exchange will maintain close liaison with Scheduled Castes and Scheduled Tribes organisations for the purpose of enriching the live register in categories of occupation in which applicants are short.

(d) The exchange will monitor these cases and will also verify the establishment (C.R.S., 1982: 115-116).

CONCESSIONS PROVIDED TO SCHEDULED CASTE CANDIDATES FOR ENTRY INTO STATE GOVERNMENT SERVICES

Under Section 8 of the ORV Act, the following concessions have been given to the Scheduled Caste candidates for easy entry into Government services in the initial recruitments.

(i) **Relaxation in age:** The upper age limit prescribed for recruitment is raised by 5 years.

(ii) **Relaxation of Qualification and experience:** Qualifying experience, if any, may be relaxed upto two years, provided such relaxation is not inconsistent with efficiency.

(iii) **Fee Concession:** Fees prescribed for admission into any competitive examination or interview for recruitment is exempted.

(iv) **Concession in travelling allowance:** The actual fare (to and fro) for the journey to attend a written examinations/viva voice is paid to the candidates by the employer according to provisions under Rule 6 of the ORV rules. This concession is not applicable to candidates who are already in government service.

PRE-EXAMINATION TRAINING FACILITY

In order to help candidates belonging to the Scheduled Castes seeking jobs perform better and improve their chances of succeeding in national and state level civil service examinations conducted by UPSC, OPSC, Government have provided for various pre-recruitment training centres which function under the supervision of heads of different educational institutions. Apart from this, intensive coaching facility is also provided to them at different pre-examination training centres for banking services, Staff Selection Commission, LIC, GIC and other Public Sector undertakings and other recruitment examinations. Pre-examination training programmes are also being organised every year through 'Rajya Sainik Board' for candidates appearing at Armed Forces recruitments (G.O.O, 1991: 1-4).

FACILITY FOR TRAINING IN VARIOUS TRADES

Besides the above reservation and pre-examination training facilities, there are three technical training institutes including two training-cum-production centres which impart technical training to those interested from amongst Scheduled Castes in various trades. In addition to modern trades on the pattern of the ITI (Industrial Training Institute), like motor mechanic, welder, wireman, training in traditional calling such as tailoring and cutting (for girls) and shorthand and typing facilities have been introduced in different secondary high schools of the Harijan & Tribal Welfare Department to impart technical training to these students for their gainful employment after completion of their education (G.O.O 1982: 12).

(e) Programme for removal of Untouchability:

Over and above the development measures, adequate legislative and regulatory measures have been taken up by the Government of Orissa to eradicate the evil practice of untouchability from society. The noteworthy measures are the following:

1. An Atrocity Enquiry Committee has been constituted at the state level comprising prominent members of the state legislature, with the prime objective to enquire into cases of atrocities committed against members of the Scheduled Castes, and to submit its report to Government. Similar committees have also been formed at the district and sub-divisional levels. Further, for the effective implementation of the Untouchability Removal Act, at the grassroot level, Government have issued a circular to all the Panchayat Samities and local bodies, which

act as watchdogs in eradicating the practice of untouchability at their respective levels. The Gram Panchayats have been impressed upon the moral and legal implications arising out of the practice of untouchability. They are further given a clear understanding that if the Scheduled Castes are debarred from using public wells/tanks in the village, and are denied social justice, then Government, as a punitive measure, will withhold all financial assistance to them. In most cases this is an adequate deterrent.

2. Police officers are warned to strictly implement the Act and to punish rigorously any culprit who violates its provisions. The Committee on the Welfare of Scheduled Castes and Scheduled Tribes, in its 8th report has found that the penal provision of the PCR Act, 1955 plays a rather limited role in dealing with the problem of untouchability. The Committee suggested more concentrated efforts in dealing with the problems of untouchability by all the Government agencies at various levels. The official machinery is required to be made to feel more responsible, and involved in the task of eradicating the practice. Government in response has recently arranged to provide incentive for successful investigation and prosecution of cases under the PCR Act and specific cases of atrocities committed against members of the Scheduled Castes. Such incentives include cash rewards which may be sanctioned by the D.G. and D.I.G. of Police and special mention in CC rolls of the Investigative Officers (G.O.O, 1992: 1).
3. The victims of atrocities belonging to Scheduled Castes are provided with monetary relief.
4. The scheme of providing legal aid to these people are also in operation.
5. An action plan is in operation, both by Government and NGO activists (assisted by state funding), in creating social awareness among the people through sticking of posters, hand bills, organisation of themes, group discussions, mobile drama groups at important public places exhorting people to shun the practice of untouchability. The Department of information and public relations is impressing upon the people through radio talks, and spreading messages in village fairs and markets the desirability of being united, as also the legal implications of violating provisions against untouchability.

6. With a view to fostering social harmony, integration and oneness between the caste Hindus and untouchables, a scheme of intermarriage was introduced in 1980. According to the scheme if an inter-caste marriage takes place, the couple is entitled to an award of Rs. 3000 together with a certificate of appreciation from the Government, i.e., the concerned Collector. Their children are also entitled to have non-statutory facilities of education.

Apart from this, community halls have been constructed and are functioning in a number of *Harijan* basties. To such community halls, library books, magazines, newspapers etc. are being supplied either by Government or NGOs assisted with state funds. Very often adult education programmes run in these halls in association with young men or women of caste Hindu community. Sometimes community dinners are also organised to inculcate the feeling of oneness (G.O.O, 1991: 1-2, and Mukherjee, 1985: 49-50).

3.2 DEVELOPMENT PLANNING AND DEMOCRATIC DECENTRALISATION

Five-Year Plans (FYPs) have been an instrument of realising the aims and objectives of securing social development and social justice as laid down in the Constitution. The Government of India by a resolution on March 15, 1950, based on Articles 38 and 39(a), (b) and (c) of the Constitution, set up a Planning Commission for effective, balanced and optimal utilisation of the country's resources with an emphasis on social justice. Since then the Commission has been functioning as the kingpin of national development. It was made clear that the socio-economic development reach one and all in free India, so that it could facilitate the eradication of the existing socio-economic inequalities between the weaker sections and the rest of society. Thus, to satisfy the constitutional provisions laid down in Article 46, the planners chalked out specific programmes for the downtrodden in general, and Scheduled Castes, in particular, and made separate financial allocation in each five year plan.

So far, the Commission has formulated eight five year plans and completed implementation of seven such plans with the objectives almost unchanged. Special emphasis has been laid on the socio-economic development of Scheduled Castes. The Commission has also been giving great importance to eradication of the evil practice of untouchability since the inception of planning, and to draw these sections into the mainstream of social and political life of the Indian democracy.

THE FIRST FIVE YEAR PLAN (1951-56)

Against this background, the task of bringing about rapid socio-economic transformation of the vast rural masses, grew the Community Development and National Extension Services Programmes, launched on the 2nd October, 1952. These included various specific sectoral schemes in the areas of housing, education, the removal of untouchability, and improving the lot of the Scheduled Castes. As the Scheduled Castes were mostly landless, nearly one million new houses were provided, and mainly settled in newly constructed colonies. Special grants were sanctioned for educational development of these people. This included pre-matric and post-matric scholarships, free distribution of study material and other allied incentives including construction of hostels.

To eradicate untouchability, the plan implemented a four-fold programme which aimed at removing the practice by law, by persuasion, by building social awareness, and by encouraging democratic practices in the life of common man. Besides, the Plan also provided economic and health programmes but not to a distinct level (G.O.I., 1952: 55).

THE SECOND FIVE YEAR PLAN (1956-61)

The second FYP was launched in 1st April, 1956. This was an ambitious effort on a much larger scale than the first one. It envisaged a socialistic pattern of development which was objectively based on industrial growth, intensive agricultural programme, rise in living standard, expansion of employment opportunity and reduction of inequality in income and wealth. But as it was felt necessary to improve the educational standards as a prerequisite to providing employment, and the consequential rise in living standards, this plan laid much stress on continuing and expanding of educational plans and programmes provided in the first FYP. Under the economic programmes, assistance was mainly provided in the agricultural sector in the form of agricultural implements and assets like plough, bullocks, seeds and manure through the agricultural co-operatives established under Intensive Agricultural Programme. Self-employment schemes were introduced through sewing and training programmes. The housing programmes as envisaged in the first FYP was continued, and the Scheduled Castes were provided with high subsidy facility to construct houses (G.O.I, 1956).

THE THIRD FIVE YEAR PLAN (1961-66)

In the third FYP the sectoral emphasis on investment of the two previous plans was continued. But this Plan stressed on accelerating the process of development of the Scheduled Castes. In addition to the implementation of previous educational schemes for development, this plan provided for girls' hostels, thereby giving an impetus to the education of girl children of these people. Thus, the accent on education was stronger than those of the previous plans. This apart, though the plan gave extra attention to improving the health and hygiene of the Scheduled Castes and to providing housing facility on a larger scale, the economic programmes focused on agriculture, co-operatives, industries etc. as in earlier plans. The third FYP came to an end on 31st March 1996 and the fourth FYP should have ordinarily commenced from the 1st April 1967 but its finalisation was delayed due to several reasons. In September 1967 the Planning Commission was reconstituted, and it decided to have annual plans from 1966-69. During these annual plans no significant innovation could be formulated for the Scheduled Castes. As a result of which all the three annual plans broadly followed the programmes of the third FYP (G.O.I., 1961).

THE FOURTH FIVE YEAR PLAN (1969-74)

The fourth FYP officially commenced on April 1, 1969 with publication of the draft plan. The plan reaffirmed the thematic aims of Indian planning with a resolve to ameliorate rural poverty and to raise the living standards and economic status of the under-privileged. It was specified in the draft Plan that planning should result in greater equality in income and wealth, and that there should be progressive reduction in the concentration of income, wealth and economic power, and further that the benefits of development should accrue more and more to the relatively less privileged classes of society, whose economic and educational interests have to be promoted with special care (G.O.I., 1971-4).

In the fourth Plan, the Union Government directed the State Governments to implement the plan and programmes meant for the socio-economic development of the Scheduled Castes with special care. Consequently, in addition to the implementation of the Untouchability Offence Act, 1955 and its vigorous enforcement, the Plan offered a good package of inputs relating to sanction of housing sites and built-up houses through the creation of special housing corporations in the states, and the introduction of a number of other new schemes such as Drought Prone Area Programme (DPAP), Small Farmers Development Agency (SFDA), Marginal Farmers and Agricultural Development Agency (MFAL), Minimum Needs Programmes, Command Area Development Programme (CADP), schemes for rural employment etc.

The DPAP was specifically meant for the drought-prone districts of the country. But SFDA and MFAL programmes were introduced all over the country with the objectives of creating rural employment and increasing income level among the Scheduled Castes and other target groups.

In addition to the already existing educational programmes, the fourth Plan also introduced new educational schemes like pre-examination training facility for the Scheduled Caste candidates appearing for competitive examinations for employment under both Union and State Governments and other allied jobs.

THE FIFTH FIVE YEAR PLAN (1974-79)

With the twin goals of removing poverty with the slogan *Garibi Hatao* and attainment of self-reliance, the fifth FYP was launched on April 1, 1974. The plan played a vital role in formulating schemes for the socio-economic and educational development of the Scheduled Castes. The Plan provided a new strategy for shortening the economic gap between these people and rest of the country. For reduction and ultimate eradication of poverty from amongst the Scheduled Castes and other weaker sections, the Plan introduced various schemes like Hill Area Development Programme (HADP) Special Live-stock Production Programme (SLPP), Desert Development Programme (DDP), Whole Village Development Programme (WVDP), Training for Rural Youth and Self Employment (TRYSEM) and Integrated Rural Development Programme (IRDP) in different time phases. Of these the last programme i.e. IRDP is the single largest anti-poverty programme ever taken up in the country with the objective of creating additional employment and raising the income level of the Scheduled Castes and other target groups living below the poverty line within a stipulated time-frame. Various schemes ranging from agriculture, dairy and poultry, rural industrialisation and rural artisanship were taken up. Intensive training facility were provided and financial assistance from nationalised banks arranged with a view to foster industrial units for self-employment. The programme was family-based. Initially twenty per cent of the total investment was reserved for the benefit of the Scheduled Castes, but as the quantum of the benefit accruing to these people from various schemes included in the programme was not adequate, it was later raised to about 50 per cent (Shishir Kumar, 1980: 110-112).

The earlier schemes like SFDA, MFAC etc. were merged with the IRDP, and the Scheduled Castes were provided with improved varieties of seeds, manure and fertiliser along with agricultural implements either free of cost or at subsidised rates. For the proper management of water, irrigation facility was developed through irrigation tanks, construction of new wells and renovation of old wells, establishment of lift irrigation points energised by diesel or electricity. The Scheduled Castes were also endowed with a variety of other "Productive assets under agriculture and allied sectors (Rao and Babu, 1994: 3).

With a view to providing minimum needs to these people, the plan introduced various allied schemes with a new thrust relating to health services including developing drinking water facilities, rural electrification and greasing the previous plan in providing homestead land and constructing new houses, apart from deriving benefit of general housing schemes such as "Integrated Subsidised Housing Scheme, Village Housing Scheme, Low and Middle-income group Housing Scheme, Land Acquisition and Development Scheme" (Chetty, 1991: 28).

Besides promoting economic schemes, the Plan also accelerated the educational programmes of the previous plans. It enhanced the pre-matric stipend and scholarship, exempted students of Scheduled Castes from paying tuition and examination fees, made provision of free school uniforms and mid-day meals, created book bank facility, established residential schools and also provided educational equipment and stationery (G.O.I, 1974).

THE SIXTH FIVE YEAR PLAN

The sixth FYP was formulated after taking into account the achievements and shortcomings of the previous five-year and annual plans. It was a long-term perspective rolling Plan which mainly stressed on removal of poverty and creating of more employment with the objective of reducing the economic disparity between the Scheduled Castes and the rest of the people to an insignificant level. For this, the Plan emphatically prepared different schemes to improve the quality of life and to promote self-reliance and social equality.

The major strategy of the sixth FYP was to try to develop full employment and raise productivity. Rural employment was to be provided to meet minimum needs through the transfer of public works programmes to the Blocks. According to the measure necessary skills were imparted to the Scheduled Castes beneficiaries in order to improve their employability through decentralision of work to the block level (G.O.I, 1980).

Even though the Plan introduced new schemes like National Rural Employment Programme (NREP), the prime minister's new twenty-point programme laid great stress on the development of women and children in the rural areas, including the Scheduled Castes etc. IRDP, the nation's massive poverty alleviation programme of the fifth FYP, actually commenced in a full-fledged manner during this plan. It was started in a very few blocks but "the programme was extended to all the 5011 blocks of the country on Gandhi Jayanti i.e. 2nd October, 1980". (Rao & Babu, 1994: 3). Unlike IRDP, NREP, of this plan period, is a direct wage employment programme which aimed at eradicating the problem of rural unemployment and underemployment ..... which can at the same time contribute directly to the creation of durable assets for the community (Singh, 1986: 205).

The previous plans and programmes for the Scheduled Castes were continued but the sixth FYP initiated a major strategy for full employability, raising productivity and meeting the minimum needs by the Scheduled Castes. Still one more measure was meant for organising the Scheduled Castes in order to plug loopholes in the redistribution programme. This was expected to improve the bargaining power of the Scheduled Castes and help them enjoy the benefits that accrued from planned development (G.O.I. 1980). Further, the plan provided special incentives for implementing programmes for Scheduled Castes and for translating the objectives of the plan into reality. It envisaged the adoption of a number of redistributive measures. Under one of the measures, Blocks with a high concentration of Scheduled Caste people were selected. People were provided with credit, irrigation and electricity facility including the facility of redistributive measures on distribution of essential goods and services. The Scheduled Castes were helped in providing essential consumer goods, farm inputs and implements with the help of credit facility from banking and other financial institutions. The plan also continued paying due importance to previous educational and other allied programmes (*ibid*).

THE SEVENTH FIVE YEAR PLAN

The most important feature of the seventh FYP is introduction of Special Component Plan (SCP) for intensive development of the

Scheduled Castes. In spite of substantial flow of finance for the betterment of these people resulting in expansion of infrastructure and enlargement of coverage and there was limited involvement of Scheduled Castes in the formulation and execution of programmes resulting in failure of schemes / policies to cater to their specific needs. During the plan period an amount of Rs. 7842.92 crore was spent under special component plan, compiled from state plans to SCP, special control assistance and contribution of National SC & ST Finance and Development Corporation (G.O.I., 1985, 92-93).

This plan laid much emphasis on the educational development of the Scheduled Castes. Pre-matric stipend and scholarship were given by the State Government. Other incentives included free supply of school uniforms, stationery and textbooks. A large chunk of money was earmarked for post-matric and post-secondary courses in Arts, Science, and Commerce as well as professional and technical degrees/ diploma and certificate courses on the basis of graded means test. The book bank facility, initiated in 1978-79, was activated further and covered a larger number of students. Hostel facilities underwent a remarkable expansion along with a better and safer study environment for students.

To enhance the competitive ability of the students of Scheduled Castes and Scheduled Tribes, a total number of about 8,000 seats were created in 101 pre-examination training centres, where coaching facility was rendered to these candidates appearing in competitive examinations for entry into public and other allied services.

During the plan period, a national level institution namely National Scheduled Caste and Scheduled Tribe Finance and Development Corporation was set up for rapid economic development of these people. This acts primarily as a catalytic agent in developing schemes for employment generation and financing pilot projects. The state level SC & ST Finance and Development Corporations continued to provide economic assistance for self-employment projects. During the plan economic assistance was provided to 118.82 lakh Scheduled Caste families under various programmes including IRDP and margin money loan was distributed to about 22.56. lakh families through 21 state level Scheduled Caste Development Corporations.

During the plan, special consideration was accorded to the Scheduled Castes and Scheduled Tribes in the Integrated Rural Development Programme. The target coverage was fixed at 30 per cent of the total beneficiaries but at the end of the plan, the actual coverage came to 32.05 per cent in case of the Scheduled Castes.

However, a target of 50 per cent has been set with effect from April 1, 1990. Prior to 1990-91 the subsidy admissible for Scheduled Castes families was only 33.5 per cent which is now enhanced to 50 per cent upto a ceiling of Rs. 5000. In the wage employment programme of Jawahar Rojgar Yojana, preference is given to Scheduled Castes families and Bonded labourers.

To eradicate the practice of untouchability from society and to protect the Scheduled Castes from atrocities, Scheduled Castes and Scheduled Tribes (Prevention of Atrocities) Act, 1989 was introduced and special courts were set up in eight states for trial of offences under the Protection of Civil Rights Act. Similarly, in implementing the Scheduled Castes and Scheduled Tribes (Prevention of Atrocities) Act, State Governments and Union Territories have declared existing district and sessions courts as special courts for trial of offences under the acts and exclusive special courts were set up in Rajasthan and Andhra Pradesh. Schemes were prepared to give monetary relief as also to encourage inter-caste marriage. Programmes based on the themes against untouchability were disseminated through the media, both formal and non-formal.

In addition to all these, special programmes were also introduced to eliminate manual scavenging through conversion of service latrines in different towns of the country into pour/flush latrines and it is reported that at the end of the Seventh Plan, 9.63 lakh dry latrines were converted, 14,529 scavengers rehabilitated and scavenging abolished in about 40 towns of the country (G.O.I., 1985 and G.O.I., 1992).

DEVELOPMENT PLAN IN THE STATE OF ORISSA

Prior to the beginning of planned efforts after independence, several socio-economic programmes relating to education, economic status, health and social life of the Scheduled Castes were already in operation with the establishment of a separate department in November, 1946 on the suggestion of the Thakar Committee. But these programmes were being implemented on a very small scale owing to paucity of funds and unorganised manpower. Concerted planned effort started with the first Plan. More intensive programmes followed in full swing in the sectors of education, economy, health and sanitation, housing and other subsidiary aspects in the second Plan.

Since the role of education in the process of development cannot be ignored, spreading of education among the Scheduled Castes became one of the most important sectors in all the plans. An amount of Rs. 35.71 lakh was spent in the second Plan, which increased to

Rs. 92.96 lakh in the fourth Plan, followed by rupees 40.56 lakh in the fifth FYP period in promoting education among these people. The major schemes under the head comprised pre- and post-matric scholarship and stipend, exemption of tuition and examination fees, supply of books, stationery, school uniforms, mid-day meals, boarding grants, and construction of schools and hostel buildings in the areas of high concentration of Scheduled Tribes and Scheduled Caste population.

The major economic schemes included in the first Plan were development of irrigation facility, development of village industries such as bee-keeping, training of artisans etc., establishment of village welfare centres, supply of agricultural inputs including bullocks, and development of horticulture and animal husbandry programmes. These were further expanded in the second Plan but the "allocation made during these two plans did not follow any pre-determined targets. Schemes were taken up in an *ad hoc* manner without long-term perspectives and without close follow-up programme" (C.R.S., 1982: 196). Further, during subsequent plan periods, programmes on development of communication, social education, health and hygiene, housing etc. were taken up. In the fourth Plan these schemes continued but the schemes like supply of improved seeds, development of minor irrigation facility, land reclamation and establishment of village and cottage industries received greater emphasis. In the fifth Plan stress was given on employment generation, reduction of poverty and provisions of basic needs and services among the Scheduled Castes. In this plan, blocks with 20 per cent Scheduled Caste population were selected for intensive assistance through loans and grants for agricultural inputs and for development of horticulture and animal husbandry. Special programmes were made to substantially expand khadi, handloom and other small-scale industries in order to generate new employment opportunity for the skilled and unskilled Scheduled Caste families.

The Scheduled Castes normally stay in unhygienic habitation as a result of which they suffer from various chronic diseases. For this, concerted efforts were made over different plan periods to provide medical, drinking water and housing facilities. During the first plan period, some allopathic and ayurvedic dispensaries were set up and healthcare facilities made available. Rural drinking water facility was extended through dug-wells and water tanks. All these programmes continued in the subsequent plan periods and housing schemes were taken up with monetary assistance from the Union Government during the second, third and fourth FYP and a provision was introduced to grant subsidies to the Scheduled Castes beneficiaries for purchase of house sites and construction of houses. In the fifth Plan a massive plan of Rs. 10 crore was made for this purpose for the benefit of both the Scheduled Castes and Scheduled Tribes.

SIXTH FIVE YEAR PLAN

It was for the first time in developmental process a systematic and thoughtful effort was made for an overall development of the Scheduled Castes through the introduction of Special Component Plan in the sixth Plan with two main objectives: (i) implementing family and individual-oriented income-generating programmes for the economic development of the Scheduled Castes, and (ii) providing minimum essential facilities and services in Scheduled Castes localities to ameliorate the working and living conditions. Funds were quantified from the divisible component of all development sectors to the special component plan to meet the above objectives. This was supplemented by proportionate central share under relevant central/centrally sponsored plan schemes and special central assistance was made available to the State by the Union Government under Special Component Plan (G.O.I., 1985: 75).

The major schemes taken up under the special component plan covers dairy development, fishery development, supply of agricultural inputs including bullocks, providing of drinking water facility through dug and tube-wells, construction of village link roads, electrification of *Harijan* localities and settlements, construction of community centres, land reclamation etc. Special attention was given to the development and refinement of traditional occupations of the Scheduled Castes such as weaving, fishing, cottage industries such as bamboo-works and basket making, leather works etc.

During this Plan, a provision was made to conduct a detailed socio-economic survey of the Scheduled Castes residing in important urban areas like Cuttack, Berhampur, Sambalpur, Bhubaneswar and Puri on the basis of which need-based action plans were implemented. Special attention was given to the development of the specially vulnerable group among the Scheduled Castes and a provision of housing scheme was made for those Scheduled Castes residing in urban areas and engaged in unclean occupations.

During the sixth Plan period another important and new programme called Economic Rehabilitation of Rural Poor (ERRP) was launched in 1980. This programme is unique to Orissa. The programme aimed at raising the economic status of the rural poor above the poverty line by selecting the poorest of the poor Scheduled Castes of villages unable to earn even Rs. 1200 per annum. For this purpose, a number of schemes relating to agriculture, animal husbandry, fishery etc. Non-agricultural sector schemes like sericulture, tailoring, laundry, small shops, bullock carts etc. were also devised and the programme with no loan component in the schemes was intensified. Highest priority was given in executing land-based schemes and provision was made to develop their assets until an optimum income level was reached before withdrawal of their assistance.

At the initial stage of the sixth Plan, Integrated Rural Development Programme was introduced in 114 blocks. Later, the programme was extended to all the 314 blocks of the State with effect from 2nd October, 1980 (G.O.O. 1994: 6). Training of Rural Youth for Self Employment (TRYSEM), being a supporting component of IRDP, was started in August 1979 with a view to facilitating diversification of the activities of this programme, away from the primary sector to the secondary and tertiary sectors through both acquisition and upgradation of skills (*ibid*: p.10). This programme aims at providing basic technical and managerial skills to the rural youths in the age group of 18-35 from families below the poverty line, to enable them to take up self-employment and wage-employment in agriculture and allied sectors, industries, services and business activities (*ibid*).

A programme called Development of Women and Children in Rural Areas (DWCRA) was initially launched as a pilot programme in 5 selected districts of Orissa in 1983-84 with assistance from UNICEF to strengthen the women's component in poverty alleviation programme. Now it covers all the districts.

The main objective of the programme is to raise the income level of women of the poor households so as to secure their organised participation in social development in the direction of economic self-reliance through formation of women groups at the village level for delivery of services like credit and skill training, cash and infrastructure support for self-employment. Through the strategy of forming women groups, it is intended to give women access to basic social services like health, education, child care, nutrition, water and sanitation (*ibid*: p.9).

Under this programme, groups of poor women consisting of 10-15 persons are assisted through a package including subsidies (under IRDP) training for skill upgradation (under TRYSEM), group revolving fund, group work centres (under JRY) and special extension staff. Each group is given a one-time grant of Rs. 15,000 as revolving fund contributed by the Government of India, the State Government and the UNICEF for infrastructure, purchase of raw materials, marketing, child care etc. (*ibid*).

Towards the end of the sixth Plan, *Indira Awas Yojana* which aims at constructing dwelling units free of cost for the poorest of the poor Scheduled Castes and other target groups was started in Orissa in May, 1985. According to the revised cost, the present unit cost stands at Rs. 14,000 in plains, and Rs. 15,800 in hilly and difficult areas. From 1.4.94 the average cost of a dwelling unit under the Yojana stands at Rs. 14,000. Again 10 per cent of the resources under JRY are earmarked for those freed from being bonded labourers. Scheduled Caste and Scheduled Tribe households who are victims of atrocities, floods and other natural calamities and those below the poverty line headed by widows and unmarried women are selected as beneficiaries under the programme. The programme specified that the allotment of houses should be in the name of the female members of the beneficiary households with a view to reducing atrocities on women in society. Alternatively, this may be in the name of both the wife and husband if there is an agreement between the parties (*ibid*: pp. 2-3).

As a whole, the sixth FYP targeted assistance to four lakh Scheduled Castes families, but in fact a total number of 4,64,081 such families were benefited from different programmes. Out of this, a total number of 1,90,606 families were benefited from IRDP, 2464 from ERRP, 6798 under rehabilitation of bonded labour programmes, and 1,63,313 from other subsidiary programmes. Some of the most important achievements made in the sixth FYP are providing of 6776 rural and sanitary wells in Scheduled Caste basties, construction of 161 community centres, electrification of 410 villages with a concentration of Scheduled Castes population, providing street lights in 1669 Scheduled Castes basties. Housing facilities were provided to Scheduled Castes in 22,505 villages and 36,123 Scheduled Castes families were provided with housing sites, 12,282 Scheduled Castes persons were given 11,637 acre surplus land under the Land Ceiling Act, 34,446 acre of Government land was provided for agricultural purpose to 16,669 Scheduled Caste persons, 63 hostels were constructed for Scheduled Caste girl students and a total number of 1934 dry latrines were converted into pour/flush sanitary latrines with a view to eradicating manual scavenging (G.I.O, 1990: 246).

Apart from all these, the previous educational, health and other programmes were continued but the process was speeded up with a view to quickening the pace of improvement and the quality of life of the Scheduled Castes.

SEVENTH FIVE YEAR PLAN (1985-90)

Keeping in view the experience of previous plans, special emphasis was laid on schemes aimed at developing infrastructures. Beneficiary oriented programmes like minor irrigation, soil and water conservation, cooperation, rural roads and land reforms were given importance. In the social service sector, emphasis was given on drinking water supply, general education, technical education and health. In the production sector the emphasis was on agriculture, animal husbandry, dairy development, fisheries, small village and cottage industries.

At the beginning of the seventh FYP, 5.70 lakh Scheduled Castes families were expected to remain below the poverty line. Of these 3.10 lakh families were expected to require second and subsequent assistance for adequate income generation and rise above the poverty line. Of the remaining 2.60 lakh families were prepared to be newly covered during this plan period and altogether 5.10 lakh Scheduled Caste families were proposed to be given assistance during this plan for their economic development with the objective of enabling at least 50% i.e. about 2.50 lakh families to cross the poverty line within the plan period (G.O.I., 1985: 76-77). All the 5.1 lakh Scheduled Caste families proposed to be assisted were categorised for coverage under specific programmes i.e. 1,88,000 in IRDP, 1,80,000 in ERRP, 1,350 in Fishery schemes (state plan), 1,500 in Handloom sector (state plan), 1,700 in sericulture (mulberry) sector (state plan), and 1,36,950 in special programmes with special central assistance (*ibid*, p. 77).

The Economic Rehabilitation of Rural Poor (ERRP) which was launched in sixth Plan period continued during this plan with certain modifications regarding its linkage with all sectoral schemes with loan system. During this plan period it was tried to avoid selecting undeserving beneficiaries through the introduction of selection procedure of assisting at least 10 per cent of families per village in the plan area (G.O.O., 1987 :12).

During this plan Million Wells Schemes (MWS) was launched during 1988-89 as a sub-scheme of National Rural Employment Programme (NREP)/Rural Landless Employment Guarantee Programme (RLEGP). The scheme is now an integral part of Jawahar Rozgar Yojana (JRY) and 30 per cent of the total JRY allocation is earmarked for Million Wells Scheme. The main objective of the scheme is to provide open irrigation wells free of cost to the small and marginal farmers belonging to Scheduled Castes and Scheduled Tribes and Freed Bonded Labourers below the poverty line. Expenditure on the non-SC/ST poor families is limited to only 10 per cent of the total expenditure (*ibid*, p. 2).

Towards the end of the seventh FYP, i.e. on 1st April, 1984, two national level employment programmes (NREP & RLEGP) were merged into a single rural employment programme called Jawahar Rozgar Yojana (JRY). Its main objective is to generate gainful employment for the Scheduled Castes, Scheduled Tribes and Freed Bonded Labourers below the poverty line. The Scheme also reserved 30 per cent employment opportunity for women. The secondary objective of the scheme includes creating assets in favour of the rural poor which will be beneficial in their daily lives, positive impact on wage levels creating community and social assets, creation of sustained employment by strengthening the rural economic infrastructure and overall improvement in the quality of life in rural areas. Thus the programme aimed to develop communal infrastructure on the one hand and direct employment on the other (*ibid*, p. l).

The strategy for the special component plan for the development of Scheduled Castes aimed at economic and educational development and bringing about improvement of their working and living conditions. The main thrust of the programme was based on the following aspects.

(a) To promote economic development through beneficiary-oriented programmes for raising their income. For this, the plan aimed to assist at least 50 per cent of Scheduled Castes families living below the poverty line.
(b) Promote bastee-oriented schemes providing essential services like drinking water, drainage, street lighting, link roads, primary and adult education institutions, health units etc.,
(c) Encourage elimination of scavenging through an accelerated drive for conversion of dry latrines into water-borne latrines,
(d) educational development, and
(e) strengthen the implementing machinery.

To satisfy the first objective i.e., assisting 51 per cent of the Scheduled Caste families living below the poverty line, composite programmes were organised for the main occupational groups; among them like weavers, leather-workers, fishermen, cultivators, sericulturists etc. with provision for supply of raw materials, marketing of products, development of skill and technology and the introduction of modern tools. Emphasis was laid on traditional occupational pattern in implementing various income-generating schemes. Availability of necessary backup services and linkage to the beneficiaries was ensured by the implementing departments and agencies. Special attention was paid to the economic development of specially vulnerable groups among Scheduled Castes. Self-employment schemes for Scheduled Castes residing in urban areas were also implemented with arrangement for loan and subsidy facility (G.O.O., 1984: 76-77).

The seventh Plan also stressed on the educational development of the Scheduled Castes since in spite of all possible efforts made during previous plans, the literacy level of these people had not improved appreciably.

The important educational programme for which funds were provided in this Plan period includes continuance of many earlier schemes like pre-matric stipend/scholarship, distribution of textbooks, completion of incomplete hostels and school buildings taken up in the sixth Plan period, continuance of High School, Ashram Schools and residential Sevashram, upgradation of LP/UP Sevashrams to residential Sevashrams, providing drinking water facility in residential schools, electrification of educational institutions and maintenance of low cost hostels for primary students. The other programmes included supply of science apparatus, beds and utensils to residential schools, supply of library books and conversion of residential sevashrams and Ashram Schools to Ashram Schools and High Schools respectively.

Democratic Decentralisation

Decentralisation is defined and understood "as the transfer of planning, decision making or administrative authority from Central Government to its field organisation, local administrative units and semi-autonomous and parasitical organisation, local government or non-governmental organisation" (Rondinelli & Cheema, 1983: 18 quoted in Das, 1990: 40). In the "decentralisation process of planning, multi-level planning is basically an exercise and it ensures higher standard of living to all" (Das, 1990: 43). It "involves decentralisation of authority of the centre as well as devolution of power among formally constituted local authorities" (Khan: 1993: 34).

In India, presently a four-tier multi-level planning is in operation, starting from national planning at the central level to the Block at the grassroot level. State and district planning act as the intermediaries between these two. This four-tier multi-level planning system may be seen below:

National
(Sectoral-cum-Inter State/Inter Regional Planning)

↕

State
(Sectoral-cum-Inter District/Inter Regional Planning)

↕

District
(Regional Planning)

↕

Block
(Area Planning)

NATIONAL PLANNING

In India, National Planning Commission is the apex planning authority at the Central level. It has a number of specialists from different streams as members, and the Prime Minister as chairman. The main functions of the Commission are to indicate policy statements, deciding planning priorities, co-ordination of planning and research, control of foreign component in financing development, input-price control etc., (Nandekar, 1991: 59). The activities of the Commission is overseen by the National Development Council (NDC), the Central Ministers and the constituent states" (Das, 1990: 51-52).

The National Planning Commission prepares three types of development plans. These are:

(1) Perspective plans for 15-25 years
(2) Five Year Plans and
(3) Annual Plans within the framework of Five Year Plans.

The perspective plan is a long term plan. But the five year plans are the medium term plans which attempt to lead the economy in the direction set up by the perspective plans. On the contrary the annual plans are essentially subjective plans targeted for completion within one year and hence the scope of these plans remains limited.

STATE PLANNING

In 1962, the Planning Commission impressed on the states the need to set up planning units in the states. Their objective was to prompt the National Planning Commission through State Planning Boards, headed by the Chief Minister with other experts appointed by the State Government. State Planning is crucial to the entire planning edifice of our country "as all the state plans put together constitute nearly fifty per cent of the total national public sector plan..... and much of the central plan is also closely inter-linked with the state's plan". (Sinha, 1993: 179)

The main tasks of the State Planning Board as formulated and set by National Planning Commission in 1974 are critical quantitative and qualitative appraisal of ongoing projects, assessment of the level of development in important sectors, determination of the priorities, preparation of resource inventories, and synthesising spatial and sectoral plans into balanced or operationally integrated plans (Das, 1990: 53).

DISTRICT PLANNING

During the third five year plan, the district level planning was set for with the broad idea of carrying out planning as close to the people as possible through providing of "basic services and to satisfy urgently felt needs of the people, both rural and urban" (Nath, 1993: 65). Its main function involves "Integration of block (Mandal) plans, reappropriation of allocation from district pool, adopting centre-state prototype schemes to district variations, arranging technical inputs, compiling purposive statistics of district level, implementing training and conducting research, (Nandekar, 1991: 59-60).

The district is considered as a unit of planning because it is the next administrative unit within the state, having a base of administrative and technical expertise. The other reasons to choose the district as the third level unit of planning were:

(1) The Zilla Parishad elected by the people provided adequate leadership to carry out the task of planning and development and

(2) It was the only territorial unit nearest the grassroots where adequate finances and information required by Planning agencies were readily available (cf. Das, 1990: 54).

BLOCK LEVEL PLANNING

When the Janata Government came to power at the Centre in March '77, it advocated decentralisation of planning down to the block levels as the district was considered too large for proper implementation of action plans. Block level planning provides a hierarchy of levels; a cluster of villages within the block, the district, and state above it. It acts as an observation platform in close proximity with the people for whom the planning is meant, and hence, block level planning makes a bridge between the people at the grassroots and the planners at the top.

The main objectives of block level planning are as follows:

1. Optimum utilisation of growth potential of an area leading to increase in income and employment;
2. Ensuring that a larger than proportionate gains of development accrue to weaker sections of the population, small and marginal farmers, share-croppers, agricultural labourers, rural artisans etc.;
3. Fulfilment of minimum needs programme, health and medical facilities, drinking water, housing, education and supply of essential goods through a public distribution system;
4. Building up of social and economic infrastructure to achieve the above objectives;
5. Reorienting the existing institutions/organisations in order to protect the interests of the poor;
6. Building up of appropriate organisations of the poor especially to protect them from exploitation;
7. Promotion of a progressively more egalitarian structure of ownership of assets;
8. Augmenting the duration and productivity of employment of the poor and the under-employed in their existing occupations (*ibid*, pp. 55-56).

3.3 STRUCTURE OF DEVELOPMENTAL AGENCIES

Development agencies, associated at different stages in a descending order, range from Central to the Block level through intermediaries viz., in the State and district administration. Hence, the structure and organisational set up of the development agencies working for the welfare of the Scheduled Castes are discussed under these broad heads.

At the Central level, the job of welfare of the Scheduled Castes rests on a division looking after the welfare of the Backward classes in the Ministry of Home Affairs. The Division is headed by a Director-

General, who is also an *ex-officio* Joint Secretary in the Ministry of Home Affairs. He is assisted by a Deputy Director and five Zone Directors. The main functions of the Director-General are:

(1) to formulate programmes for Backward classes;
(2) to liaison with the State Government;
(3) to monitor the implementation of the schemes;
(4) to remove bottlenecks encountered in the implementation of schemes;
(5) to critically assess the working and impact of the schemes; and
(6) to extend all assistance and co-operation, particularly in obtaining information for the Commissioner of Scheduled Castes and Scheduled Tribes whenever wanted by the Commissioner (Dubey, 1973: 35).

There is a Commissioner for the Scheduled Castes and Scheduled Tribes at the Central Level. He is appointed by the President of India. Article 338 of the Indian Constitution spells out the duty of the Commission in the following words as "to investigate all matters relating to the safeguards provided for the Scheduled Castes........ and report to the President upon the working of these safeguards at such intervals as the President may direct and the President shall cause all such reports to be laid before each house of Parliament".

At the state level, the structural arrangement is somewhat different from that of the Centre. Here, in order to administer the programme for the welfare of Scheduled Castes, the organisation set-up comprises a Minister of Social Welfare, a Secretariat and a Directorate of Backward Classes/Social Welfare. But the organisational set-up at the level of Secretariat is not uniform (*ibid*) in all the states. However, apart from the Secretariat at the state level, Directorate functions below the Secretariat. It deals with welfare programmes for the Scheduled Castes and is directly related with the field. In some states, welfare programmes for the Scheduled Castes are a part of the Directorate either of the Backward Classes, or of Welfare, while in other states this forms a part of the Directorate of Social Welfare (*ibid*, pp. 35-36).

Since planning is made at a higher level and action plans are implemented at the district level, it is understood as an important unit in the organisational set-up of the Welfare of the Scheduled Castes. The organisational units responsible for the implementation of the programmes for the welfare of the Scheduled Castes at the district level consists of various governmental machinery and the Panchayati

Raj institutions. In most of the states there are District Social Welfare Officers to implement the welfare programmes for Scheduled Castes at the district level in addition to Additional District Social Welfare Officer for land acquisition for housing sites for Scheduled Castes. The Collector acts as the head of the technical as well as of the District Social Welfare Officers and supervises their work at the district level.

Similarly, there is another organisational unit called Zilla Parishad at the district level which also deals with the implementation of the welfare schemes and measures for the Scheduled Castes. The Zilla Parishad, being the main unit in the Panchayat Raj institutions, works through various sectoral Committees. However, there is a specific Social Welfare Committee which deals with matters concerning the Scheduled Castes. It is responsible for planning, co-ordinating and in some states for execution of the development programmes" (Dubey, 1973: 38). Consequently in many states, most of the development programmes have been transferred to the Zilla Parishads, and hence, the district Technical Officers are controlled by the President of the Zilla Parishad (*ibid*, pp. 37-38).

The last unit which implements development schemes for Scheduled Castes within the district is the Panchayat Samiti. The Block Development Officer is the chief administrative officer who is assisted by different sectoral officers for smooth implementation of the programmes of the Block. He looks after the welfare programmes of the Scheduled Castes in addition to other duties.

In Orissa, the *Harijan* & Tribal Welfare Department was the nodal department for development and welfare of the Scheduled Castes and Scheduled Tribes of the state. But with a view to implementing the action plans more effectively and for smooth and efficient functioning of the administration, the integrated *Harijan* & Tribal Welfare Department came to be divided into two different departments; the Tribal Welfare Department and *Harijan* Welfare Department in 1995 under the control and supervision of the Ministry of *Harijan* and Tribal Welfare. The Development and Welfare of the Scheduled Castes have been under the control of the Principal Secretary-cum-Commissioner to Government. One post of Director for the Welfare of these people has also been created and the three Revenue Divisional Commissioners are there to ensure smooth and speedy implementation of various programmes relating to the upliftment of the Scheduled Castes in their respective divisions. To assist the Revenue Divisional Commissioners, one Joint Director is appointed in each Revenue Division. At the district level, the Collector is in overall charge of the programmes and is assisted by the District Welfare Officer including some other officials engaged in the matter (cf. G.O.O., 1994: 1).

SOCIO-ECONOMIC DEVELOPMENT INPUTS: THE BAURI BENEFICIARIES

(i) Poverty Alleviation, Rural Employment Generation and Asset Building Programmes, and the Bāuris

With a view to bringing the Scheduled Castes and the poor above the poverty line, the Government of Orissa have taken up various anti-poverty programmes, Rural Productive Employment Generation programmes and asset building programmes of the Central Government as well as some of their own. These programmes include Integrated Rural Development Programme (IRDP), Economic Rehabilitation of Rural Poor (ERRP), National Rural Employment Programme (NREP), Rural Landless Employment Guarantee Programme (RLEGP), Indira Awas Yojana (IAY), Training of Rural Youth for Self Employment (TRYSEM), Jawahar Rojagar Yojana (JRY), Development of Women and Children in Rural Areas (DWCRA) etc. which have been implemented during the sixth and seventh Five Year Plans. Apart from these major programmes, Bonded Labour Rehabilitation Programme (BLRP), Fishery Extension Programme, Disability Pension Scheme and Schemes on creation of durable assets for generating additional income through shopping complex, fishery, poultry, dairy, plantation etc. of Orissa Scheduled Caste Scheduled Tribe Development Finance Co-operative Corporation Limited (OSCSTDFCC) etc. have also been implemented in the state of Orissa during the same period.

Of these plans and programmes, IRDP, ERRP, Bonded Labour Rehabilitation programme and the sectoral schemes of Orissa Scheduled Caste Scheduled Tribe Development Finance Co-operative Corporation are the main programmes. Under these programmes, the Bāuri beneficiaries of the villages of Hirāpur and Āmbadiha were sanctioned margin money-cum-subsidy assistance of loan, both in cash and in kind, during the sixth and seventh plan periods. As a result these people who have received assistance under these programmes have been taken as beneficiaries. Those who have got daily employment under NREP and RLEGP for temporary periods are not considered as such.

It may be seen from the Table 3.1 that out of the total of 55 beneficiary households in Hirāpur, a total of 23 and 32 households, constituting about 41.81 and 58.18 per cent have been assisted under IRDP, ERRP, sectoral schemes of Orissa Scheduled Caste Scheduled

Tribe Development Finance Co-operative Corporation Ltd. (OSCST DFCC) and Bonded Labour Rehabilitation Programme, during sixth and seventh Plan periods, respectively. The corresponding figures for Āmbadiha are 29 and 21 representing 58.00 and 42.00 per cent .

TABLE 3.1

Distribution of beneficiary households according to assistance received under different programmes during 6th FYP and 7th FYP

Plan period & village / Programmes	6th FYP		7th FYP		Total	
	Hirāpur	Āmbadiha	Hirāpur	Āmbadiha	Hirāpur	Āmbadiha
(1)	(2)	(3)	(4)	(5)	(6)	(7)
IRDP	5 (9.09)	12 (24.00)	10 (18.18)	11 (22.00)	15 (27.27)	23 (26.13)
ERRP	5 (9.09)	5 (10.00)	9 (16.36)	13 (6.00)	14 (25.45)	8 (16.00)
Sectoral Schemes of OSSCSTFDCC	3 (5.45)	1 (2.00)	10 (18.18)	4 (8.00)	13 (23.64)	5 (10.00)
Bonded labour rehabilitation programme	10 (18.18)	11 (22.00)	3 (5.45)	3 (6.00)	13 (23.64)	14 (28.00)
Total	23 (41.81)	29 (58.00)	32 (58.18)	21 (42.00)	55 (100.00)	50 (100.00)

Note: Figures in brackets represent %age

A cursory look at the same table further indicates that during both these plan periods, the beneficiaries assisted under IRDP, ERRP and the sectoral schemes of OSCSTDFFCC are found to be larger in number in case of Hirāpur than that of Āmbadiha. While it is 14 (27.27%), 14 (25.45%), and 13 (23.64%) in case of the former village, it is 23 (26.00%) 8 (16.00%) and 5 (10.00%) for the latter village respectively. But the number of beneficiaries assisted under Bonded Labour Rehabilitation Programme is found to be more i.e. 14 (28.00%) in the village Āmbadiha than that of Hirāpur which is having 13 (23.64%) beneficiaries under this programmes.

PROGRAMMES AND SECTORAL SCHEMES

(a) Integrated Rural Development Programmes (IRDP)

The schemes launched under this programme are in many ways directly linked with employment creation, income and asset generation among the beneficiaries. To some extent, the schemes are also indirectly linked with some issues like removal of illiteracy, improvement of health, family welfare, greater political participation in case of both the beneficiary as well as non-beneficiary people.

This Programme includes mainly three sectors under which individual beneficiaries are selected and sanctioned loans, either in cash or in kind or both. There are: (i) the primary sector, (ii) the secondary sector, and (iii) the tertiary sector.

The primary sector covers schemes on agriculture, minor irrigation, animal husbandry and allied sectors. Further, the schemes under agriculture covers land reclamation, provision of plough, bullock, and horticulture. The sub-schemes on irrigation includes provision of dug wells and pump sets and animal husbandry and allied sectors including dairy, goat-farming, sheep-farming, pig-farming, poultry and pisciculture.

The schemes in the secondary sector cover units like blacksmithy, bamboo-work, carpentry, mat-making, pottery, stone-work, oilseed-crushing, weaving, leather-work etc., all of which are skill-based. The tertiary sector includes petty trade and business, shops, operating cycle-rickshaws, trolleys and other allied units as felt necessary by the beneficiaries. Hence, these sectoral schemes vary from area to area and in some cases even from block to block also.

The sectoral schemes, under which the Bāuri beneficiaries in both the study villages have been provided with financial assistance are: selling of paddy, vegetable selling, stationery and grocery shop, business of betel leaf, dairy farming, and goat-farming units.

Table 3.2 illustrates that out of a total of 15 beneficiaries under IRDP in Hirāpur, as many as 12 or 80 per cent have been assisted under the trade and business sector that includes 33.33 per cent beneficiaries for paddy and rice business, 26.67 per cent for grocery and stationery shops and 20 per cent for vending vegetables. Conversely, of a total of 23 beneficiaries of Āmbadiha, maximum beneficiaries, i.e. 60-70 per cent have also been covered under this sector. But while 30-43 per cent or 7 beneficiaries of Āmbadiha have been assisted in the animal husbandry sector covering 5 (21.75%) under the dairy scheme, and 2 (8.70%) under goat-farming scheme, it is merely 13.33 per cent or 2 beneficiaries in Hirāpur. Both these beneficiaries are covered in the dairy scheme. Remarkably, when a majority of beneficiaries in both the villages have been covered by trade and business and animal husbandry schemes, very few beneficiaries are found to have been assisted under agricultural sector in both the study villages.

TABLE 3.2

Beneficiary under sectoral schemes of IRDP

Sector and Scheme / Village	Agri. Plough Block	Animal Husbandry			Trade Business					Grand total
		Dairy	Goatery	Total	Paddy & rice	Vegetables	Betel Leaf	Grocery/ Stat.	Total	
(1)	(2)	(3)	(4)	(5)	(6)	(7)	(8)	(9)	(10)	(11)
Hirāpur	1 (6.67)	2 (13.33)	-	2 (13.33)	5 (33.33)	3 (20.00)	-	4 (26.67)	12 (80.00)	15 (100.00)
Āmbadiha	2 (8.70)	5 (21.74)	2 (8.70)	7 (30.43)	5 (21.74)	2 (8.70)	5 (21.74)	2 (8.70)	14 (60.70)	23 (100)

Note: Figures in brackets represent %age.

When only 1 beneficiary constituting 6.67 per cent has been assisted under agriculture sector in the village Hirāpur, there are 2 beneficiaries who account for 8.70 per cent of the total beneficiaries assisted under this programme in Āmbadiha.

(b) Economic Rehabilitation of Rural Poor (ERRP)

Like IRDP, ERRP also features three different sectors such as (i) Primary Sector (ii) Secondary Sector and (iii) Tertiary Sector.

The primary sector includes agriculture and animal husbandry schemes. But the secondary sector covers a wide range of schemes viz. bamboo-works, blacksmithy, carpentry, weaving and other skill-based schemes and the tertiary sector covers schemes on petty business, operating of cycle-rickshaws and trolleys, tailoring etc.

The beneficiaries of the study villages have been assisted under two broad sectors. The primary sector which exclusively includes schemes in animal husbandry like dairy, goat-farming and sheep-farming, covers 11 beneficiaries in Hirāpur. It works out to 78.57 per cent of the total of 14 beneficiaries of the village assisted under this programme. The rest 3 or 21.43 per cent beneficiaries have been given assistance in schemes of transport along with animal husbandry unit (Table 3.3).

It is worth mentioning here that all the beneficiaries of Āmbadiha assisted under ERRP have been assisted in the primary sector with animal husbandry schemes. Hence, it would be safe to conclude that under ERRP, animal husbandry has been given highest priority in case of both the study villages.

The same table also indicates that in both the villages dairy scheme has covered a larger number of beneficiaries, in comparison with sheep-farming. There are 3 (21.43%) beneficiaries in Hirāpur who have received assistance for transport schemes, as also for animal husbandry. A total number of 2 (14.29%) beneficiaries have been given cycle-rickshaws along with 7 goats each and the single remaining person (7.14%) has been provided with a trolley and 6 goats.

(c) Schemes of Orissa Scheduled Caste Scheduled Tribe Development Finance Co-operative Corporation Ltd.

The Orissa SC & ST Development Finance Co-operative Corporation has assisted a large chunk of the Scheduled Castes living below the poverty line under various sectoral schemes. But the major thrust of the corporation remains on the sector of trade and business

TABLE 3.3

Beneficiary under sectoral schemes of ERRP

Sector and Scheme / Village	Animal Husbandary				Transport alongwith Animal Husbandary			Grand total
	Dairy	Goatery	Sheepary	Total	Cycle Rick-shaw with goatery	Trolley with goatery	Total	
(1)	(2)	(3)	(4)	(5)	(6)	(7)	(8)	(9)
Hirāpur	5 (35.71)	3 (21.43)	3 (21.43)	11 (78.57)	2 (14.29)	1 (7.14)	3 (21.43)	14 (100.00)
Āmbadiha	3 (37.50)	3 (37.50)	2 (35.00)	8 (100.00)	-	-	-	8 (100)

Note: Figures in brackets represent %age.

in both the study villages. It is seen from Table 3.4 that, while all the 13 beneficiaries of Hirāpur have been assisted in this sector, 60 per cent or 3 of 5 beneficiaries assisted in Āmbadiha, also belong to this sector.

Among the beneficiaries assisted under the trade and business sector in Hirāpur, beneficiaries opting for paddy and rice business form the largest group. It forms 38.46 per cent of the total 5 beneficiaries followed by 23.08 per cent beneficiaries under betel leaf business. The beneficiaries under grocery and stationery in it also represent 23.08 per cent of coverage. Vegetable vending gets a low profile as it covers only 2 beneficiaries accounting for 15.38 per cent of the total beneficiaries assisted under the said scheme in this village.

It is noteworthy that there are only 5 beneficiaries under the sectoral programmes of OSCSTFDCC in Āmbadiha, of which 3 or 60 per cent have been assisted in the business category and the rest 2 or 40 per cent in the animal husbandry category. The 3 beneficiaries who have been assisted under trade and business sector have opted for trading in betel leaf.

(d) Bonded Labour Rehabilitation Programme

Bonded Labour Rehabilitation is a fully subsidised programme under which persons working as *Haliā* or *Kothiā* have been rendered economic assistance for their rehabilitation.

Of the total 13 persons assisted under this programme in Hirāpur, largest number of beneficiaries constituting 38.46 per cent have been covered by the transport scheme, and have been provided cycle-rickshaws along with goat-farming, followed by 30.77 per cent beneficiaries in trolleys along with goat-farming, and the lowest i.e., 23.08 per cent in the bullock and cart scheme. The case is just reverse in the case of Āmbadiha. It is because of the fact that there is no demand for rickshaws and trolleys due to the poor condition of the road.

Under the trade and business sector, while only 1 (7.69%) beneficiary of the former village is found to have been assisted under the scheme of trade and business for a shop, there are as many as 5 (35.71%) beneficiaries assisted under this sector in the latter village. Of the total 14 beneficiaries assisted under this programme, 3 (21.43%) have chosen trading of betel leaf and the rest 2 (14.29%) have chosen for running of stationery or grocery shop (Table 3.5).

TABLE 3.4

Beneficiary households under sectoral schemes of Orissa State Scheduled Caste Scheduled Tribe Finance Development Co-op. Corporation Ltd.

Sector and Scheme / Village	Trade & Business					Animal & Husbandry	Grand total
	Paddy & rice	Vegetables	Betel Leaf	Grocery/ Stationery	Total		
(1)	(2)	(3)	(4)	(5)	(6)	(7)	(8)
Hirāpur	5 (38.46)	2 (15.38)	3 (23.08)	3 (23.08)	13 (100.00)	-	13 (100.00)
Āmbadiha	-	-	3 (60.00)	-	3 (60.00)	2 (40.00)	5 (100.00)

Note: Figures in brackets represent %age.

TABLE 3.5

Bāuri beneficiary under various sectoral schemes of Bonded Labour Rehabilitation Programme

Sector and Scheme / Village	Transport with Animal Husbandry				Trade & Business			Grand Total
	Cycle-Rickshaw	Trolley & Goatery	Bullock & Cart	Total	Betel	Stationery	Total	
(1)	(2)	(3)	(4)	(5)	(6)	(7)	(8)	(9)
Hirāpur	5 (38.46)	4 (30.77)	3 (23.08)	12 (92.31)	-	1 (7.69)	1 (7.69)	13 (100.00)
Āmbadiha	1 (7.14)	-	8 (57.14)	9 (64.29)	3 (21.43)	2 (14.29)	5 (35.71)	14 (100.00)

Note: Figures in brackets represent %age.

All Programmes

When all the sectoral schemes of each of the above programme are put together a different picture emerges.

Table 3.6 indicates that, in case of both the villages, trade and business has attracted maximum number of beneficiaries compared to other sectors like animal husbandry, transport along with animal husbandry, and agriculture. It can also be seen from the same table that of the 55 beneficiaries of Hirāpur, 26 (47.27%) have been assisted under the trade and business sector followed by 13 (23.64%) in animal husbandry, 15 (27.27%) in transport along with animal husbandry, and only 1 (1.82%) beneficiary in agricultural sector as against 22 (44%) beneficiary of Āmbadiha in trade and business category, 17 (34%) in animal husbandry, 9 (18%) in transport along with animal husbandry sector and the rest 2 (4%) beneficiaries in the agricultural sector.

Further, it is a remarkable feature that while highest percentage (22) of beneficiaries of Āmbadiha have been assisted for trading in betel leaf, it is only 5.45 per cent in the case of Hirāpur. Whereas 10 beneficiaries constituting 18.18 per cent of Hirāpur have gone for trading in rice and paddy, it is only 5 per cent in the case of Āmbadiha. Under the Animal Husbandry sector dairy unit has the highest priority in terms of coverage of beneficiaries followed by goat and sheep-farming in both these study villages.

In the former village most of the beneficiaries have been assisted under rickshaw and trolley along with goat scheme and very few i.e. 3 (5.45%) of the total beneficiaries have been assisted under bullock-and-cart scheme along with animal husbandry sector. The trend is just reverse in a case of the latter village where out of 9 beneficiaries assisted in this category, as many as 8 have received bullock-and-cart followed by only one beneficiary who has been provided assistance for rickshaw along with goat scheme.

(ii) Selection of Beneficiaries, Funding Agencies and Mechanism of Fund Sanctioned, and the Bauris

The process of selection of the beneficiaries under IRDP, ERRP, sectoral schemes of OSSCSTFDCC and BLRP constitutes an important aspect since the objective of the above programme is to assist the poor Scheduled Castes and other such poor falling below the poverty line, and to rehabilitate the bonded labourers. To identify such persons, household survey is conducted by the Block officials during each plan period, under the guidance of District Rural Development Agency (DRDA). After the survey, households below the poverty line and the

TABLE 3.6

Beneficiary households under various sectoral schemes of all programmes (IRDP, ERDP, sectoral schemes of OSSCSTFDCL & bonded labour rehabilitation programme

Sector and Scheme / Village	Agri-culture	Trade & Business					Animal Husbandary				Transport with animal husbandry				Grand Total
	Plough & Bullock	Paddy & Rice	Vege-table	Betel Leaf	Station-ery	Total	Dairy	Goat	Sheep	Total	Rikshaw with goat	Trolley with goat	Bullock and cart	Total	
(1)	(2)	(3)	(4)	(5)	(6)	(7)	(8)	(9)	(10)	(11)	(12)	(13)	(14)	(15)	(16)
Hirāpur	1 (1.82)	10 (18.18)	5 (9.09)	3 (5.45)	8 (14.55)	26 (47.27)	7 (12.73)	3 (5.45)	3 (5,45)	13 (23.64)	7 (12.73)	5 (9.09)	3 (5.45)	15 (27.20)	55 (100.00)
Āmbadiha	2 (4.00)	5 (10.00)	2 (4.0)	11 (22.00)	4 (8.00)	22 (44.00)	10 (20.00)	5 (10.00)	2 (4.00)	17 (34.00)	1 (2.00)	–	8 (16.00)	9 (18.00)	50 (100.00)

Note: Figures in brackets represent %age.

bonded labourers are listed and referred to a village committee for comments and approval. After approval of the list at this level, the list is sent to DRDA for its final approval at the district level. In accordance with instructions and guidelines of various individual programmes, the beneficiaries are selected by the blocks giving priority to destitute groups of the target population for coverage in the programmes. But, in reality, the procedure has neither been properly followed in the Balianta block nor in Balipatna block in selecting beneficiaries of the study villages. It can be seen for Table 3.7 that of the total 55 beneficiaries of Hirāpur, as many as 13 or 23.64 per cent have induced their names in the eligibility list (below poverty line) during household survey at the village level by personal request or by any other means followed by a total number of 7 or 14 per cent beneficiaries of Āmbadiha who have managed to be listed in the same way. But while later on about 25 per cent beneficiaries in the former village could introduce their names from the ineligible to the eligible list, it is only 8 per cent in case of the latter village. The rest of the beneficiaries argue that their identification of being eligible for getting financial assistance from Government is quite justified.

TABLE 3.7

Identification of beneficiaries

Village	Total Beneficiaries	Mis-identified at village level during survey	Mis-identified at block level	Reset
(1)	(2)	(3)	(4)	(5)
Hirāpur	55 (100.00)	13 (23.64)	14 (25.45)	28 (50.91)
Āmbadiha	50 (100.00)	7 (14.00)	4 (8.00)	39 (78.00)

Note: Figures in brackets represent %age.

INFORMATION REGARDING DEVELOPMENT PROGRAMMES AND THE BAURI BENEFICIARIES

So far as information regarding the above development programmes is concerned, the main source has been the block office in case of Hirāpur and the local petty politicians, like the *Sarpanch* and ward Members in the case of Āmbadiha. As it may be observed from Table 3.8 that, of the total 55 beneficiaries of the former village,

TABLE 3.8

Distribution of beneficiaries by informers about different programmes

Village	Total Beneficiaries	Informers						
		Block Officials	Exclusively VLW	Bank Officials	Sarpanch/ Ward Members	Local Caste Hindus	Members of own caste	Local Brokers/ Middlemen
(1)	(2)	(3)	(4)	(5)	(6)	(7)	(8)	(9)
Hirāpur	55 (100.00)	16 (29.09)	3 (5.45)	6 (10.91)	11 (20.00)	6 (10.91)	10 (18.18)	3 (5.45)
Āmbadiha	50 (100.00)	6 (12.00)	7 (14.0)	1 (2.00)	12 (24.00)	5 (10.00)	9 (18.00)	10 (20.00)

Note: Figures in brackets represent %age.

as many as 16 (29.09%) have gained information from the local block officials as against 12 or 24 per cent of the total beneficiaries of 50 of the latter village who have got to know about the programmes from the local *Sarpanch* and the Ward Members. It can also be observed from the same table that while the local *Sarpanch* and the Ward Members constitute the second major sources of information forming about 20 per cent of beneficiaries in case of Hirāpur, it is the local brokers and mediators (20%) in case of the village Āmbadiha who make a bridge between the beneficiaries and the local block and bank officials. The third major source, as may be seen from the same table, are the members of their own community in case of both the villages, followed by other important sources being the VLW (14%) Block Officials (12%), local caste Hindus (10%) and Bank officials (2%) in the case of Āmbadiha. For Hirāpur it is bank officials (10.91%), local caste Hindus (10%), V.L.W. (5.45%) and local brokers (5.45%).

AGENCIES INVOLVED IN SELECTION OF BENEFICIARIES

Regarding the agencies involved in selection of the Bāuri beneficiaries Table 3.9 points out that while in both the study villages lowest percentage of beneficiaries have been selected with the involvement of Grama Sabha, the block officials have been responsible for selection of highest percentage of beneficiaries. Hence, while the involvement of Gram Sabha was only for 3.6 per cent of beneficiaries

TABLE 3.9

Agencies involved in selection of beneficiaries

Village	Total Benefi-ciaries	Agencies/Persons involved				
		Block Officials	Bank Officials	Gram Sabha	Sarpanch/ Ward Members	Local Brokers/ Middle-men
(1)	(2)	(3)	(4)	(5)	(6)	(7)
Hirāpur	55 (100.00)	39 (70.91)	9 (16.36)	2 (3.64)	3 (5.45)	2 (3.64)
Āmbadiha	50 (100.00)	27 (54.00)	4 (8.00)	3 (6.00)	7 (14.00)	9 (18.00)

Note: Figures in brackets represent %age.

in the village Hirāpur, it was 6 per cent in Āmbadiha. Likewise, while the block officials were responsible for selection of 70.91 per cent beneficiaries in Hirāpur, it was 54 per cent in case of Āmbadiha. Further, there are about 16 per cent of beneficiaries in the village Hirāpur who have been motivated because of the intervention of the local bank officials. The corresponding figure is just half, i.e. 8 per cent in case of the village Āmbadiha. A cursory look at the same table also reveals the fact that when there are only 5.45 and 3.64 per cent of the beneficiaries in the village Hirāpur, who have been able to include their names in the beneficiary list with the involvement of local petty politicians and local brokers respectively, it is as high a 14 and 18 per cent in case of the village Āmbadiha.

NO. OF VISITS PAID, AMOUNT OF MONEY SPENT TOWARDS SATISFYING DIFFERENT OFFICERS, TRAVELLING AND FOOD EXPENSES, AND THE BAURI BENEFICIARIES

The beneficiaries of both the villages are found to have paid a number of visits to different agencies in order to pursue securing financial assistance in their favour. It is important to note here that when a single visit of a beneficiary of the village Āmbadiha to its block office consumes a whole working day, it is not so in case of the village Hirāpur because of its proximity to the block headquarters.

It may be observed from Table 3.10 that in the village Hirāpur, more than 60 per cent beneficiaries (61.82%) have paid 1 to 5 visits, 27.27 per cent , 6 to 10 visits and the rest 10.91 per cent 11 or more than 11 visits to various agencies in order to ensure their names featuring in the select list, pursue the forwarding of their loan applications to the Bank, the sanction of margin money with subsidy, and finally for the disbursement respectively. The trend is just reverse in case of the village Āmbadiha as it may be noted from the same table that of the total number of 50 beneficiaries as many as 28 (58%) have visited different agencies for more than 11 times, it is only 8 or 16 per cent of the beneficiaries who are found to have visited between 1–6 times only. Further, it is worth mentioning that even though in both the study villages, the beneficiaries are found to have bribed officials in different agencies, it is more so in case of Hirāpur than Āmbadiha. As Table 3.11 reveals, it can be seen that while 17 (30.91%), 9 (16.36%), and 2 (3.64%) altogether 28 or 50.91 per cent beneficiaries have given bribes of varying amounts in cash to different officials of the Block, Bank, and the local brokers respectively, it is 4 (8%) 1 or (2%) and 9 (18%) in case of the village Āmbadiha which constitutes a total number

TABLE 3.10

No. of visits paid to different agencies/officers to obtain assistance

Village & no. of days visited / Agents Involved	Hirāpur				Āmbadiha			
	Total	1-5	6-10	11+	Total	1-5	6-10	11+
(1)	(2)	(3)	(4)	(5)	(6)	(7)	(8)	(9)
Block Officials	39 (100.00)	22 (56.41)	11 (28.21)	6 (15.38)	27 (100.00)	2 (7.41)	6 (22.22)	19 (70.37)
Bank Officials	9 (100.00)	6 (66.67)	3 (33.33)	-	4 (100.00)	-	3 (75.00)	1 (25.00)
Gram Sabha	2 (100.00)	2 (100.00)	-	-	3 (100.00)	3 (100.00)	-	-
Sarpanch/Ward Member	3 (100.00)	2 (66.67)	1 (33.33)	-	7 (100.00)	3 (42.86)	3 (42.86)	1 (14.29)
Local Brokers/ Middlemen	2 (100.00)	2 (100.00)	-	-	9 (100.00)	-	2 (22.22)	7 (77.73)
Total	55 (100.00)	34 (61.82)	15 (27.27)	6 (10.91)	50 (100.00)	8 (16.00)	14 (28.00)	28 (58.00)

Note: Figures in brackets represent %age.

of 14 that accounts for 28 per cent beneficiaries. Hence, it can be said that while higher percentage of beneficiaries of the former village have given bribes to the block officials, it is lower in case of the beneficiaries of the latter one. Larger number of beneficiaries of Āmbadiha have given bribes to the local brokers and middlemen. Not a single person of any of the village is found to have given any bribe either to any member of the Gram Sabha or to the local petty political leaders.

TABLE 3.11

Beneficiaries given bribe to different officials in obtaining assistance

Village	Total Benefi-ciaries	Agencies/Persons involved					
		Block Officials	Bank Officials	Gram Sabha	Sarpanch/ Ward Members	Local Brokers/ Middle-men	Total
(1)	(2)	(3)	(4)	(5)	(6)	(7)	(8)
Hirāpur	55 (100.00)	17 (30.91)	9 (16.39)	–	–	2 (3.64)	28 (50.91)
Āmbadiha	50 (100.00)	4 (8.00)	1 (2.00)	–	–	9 (18.00)	14 (28.00)

Note: Figures in brackets represent %age.

So far as the amount of bribe given to different persons is concerned, it can be seen from the Table 3.12 that of the total 28 beneficiaries of Hirāpur, as many as 15 (53.57%) have given more than Rs. 600 as bribe to various officials of the Block and Bank and also to the local brokers followed by only 3 or 10.71 per cent beneficiaries who have given less than Rs. 300 to the above officials. The rest of the persons are found to have given between Rs. 300 to Rs. 600. But the trend is somewhat different in case of the village Āmbadiha as it is observed from the same table that out of the total 14 beneficiaries who have given bribe to different officials, 6 (42.86%) have given between Rs. 300 and Rs. 600 followed by only 3 or 21.43 per cent who have given less than Rs. 300 as bribe. There are as many as 5 (55.55%) beneficiaries who have given more than Rs. 600 as bribe to various officials. A further cursory look at the same table reveals the fact that while most of the beneficiaries of Hirāpur have bribed the Block and Bank Officials, it is the local brokers or

TABLE 3.12

Amount spent for different officials in obtaining assistance

Agents Involved	Hirāpur Range of Bribe (in Rs.)				Āmbadiha Range of Bribe (in Rs.)			
	Total beneficiaries given bribe	300	300-600	600	Total beneficiaries given bribe	300	300-600	600
(1)	(2)	(3)	(4)	(5)	(6)	(7)	(8)	(9)
Block Officials	17 (100.00)	-	6 (35.29)	11 (64.71)	4 (100.00)	2 (50.00)	2 (50.00)	-
Bank Officials	9 (100.00)	3 (33.33)	4 (44.44)	2 (22.22)	1 (100.00)	-	1 (100.00)	-
Local Brokers/ Ward Members	2 (100.00)	-	-	2 (100.00)	9 (100.00)	1 (11.11)	3 (33.33)	5 (55.55)
Total	28 (100.00)	3 (10.71)	10 (35.71)	15 (53.57)	14 (100.00)	3 (21.43)	6 (42.86)	5 (35.71)

Note: Figures in brackets represent %age.

middlemen who have extracted money as bribe from most of the beneficiaries of Āmbadiha.

Further, while more than 50 per cent (52.73%) beneficiaries of the former village have not spent any money towards their transport and food expenses while visiting different officials for persuading margin money-cum-subsidy loan assistance from the Block in their favour, all the beneficiaries of the latter village have spent money for these purposes ranging from below Rs. 50 to above Rs. 150 (Table 3.13). Thus, from the above discussions it can be concluded that:

(i) The beneficiaries of Hirāpur have visited or met different agents or officials for less number of times and have bribed them more heavily. However, the beneficiaries of Āmbadiha have, in spite of greater distance from the Block and Bank offices, visited different agents or officials more number of times, but have given less bribe.

(ii) The beneficiaries of the former village have spent less amount of money on transport and fooding expenses while visiting the officials than those of the latter village, presumably because of its shorter distance.

TABLE 3.13

Amount spent on visits to different officials in obtaining assistance

Village	Total benefi-ciaries	Range of amount spent (in Rs.)				
		Nil	<50	50-100	100-150	150>
(1)	(2)	(3)	(4)	(5)	(6)	(7)
Hirāpur	55 (100.00)	29 (52.73)	8 (14.55)	9 (16.36)	7 (12.73)	-
Āmbadiha	50 (100.00)	-	8 (16.00)	24 (48.00)	16 (32.00)	2 (4.00)

Note: Figures in brackets represents %age.

It is obvious that the beneficiaries residing near the block head-quarters should pay more number of visits to different officials but in practice it has not happened so in case of the beneficiaries of the village Hirāpur which is located nearer to the Block headquarters. This is because of the fact that the people of this village remain very busy in Bhubaneswar in connection with their daily economic pursuits, and hence, do not like to spoil much of their time in visiting officials time and again. They rather prefer to bribe the concerned officials and make them agree to ensure and expedite their cases. They came just on the day of disbursement of margin money loan.

PROCEDURAL DELAY IN OBTAINING FINANCIAL ASSISTANCE

The statistical information pertaining to procedural delay in obtaining margin money and loan assistance is mentioned in Table 3.14. It is seen that a total number of 4 or 4.27 per cent of the beneficiaries experienced delay (beyond 3 months) in forwarding their loan applications to the Banks. They are followed by 7 or 12.73 per cent beneficiaries whose applications for sanction of margin money and loan assistance were delayed in their favour and 8 or 14.55 per cent while disbursing the loan. All these 19 beneficiaries together account for 34.55 per cent of the total 55 beneficiaries of Hirāpur. The corresponding figures are found to be 6 or 12 per cent , 10 or 20 per cent , 13 or 26 per cent and 29 or 58 per cent in case of Āmbadiha. Thus, while about 35 per cent of the beneficiaries of the former village have experienced delay at various stages of processing of their applications it is as high as 58 per cent in case of the latter village. The rest of the beneficiaries have not complained of having experienced any procedural delay at any stage of processing on their applications.

TABLE 3.14

Procedural delay in obtaining assistance (more than three months)

Village	Total beneficiaries	Forwarding of application	Sanction of loan assistance	Delay in disbursement	Total
(1)	(2)	(3)	(4)	(5)	(6)
Hirāpur	55 (100.00)	4 (7.27)	7 (12.73)	8 (14.55)	19 (34.55)
Āmbadiha	50 (100.00)	6 (12.00)	10 (20.00)	13 (26.00)	29 (58.00)

Note: Figures in brackets represent %age.

PROGRAMME-WISE ASSISTANCE AND SUBSIDY, AND THE BAURI BENEFICIARIES

So far as the total amount of assistance and subsidy received by the individual beneficiary is concerned, it can be noted from Table 3.15 that whereas in Hirāpur, the average margin money-cum-subsidy

TABLE 3.15

Programme-wise assistance and subsidy received (in Rs.) by the beneficiary households

Programme	Hirāpur (N=55)						Āmbadiha (N=50)					
	Total beneficiaries	Total assistance received	Avg. per beneficiary	Total subsidy sanctioned	Avg. per beneficiary	%age to avg. assistance per beneficiary	Total beneficiaries	Total assistance received	Avg. per beneficiary	Total subsidy sanctioned	Avg. per beneficiary	%age to avg. assistance per beneficiary
(1)	(2)	(3)	(4)	(5)	(6)	(7)	(8)	(9)	(10)	(11)	(12)	(13)
IRDP	15	43850	2923.33	14997	999.80	34.20	23	60300	2621.74	23847	1036.83	39.55
ERRP	14	42000	3000.00	25722	1837.29	61.24	8	24450	3056.25	14211	1776.38	58.12
OSSCSTF	13	49550	3811.54	28903	2223.31	58.33	5	18000	3600.00	10500	2100.00	58.33
DCL												
BLRP	13	48750	3750.00	48750	3750.00	100.00	14	64600	4614.29	64000	6460.00	100.00
Total	55	184150	3348.18	118372	2152.22	64.28	50	167350	3347.00	113158	2263.16	67.62

loan assistance per beneficiary is found to be Rs. 3811.54, Rs. 3000 and Rs. 2923.33 in case of the beneficiary assisted under different sectoral schemes of Scheduled Caste Finance Development Co-operative Corporation, ERRP and IRDP respectively, it is Rs. 3600, Rs. 3056.25 and Rs. 2621.75 in case of the village Āmbadiha. So far as assistance received under the bonded labour rehabilitation programme is concerned, the average amount of assistance per beneficiary comes to Rs. 3750 in the case of Hirāpur as against Rs. 4614.29 of Āmbadiha.

When all the programmes are taken into consideration together, the average assistance per beneficiary is found to be Rs. 3348.18 in case of the former village as against Rs. 3347 of the latter one. But when the expenditure incurred towards travelling, food expenses and bribe given to different officials before establishing the Project by the individual beneficiaries are considered, the average net assistance received per beneficiary varies from programme to programme in either villages. Thus, in Hirāpur, under bonded labour rehabilitation programme, the average assistance received per beneficiary comes to be highest, i.e. Rs. 3411.92 but it is lowest, i.e. Rs. 2274 in case of the beneficiaries assisted under IRDP. This amount comes to Rs. 3160.62 per beneficiary covered under different sectoral programmes of Scheduled Caste Finance Development Co-operative Corporation as against Rs. 2876.79 per beneficiary assisted under ERRP. The pattern is almost same in case of the village Āmbadiha but the average assistance received by the individual beneficiaries assisted under Bonded Labour Rehabilitation Programme is found to be as high as Rs. 4319.71 (Table 3.16). This is because of the fact that most of the beneficiaries under this programme have been provided with bullock and cart which costs more than any other scheme.

The pattern of subsidies is upto 50 per cent in case of IRDP, 75 per cent in ERRP as also in the case of sectoral programmes of the Scheduled Caste Finance Development Co-operative Corporation Ltd. The Bonded Labour Rehabilitation Programme is fully subsidised.

The subsidy component varies in the sectoral schemes of the above programmes depending upon the income level of the beneficiaries. As a result the average percentage of subsidy per beneficiary has varied from programme to programme in both these study villages. Thus, looking at the subsidy component, one can notice that while the average percentage of subsidy assistance per beneficiary is found to be 61.24 in case of ERRP, 58.33 under Sectoral Schemes of OSCFDCC and 34 under IRDP in Hirāpur village, the figures for the beneficiaries of Āmbadiha are 58.33, 58.12 and 39.55 for programmes of sectoral

Table 3.16

Programme-wise net assistance received by the beneficiaries

Pro-gramme	Hirāpur							Āmbadiha						
			Total expenditure incurred on							Total expenditure incurred on				
	Total benefi-ciary	Total assistance received	Travell-ing and fooding	Bribe	Total	Net assistance received	Avg. per benefi-ciary	Total benefi-ciary	Total assistance received	Trave-lling and fooding	Bribe	Total	Net assistance received	Avg. per benefici-ary
(1)	(2)	(3)	(4)	(5)	(6)	(7)	(8)	(9)	(10)	(11)	(12)	(13)	(14)	(15)
IRDP	15	43850	585	2400	2985	40865	2724	23	60300	2233	2400	4633	55667	2420.30
ERRP	14	42000	575	1150	1725	40275	2876.79	8	24450	557	1100	1657	22793	2849.13
OSSCST FDCL	13	49550	587	7875	8462	41088	3160.62	5	18000	428	1600	2028	15975	3195.00
BLRP	13	48750	145	4250	4395	44355	3411.92	14	64600	1224	2900	4124	60476	4319.71
Total	55	184150	1892	15675	17567	166583	3028.78	50	167350	4442	800	12442	154911	3098.22

schemes of OSCFDCC, ERRP and IRDP respectively. The Bonded Labour Rehabilitation Programme being fully subsidised, the proportion of subsidy is 100 per cent in both the villages. However, of the total assistance received by all the beneficiaries in all programmes, the subsidy constitutes 64.28 per cent in case of Hirāpur and 67.62 per cent in case of Āmbadiha.

(iii) Utilisation of Assistance and the Bauri Beneficiaries

Agriculture Sector

According to the data available in Table 3.6, there is only one beneficiary in Hirāpur as against 2 beneficiaries of the village Āmbadiha who had been rendered margin money-cum-subsidy loan assistance in agriculture sector. Each beneficiary had been provided with a plough and a pair of bullocks. At the time of survey, none of the beneficiaries was found to have mis-utilised the assistance. But the beneficiaries who had been covered up under the sector of trade and business, animal husbandry, and transport along with animal husbandry, reflect a different pattern of utilisation of the assistance received. The following analysis reveals the extent of utilisation or otherwise.

Trade and Business Sector

Under the trade and business sector, of the total of 26 beneficiaries in the village of Hirāpur, 11 or 42.31 per cent beneficiaries have continued the original schemes, and as many as 7 or 26.92 per cent beneficiaries who have sold their respective original assets and utilised the money in other productive units according to their own choice and convenience. Only 2 (7.09%) of the total beneficiaries are found to have partly sold their assets received and utilised the money in other productive units but the percentage is found to be 15.38 that constitutes a total number of 4 beneficiaries who have completely sold their assets and utilised the money in various non-productive activities like marriage ceremony, death ritual, festive occasions and in meeting day-to-day necessities. These 4 beneficiaries are followed by 2 other beneficiaries who have partly sold their assets and utilised the money in such non-productive activities.

In the village of Āmbadiha, a remarkable picture emerges from the same table. As many as 50 per cent or 11 beneficiaries are found to have continued with their original schemes and no one is found to have sold its assets and utilised the money in other productive units. However, as many as 36.36 per cent of the beneficiaries have completely sold their respective assets and utilised the money in various non-productive activities followed by 2 or 9.09 per cent who have partly sold their assets and utilised the money in non-productive activities. There is only one beneficiary who has partly sold its assets and utilised the money in other productive units (Table 3.17).

TABLE 3.17

Distribution of beneficiaries according to utilisation of assistance received under trade and business sector of all programmes (IRDP, sectoral schemes of OSSCSTFDCL & BLRP) in Hirāpur and Āmbadiha

Hirāpur

Schemes	Total beneficiaries	Continued the original scheme	Sold and utilized the money in OPU	Partly sold & utilized the money in OPU	Sold and utilized the money in NPA	Partly sold and utilized the money in NPA
(1)	(2)	(3)	(4)	(5)	(6)	(7)
Paddy & rice	10 (100.00)	3 (30.00)	4 (40.00)	-	1 (10.00)	2 (20.00)
Vegetables selling	5 (100.00)	3 (60.00)	-	1 (20.00)	1 (20.00)	-
Betel Leaf selling	3 (100.00)	2 (66.67)	-	1 (33.33)	-	-
Stationery & Grocery shop	8 (100.00)	3 (37.50)	3 (37.50)	-	2 (25.00)	-
Total	26 (100.00)	11 (42.31)	7 (26.92)	2 (7.09)	4 (15.38)	2 (7.69)

Āmbadiha

(1)	(2)	(3)	(4)	(5)	(6)	(7)
Paddy & rice	5 (100.00)	1 (20.00)	-	-	3 (60.00)	1 (20.00)
Vegetables selling	2 (100.00)	1 (50.00)	-	-	1 (50.00)	-
Betel Leaf selling	11 (100.00)	7 (63.64)	-	1 (9.09)	2 (18.18)	1 (9.09)
Stationery & Grocery shop	4 (100.00)	2 (50.00)	-	-	2 (50.00)	-
Total	22 (100.00)	11 (50.00)	-	1 (4.55)	8 (36.36)	2 (9.09)

Note: (i) OPU–Other Productive Units
(ii) NPA–Non-Productive Activities
(iii) Figures in parentheses represent %age.

Animal Husbandry Sector

In the village Hirāpur and Āmbadiha a total number of 13 and 17 beneficiaries respectively, have been assisted under the dairy, goat and sheep-farming schemes but the dairy scheme has a high profile in covering larger number of beneficiaries compared to goat and sheep-farming schemes in both the villages under study (Table 3.18). It is

TABLE 3.18

Distribution of beneficiaries according to utilisation of assistance received under animal husbandry sector of all programmes (IRDP, sectoral schemes of OSSCSTFDCL & BLRP) in Hirāpur and Āmbadiha

Hirāpur

Schemes	Total benefi-ciaries	Conti-nued the original scheme	Sold and utilized the money in OPU	Partly sold & utilized the money in OPU	Sold and utilized the money in NPA	Partly sold and utilized the money in NPA	Living assets died
(1)	(2)	(3)	(4)	(5)	(6)	(7)	(8)
Dairy	7 (100.00)	3 (42.86)	2 (28.57)	-	2 (28.57)	-	-
Goatery	3 (100.00)	2 (66.67)	-	-	-	-	1 (33.33)
Sheepary	3 (100.00)	-	2 (66.67)	1 (33.33)	-	-	-
Total	13 (100.00)	5 (38.46)	4 (30.77)	1 (7.69)	2 (15.38)	-	1 (7.69)

Āmbadiha

(1)	(2)	(3)	(4)	(5)	(6)	(7)	(8)
Dairy	10 (100.00)	5 (50.00)	-	1 (10.00)	1 (10.00)	3 (30.00)	-
Goatery	5 (10.00)	2 (40.00)	-	-	1 (20.00)	-	2 (40.00)
Sheepary	2 (100.00)	-	-	1 (50.00)	-	1 (50.00)	-
Total	17 (100.00)	7 (41.18)	-	2 (11.76)	2 (11.76)	4 (23.53)	2 (11.76)

Note: (i) Beneficiaries whose animals have partially died are included in continuance of original scheme

(ii) Figures in parentheses represent %age.

found that of the total 5 beneficiaries of the village Āmbadiha, 2 beneficiaries accounting for 40 per cent have completely lost their goats as the animals are dead, shortly after receiving these. A beneficiary, or 33.33 per cent of the total 3, in Hirāpur has also faced the same problem. From the total figures of all the schemes, it can be analysed that in the village of Hirāpur, a total number of 5 or 38.46 per cent of the beneficiaries are found to have continued their original schemes against 7 or 41.18 per cent of Āmbadiha. Further, while there are as many as 4 or 30.77 and 1 or 7.69 per cent beneficiaries in the former village who have fully and partly sold their assets respectively and utilised the money in other productive units, it is only 2 or 11.76 per cent in the latter village who have partially sold their assets and utilised the money in other productive units. The same table further indicates that in the villages of Hirāpur and Āmbadiha 2 beneficiaries each accounting for 15.38 and 11.76 per cent respectively have sold all their assets and utilised the money exclusively in various non-productive activities. But as many as 23.53 per cent of the total number of beneficiaries of the village Āmbadiha are found to have sold their assets partially and utilised the money in various non-productive activities. There is no one in the village Hirāpur who has partly sold any part of his assets originally received.

Transport and Animal Husbandry Sector

So far as this sector is concerned, in both the study villages, the beneficiaries have been provided with transport assets like rickshaw, trolley and cart along with animal husbandry assets, like goats and bullocks. While bullocks were sanctioned as indispensable to the drawing of the cart, the goats were provided to the beneficiaries who preferred rickshaw or trolley schemes as a supplement since surplus money was available in this sector. If a glance at the data available in Tables 3.19.1 and 3.19.2 is given, it renders that when assets like rickshaw, trolley and cart with bullocks are practically utilised, the animals, like goat are found to have been mis-utilised. The beneficiaries of both the villages complained that the quality of the goats and sheeps provided is very poor. So it has compelled them to diversify the assets.

Table 3.19.1 suggests that in the village Hirāpur there are as many as 93.33 per cent or 14 beneficiaries, who are found to have continued the rickshaw, trolley and cart with bullock schemes as against only 55.56 per cent or 5 beneficiaries of the village Āmbadiha. While there is only 1 or 6.67 per cent beneficiary in the former village who has sold his assets and utilised the money in other productive activities, there is no such beneficiary in the village Āmbadiha. Rather, in this village 3.38 per cent beneficiaries are found to have sold their assets and utilised the money in various non-productive activities.

TABLE 3.19.1

Distribution of beneficiaries according to utilisation of non-living assets received under transport alongwith animal husbandry sector of all programmes (ERRP & BLRP) in Hirāpur and Āmbadiha

Hirāpur

Schemes	Total benefi-ciaries	Conti-nued the original schemes	Sold and utilized the money in OPU	Partly sold & utilized the money in OPU	Sold and utilized the money in NPA	Partly sold and utilized the money in NPA
(1)	(2)	(3)	(4)	(5)	(6)	(7)
Rickshaw with Goatery	7 (100.00)	6 (85.71)	-	-	1 (14.29)	-
Trolley with Goatery	5 (100.00)	5 (100.00)	-	-	-	-
Bullock & cart	3 (100.00)	3 (100.00)	-	-	-	-
Total	15 (100.00)	14 (93.33)	-	-	1 (6.67)	-

Āmbadiha

(1)	(2)	(3)	(4)	(5)	(6)	(7)
Rickshaw with Goatery	1 (100.00)	-	-	-	1 (100.00)	-
Trolley with Goatery	-	-	-	-	-	-
Bullock & cart	8 (100.00)	5 (62.50)	1 (12.50)	-	2 (25.00)	-
Total	9 (100.00)	5 (55.56)	1 (11.11)	-	3 (33.33)	-

Note: (i) Utilisation of living assets is mentioned in a separate Table (Table 3.19.2)

(ii) The above figures represent the utilisation of assets like Rickshaw, Trolley and Cart

(iii) Figures in parentheses represent %age.

TABLE 3.19.2

Distribution of beneficiaries according to utilisation of assistance received under transport along with animal husbandry sector of all programmes (ERRP & BLRP) in Hirāpur and Āmbadiha

Hirāpur

Schemes	Total beneficiaries	Continued the original scheme	Sold and utilized the money in OPU	Partly sold & utilized the money in OPU	Sold and utilized the money in NPA	Partly sold and utilized the money in NPA	Living assets died
(1)	(2)	(3)	(4)	(5)	(6)	(7)	(8)
Rickshaw with Goatery	7 (100.00)	2 (28.57)	2 (28.57)	1 (14.29)	1 (14.29)	1 (14.29)	-
Trolley with Goatery	5 (100.00)	3 (60.00)	-	-	-	1 (20.00)	1 (20.00)
Bullock & Cart	3 (100.00)	3 (100.00)	-	-	-	-	-
Total	15 (100.00)	8 (53.33)	2 (13.33)	1 (6.67)	1 (6.67)	2 (13.33)	1 (6.67)

Āmbadiha

(1)	(2)	(3)	(4)	(5)	(6)	(7)	(8)
Rickshaw with Goatery	1 (100.00)	-	-	-	-	-	1 (100.00)
Trolley Goatery	-	-	-	-	-	-	-
Bullock & Cart	8 (100.00)	5	-	-	-	2	1
Total	9 (100.00)	5 (55.56)	-	-	-	2 (22.22)	2 (22.22)

Note: Figures in parentheses represents %age

Regarding the utilisation of the animals like goats and bullocks received under the above schemes, it can be understood from Table 3.19.2 that in Hirāpur, out of a total 15 beneficiaries, 8 or 53.33 per cent are continuing with their original schemes followed by 2 or 13.33 per cent, who have sold their original assets and utilised the money in various other productive units. An equal number of beneficiaries, i.e. 2 or 13.33 per cent have partially sold their original assets received but have utilised the money in non-productive activities followed by only 1 or 6.67 per cent beneficiary who is found to have sold his assets and utilised the money in other productive units. Out of the rest 2 beneficiaries, 1 is deceased and the other one has sold all his assets, i.e. goats and utilised the money in various non-productive activities.

In Āmbadiha, out of the total 9 beneficiaries, 5 (55.56%) are found to be continuing their original schemes. They are followed by 2 or 22.22 per cent who have partially sold their original assets and have utilised the money in various non-productive activities. The rest 2 or 22.22 per cent of beneficiaries have lost all their living assets as these did not survive because of their sudden unnatural death after receiving these living assets.

If the data available in Tables 3.17, 3.18, 3.19.1 and 3.19.2 are consolidated together, it can be found that a total number of 13 or 23.64 per cent households of Hirāpur have sold all their assets and utilised the money in some other productive units (OPU) followed by 4 or 7.27 per cent beneficiaries who have partially sold their original assets and have utilised their money in other productive units. There are only 4 or 8 per cent beneficiaries in the village Āmbadiha who are found to have sold their assets partially and utilised the money in other productive units (Table 3.20).

TABLE 3.20

Distribution of beneficiaries according to assets sold and utilisation of money in other productive units (OPU) (all programmes)

Village	Total benefi-ciaries	Households sold their assets		
		Fully and utilised the money in OPU	Partially and utilised the money in OPU	Total
(1)	(2)	(3)	(4)	(5)
Hirāpur	55 (100.00)	13 (23.64)	4 (7.27)	17 (30.91)
Āmbadiha	50 (100.00)	-	4 (8.00)	4 (8.00)

Note: Figures in brackets represent %age.

Likewise, from Table 3.21, it can be found that while a total of 6 beneficiaries of Hirāpur representing 10.91 per cent have sold all their assets and utilised the money entirely in various non-productive activities, it is as much as 10 or 20 per cent in the case of Āmbadiha. Further, from the same table it may also be noticed that where only 1 or 1.82 per cent beneficiary in the former village has lost all his goats because of their unnatural death, it is 2 or 4 per cent in case of the latter village.

TABLE 3.21

Distribution of beneficiaries according to assets sold and utilisation of money in non-productive activities and death of living assets (all programmes)

Village	Total benefi-ciaries	Households		
		Fully sold their assets and utilised the money in NPA	Lost all living assets due to unnatural death	Total
(1)	(2)	(3)	(4)	(5)
Hirāpur	55 (100.00)	6 (10.91)	1 (1.82)	7 (12.73)
Āmbadiha	50 (100.00)	10 (20.00)	2 (4.00)	12 (24.00)

Note: Figures in brackets represent %age

Utilisation of Money in Various Productive Units and the Bāuri Beneficiaries

When the Bāuri beneficiaries, who have sold their original assets received under various development inputs and used the money in other productive units is analysed, it is manifested from Table 3.22 that of the total 17 beneficiaries, 5 (29%) have purchased rickshaw followed by 2 (12%) beneficiary who have utilised their money in purchasing trolley. A total number of 7 (41.18%) beneficiaries have purchased bicycles in order to have an easy access to Bhubaneswar city in connection with their daily business activities. Apart from all these beneficiaries, 2 (11.76%) beneficiaries are found to have spent their money in establishing dry fish units. Both these beneficiaries sell dry fish in local villages as pedlars. At some later time, they also open their petty shops in different weekly markets held in Bhubaneswar city. Rest 1 (5%) beneficiary who has purchased a sewing machine is carrying on business in Bhubaneswar city.

In the village Āmbadiha, as many as 3 (75%) of the total 4 beneficiaries have purchased bicycles followed by only 1 (25%) beneficiary who has utilised his money in running a dry fish unit. But unlike the beneficiaries of the village Hirāpur, this beneficiary, sells dry fish in the nearby villages exclusively as a pedlar.

TABLE 3.22

Distribution of beneficiaries according to assets sold and utilization of money in other productive units (all programmes, viz., IRDP, ERRP, sectoral schemes of OSSCSTFDCL & BLRP)

Village	Benefi-ciaries utilising their asst. in OPU	Other productive units				
		Rick-shaw	Trolley	Cycle	Dry fish	Tailo-ring
(1)	(2)	(3)	(4)	(5)	(6)	(7)
Hirāpur	17 (100.00)	5 (29.41)	2 (11.76)	7 (41.18)	2 (11.76)	1 (5.88)
Āmbadiha	4 (100.00)	-	-	3 (75.00)	1 (25.00)	-

Note: Figures in brackets represent %age.

Position of Assets Retained and the Bauri Beneficiaries

The position of assets remaining with the beneficiaries by the time of survey is demonstrated in Table 3.23. The figures include the assets purchased under other productive units after selling the original assets received under various development programmes as inputs.

Position of Assets Retained under Agricultural Sector

The above table reveals that in case of all the beneficiaries of both the study villages assisted under this sector, the position of all the assets are intact and the beneficiaries are successfully running the scheme of bullocks and plough, which they have received.

Position of Assets Retained under Trade & Business Sector

In the village of Hirāpur, the sectoral schemes under trade and business have covered a total number of 26 beneficiaries. Of these 26, 15 or about 58 per cent beneficiaries are found to have retained their original assets intact. They are followed by 5 or 19.23 per cent beneficiaries, who have retained assets worth more than 50 per cent of the cost of the total assets originally received. The beneficiaries who have not retained any asset are found to be 4 in number. They account for 15.28 per cent of the total beneficiaries.

Further, the same table also indicates that in the village Āmbadiha, 11 or half the beneficiaries have retained all their original assets followed by 2 or 9.9 per cent beneficiaries, who have partly retained their assets valued at less than 50 per cent of the total cost of the assets received. The remaining 9 or 40.91 per cent beneficiaries of the total 22, have not kept any assets received under this sector (Table 3.23).

Position of Assets Retained under Animal Husbandry Sector

Table 3.23 also illustrates data pertaining to the position of assets received in the animal husbandry sector. It is observed that in the village Hirāpur most of the beneficiaries have retained all their assets. The percentage of such beneficiaries is 46.15. But the percentage of those who have not retained any asset is 30.77. A total number of 2 or 15.38 per cent of beneficiaries have retained some assets constituting below 50 per cent of the cost of the total assets originally received followed by a single person or 7.64 per cent of the beneficiaries who has partly retained his assets but it costs more than 50 per cent of the total value of the assets received.

In case of the village Āmbadiha 41.18 per cent of the beneficiaries have retained all their assets intact followed by 35.29 per cent or 9 beneficiaries, who have not retained any asset. A total number of 2 or 11.76 per cent beneficiaries have retained some assets costing below 50 per cent of the cost of the total assets originally received. An equal number of beneficiaries are also found to have retained some of the assets costing more than 50 per cent of the cost of the total assets originally received under the scheme.

Position of Assets Retained under Transport with Animal Husbandry Sector

The data available in the same table also demonstrates the position of assets retained under transport along with animal husbandry sector. It comes to the notice that there is a total number of 8 and 5 beneficiaries in the village Hirāpur and Āmbadiha who account for 53.33 and 44.56 per cent respectively in case of those who have retained all their assets intact. But while 13.33 per cent or 2 beneficiaries are found in the former village who do not possess any asset, it is 22.22 per cent or 2 beneficiaries in case of the latter village. Further in the village Hirāpur there are 2 (13.33%) and 3 (20%) beneficiaries in total who have retained some assets which cost below 50 per cent and more than 50 per cent of the total cost of the original assets received

TABLE 3.23

Distribution of beneficiaries of all the programmes (IRDP, ERRP, OSSCSTDCL & BLRP) according to position of assets

Schemes	Hirāpur		Partly retained			Āmbadiha		Partly retained		
	Total benefici-aries	Retained	Less than 50%	More than 50%	Not retained	Total benefici-aries	Retained	Less than 50%	More than 50%	Not retained
(1)	(2)	(3)	(4)	(5)	(6)	(7)	(8)	(9)	(10)	(11)
Agriculture	1 (100.00)	1 (100.00)	-	-	-	2 (100.00)	1 (50.00)	-	1 (50.00)	-
Trade & Business	26 (100.00)	15 (57.69)	2 (7.69)	5 (19.23)	4 (15.38)	22 (100.00)	11 (50.00)	2 (9.9)	-	9 (40.91)
Animal Husbandry	13 (100.00)	6 (46.15)	2 (15.38)	1 (7.69)	4 (30.79)	17 (100.00)	7 (41.18)	2 (11.76)	2 (11.76)	6 (35.29)
Transport with Animal husbandary	15 (100.00)	8 (53.33)	2 (13.33)	3 (20.00)	2 (13.33)	9 (100.00)	5 (55.56)	1 (11.11)	1 (11.11)	2 (22.22)
Total	55 (100.00)	30 (54.55)	6 (10.91)	9 (16.36)	10 (18.18)	50 (100.00)	25 (50.00)	5 (10.00)	3 (6.00)	17 (34.00)

Note: (i) Figures include the assets purchased under other productive units by selling of original assets.

(ii) Figures in brackets represent %age.

respectively. But in case of the village Āmbadiha, there is 1 (11.11%) beneficiary who has retained some assets which cost below 50 per cent of the total assets originally received. Similarly another beneficiary is also there who seems to have retained some assets of the total assets originally received. But the cost of the assets comes to be more than 50 per cent of the total assets received.

While the position of assets of all the sectors is taken into consideration, it is observed from the same table that in case of the village Hirāpur about 55 per cent beneficiaries are found to have retained all their original assets intact but it is exactly 50 per cent in case of the village Āmbadiha. But when as high as a percentage of 34 beneficiaries of the village Āmbadiha have not retained any asset it is only 18.18 per cent in case of the village Hirāpur. A further cursory look at the data available in the same table depicts that in the village Hirāpur a total number of 9 or 16.36 per cent of beneficiaries have retained some of their assets received originally which cost more than 50 per cent of the total cost of the total assets originally received. It is 3 or 6 per cent in case of the village Āmbadiha.

(iv) Demographic Structure of the Beneficiary and Non-Beneficiary Households

The demographic structure of the Bāuri people belonging to beneficiary and non-beneficiary households is illustrated in the Table 3.24. It can be observed from this table that there is a total number of 108 Bāuri households in Hirāpur of which 55 (50.93%) are beneficiary households and the rest 53 (49.07%) are non-beneficiary households. But on the contrary Āmbadiha has a total number of 119 households of which 50 (42.02%) are beneficiary households and the remaining 69 (57.98%) are non-beneficiary households.

The beneficiary households of Hirāpur constitute a total number of 212 population out of which 110 or 51.89 per cent are males and the rest 102 or 48.11 per cent are females. Likewise, the beneficiary households of the village Āmbadiha have a total number of 240 population. Of these 127 (52.92%) are males and the rest 113 (47.08%) are females.

The same table also speaks about the population profile of the non-beneficiary households. In case of the former village there are 232 population out of which 120 or 51.72 per cent are males as against the rest of 112 or 58.28 per cent females. The corresponding figures come out to be 165 or 51.56 per cent and 155 or 48.44 per cent of the total population of 320 non-beneficiary population of the village

TABLE 3.24

Beneficiary and non-beneficiary households according to population size and sex

Village	Households			Population								
				Beneficiary			Non-beneficiary			Total		
	Beneficiary	Non-beneficiary	Total	M	F	T	M	F	T	M	F	T
(1)	(2)	(3)	(4)	(5)	(6)	(7)	(8)	(9)	(10)	(11)	(12)	(13)
Hirāpur	55 (50.93)	53 (49.07)	108 (100.00)	110 (51.89)	102 (48.11)	212 (100.00)	120 (51.72)	112 (58.28)	232 (100.00)	230 (57.80)	214 (48.20)	444 (100.00)
Āmbadiha	50 (42.02)	69 (57.98)	119 (100.00)	127 (52.92)	113 (47.08)	240 (100.00)	165 (51.56)	155 (48.44)	320 (100.00)	292 (52.14)	268 (47.86)	560 (100.00)

Note: Figures in brackets represent %age.

Āmbadiha. Age and sex-wise break-ups of beneficiary and non-beneficiary population are presented in Table 3.25.

TABLE 3.25

Age and sex-wise breakup of population of beneficiary and non-beneficiary households of Hirāpur and Āmbadiha

Hirāpur

Age group	Beneficiary			Non-beneficiary			Total		
	M	F	T	M	F	T	M	F	T
(1)	(2)	(3)	(4)	(5)	(6)	(7)	(8)	(9)	(10)
0-5	12	9	21	16	13	29	28	22	50
6-10	14	7	21	15	13	28	29	20	49
11-15	13	12	25	17	12	29	30	24	54
16-20	13	12	25	12	7	19	25	19	44
21-25	9	11	20	4	16	20	13	27	40
26-35	18	18	36	22	13	35	40	31	71
36-45	12	17	29	15	12	27	27	29	56
46-65	16	14	30	12	13	25	28	27	55
65 and above	3	2	5	7	13	20	10	15	25
Total	110	102	212	120	112	232	230	214	444

Āmbadiha

Age group	Beneficiary			Non-beneficiary			Total		
	M	F	T	M	F	T	M	F	T
(1)	(2)	(3)	(4)	(5)	(6)	(7)	(8)	(9)	(10)
0-5	19	16	35	26	31	57	45	47	92
6-10	16	14	30	22	23	45	38	37	75
11-15	11	14	25	15	18	33	26	32	58
16-20	11	17	28	18	22	40	29	39	68
21-25	9	15	24	15	8	23	24	23	47
26-35	23	10	40	20	27	47	43	44	87
36-45	13	11	24	22	12	34	35	23	58
46-65	19	8	27	20	12	32	39	20	59
65 and above	6	1	7	7	2	9	13	3	16
Total	127	113	240	165	155	320	292	268	560

Note: Figures in brackets represent %age

Chapter IV

DEVELOPMENT IMPACT ON THE BAURI BENEFICIARIES

EDUCATIONAL DEVELOPMENT OF BAURIS

Education is considered as the most important factor for the socio-economic development of any group of people. Hence, Article 45 of the Constitution of India enjoins that "the state shall endeavour to provide within a period of ten years from the commencement of this constitution, for free and compulsory education for all children until they complete the age of fourteen years". Further, with a view to improving the educational status of the Scheduled Castes, the Indian Constitution has specified in Article 46 that "the state shall protect with special care the educational and economic interests of the weaker sections of the people, in particular of the Scheduled Castes... and shall protect them from social injustices and all forms of exploitation". Hence, at the primary stage, universal free and compulsory education was spelt out in the Constitution with the objective that it would open the gates to further and higher education, both liberal and technical. Thus, the Constitution reflects the intention of the nation to provide universal, free and compulsory education for the people in general, and the Scheduled Castes in particular, with due safeguards of protecting them from the stigma of untouchability in the educational institutions.

In the past, on the one hand, the Scheduled Castes were barred by caste Hindus from attending public educational institutions while, on the other hand, most of the Scheduled Caste people never thought of studying but of taking up one of their traditional jobs or professions. Though, nowadays, most of them have become conscious about the importance of education, and are now quite aware of its benefits. Still then on the authority of the 1991 census, the literacy among these people is found to be very low at 37.41 per cent only, as against 52.21 per cent for India as a whole and 49.09 per cent for the state of Orissa. This low level of literacy among these people is not because of any single factor, but because of a wide number of socio-economic as well as cultural factors which are inter-related with one another.

Education is undeniably the most effective agent for social change. Its spread would help the Scheduled Castes acquire higher socio-economic status in the society. But the fact is not generally accepted by most of these people as many of them are tradition-bound and are reluctant to educate themselves. In this context, when one looks at the data available in Table 4.1, it is seen that quite a significant number of the old Bāuris falling in age group above 50 years or more in both the study villages, i.e. 47.50 per cent in Hirāpur, and 55.00 per cent in Āmbadiha believe that since it is the duty of the caste Hindus to get educated and to take up white-collar jobs, the Bāuris should not go for this. They opine that they are born to render their traditional services for the well-being of caste Hindu people. They strongly believe that since time immemorial, there has been a religious taboo against their studying and reading scriptures.

TABLE 4.1

Opinion of Bāuri people regarding education and occupation

Opinion/Answer	Hirāpur		Āmbadiha	
	15-40 (N=40)	50+ (N=40)	15-40 (N=40)	50+ (N=40)
(1)	(2)	(3)	(4)	(5)
Since it is the duty of the caste Hindus to get educated and take to white collar jobs, the Bāuris, being *Harijans* should not go for this.	8 (20.00)	19 (47.50)	10 (25.00)	22 (55.00)
There is no harm if the Bāuris get educated and take to white collar jobs.	32 (80.00)	21 (52.50)	30 (75.00)	18 (45.00)

Note: (i) Sample includes 50 per cent males and 50 per cent females of the total sample size of each age group.
(ii) Figures in brackets represent %age.

Education begins with the writing of a sacred word "*OM*" symbolising the three prime Hindu deities, Brahma, the creator; Vishnu, the saviour; and Maheswar, the destroyer. Any sort of violating the taboo is not possible on their part. Hence neither they can go for educating themselves nor their children. They further believe that it is God who has assigned them the duty of blowing conch-shell on ceremonial occasions of caste Hindu people. In their perception of things, it is essential that each component of society performs duties which are divinely ordained for the smooth functioning of society as a whole. If they deviate from this age-old divinely ordained practice, they would certainly go against the will of the Almighty, and their life or peace, prosperity and happiness could be at stake. On the contrary, the rest of the old people opine that there is no harm if the Bāuris get educated and take up white-collar jobs. Conversely as many as 32 or 80 per cent young Bāuris falling in the age group of 15-40 of Hirāpur as against 30 or 75 per cent of the village Āmbadiha do not agree with the view. But the rest 8 or 20 per cent younger Bāuris of Hirāpur and 10 or 25 per cent of Āmbadiha village opine that they should not deviate from the age-old divinely ordained set practice, and firmly believe in the traditional system. However, change is in the air. With the increasing awareness, Bāuris of both younger and older generations have now realised the importance of education and its benefits. With the passage of time and development activity all around, the Bāuris are realising the significance of deriving the benefits of modern education and joining the mainstream. Consequently, they are now inclined towards educating their children, and if possible even themselves. Still then because of a number of reasons, they do not always get an opportunity for education.

(A) Present Educational Status among the Family Members of the Beneficiary and Non-Beneficiary Households

(a) Level of Literacy

The educational status of the family members of beneficiary and non-beneficiary households between the village Hirāpur and Āmbadiha is presented in table 4.2.

Literacy between the family members of beneficiary households of the villages Hirāpur and Āmbadiha

As far as literacy of the family members of the beneficiary households in the study villages is concerned, it is noticed that of the total beneficiaries numbering 191 in the village of Hirāpur, 47 persons or 24.61 per cent are literate. In the village of Āmbadiha it is 56 or 27.32 per cent out of 205 beneficiaries. Thus, the beneficiaries of Hirāpur are found to be more illiterate than those of Āmbadiha, and this difference is found to be statistically insignificant. Hence, as expected and hypothesised, the beneficiaries of Hirāpur would be educationally more progressive than those of the village of Āmbadiha because of its locational advantage to the Bhubaneswar city and to the existence of a High School and other educational institutions, practically it has not happened so. This means that the provision of financial assistance rendered to the Scheduled Caste people living on the outskirts of urban centres does not necessarily create any positive educational advancement among the family members of the beneficiary households. So the first hypothesis which reads as: "Economic development inputs, i.e. poverty alleviation programmes cause educational advancement among the family members of the beneficiary households living in proximal villages of urban centres," is hereby not borne out.

TABLE 4.2

Literacy among the family members of beneficiary and non-beneficiary households between the village Hirāpur and Āmbadiha

Village Hirāpur

Literacy	Beneficiaries			Non-beneficiaries			Total		
	M	F	T	M	F	T	M	F	T
(1)	(2)	(3)	(4)	(5)	(6)	(7)	(8)	(9)	(10)
Illite-rate	58 (59.18)	86 (92.47)	144 (75.39)	48 (46.15)	89 (89.90)	137 (67.49)	106 (53.47)	175 (91.15)	281 (71.32)
Lite-rate	40 (40.82)	7 (7.53)	47 (24.61)	56 (53.85)	10 (10.10)	66 (32.51)	96 (47.52)	17 (8.85)	113 (28.68)
Total	98 (100)	93 (100)	191 (100)	104 (100)	99 (100)	203 (100)	202 (100)	192 (100)	394 (100)

Village Āmbadiha

Literacy	Beneficiaries			Non-beneficiaries			Total		
	M	F	T	M	F	T	M	F	T
(1)	(2)	(3)	(4)	(5)	(6)	(7)	(8)	(9)	(10)
Illite-rate	62 (57.41)	87 (89.69)	149 (72.68)	82 (58.99)	112 (90.32)	194 (73.76)	144 (58.30)	199 (90.05)	343 (73.29)
Lite-rate	46 (42.59)	10 (10.31)	56 (27.32)	57 (41.01)	12 (9.68)	69 (26.24)	103 (41.70)	12 (9.95)	125 (26.71)
Total	108 (100)	97 (100)	205 (100)	139 (100)	124 (100)	263 (100)	247 (100)	221 (100)	468 (100)

Z	0.613	1.48	0.287

Note: (i) Figures exclude population falling in the age group of 0-5

(ii) Figures in brackets represent %age.

A look at the data available in Table 4.1 shows that the people of Hirāpur are found to be educationally more aware than those of Āmbadiha. But conversely, as pointed out earlier, the family members of the beneficiary households of Hirāpur are found to be less literate than those of Āmbadiha. This trend of low literacy among the beneficiaries of Hirāpur is primarily because of the illiteracy of a number of children who fall in the school-going age groups (Table 4.4). However, even though the literacy among the beneficiary people of Hirāpur is lower than those of Āmbadiha, the level of education attained among children falling in the age group of 6-15, among the beneficiary of the former village is higher than the educational level achieved among the people of the corresponding age group of the latter village. Again the higher level of education achieved among the people of the beneficiary group of the village Hirāpur is found to be in the earlier age groups (Table 4.4). This, of course, reflects greater awareness and stronger motivation in some beneficiary families in obtaining higher education for their children, and in getting them employed.

Further a cursory look at Table 4.2 reveals that literacy, in case of both males and females, is higher in Āmbadiha than in the village of Hirāpur. For Āmbadiha the figures are 42.59 and 10.31 per cent for males and females respectively, while for Hirāpur these are 40.82 and 7.53 per cent. This trend of low literacy among the members of beneficiary group of people of the village Hirāpur is mainly because of two important factors which will be discussed later on in this chapter.

Literacy between family members of the non-beneficiary households of the village Hirāpur and Āmbadiha

The literacy among the family members of the non-beneficiary households of Hirāpur is 32.51 per cent which is higher than that of Āmbadiha (26.24%). Hence, the difference is found to be statistically insignificant.

When the sex-wise literacy is examined, it is found that in case of both the males and females, the level of literacy among the concerned population of the village of Hirāpur is found to be higher than those of Āmbadiha. In case of the former village the corresponding figures are found to be 53.85 and 10.16 per cent as against 41.01 and 9.68 per cent of the latter one.

Thus, when the literacy of the family members of both the beneficiary and non-beneficiary households is combined, it is noticed that while the literacy is 28.68 per cent in case of the Hirāpur, it is 26.71 per cent for the village of Āmbadiha. Thus, even though the overall literacy is found to be higher in case of the former village, the difference is not statistically significant. This is because of the fact that a reverse trend of literacy is found between the family members of beneficiary and non-beneficiary households of these two study villages (Table 4.2).

Beneficiaries Vs. Non-Beneficiaries

From the above discussion made on the basis of the data available in Table 4.2, it is clear that literacy among the family members of the beneficiary households of Hirāpur is lower than those of Āmbadiha. Conversely it indicates that literacy among the family members of the non-beneficiary households of the former village is higher than those of the latter one. But when the literacy among the family members of both the beneficiary and non-beneficiary households of the village of Hirāpur is added together the literacy of this village as a whole comes to be slightly higher than that of Āmbadiha.

(b) Level of education among literate family members between beneficiary and non-beneficiary households

The level of education achieved among the literate members of the beneficiary and non-beneficiary households of the study villages is presented below under seven different levels viz., (i) Illiterate, (ii) Literate, but without any formal education, including educational level not classifiable, (iii) Primary, (iv) Middle, (v) High School, (vi) Under Graduation, and (vii) Graduation and above (Table 4.3).

Level of education attained by the family members of beneficiary households between the villages of Hirāpur and Āmbadiha

Of the total 191 people belonging to beneficiary households of Hirāpur, as many as 144 or 75.39 per cent are found to be illiterate. The corresponding figure for Āmbadiha is 149 or 72.68 per cent out of a total of 205. Among the literate persons, the educational level achieved ranges from primary to the graduation level in case of Hirāpur, but it is only upto the level of middle standard in case of Āmbadiha. So it can be said that even though the people belonging to the beneficiary households of Hirāpur have a lower level of literacy than those of Āmbadiha, some of them of the former village have achieved higher educational qualification than those of the latter one. But even though the educational level among the people of beneficiary households of Hirāpur ranges upto graduation level, there is only 1 person representing 0.52 per cent of the total beneficiary population, who has completed graduation and there are only 2 or 1.05 per cent who have successfully completed undergraduation.

The same table reveals that, while there is a total number of 26 persons constituting 12.68 per cent of the total beneficiary population of Āmbadiha who are just literate without having any formal education, in the case of Hirāpur it is as low as 13 or 6.81 per cent. Those having passed primary education number 16 or 8.38 per cent in case of Hirāpur as against 24 or 11.71 per cent in Āmbadiha. The figures for persons

TABLE 4.3

Level of education among family members of beneficiary and non-beneficiary households between the villages Hirāpur and Āmbadiha

Village Hirāpur

Level of Ed.	Beneficiary			Non-beneficiary			Total		
	M	F	T	M	F	T	M	F	T
(1)	(2)	(3)	(4)	(5)	(6)	(7)	(8)	(9)	(10)
Illite-rate	58 (59.18)	86 (92.47)	144 (75.39)	48 (46.15)	89 (89.90)	137 (67.90)	106 (53.47)	175 (91.15)	281 (71.32)
Lit. with-out any formal Ed. lev.	10 (10.20) [25.00]	3 (3.23) [42.85]	13 (6.81) [27.66]	30 (28.85) [53.57]	5 (5.05) [50.00]	35 (17.24) [53.03]	40 (19.80) [41.67]	8 (4.17) [47.06]	48 (12.18) [42.28]
Primary	14 (14.29) [35.00]	2 (2.15) [28.57]	16 (8.38) [34.04]	20 (19.23) [35.71]	3 (3.03) [30.00]	23 (11.33) [34.85]	34 (16.83) [35.42]	5 (2.60) [29.41]	39 (9.90) [34.51]
Middle	10 (10.20) [25.00]	1 (1.08) [14.29]	11 (5.76) [23.40]	3 (2.88) [5.36]	2 (2.20) [20.00]	5 (2.46) [7.58]	13 (6.44) [13.54]	3 (1.56) [17.65]	16 (4.06) [14.16]
High School	3 (3.06) [7.50]	1 (1.08) [14.29]	4 (2.09) [8.51]	2 (1.92) [3.57]	-	2 (0.99) [3.03]	5 (2.48) [5.21]	1 (0.52) [5.88]	6 (1.52) [5.31]
Under Gradu-ation	2 (2.04) [5.00]	-	2 (1.05) [4.26]	1 (0.96) [1.79]	-	1 (0.49) [1.52]	3 (1.49) [3.13]	-	3 (0.76) [2.65]
Gradu-ation	1 (1.02) [2.5]	-	1 (0.52) [2.13]	-	-	-	1 (0.50) [1.04]	-	1 (0.25) [0.88]
Total	98 (100)	93 (100)	191 (100)	104 (100)	99 (100)	203 (100)	202 (100)	192 (100)	394 (100)
Total Literate	40 (100)	7 (100)	47 (100)	56 (100)	10 (100)	66 (100)	96 (100)	17 (100)	113 (100)

contd.

TABLE 4.3 (contd.)
Village Āmbadiha

Level of Ed.	Beneficiary			Non-beneficiary			Total		
	M	F	T	M	F	T	M	F	T
(1)	(2)	(3)	(4)	(5)	(6)	(7)	(8)	(9)	(10)
Illiterate	62 (57.41)	87 (89.69)	149 (72.68)	82 (58.99)	112 (90.32)	194 (73.76)	144 (5830)	199 (90.05)	343 (73.29)
Lit. without any formal Ed. lev.	18 (16.67) [39.13]	8 (8.25) [80.00]	26 (17.68) [46.43]	28 (20.14) [49.12]	7 (5.65) [58.33]	35 (13.31) [50.72]	46 (18.62) [44.66]	15 (6.79) [68.18]	61 (13.03) [48.80]
Primary	22 (20.37) [47.83]	2 (2.06) [20.00]	24 (11.71) [42.86]	19 (13.67) [33.33]	5 (4.03) [41.67]	24 (9.13) [34.78]	41 (16.60) [39.81]	7 (3.17) [31.82]	48 (10.26) [38.40]
Middle	6 (5.56) [13.04]	-	6 (2.93) [10.71]	9 (6.47) [15.79]	-	9 (3.42) [13.04]	15 (6.07) [14.56]	-	15 (3.21) [12.00]
High School	-	-	-	1 (0.77) [1.75]	-	1 (0.38) [1.45]	1 (0.40) [0.97]	-	1 (0.21) [0.80]
Under Graduation	-	-	-	-	-	-	-	-	-
Graduation	-	-	-	-	-	-	-	-	-
Total	108 (100)	97 (100)	205 (100)	139 (100)	124 (100)	263 (100)	247 (100)	221 (100)	468 (100)
Total Literate	46 (100)	10 (100)	56 (100)	57 (100)	12 (100)	69 (100)	103 (100)	22 (100)	125 (100)

Note: (i) Figures in upper brackets represent %age to total population.
(ii) Figures in lower brackets represent %age to total literates.

having completed middle education is 11 or 5.76 per cent in case of Hirāpur as against only 6 or 2.93 per cent in Āmbadiha. While among the beneficiaries of Hirāpur, those having passed Matriculation constitute a body of 4 or 2.09 per cent, there is no one in Āmbadiha who has passed this level of education.

A further look at the same table also shows that if the total number of literate persons is taken into account, it is found out that while about 90 per cent of literates of Āmbadiha are concentrated in the first two levels of education viz., literate without having any formal education and the primary level, it is only about 62 per cent in case of Hirāpur. The rest have completed education ranging from middle standard to completion of college education.

So far as sex-wise literacy is concerned, only 2 girls of the village Āmbadiha accounting for 2.06 per cent of the total female population have passed primary education as against 2 or 2.15 per cent of the village Hirāpur. There is not a single girl in the former village who has achieved middle education but in the latter village there is 1 (1.08%) girl who has passed high school education.

Level of education attained among the family members of non-beneficiary households between the village Hirāpur and Āmbadiha

Among the family members of the non-beneficiary households of the study villages, the highest educational qualification attained by the literate persons is observed to be undergraduation in case of Hirāpur and it is high school education in case of Āmbadiha. But in both the villages there is only one male each who has completed these levels of education respectively.

So far as the extent of literacy is concerned, in Hirāpur it is found that of the total number of 203 family members of non-beneficiary households, as many as 137 or 67.49 per cent are found to be illiterate followed by 35 or 17.24 per cent of people who are simply literate without having any formal education. Among the rest, 23 or 11.33 per cent, 5 or 2.46 per cent, and 2 or 0.99 per cent have completed primary, middle and high school education respectively. There is only 1 person or 0.49 per cent, who is an undergraduate. But when the case of Āmbadiha is examined, it is seen that of the total number of 263 family members of the non-beneficiary households as many as 194 or 73.76 per cent are illiterate. They are followed by 35 or 13.31 per cent people who are found to be simply literate, while a total number of 24 persons accounting for 9.13 per cent have passed primary education. Only 3.42 per cent and 1 or 0.38 per cent have completed middle and high school education, respectively.

When the total number of literate persons of each study village is taken into consideration, it is observed that in case of both the villages more than 50 per cent of the literates are found to be simply literate without having any formal education. It accounts for 53.03 per cent in case of Hirāpur as against 50.72 per cent of Āmbadiha.

(c) Education and Age

Tables 4.4 and 4.5 present the educational level of the beneficiary and non-beneficiary population of the two study villages by age and sex respectively. Data are presented for the age groups of 6-10, 11-15, 16-20, 21-25, 26-35,36-45, 46-65 and those above 65.

As in both the study villages, children falling in the age group of 0-5 years are neither enrolled in any of the educational institutions; whether formal or non-formal, nor is any one of them is found to be literate, this age group has therefore, been excluded from the analysis. However, so far as the population strength of this age group is concerned, it may be ascertained from Table 3.25. While there is a total number of 50 children in Hirāpur, it is as many as 92 in Āmbadiha. All these children are illiterate.

The Bāuris do not generally prefer to admit their children in any educational institution at an early age. They claim that it is essential that a child must be psychologically free from its mother before admission, otherwise it may create a negative impact on it. Hence, in many cases, a Bāuri child of 6 or 7 or sometimes even 8 years old is observed for its attachment to mother, and hence not sent to any school.

Beneficiaries

Age group 6-10

Amongst a total number of 21 children of Hirāpur and 30 of Āmbadiha, there are as many as 15 or 71.43 per cent in the former village as against only 10 or 33.33 per cent of the latter one who are literate. This means that in this particular age group, literacy among the children of Hirāpur is much lower than those of the village Āmbadiha.

Among the rest of the children of this age group belonging to Hirāpur, 14.29 per cent are simply literate without having any formal education. But an equal percentage of children has completed primary education. The corresponding figures for Āmbadiha are found to be 50 per cent and 16.67 per cent, respectively. This indicates that in each of these two educational levels there are less children in the village of Hirāpur than in Āmbadiha.

Age group 11-15

This age group has a total number of 25 children each in the village Hirāpur and Āmbadiha. But it includes more illiterate children in Āmbadiha than in Hirāpur. It is found that while there is a total number of 16 or 64 per cent illiterate children in Āmbadiha, the figure is 15 or 60 per cent in the case of Hirāpur. Further, it is also observed that while there is only one boy accounting for 4 per cent of Hirāpur who has passed high school examination, there is no one in Āmbadiha who seems to have passed this level of education. As for the rest of the children, 12 per cent have passed primary, and 16 per cent have passed middle level education in Hirāpur as against 20 and 13 per cent respectively in Āmbadiha.

Age group 16-20

This age group represents a total number of 25 and 28 persons in case of the village Hirāpur and Āmbadiha respectively. Like the above age group, i.e. 11-15, in this age group, the extent of literacy among the persons is almost same. A striking feature of this age group is that in case of both the villages, there is not a single person who is found to be a simple literate without having any formal education. Every one who had started has completed at least primary education. However, in this age group, there is also one person in Hirāpur, who has completed high school education. The highest educational level attained is found to be middle standard in case of 2 or 7.14 per cent in Āmbadiha, as against 4 or 16 per cent in Hirāpur.

Age group 21-25

This age group includes a total number of 20 persons in Hirāpur and 24 in Āmbadiha. Of those in Hirāpur, 15 persons, accounting for 75.10 per cent, are found to be illiterate as against 19 or 79.17 per cent in Āmbadiha. This age group, as the previous one, shows the same trend of high illiteracy among the people of Āmbadiha, and high literacy among the people of Hirāpur. Even though the highest educational level attained by some persons of the village Āmbadiha is still found to be middle standard, it is graduation in the case of Hirāpur. However, there is only one man accounting for 5 per cent of the total population who has attained this level.

Age group 26-35

In this age group, there are 36 persons in Hirāpur as against 40 in Āmbadiha. Of this number in the former village, as many as 28 or 77.78 per cent are illiterate as against 32 or 80 per cent in the latter one. While the highest education level attained by the highest qualified person of this age group in Hirāpur is graduation, it is just primary in the case of Āmbadiha. Many of the people, i.e. 6 or 26.09 per cent in Āmbadiha are found to be just literate without having any formal education as against only 1 or 2.78 per cent in Hirāpur. In Hirāpur,

TABLE 4.4

Percentage distribution of educational level among family members of beneficiary households according to age and sex in Hirāpur and Āmbadiha

Age group	Village	Illiterate			Literate without any educational level			Primary			Middle		
		M	F	T	M	F	T	M	F	T	M	F	T
(1)	(2)	(3)	(4)	(5)	(6)	(7)	(8)	(9)	(10)	(11)	(12)	(13)	(14)
6-10	H	71.43 (10)	71.43 (5)	71.43 (15)	14.29 (2)	14.29 (1)	14.29 (3)	14.29 (2)	14.29 (1)	14.29 (3)	-	-	-
	A	18.75 (3)	50.00 (7)	33.33 (10)	50.00 (8)	50.00 (7)	50.00 (15)	31.25 (5)	- -	16.67 (5)	-	-	-
11-15	H	46.15 (6)	75.00 (9)	60.00 (15)	7.69 (1)	8.33 (1)	8.00 (2)	15.38 (2)	8.33 (1)	12.00 (3)	23.08 (3)	8.33 (11)	16.00 (4)
	A	36.36 (4)	85.71 (12)	64.00 (16)	-	7.14 (1)	4.00 (1)	36.36 (4)	7.14 (1)	20.00 (5)	27.27 (3)	-	12.00 (3)
16.20	H	46.15 (6)	91.67 (11)	68.00 (17)	-	-	-	23.08 (3)	-	12.00 (3)	30.77 (4)	-	16.00 (4)
	A	54.55 (6)	94.12 (16)	78.57 (22)	-	-	-	27.27 (3)	5.88 (1)	14.29 (4)	18.18 (2)	-	7.14 (2)
21-25	H	55.56 (5)	90.91 (10)	75.00 (15)	11.11 (1)	9.09 (1)	10.00 (2)	-	-	-	11.11 (1)	-	5.00 (1)
	A	44.44 (4)	100.00 (15)	79.17 (15)	-	-	-	44.44 (4)	-	16.67 (4)	11.11 (1)	-	4.17 (1)

contd.

TABLE 4.4 (contd.)

Age group	Village	Illiterate			Literate without any educational level			Primary			Middle		
		M	F	T	M	F	T	M	F	T	M	F	T
(1)	(2)	(3)	(4)	(5)	(6)	(7)	(8)	(9)	(10)	(11)	(12)	(13)	(14)
26-35	H	55.50 (10)	100.00 (18)	77.78 (28)	5.56 (1)	-	2.78 (1)	16.67 (3)	-	8.33 (3)	11.11 (2)	-	5.56 (2)
	A	65.22 (15)	100.00 (17)	80.00 (32)	26.09 (6)	-	15.00 (6)	8.70 (2)	-	5.00 (2)	-	-	-
36-45	H	58.33 (7)	100.00 (17)	82.76 (24)	16.67 (2)	-	6.90 (2)	25.00 (3)	-	10.34 (3)	-	-	-
	A	69.23 (9)	100.00 (11)	83.33 (20)	15.38 (2)	-	8.33 (2)	15.38 (2)	-	8.33 (2)	-	-	-
46-65	H	68.75 (11)	100.00 (14)	83.33 (25)	18.75 (3)	-	10.00 (3)	6.75 (1)	-	3.33 (1)	-	-	-
	A	78.95 (15)	100.00 (8)	85.19 (23)	10.53 (2)	-	7.41 (2)	10.53 (2)	-	7.41 (2)	-	-	-
65 & above	H	100.00 (3)	100.00 (2)	100.00 (5)	-	-	-	-	-	-	-	-	-
	A	100.00 (6)	100.00 (1)	100.00 (7)	-	-	-	-	-	-	-	-	-
Total	H	59.18 (58)	92.47 (86)	75.39 (144)	10.20 (10)	3.23 (3)	6.81 (13)	14.29 (14)	2.15 (2)	8.38 (16)	10.20 (10)	1.08 (1)	5.76 (11)
	A	57.41 (62)	89.69 (87)	72.68 (149)	16.67 (18)	8.25 (8)	12.68 (26)	20.37 (22)	2.06 (2)	11.71 (24)	5.56 (6)	-	2.93 (6)

contd.

TABLE 4.4 (contd.)

Age group	Village	High School			Under Graduation			Graduation			Total		
		M	F	T	M	F	T	M	F	T	M	F	T
(1)	(2)	(3)	(4)	(5)	(6)	(7)	(8)	(9)	(10)	(11)	(12)	(13)	(14)
6-10	H	-	-	-	-	-	-	-	-	-	100.00 (14)	100.00 (7)	100.00 (21)
	A	-	-	-	-	-	-	-	-	-	100.00 (16)	100.00 (14)	100.00 (30)
11-15	H	7.69 (1)	-	4.00 (1)	-	-	-	-	-	-	100.00 (13)	100.00 (12)	100.00 (25)
	A	-	-	-	-	-	-	-	-	-	100.00 (11)	100.00 (14)	100.00 (25)
16-20	H	-	2.33 (1)	4.00 (1)	-	-	-	-	-	-	100.00 (13)	100.00 (12)	100.00 (25)
	A	-	-	-	-	-	-	-	-	-	100.00 (11)	100.00 (17)	100.00 (28)
21-25	H	11.11 (1)	-	5.00 (1)	11.11 (1)	-	5.00 (1)	-	-	-	100.00 (9)	100.00 (15)	100.00 (20)
	A	-	-	-	-	-	-	-	-	-	100.00 (9)	100.00 (15)	100.00 (24)
26-35	H	5.56 (1)	-	2.78 (1)	-	-	-	5.56 (1)	-	2.78 (1)	100.00 (18)	100.00 (18)	100.00 (36)
	A	-	-	-	-	-	-	-	-	-	100.00 (23)	100.00 (17)	100.00 (40)

contd.

TABLE 4.4 (contd.)

Age group	Village	High School			Under Graduation			Graduation			Total		
		M	F	T	M	F	T	M	F	T	M	F	T
(1)	(2)	(3)	(4)	(5)	(6)	(7)	(8)	(9)	(10)	(11)	(12)	(13)	(14)
36-45	H	-	-	-	-	-	-	-	-	-	100.00 (12)	100.00 (17)	100.00 (29)
	A	-	-	-	-	-	-	-	-	-	100.00 (13)	100.00 (11)	100.00 (24)
46-65	H	-	-	-	6.25 (1)	-	3.33 (1)	-	-	-	100.00 (16)	100.00 (14)	100.00 (30)
	A	-	-	-	-	-	-	-	-	-	100.00 (19)	100.00 (8)	100.00 (27)
65 & above	H	-	-	-	-	-	-	-	-	-	100.00 (3)	100.00 (2)	100.00 (5)
	A	-	-	-	-	-	-	-	-	-	100.00 (6)	100.00 (1)	100.00 (7)
Total	H	3.06 (3)	1.08 (1)	2.09 (4)	2.04 (2)	-	1.05 (2)	1.02 (1)	-	0.52 (1)	100.00 (98)	100.00 (93)	100.00 (191)
	A	-	-	-	-	-	-	-	-	-	100.00 (108)	100.00 (97)	100.00 (205)

Note: (i) Figures in brackets represent absolute numbers.
(ii) H–Hirāpur, A–Āmbadiha

TABLE 4.5

Percentage distribution of educational level among family members of non-beneficiary households according to age and sex in Hirāpur and Āmbadiha

Age group	Village	Illiterate			Literate without any educational level			Primary			Middle		
		M	F	T	M	F	T	M	F	T	M	F	T
(1)	(2)	(3)	(4)	(5)	(6)	(7)	(8)	(9)	(10)	(11)	(12)	(13)	(14)
6-10	H	33.33 (5)	61.54 (8)	46.43 (13)	40.00 (6)	30.77 (4)	35.71 (10)	26.67 (4)	7.69 (1)	17.86 (5)	-	-	-
	A	40.91 (9)	73.91 (17)	57.78 (26)	36.36 (8)	17.39 (4)	26.67 (12)	22.72 (5)	4.35 (1)	13.33 (6)	-	-	-
11-15	H	29.41 (5)	25.00 (9)	42.28 (14)	29.41 (5)	8.33 (1)	20.69 (6)	35.24 (6)	16.67 (2)	27.59 (6)	5.88 (1)	-	3.45 (1)
	A	46.67 (7)	72.22 (13)	60.61 (20)	13.33 (2)	11.11 (7)	12.12 (4)	20.00 (3)	22.22 (4)	21.21 (7)	20.00 (3)	-	9.09 (3)
16.20	H	50.00 (6)	71.43 (5)	57.89 (11)	25.00 (3)	-	15.79 (3)	25.00 (3)	-	15.29 (3)	8.33 (1)	14.29 (1)	10.53 (2)
	A	55.56 (10)	95.45 (21)	77.50 (31)	-	4.55 (1)	2.50 (1)	22.22 (4)	-	10.00 (4)	22.22 (4)	-	10.00 (4)
21-25	H	50.00 (2)	93.75 (15)	85.00 (17)	-	-	-	-	-	-	-	6.25 (1)	5.00 (1)
	A	60.00 (9)	100.00 (8)	73.91 (17)	6.67 (1)	-	4.35 (1)	13.33 (2)	-	8.70 (2)	13.33 (2)	-	8.70 (2)

contd.

TABLE 4.5 (contd.)

Age group	Village	Illiterate			Literate without any educational level			Primary			Middle		
		M	F	T	M	F	T	M	F	T	M	F	T
(1)	(2)	(3)	(4)	(5)	(6)	(7)	(8)	(9)	(10)	(11)	(12)	(13)	(14)
26-35	H	50.00 (11)	100.00 (13)	68.57 (24)	36.36 (8)	-	22.86 (8)	4.55 (1)	-	2.86 (1)	4.55 (1)	-	2.86 (1)
	A	60.00 (12)	100.00 (27)	82.98 (39)	15.00 (3)	-	6.38 (3)	25.00 (3)	-	10.64 (5)	-	-	-
36-45	H	53.33 (8)	100.00 (12)	74.07 (20)	26.67 (4)	-	14.81 (4)	20.00 (3)	-	11.11 (3)	-	-	-
	A	63.64 (14)	100.00 (12)	76.47 (26)	36.36 (8)	-	23.53 (8)	-	-	-	-	-	-
46-65	H	58.33 (7)	100.00 (13)	80.00 (20)	16.67 (7)	-	80.00 (2)	25.00 (3)	-	12.00 (3)	-	-	-
	A	70.00 (14)	100.00 (12)	81.25 (26)	30.00 (6)	-	18.75 (6)	-	-	-	-	-	-
65 & above	H	71.43 (5)	100.00 (13)	90.00 (18)	28.57 (2)	-	10.00 (2)	-	-	-	-	-	-
	A	100.00 (7)	100.00 (2)	100.00 (9)	-	-	-	-	-	-	-	-	-
Total	H	46.15 (48)	89.90 (89)	67.49 (137)	28.85 (30)	5.05 (5)	17.24 (35)	19.23 (20)	3.03 (3)	11.33 (23)	2.88 (3)	2.02 (2)	2.46 (5)
	A	58.99 (82)	90.32 (112)	73.76 (194)	20.14 (28)	5.65 (7)	13.31 (35)	6.47 (9)	4.03 (5)	9.13 (24)	6.47 (9)	-	3.42 (9)

contd.

TABLE 4.5 (contd.)

Percentage distribution of educational level among family members of non-beneficiary households according to age and sex in Hirāpur and Āmbadiha

Age group	Vilage	High School			Under Graduation			Total		
		M	F	T	M	F	T	M	F	T
(1)	(2)	(3)	(4)	(5)	(6)	(7)	(8)	(9)	(10)	(11)
6-10	H	-	-	-	-	-	-	100.00 (15)	100.00 (13)	100.00 (28)
	A	-	-	-	-	-	-	100.00 (22)	100.00 (23)	100.00 (45)
11-15	H	-	-	-	-	-	-	100.00 (17)	100.00 (12)	100.00 (29)
	A	-	-	-	-	-	-	100.00 (15)	100.00 (18)	100.00 (33)
16-20	H	-	-	-	-	-	-	100.00 (12)	100.00 (7)	100.00 (19)
	A	-	-	-	-	-	-	100.00 (18)	100.00 (22)	100.00 (40)
21-25	H	25.00 (1)	-	5.00 (1)	25.00 (1)	-	5.00 (1)	100.00 (4)	100.00 (16)	100.00 (20)
	A	6.67 (1)	-	4.35 (1)	-	-	-	100.00 (15)	100.00 (8)	100.00 (23)

contd.

TABLE 4.5 (contd.)

Age group	Vilage	High School			Under Graduation			Total		
		M	F	T	M	F	T	M	F	T
(1)	(2)	(3)	(4)	(5)	(6)	(7)	(8)	(9)	(10)	(11)
26-35	H	4.55 (1)	-	2.86 (1)	-	-	-	100.00 (22)	100.00 (13)	100.00 (35)
	A	-	-	-	-	-	-	100 (20)	100 (27)	100 (47)
36-45	H	-	-	-	-	-	-	100.00 (15)	100.00 (12)	100.00 (27)
	A	-	-	-	-	-	-	100.00 (22)	100.00 (12)	100.00 (34)
46-65	H	-	-	-	-	-	-	100.00 (12)	100.00 (13)	100.00 (25)
	A	-	-	-	-	-	-	100.00 (20)	100.00 (12)	100.00 (37)
65 & above	H	-	-	-	-	-	-	100.00 (7)	100.00 (13)	100.00 (20)
	A	-	-	-	-	-	-	100.00 (7)	100.00 (2)	100.00 (9)
Total	H	1.92 (2)	-	0.99 (2)	0.96 (1)	-	0.49 (1)	100.00 (104)	100.00 (99)	100.00 (203)
	A	0.72 (1)	-	0.36 (1)	-	-	-	100.00 (139)	100.00 (124)	100.00 (263)

Note: (i) Figures in brackets represents absolute numbers.
(ii) H–Hirāpur, A–Āmbadiha

8.33 per cent, 5.56 per cent and 2.78 per cent people are there, who have completed primary, middle and high school education respectively. But in Āmbadiha, the only formal education completed by 5 per cent people in this age group is primary.

Age group 36-45

This age group constitutes a total number of 29 persons in Hirāpur and 24 persons in Āmbadiha. In this age group, almost an equal number of people are illiterate in both the villages. The percentage is 82.76 in case of the former village as against 83.33 of the latter one. The highest level of education achieved among the literate persons is also found to be same, i.e. primary in case of both the villages. But while 10.34 per cent of the people in the former village have completed primary education, it is 8.33 per cent in case of the latter one. There are two persons each in the village Hirāpur and Āmbadiha constituting 6.90 and 8.33 per cent of the total population of the former and latter village respectively, who are simply literate without having any formal education.

Age group 46-65

In this age group, there are 30 persons in Hirāpur as against 27 of Āmbadiha. While as many as 25 or 83.33 per cent are found to be illiterate in case of Hirāpur, it is 23 or 85.11 per cent in case of Āmbadiha. Hence, as in all previous age groups, this one also reflects the same trend of literacy between the people of these two villages. Only one person accounting for 3.33 per cent of the village Hirāpur is found to have completed undergraduation.

Age group 66 & above

This age group is constituted by 5 people in case of Hirāpur as against 7 of Āmbadiha. They are all illiterate in both the cases.

Conclusion

From the above data it may be concluded that the literacy of the people of Āmbadiha falling in the age group of 6-10 is higher than that of the village of Hirāpur. But a reverse trend is seen in the next succeeding age group of 11-15, and in all other subsequent age groups, except the last, i.e. 66 and above, where all the people of both the study villages are found to be illiterate. Still looking at the total figures, the trend of literacy among the people belonging to the age group of

6-10 comes to the mind. It is found that of the total population of 191 of the village Hirāpur, there are as many as 144 or 75.39 per cent illiterate children, but it is 149 or 72.68 per cent in case of Āmbadiha. Thus, the literacy among the people of the beneficiary households of Āmbadiha is found to be higher than those of the village Hirāpur.

Further when a cursory look at each of the above age groups is given, it is observed that in case of both the villages, literacy gradually reduces from the age group of 11-15 to the last one, i.e. 66 and above. Hence, it can be concluded that:

(i) Higher the age groups lower the literacy and
(ii) Lower the age groups higher the literacy.

It also indicates that in the age group of 11-15, 15-20 and 46-65 some of the literates of the village Hirāpur have attained higher educational qualification as compared to those of the village Āmbadiha. But in case of the age group of 36-45, there is not a single person in either of the villages who is found to have attained education beyond the middle standard.

Non-Beneficiary

Age group 6-10

There is a total number of 28 and 45 children in the village Hirāpur and Āmbadiha respectively who are represented in this age group. In case of Hirāpur, about 46 per cent of the children are found to be illiterate, as against 58 per cent of Āmbadiha. Thus, in comparison with the beneficiaries belonging to this age group, a reverse trend is observed. This trend otherwise speaks that in this age group there are more literate children in Hirāpur than in Āmbadiha. Among the rest of the children of this age group, 17.86 per cent of the former village as against 13.33 per cent of the latter one have got primary education. As many as 10 or 35.71 per cent children of Hirāpur 12 or 26.67 per cent children of Āmbadiha are found to be just literate without having any formal education.

Age group 11-15

This age group is constituted of 29 children in the village of Hirāpur and 33 of Āmbadiha. Of this, while the number of illiterates is 14 or 48.14 per cent in Hirāpur, it is 20 or 60.04 per cent in Āmbadiha.

Among these literates, 20.69 per cent or 6 children of the village Hirāpur are found to be just literate without having any formal education, whereas it is 12.12 per cent and 4 children in case of Āmbadiha. Likewise, the percentage of the people who have passed primary education is higher in case of Hirāpur than that of Āmbadiha. But while 3 children or 9.09 per cent of Āmbadiha have passed middle education, it is only one child or 3.45 per cent in case of the village of Hirāpur.

Age group 16-20

This age group is represented by 19 persons of Hirāpur and 40 persons of Āmbadiha. The illiterate persons of Hirāpur falling in this age group are fewer than those of Āmbadiha. It comes to be 57.89 per cent for the former village as against 77.50 per cent of the latter one. The highest education level attained is middle education in case of both the villages. So far as primary and middle education is concerned, a higher percentage of people have passed in Hirāpur than in Āmbaḍiha. The same is the case of people who are simply literate without having any formal education.

Age group 21-25

A total number of 20 persons of Hirāpur and 23 of Āmbadiha are found in this age group. It is interesting to note that, in this age group, illiteracy is as high as 85 per cent for Hirāpur as against 73.91 per cent for Āmbadiha. Of the total 2 literate men in Hirāpur, one has passed matriculation and the other one is an undergraduate. The only literate woman of this village belonging to this age group is found to have passed middle education. In Āmbadiha, there are only 2 or 8.70 per cent people each in primary and middle level education. There is only one male who is found to have completed high school education and holds the highest educational qualification attained by any person of this age group in Āmbadiha.

Age group 26-35

This age group includes 35 persons in Hirāpur and 47 in Āmbadiha. Hirāpur has 68.57 per cent illiterates and it is as high as 82.98 per cent in case of the village Āmbadiha. A total number of 3 persons accounting for 6.38 per cent are there in the village Āmbadiha as against 8 or 22.86 per cent in Hirāpur who are simply literate without having any formal education. However, a reverse trend is observed in the case of primary education as it is seen that while there are more people (10.64%) in the village Āmbadiha, it is only 2.80 per cent in the case of Hirāpur. In Hirāpur, there is one person each in primary, middle and high school thereby indicating high school examination being the highest education level attained.

Age group 36-45

This age group is represented by a total number of 27 persons in Hirāpur and 34 person in Āmbadiha. Of this, while of 20 or 74.07 per cent are found to be illiterate in the former village, it is 26 or 76.47 per cent in the latter one. All the literates of the village Āmbadiha are observed to be simply literates without having any formal education. In Hirāpur, there are 3 or 11.11 per cent people who have passed primary education, followed by 4 or 14.81 per cent being simply literate, without having any formal education.

Age group 46-65

This age group comprises 25 persons in Hirāpur, as against 32 in Āmbadiha. A very large number of people belonging to this age group are found to be illiterate. But the proportion of illiteracy among the people of these two study villages is almost equal. Where it is 80 per cent in Hirāpur, it is 81.25 per cent in Āmbadiha. The rest of the people of Āmbadiha are simply literate without having any formal education. But in case of Hirāpur, however, 8 per cent of the people are simply literate and the rest 12 per cent have completed primary education.

Age group 66 and above

In this age group there is a total number of 20 persons in Hirāpur as against 9 in Āmbadiha. Exactly 90 per cent of those in Hirāpur are illiterate as against all the people of Āmbadiha. The remaining 10 per cent people of Hirāpur are simple literates without having any formal education.

Conclusion

A cursory look at Table 4.5 reveals that in Hirāpur there are some literate persons in all age groups, except the age group of 21-25. This is not so in the cause of Āmbadiha. Barring the age group of 21-25, it may be observed that in Hirāpur, the literacy decreases when the age group increases. But this trend is not seen in Āmbadiha. The total figures show that literacy among the people of Hirāpur is higher than that of the village of Āmbadiha and that in each educational level expect the primary standard, the former village represents a higher percentage of literate people than in the village of Aímbadiha. In case of the village of Hirāpur undergraduation is the highest educational level reached, whereas in Āmbadiha it is matriculation level.

(B) Causes of Illiteracy, Non-enrolment and Dropout

Beneficiary

In order to find out the reasons of illiteracy among the family members of the beneficiary and non-beneficiary households of both the study villages, a total number of 80 persons of each category of people in each village were interviewed. A total of seven reasons have stood out. There are, however, two important reasons which are found to be responsible in reducing literacy among the family members of the beneficiary households of Hirāpur. A view of the data available in Table 4.6 makes it clear that out of the total number of 80 sample respondents in this village, as many as 62 or 77.5 per cent as against merely 4 or 5 per cent in the village of Āmbadiha opine that the poor economic condition of parents, combined with easy availability of job opportunities for both the adult and young illiterate people in Bhubaneswar city, are primarily responsible for this. Those intending to educate their children are helpless as adult male, or sometimes both the parents come over to Bhubaneswar city early in the morning and go back home late in the evening. This pattern of engagement of adult male members in Bhubaneswar city apparently creates a negative impact on the education of their children. On the other hand the women who do not come over to Bhubaneswar do not take a keen interest in the education of their children. Consequently, the children become wayward and most often they try to remain away from school. Thus, a total number of 49 respondents accounting for 61.25 per cent of the former village as against merely 2 or 2.5 per cent of the latter one claim that it is also because of the negligence of parents.

The third major reason which is pointed out by as many as 43 or 53.75 per cent people of the village Hirāpur is that the poor economic condition of parents combined with easy availability of job opportunities for the young persons in Bhubaneswar city along with the problem of unemployment of many educated youths together does not create any interest among the parents to give due importance to the education of their children. They point out that it is wiser for the children to learn daily activities that help to earn one's bread early than to simply spend time within the four walls of the classroom. Further they point out that the Bāuri children who have been educated

TABLE 4.6

Causes of non-enrolment, dropout and illiteracy between family members of beneficiary and non-beneficiary households of Hirāpur and Āmbadiha

Reasons	Village	Benefi-ciary (N=80)	Non-Bene-ficiary (N=80)	Total (N=160)
(1)	(2)	(3)	(4)	(5)
Poor economic condition of parents combinedly with easy and better availability of job opportunities for both adult and younger people in Bhubaneswar city.	Hirāpur	(62) 77.5	(38) 47.5	(100) 62.5
	Āmbadiha	(4) 5.0	(3) 3.75	(7) 4.38
Negligence of parents towards the education of their children as they mostly spend their time in different economic activities in Bhubaneswar city.	Hirāpur	(49) 61.25	(36) 45.0	(85) 53.13
	Āmbadiha	(2) 2.5	(1) 1.25	(3) 1.88
Unemployment of educated youths along with poor economic condition of parents.	Hirāpur	(43) 53.75	(39) 48.75	(82) 51.25
	Āmbadiha	(52) 65.00	(61) 76.25	(113) 70.63
Poor economic condition of parents causing inferiority complex of Bāuri children at school.	Hirāpur	(43) 53.75	(44) 55.00	(87) 54.38
	Āmbadiha	(47) 58.75	(67) 83.75	(114) 71.25
Repeated failure in class promotion examination/unsatisfactory performance in school education.	Hirāpur	(14) 17.5	(10) 12.5	(24) 15.00
	Āmbadiha	(16) 20.00	(16) 20.00	(32) 20.00
Ill-treatment of caste Hindu friends/classmates at school.	Hirāpur	(11) 13.75	(9) 11.25	(20) 12.50
	Āmbadiha	(15) 18.75	(11) 13.75	(26) 16.25
Looking after younger siblings during absence of parents and helping them in different day-to-day household and economic activities.	Hirāpur	(39) 48.75	(57) 71.25	(96) 60.00
	Āmbadiha	(74) 92.5	(70) 87.5	(144) 90.00

Note: Figures in brackets represent absolute numbers.

are mostly unemployed and have become very prestige conscious because of their education. As a result of this neither they help their parents in daily economic pursuits, nor do they go for wage-earning to supplement their family income. Hence, the unemployed youths remain unproductive and a burden of their illiterate wage-earning parents. In such a situation the parents find it very difficult on their part to feed their children out of their hard earned daily income. So, when education does not provide them employment and the educated unemployed youth do not like to perform menial jobs or those requiring manual labour and work as daily wage-earners, their parents feel frustrated and do not give much importance to the education of their children. Hence, a total number of 52 or 65 per cent of the respondents of Āmbadiha highlight that unemployment of educated youth along with poor economic condition of their parents, together cause a low level of literacy among them. They do not point out the fact of easy availability of jobs in Bhubaneswar city as they are far away from it, and hence, have very little scope of access to job opportunities in the city. The next factor which is also pointed out by an equal percentage of people of the village Hirāpur is the poor economic condition of the parents and the inferiority complex from which the Bāuri children suffer due to their lacking in proper dress and adequate study materials. They feel embarrassed to attend classes with the caste Hindu friends who have fine school dress and all or most of the required study materials. This factor is focused by 47 or 58.75 per cent of the respondents of the village of Āmbadiha.

The next factor, i.e. looking after younger sibling during daily absence of their parents and helping parents in their daily household chores and economic activities is highlighted by a total number of 39 or 48.75 per cent of the people of the former village as against 74 or 29.5 per cent in case of the latter one. Further, a total number of 14 or 17.5 per cent respondents of the village Hirāpur as against 16 or 20 per cent of Āmbadiha point to repeated failure of their children in class promotion examinations, consequent frustration of both children and parents leading to disillusionment and hence, dropping out from school for not wanting to waste scarce money on the education of their children, as another reason for lack of education. On the other hand 11 or 13.75 per cent respondents of the village Hirāpur as against 15 or 18.75 per cent of the village Āmbadiha complain of ill-treatment of caste Hindu students towards their Bāuri classmates at school. It made a strong negative impact on Bāuri students demotivating them from attending school even if their parents sent them there.

Non-Beneficiary

So far as the reasons pointing to responsibility for illiteracy among the family members of the non-beneficiary households of the villages of Hirāpur and Āmbadiha are concerned, it can be observed from the Table 4.6 that looking after younger siblings during the absence of parents at work, and helping them in different household chores and daily economic activities is found to be the single most important reason. This factor is pointed out by 71.25 per cent people of Hirāpur against 87.5 per cent of Āmbadiha. The next important reason seems to be poor economic condition of parents combined with inferiority complex of Bāuri students at school as their children do not possess required study materials and look unkempt because of their lack of hygiene, wearing shabby dress, and appearing dishevelled. This reason is mentioned by 55 per cent of respondents of the former village against as high a percentage as 83.75 of the latter one. Interestingly 48.75 per cent of the respondents of Hirāpur as against 76.25 per cent of Āmbadiha attribute unemployment of educated youth along with poor economic condition of parents as the third major reason for considerably reducing literacy among their people. Poor economic condition of parents combined with easy and better availability of job opportunity for both the adult and young Bāuris in Bhubaneswar city is the fourth important factor believed to have delayed the spread of education among the people of non-beneficiary households of the village Hirāpur and is identified by 47.5 per cent of respondents of this village. But this factor does not have any major effect on the corresponding group in the village of Āmbadiha as this village is far away from Bhubaneswar. Hence, this being a factor responsible for bringing down literacy among the people of Āmbadiha, is pointed out by only by 3.75 per cent of the respondents. The next important reason considered to have been responsible for reducing literacy in the village Hirāpur is pointed out by 45 per cent respondents of this village as against merely 1.25 per cent of Āmbadiha. The reason seems to be want of sufficient motivation in parents to educate their children. These parents, or at least the father, spend most of their time in Bhubaneswar city in order to earn more than what they could possibly earn in their village.

Intensity of causes of illiteracy

To determine the intensity of each of the above reasons, a three-point rating scale technique has been applied. Each reason has been rated as (i) to great extent (with 2 weight points) (ii) to some extent (with 1 weight point), and (iii) not at all (with 0 weight point). The intensity of each reason is rendered in table 4.7 which is self-explanatory.

TABLE 4.7

Intensity of factors responsible for non-enrolment, dropout and illiteracy between the family members of beneficiary and non-beneficiary household of Hirāpur and Āmbadiha

Sl. No.	Reasons	Category of people	To a great extent		To some extent		Not at all	
			Hirāpur	Āmbadiha	Hirāpur	Āmbadiha	Hirāpur	Āmbadiha
(1)	(2)	(3)	(4)	(5)	(6)	(7)	(8)	(9)
1.	Poor economic condition of parents combinedly with easy and better availability of job opportunities for both adult and younger people in Bhubaneswar city.	Beneficiary	(62) 87.94	(4) 53.33	(17) 12.06	(7) 46.67	(1) 0	(69) 0
		Non-Beneficiary	(38) 73.08	(3) 50.00	(28) 26.92	(6) 50.00	(14) 0	(71) 0
		Total	(100) 81.63	(7) 51.85	(45) 18.36	(13) 48.15	(15) 0	(140) 0
2.	Negligence of parents towards the education of their children as they mostly spend their time in different economic activities in Bhubaneswar city.	Beneficiary	(49) 77.78	(2) 50.00	(28) 22.22	(34) 50.00	(3) 0	(74) 0
		Non-Beneficiary	(36) 72.73	(1) 40	(27) 27.27	(3) 60.00	(17) 0	(76) 0
		Total	(85) 75.56	(3) 46.15	(55) 24.44	(7) 53.85	(20) 0	(150) 0
3.	Unemployment of educated youths along with poor economic condition of parents.	Beneficiary	(43) 70.49	(52) 78.79	(36) 29.51	(28) 21.21	(1) 0	(0) 0
		Non-Beneficiary	(39) 67.24	(61) 86.52	(38) 32.76	(19) 13.48	(3) 0	(0) 0
		Total	(82) 68.91	(113) 82.78	(74) 31.09	(47) 17.22	(4) 0	(0) 0

contd.

TABLE 4.7 (contd.)

Sl. No.	Reasons	Category of people	To a great extent		To some extent		Not at all	
			Hirāpur	Āmbadiha	Hirāpur	Āmbadiha	Hirāpur	Āmbadiha
(1)	(2)	(3)	(4)	(5)	(6)	(7)	(8)	(9)
4.	Poor economic condition of parents causing inferiority complex of Bāuri children at school.	Beneficiary	(43) 75.44	(47) 75.20	(28) 24.56	(31) 24.8	(9) 0	(2) 0
		Non-Beneficiary	(44) 75.21	(67) 92.41	(29) 24.29	(11) 7.59	(7) 0	(2) 0
		Total	(87) 75.32	(114) 84.44	(57) 24.68	(42) 15.56	(16) 0	(4) 0
5.	Repeated failure in class promotion examination/unsatisfactory performance in school education.	Beneficiary	(14) 54.90	(16) 53.33	(23) 45.10	(28) 46.67	(43) 0	(46) 0
		Non-Beneficiary	(10) 41.67	(16) 49.23	(28) 58.33	(33) 50.77	(42) 0	(31) 0
		Total	(24) 48.48	(32) 51.2	(51) 51.52	(61) 48.8	(85) 0	(67) 0
6.	Ill-treatment of caste Hindu friends/classmates at school.	Beneficiary	(11) 48.89	(15) 44.12	(23) 51.11	(38) 55.88	(46) 0	(27) 0
		Non-Beneficiary	(9) 47.37	(11) 42.31	(20) 52.63	(30) 57.69	(51) 0	(39) 0
		Total	(20) 48.19	(26) 43.33	(43) 51.81	(68) 56.67	(97) 0	(66) 0
7.	Looking after younger siblings during absence of parents and helping them in different day-to-day household and economic activities.	Beneficiary	(39) 69.03	(74) 96.10	(35) 30.97	(6) 3.90	(6) 0	(0) 0
		Non-Beneficiary	(57) 85.07	(70) 95.24	(20) 14.93	(7) 4.76	(3) 0	(3) 0
		Total	(96) 77.73	(144) 95.68	(55) 22.27	(13) 4.32	(9) 0	(3) 0

Note: Figures in brackets represent absolute numbers.

4.2 ECONOMIC IMPACT THROUGH DEVELOPMENT PROGRAMMES

Caste and occupation are inter-related concepts. In the traditional Indian society, different occupations have been specified for different castes. As a result of this, a child born in a family automatically inherits the social and occupational status of his father in a patrilineal society. The case is also same in case of matrilineal societies where daughters inherit the occupational status of their mothers. It signifies the ascriptive nature of caste system, and thus the caste system assigns a particular occupation to a person of a particular caste or community. But nowadays, in many societies of India, the social structure along with the *Jajmani* system has considerably weakened, and in many cases it has been completely broken down. So, in such societies the individuals enjoy full freedom to change their ascribed occupations depending upon their need, suitability and profitability. Apart from this, the intensive interference of Government and increasing awareness among the rural people in general and Scheduled Caste in particular have also opened a wider scope for giving up their menial, unclean and low-income oriented traditional caste occupations, taking to a wide variety of new or modern occupations.

The Bāuris who had traditionally been depending upon agriculture of the local caste Hindus and had been earning an income that allowed a hand-to-mouth living as agricultural labourers and wage-earners are also nowadays experiencing greater change in their traditional social structure. Earning one's bread as agricultural labour or as a wage-earning worker is neither menial nor unclean, but it is not so rewarding, both economically and socially. For this, the Bāuris have taken to a number of non-traditional occupations.

(i) New Occupations

In order in know the occupational changes which have taken place among the beneficiary and non-beneficiary households of the villages of Hirāpur and Āmbadiha, the data available in Table 4.8 may be referred. This table portrays that in all, a total number of 7 traditional and 8 non-traditional occupations are there, of which the beneficiary and non-beneficiary households earn their livelihood as their primary and subsidiary sources of income. (The primary occupations are considered to be those from which maximum income is incurred by the household, and the subsidiary occupations are those from which the amount of income ranks next to that of the primary occupation).

Occupation of Beneficiary Households:

Traditional occupations

1. (a) Agricultural/ Wage Labourer

Agricultural labour includes common activities like ploughing, levelling the field, sowing seeds, transplantation of seedling, weeding, harvesting etc. But wage-labour includes different activities in different villages. In case of the village of Hirāpur, it includes brick manufacturing in different brick kilns located on the outskirts of Bhubaneswar, skilled and unskilled labour in different transport vehicles like trucks, tractors etc. These works are more easily available for the Bāuris of the village Hirāpur. But in case of the village Āmbadiha, it includes only home-based activities as a result of which work is not so frequently available for the Bāuris of this village.

The wage for agricultural labour is about Rs. 20 per day but the wage for working in kilns and in transport vehicles is a little less (around Rs. 18) than the daily agricultural wage. Still most of the Bāuris of Hirāpur prefer working in brick kilns and also in transport vehicles as these jobs are available to wage earners on contract basis for a week, a month, a season, or even for a year.

From Table 4.8 it is found that among the beneficiary households, while there are only about 25 per cent (25.45) households in Hirāpur who primarily earn their daily bread as agricultural or wage labour, it is 60 per cent in case of Āmbadiha. But so far as the subsidiary occupation is concerned about 55 per cent (54.55) households of the former village earn their daily bread from this source of income. It is only 12 per cent in case of the latter one.

b) Haliā/Kothiā

The Bāuris who are especially employed for ploughing agricultural fields apart from doing allied agricultural activities are called as *Haliā* or ploughman. They are especially appointed for a specific agricultural generation or for both the agricultural generations of a year. For the purpose of ploughing the field, a *Haliā* can either use his own plough and bullocks, or those of his employer.

A *Haliā* works under a bond of mutual contract and is paid either on daily basis or half yearly or annually depending upon his labour use and contract made with the employer. When a *Haliā* uses his personal plough and bullocks for ploughing the fields of his employer, he gets more money and a secured income either in cash or in kind, or in both. However, for a *Haliā,* who does not own any bullock, his job and income is also secured. Hence, if a Bāuri *Haliā* has a plough and a pair of bullocks, he earns more than otherwise. So each Bāuri household has a craze to own these agricultural assets in order to earn more, and thereby improve his economic condition.

TABLE 4.8

Distribution of beneficiary and non-beneficiary households according to occupations

Category of Occupation	Sl. No.	Occupation	Beneficiary			
			Hirāpur (N=55)		Āmbadiha (N=50)	
			P	S	P	S
(1)	(2)	(3)	(4)	(5)	(6)	(7)
Traditional	1.	Daily/Annual Labourer	18 (32.73)	30 (54.55)	39 (78.00)	9 (18.00)
	a.	Agricultural/Wage Labourer	14 (25.45)	30 (54.55)	30 (60.00)	6 (12.00)
	b.	Halia/Kothia	4 (7.27)	-	9 (18.00)	3 (6.00)
	2.	Coconut plucking	1 (1.82)	1 (1.82)	3 (6.00)	2 (4.00)
	3.	Transport Business with bullock & cart	2 (3.64)	-	1 (2.00)	-
	4.	Stone dressing	2 (3.64)	-	-	-
	5.	Animal husbandry	2 (3.64)	-	-	-
	a.	Goat rearing	1 (1.82)	-	-	-
	b.	Poultry farming	1 (1.82)	-	-	-
	6.	Cow herding	-	1 (1.82)	-	-
	7.	Mat weaving	-	3 (5.45)	-	4 (8.00)

contd.

The *kothiās* are those who are normally employed for performing both the agricultural as well as domestic activities of the employer. But their main work concentrates in agricultural activities.

The appointment for both the posts is normally made in the month of *Phālguna* (February-March) on the day of *Dolā* festival. Even though the appointment for such post is ordinarily made for one year, it may continue for years with the mutual consent of either parties. Within the contract period neither the employer nor the employee can break the agreement.

The *kothiās* are usually paid a lower daily wage which is almost half of the daily agricultural wage. But in addition to this, they get a

TABLE 4.8 (contd.)

Non-Beneficiary				Total			
Hirāpur (N=53)		Āmbadiha (N=69)		Hirāpur (N=108)		Āmbadiha (N=119)	
P	S	P	S	P	S	P	S
(8)	(9)	(10)	(11)	(12)	(13)	(14)	(15)
35 (66.04)	13 (24.53)	64 49.28	1 (1.45)	53 (49.07)	44 (40.74)	103 (86.55)	10 (8.40)
31 (58.49)	9 (16.98)	57 (82.61)	1 (1.45)	45 (41.67)	40 (37.03)	87 (73.11)	7 (5.88)
4 (7.55)	4 (7.55)	7 (10.14)	-	8 (7.41)	4 (3.70)	16 (13.45)	7 (5.88)
2 (3.77)	1 (1.89)	3 (4.35)	-	3 (2.78)	2 (1.85)	6 (5.04)	2 (1.68)
-	-	-	-	2 (1.85)	-	1 (0.84)	-
1 (1.89)	-	-	-	3 (2.78)	-	-	-
-	-	-	-	2 (1.85)	-	-	-
-	-	-	-	1 (0.93)	-	-	-
-	-	-	-	1 (0.93)	-	-	-
-	1 (1.89)	-	2 (2.90)	-	2 (1.85)	-	2 (1.68)
-	4 (7.55)	-	7 (10.14)	-	7 (6.48)	-	3 (2.52)

contd.

fixed amount of money at the end of the year. Normally, this amount ranges from Rs. 1000 to Rs. 3000 depending upon the work pressure on the employee. Apart from this, they are also entitled to get a napkin and a *dhoti* on the day of *Dola* festival as incentive. Substituting the annual salary or in addition to it, the employee may also get a piece of agricultural land, possibly a paddy field called *Hetā*. But it depends upon the work pressure on the employee. So long as the *kothiā* works for his employer, he enjoys the *Hetā* which is solely cultivated by his family members and the whole produce is enjoyed by them. The employer takes back his land only when the contract is over or broken

TABLE 4.8 (contd.)

Category of Occupation	Sl. No.	Occupation	Beneficiary			
			Hirāpur (N=55)		Āmbadiha (N=50)	
			P	S	P	S
(1)	(2)	(3)	(4)	(5)	(6)	(7)
Non-Traditional	1.	Rickshaw/Trolley Pulling	9 (16.36)	1 (1.82)	-	-
	2.	Petty Business	8 (14.55)	7 (12.73)	5 (10.00)	-
	a.	Shop Keeping	1 (1.82)	3 (5.45)	1 (2.00)	-
	b.	Vegetable Selling	3 (5.45)	3 (5.45)	-	-
	c.	Selling of betel leaf	2 (3.64)	-	2 (4.00)	-
	d.	Rice Selling	1 (1.82)	-	-	-
	e.	Dry fish selling	1 (1.82)	1 (1.82)	2 (4.00)	-
	3.	Tailoring	1 (1.82)	2 (3.64)	-	-
	4.	Share-cropping	6 (10.91)	6 (10.91)	2 (4.00)	2 (4.00)
	5.	Horticulture	1 (1.82)	-	-	-
	6.	Construction work	3 (5.45)	-	-	-
	a.	Mason	1 (1.82)	-	-	-
	b.	Apprentice Mason	2 (3.64)	-	-	-
	7.	Carpenter	1 (1.82)	-	-	-
	8.	Net weaving & selling	1 (1.82)	4 (7.27)	-	2 (4.00)

contd.

by either. Thus, usually the annual income of a *kothiā* exceeds that of a casual agricultural labourer or wage earner as an agricultural labourer or wage earner does not get a constant earning opportunity throughout the year.

TABLE 4.8 (contd.)

Non-Beneficiary				Total			
Hirāpur (N=53)		Āmbadiha (N=69)		Hirāpur (N=108)		Āmbadiha (N=119)	
P	S	P	S	P	S	P	S
(8)	(9)	(10)	(11)	(12)	(13)	(14)	(15)
3 (5.66)	-	-	-	12 (11.11)	1 (0.93)	-	-
5 (9.43)	-	-	1 (1.45)	13 (12.04)	7 (6.48)	5 (4.20)	1 (0.84)
-	-	-	-	1 (0.93)	3 (2.78)	1 (0.84)	-
3 (5.66)	-	-	-	6 (5.56)	3 (2.78)	-	-
1 (1.89)	-	-	-	2 (1.85)	-	2 (1.68)	-
-	-	-	-	1 (0.93)	-	-	-
1 (1.89)	-	-	1 (1.45)	2 (1.85)	1 (0.93)	2 (1.68)	1 (0.84)
-	-	-	-	1 (0.93)	2 (1.85)	-	-
5 (9.43)	2 (3.77)	2 (2.90)	-	11 (10.19)	8 (7.41)	4 (3.36)	2 (1.68)
-	-	-	-	1 (0.93)	-	-	-
1 (1.89)	-	-	-	4 (3.70)	-	-	-
-	-	-	-	1 (0.93)	-	-	-
1 (1.89)	-	-	-	3 (2.78)	-	-	-
-	-	-	-	1 (0.93)	-	-	-
1 (1.89)	1 (1.89)	-	1 (1.45)	2 (1.85)	5 (4.63)	-	2 (1.68)

Note: (i) Figures in brackets represent %age
(ii) P = Primary, S = Subsidiary

Hence, as this occupation is found profitable for the Bāuris, there is a total number of 4 households accounting for 7.27 per cent in the village Hirāpur and 9 or 18 per cent in the village Āmbadiha who primarily earn their daily bread out of this occupation. In the latter village a total number of 3 households accounting for 6 per cent are there who practise this occupation as their subsidiary source of income.

2. Coconut Plucking

The study area is situated in the coastal belt and this belt is very suitable for coconut cultivation. So most of the local caste Hindu landlords cultivate this crop and earn substantially. The people belonging to Bāuri caste normally work as coconut pluckers. The remuneration for plucking coconut is one coconut or Rs. 2.50 per tree. If a plucker climbs up for plucking only green coconuts he is entitled to have a green coconut or Rs. 2 as his wage. At the time of annual cleaning of the tree, as the job is tough and frought with some danger, the plucker gets 2 coconuts or Rs. 5 per tree. Normally, a plucker can pluck coconuts from 20-30 trees in a day. Hence, he can earn upto Rs. 50 to Rs. 75 depending upon the availability of the job. Hence, as this source of income is more profitable than working as a wage-earner or agricultural labourer, some Bāuris of both the study villages have specialised themselves in this sector and earn accordingly. There are some Bāuri pluckers in Hirāpur, who not only work as such in the rural areas, but also go over to Bhubaneswar and earn more than what they would ordinarily earn in villages.

If one looks at the same table it may be noticed that there is a total number of 1 (1.82%) and 3 (6%) households in the village Hirāpur and Āmbadiha respectively, who have this job as their primary occupation. Likewise, 1 or 21.82 per cent and 2 or 4 per cent households are also there in the former and latter villages respectively, who earn their livelihood out of this source of income as their subsidiary occupation.

3. Transport Business with Bullocks and Cart

In both the study villages, the Bāuri cart-owners use their bullocks and cart for agricultural purpose of the local caste Hindu landowners. But in Hirāpur there is a greater demand for the cart-owners for transporting of various materials, like sand from the river bed, bricks from the local kilns, bundled hay for selling in Bhubaneswar etc.

Ordinarily a cart-owner earns Rs. 50 per day on an average. So looking at the demand and profitability of this job, 2 households accounting for 3.64 per cent of Hirāpur followed by 1 (2%) household of Āmbadiha primarily earn their livelihood out of this occupation.

4. Stone Dressing

Two Bāuri households of Hirāpur have learnt the art of stone dressing and they practise this job both in Bhubaneswar as also in other areas. The normal wage for dressing a piece of literate stone is Rs. 1.50. A stone-dresser can dress about 30 to 40 such stone blocks in a day and can earn accordingly.

5. Animal Husbandry

(a) Goat and Sheep Rearing (Commercial Enterprise)

Of the total number of 6 beneficiary households in Hirāpur assisted under goat and sheep-farming units, only 1 (1.82%) household is found to have been very successful. And this household primarily earns its livelihood from this occupation as its primary source of income. There is no household in Āmbadiha which earns its livelihood from this source of income, either as primary or subsidiary occupation.

(b) Poultry Farming (Commercial Enterprise)

The Bāuris traditionally rear country birds for their personal use but it is found that only 1 (1.82%) household of the village Hirāpur has made it a commercial enterprise and earns its daily bread primarily from this occupation.

(c) Cow Herding

There is only 1 (1.82%) household in Hirāpur and none in Āmbadiha, who is engaged in this job. The income from cow herding is a subsidiary source of income.

6. Mat Weaving and Trading

Most of the Bāuri people make jute ropes for weaving of mats. They have indigenous technique for weaving mats. Generally both men and women collect wild grass from the local swampy areas during winter, and sell it for Rs. 30 to Rs. 40 per piece depending upon its size. There are 3 or 5.45 per cent households in Hirāpur village who have made it as their subsidiary occupation. In the case of Āmbadiha 4 or 8 per cent households also earn their livelihood from this source of income as their subsidiary occupation.

Non-Traditional Occupation

1. Rickshaw / Trolley drawing

Among the beneficiary households of the village Hirāpur a total number of 9 accounting for 16.36 per cent have taken to rickshaw and trolley pulling as their primary occupation followed by only 1 or 1.82 per cent household who earns its daily bread subsidiarily from this source of income. There is not a single household in the village Āmbadiha which is found to have adopted this occupation. This is, as mentioned earlier, because of undeveloped road communication. The rickshaw and trolley pullers of Hirāpur generally prefer to play their vehicles in Bhubaneswar city and earn about Rs. 35 per day on an average.

2. Petty Business

The petty business which have been adopted by the beneficiary households of either study village include (a) shopkeeping (Grocery-cum-stationery and betel shop), (b) Vegetable selling, (c) selling of betel leaf, (d) rice selling, (e) dry fish selling. Each of the household doing this occupation has a bicycle for easy transportation of tradable commodities.

It is also observed from the same table that in Hirāpur, a total number of 8 and 7 households accounting for 14.55 and 12.73 per cent respectively have adopted this source of income as their primary and subsidiary occupations. In the village Āmbadiha there are 5 or 10 per cent households who earn their livelihood primarily from this source of income. Sector-wise business taken up by the beneficiary household is described below:

(a) Shopkeeping (Grocery-cum-Stationery and Betel Shop)

In the village Hirāpur there is only 1 (1.82%) household who has opened a betel shop in Bhubaneswar city and primarily earns its livelihood out of this occupation followed by 3 or 5.45 per cent of households who have opened 3 small grocery-cum-stationery shops inside their own hamlets and earn their daily bread subsidiarily from this source of income. These 3 households sell the commodities among themselves and no customer belonging to caste Hindus comes to their shop because of the stigma of untouchability attached with them. Sometimes, these shopkeepers also take petty mobile shops to different weekly markets held in Bhubaneswar city and other areas and earn about Rs. 40 on an average per market day. But their profit remains within Rs. 10 to Rs. 15 during non-market days. The household who has opened a betel shop in Bhubaneswar city profits Rs. 30 on an average per day.

In the village Āmbadiha there is only 1 or 2 per cent household who primarily depends on this source of income. This household runs a grocery shop inside his hamlet and like the village Hirāpur, in this case the customers also remain confined to the population of its own caste.

(b) Vegetable Selling

The Bāuri businessmen generally purchase different vegetables from the local rural area in cheap rate and sell it in Bhubaneswar city. A total number of 3 or 5.45 per cent households of the village Hirāpur have taken to this source of income as their primary occupation. An equal number of households are also there in this village who have taken to this occupation as their subsidiary occupation. But there is none in the village Āmbadiha who has taken to this occupation either as its primary or subsidiary source of income.

(c) Selling of Betel Leaf

Banamalipur area, where betel cultivation is practised to a large extent by a number of local cultivators is about 30 kms. away from Hirāpur and about 10 kms. away from Āmbadiha. So, as betel leaf trading is a profitable business, 2 (3.64%) households of Hirāpur have taken to this job as their primary occupation. They go to Banamalipur area, purchase betel leaf and trade it in different markets of Bhubaneswar city. Likewise, a total number of 2 households accounting for 4 per cent of Āmbadiha have also adopted this source of income as their primary occupation. The average income per day per household doing this business comes to about Rs. 40 per day.

(d) Rice Selling

In Hirāpur only 1 (1.82%) household has taken to this job as its primary occupation. This household purchases paddy from local agriculturists during harvesting season, and stores it for peak seasons. When the market rate of paddy is hiked, it sells rice in different markets in Bhubaneswar city. The average income comes to about Rs. 40/-.

(e) Dry Fish Selling

In Hirāpur 1 (1.82%) household is found to have established a dry fish unit as its primary occupation. Another household is also there in this village which has taken to this occupation as its secondary source of income. Both these beneficiary households sell dry fish in local markets as well as in Bhubaneswar city. While the household who has taken to this job as primary occupation has a larger unit and earns about Rs. 50 on an average per day, it rests on Rs. 30 on an average per day in case of another household that has adopted it as its subsidiary occupation. In Āmbadiha, 2 or 4 per cent households have taken to this job as their primary source of income.

3. Tailoring

One beneficiary household (1.82%) of Hirāpur has purchased a sewing machine and carries out its business in Bhubaneswar city as its primary occupation. Its earning comes to be about Rs. 70 on an average per day. There are also two other households in this village who earn their livelihood out of this source of income as their subsidiary occupation. They run their units in their own villages.

4. Share-Cropping

A total number of 6 or 10.91 per cent households of Hirāpur earn their livelihood primarily from this occupation. An equal number of households are also there in this village who have taken to this occupation. In Āmbadiha there are 2 or 4 per cent households who have adopted this occupation as their primary source of income followed by an equal number of households who have taken to this source of income as their subsidiary occupation. Hence it becomes manifested that more number of households of Hirāpur than Āmbadiha have taken to this occupation as their primary and subsidiary occupation. This is because of the following factors:

(i) the caste Hindus of this village have considerably given up their traditional occupations in general and cultivation in particular and taken to various profitable occupations outside the village, preferably in Bhubaneswar city combined with high increase of daily wage and price hike of agricultural pesticides, manure, fertilisers etc. As a result of this, they like to dispose of their agricultural fields for share cultivation.

(ii) the land which are either located at a distance place or not so productive are disposed of for share-cropping, and

(iii) due to the cordial master and servant relationship, the caste Hindus transfer agricultural fields to Bāuri clients for share-cropping.

5. Horticulture

Only 1 (1.82%) household of Hirāpur is found to have adopted this source of income as its primary occupation. This household has taken a piece of cultivated land, about 2 acres on contract basis from a local *Brahman* landlord and grows different green vegetables and sells the products either on the spot on wholesale basis or carries it to Bhubaneswar city for selling.

6. Construction work

(a) Mason

This occupation has been taken up by only 1 (1.82%) household of Hirāpur as its primary source of income. The person preferably works as such in Bhubaneswar city and earns an amount of Rs. 60 per day on an average. There is none in Āmbadiha who is found to have taken to this either as its primary or subsidiary occupation.

(b) Apprentice Mason

In Hirāpur, two apprentice mason households are also there who primarily earn their daily bread out of this occupation. These people prefer working in Bhubaneswar city where they are able to get Rs. 40 on an average per day.

7. Carpenter

This occupation has been adopted by one household (1.82%) in Hirāpur who works in a workshop in Bhubaneswar city and earns about Rs. 45 per day on an average. This occupation is considered as its primary occupation.

8. Net Making and Selling

Net making is the traditional caste occupation of the local fisherman people. But some of the Bāuris have learnt this skill and taken to this occupation as one of their source of income. It is observed that in Hirāpur when there is only one household (1.82%) who has taken to this source of income as its primary occupation, there are as many as 7.27 per cent households in the same village who have taken to this job as their subsidiary occupation. In Āmbadiha even though there is none who earns primarily from this source of income, there is a total number of 2 (4%) households who have taken to this job as their subsidiary occupation.

Occupation of Non-Beneficiaries

Traditional Occupations

The traditional occupations of the non-beneficiary households of the study villages include agricultural labour/wage earning, *Haliā/ Kothiā*, coconut plucking, stone-dressing, cow-herding and mat-weaving (Table 4.8).

1. (a) Agricultural Labour/Wage Earning

It is observed from the Table 4.8 that 31 or 58.49 per cent of the households of Hirāpur primarily earn their livelihood out of this occupation. But in case of Āmbadiha there are as many as 57 or 82.61 per cent of the total 69 such households which also practically earn their daily bread out of this source of income. So far as the subsidiary occupation is concerned, while a total number of 9 or 16.98 per cent of households of Hirāpur depend on this source of income, it is only 1 (1.45%) household in case of Āmbadiha.

(b) Halia/Kothia

In Hirāpur 4 or 7.55 per cent households are employed as *Haliā/ Kothiā*, and earn their livelihood primarily from this source. This is followed by the same number of households which consider this source as their subsidiary occupation. About 10 per cent or 7 households of Āmbadiha have taken to this source of income as their primary occupation.

2. Coconut Plucking

This occupation has been retained by 2 (3.77%) households of Hirāpur as against 3 or (4.35%) of Āmbadiha who have been found to earn their livelihood primarily from this occupation. In the former village there is also 1 (1.89%) household for which this is its subsidiary occupation.

3. Stone Dressing

This occupation has been adopted by only 1 (1.89%) household of Hirāpur which primarily earns its livelihood out of this source of income.

4. Cow Herding

This is found to be a subsidiary occupation in case of both the villages. While in case of Hirāpur there is only 1 (1.89%) household, It is 2 or 2.90 per cent in case of Āmbadiha who earn their livelihood out of this source of income.

5. Mat Weaving and Selling

Like cow herding, mat weaving and selling it in the local markets, is also a subsidiary occupation for some of the households in both the villages. In case of Hirāpur, 4 households accounting for 7.55 per cent derive their subsidiary income from this occupation. But it is as high as 7 or 10.14 per cent households in the case of Āmbadiha.

Non-Traditional Occupation

The non-traditional occupations adopted among the non-beneficiary households include rickshaw/trolley pulling, petty business, like vegetable selling, selling of betel leaf, dry fish selling, share-cropping, masonry and mat weaving and selling.

1. Rickshaw/Trolley pulling

This occupation is found to have been adopted by 3 or 5.66 per cent households of Hirāpur as their primary occupation, whereas there is no one in Āmbadiha who has taken to this occupation either as a primary or as a subsidiary source of income.

2. Petty Business

A total number of 5 or 9.09 per cent of the households of Hirāpur have taken to different petty business, like vegetable selling by 3 households (5.66%), selling of betel leaf by 1 household (1.89%), and the selling of dry fish by 1 household (1.89%) of Hirāpur village. There is none in Āmbadiha who has taken to any one of these occupations.

3. Share-Cropping

So far as share-cropping is concerned, it is found that 5 households in Hirāpur and 2 in Āmbadiha, representing 9.43 and 2.90 per cent respectively, have taken to it as their primary occupation. In Hirāpur 2 households (3.77%) have taken to this as their subsidiary occupation.

4. Apprentice Masonry

In Hirāpur only 1 (1.89%) household primarily earns its livelihood from apprentice masonry. There is no household in Āmbadiha found adopting this as a source of income, either as its primary or as subsidiary occupation.

5. Mat Weaving and Selling

This occupation has been adopted by 1 (1.89%) household of Hirāpur as its primary source of income. Another household is also there which is found to have adopted this source of income as its subsidiary occupation.

Occupation among Total Households

Traditional Occupation

When one looks at the total figures of beneficiary and non-beneficiary households of Hirāpur and Āmbadiha available in Table 4.8, it is found that while a total number of 53 households of the former village (49.07%) earn their livelihood primarily as agricultural labourers or as wage-earners or as *Haliā* and *Kothiā,* it is as many as 103 or 86.55 per cent in the case of Āmbadiha. In the former village, a total number of 44 or 40.74 per cent households derive subsidiary income from this occupation as a whole, while for Āmbadiha, it is only 10 or 8.40 per cent of the households.

So far as coconut plucking is concerned, in the village of Hirāpur, 3 (2.78%) and 2 (1.85%) per cent of the non-beneficiary households earn their livelihood from this source as their primary and subsidiary income respectively. But it is 6 or 5.04 per cent and 2 or 1.68 per cent respectively, in case of Āmbadiha.

The occupation of transport business with bullock and cart has been taken up as a primary occupation in case of 2 (1.85%) households of Hirāpur and 1 (0.84%) household of Āmbadiha. But stone-dressing and goat-rearing are found to have been the primary source of income in case of 3 or 2.75 per cent and 1 or 0.93 per cent household of Hirāpur respectively. Another household in Hirāpur earns its livelihood primarily from goat-rearing. The job of cow-herding is not found to have been acceptable as a primary source of income by any household in either of the villages, rather there are 2 (1.85%) households in Hirāpur, and 1 (1.68%) in Āmbadiha, which benefit from this as a subsidiary occupation. Likewise, mat-weaving and its sale is not considered to be a primary occupation for any of the households either in Hirāpur or in Āmbadiha. However, 7 or 6.48 per cent and 3 or 2.52 per cent households of Hirāpur and Āmbadiha are engaged in this occupation as their secondary source of income.

Non-Traditional Occupation

The Table 4.8 also reveals that in Hirāpur a total number of 12 (11.1%) households have taken to rickshaw and trolley pulling as their primary occupation. There is only 1 household in this village which has taken to this occupation as its subsidiary occupation. But, there is none in Āmbadiha which is found to have adopted this as a source of income, either primary or subsidiary.

Regarding adoption of petty business, 13 or 12.04 per cent households of Hirāpur as against 5 or 4.20 per cent households of Āmbadiha have taken to this job as their primary occupation. Among these 13 households of the former village, 1 (0.93%), 6 (5.65%), 2 (1.83%),1 (0.93%) and 2 (1.83%) households have adopted shop-keeping, vegetable selling, dealing in betel leaf, selling of rice and selling of dry-fish respectively as their primary occupations. Likewise of the total 5 households of Āmbadiha 1 (0.84%), 2 (1.68%) and 2 (1.68%) household have taken to shop-keeping, selling of betel leaf and dry-fish respectively as their primary occupation. There are as many as 7 or 6.48 per cent household in Hirāpur as against only 1 or 0.84 per cent in Āmbadiha who practise various petty business as their subsidiary occupation. These households have adopted different petty business as their subsidiary occupations including shop-keeping (6.48%), vegetable selling (6.48%), and selling of dry fish (0.93%). There is only 1 household (0.84%) in Āmbadiha that has adopted selling of dry fish.

So far as the job of tailoring is concerned, it is 1 or 0.93 per cent and 2 or 1.25 per cent households in case of the village Hirāpur which depend on this source of income as their primary and subsidiary occupation respectively.

Regarding share-cropping it may be said that in Hirāpur there are as many as 11 or 10.19 per cent households as against only 4 or 3.36 per cent in Āmbadiha, who primarily earn their livelihood out of this source of income. Interestingly, a greater number of households (8 or 7.41%) of Hirāpur have also taken to this source of income as their subsidiary occupation than those of Āmbadiha having only 2 or 1.68 per cent.

The same table also reveals that, while in Hirāpur 3 or 2.78 per cent of households have adopted apprentice masonry as their primary occupation, only 1 (1.93%) household of Āmbadiha earns its primary livelihood out of masonry followed by another household (0.93%) with horticulture as its primary occupation. In this village there are 2 (1.85%) households which have taken to net weaving and its sale as their primary occupation. They are followed by 5 or 4.63 per cent households which have taken to this job as their subsidiary occupation. In Āmbadiha only 2 or 1.68 per cent households have taken up net weaving as their subsidiary occupation.

Summary Findings

All households considered occupation-wise have been summed up in Table 4.9. The summary findings are also pictographically presented in Diagram 4.1.

TABLE 4.9

Traditional and non-traditional occupations among beneficiary and non-beneficiary households

Category of Occupation	Beneficiary				Non-Beneficiary				Total			
	Hirāpur (N=55)		Āmbadiha (N=50)		Hirāpur (N=53)		Āmbadiha (N=69)		Hirāpur (N=108)		Āmbadiha (N=119)	
	P	S	P	S	P	S	P	S	P	S	P	S
(1)	(2)	(3)	(4)	(5)	(6)	(7)	(8)	(9)	(10)	(11)	(12)	(13)
Traditional	25 (45.45)	35 (63.64)	43 (86.00)	15 (30.00)	38 (71.70)	19 (35.85)	67 (97.10)	11 (15.94)	68 (62.96)	54 (50.00)	110 (92.44)	26 (21.85)
Non-Traditional	30 (54.55)	20.00 (36.36)	7 (14.00)	4 (8.00)	15 (28.30)	3 (5.66)	2 (2.90)	2 (2.90)	45 (41.67)	23 (21.30)	9 (7.56)	6 (5.04)
'Z' value	a = 4.93 b = 3.72				a = 3.91 b = 0.74				a = 6.45 b = 3.64			

Note: (i) Figures in brackets represent %age
(ii) P = Primary, S = Subsidiary
(iii) 'Z' value is calculated out of data relating to primary occupations (a) and subsidiary occupations (b).

Beneficiary Households

The Table 4.9 illustrates that of the total 55 beneficiary households of Hirāpur more than half, i.e., 30 or 54.55 per cent households have taken to various non-traditional occupations as their primary source of income, as against a mere 14 per cent or 7 households of the total 50 such households in Āmbadiha. The rest of the households of each village earn their livelihood primarily from different traditional occupations. So far as subsidiary occupations are concerned, while about 36.36 per cent or 20 households of the former village earn their daily bread from different non-traditional occupations, it forms merely 8 per cent or 4 households in the case of Āmbadiha.

Diagram 4.1

Traditional and non-traditional occupation among beneficiary and non-beneficiary households of village Hirāpur and Āmbadiha

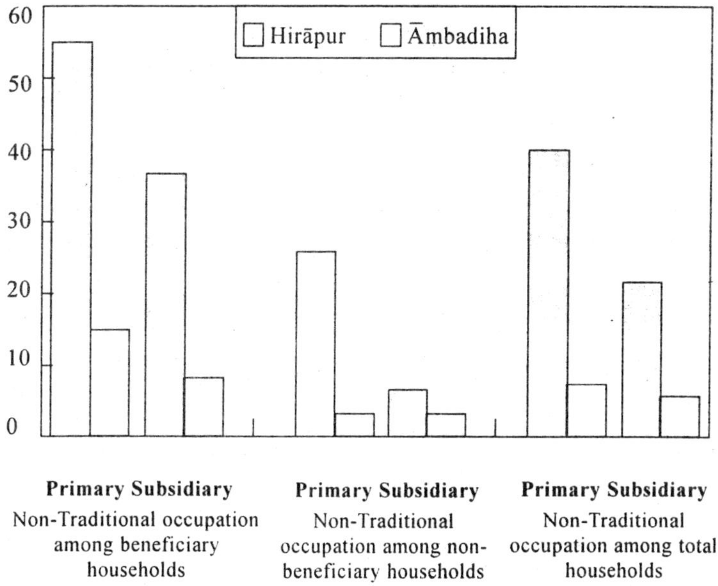

contd.

Diagram 4.1 (contd.)

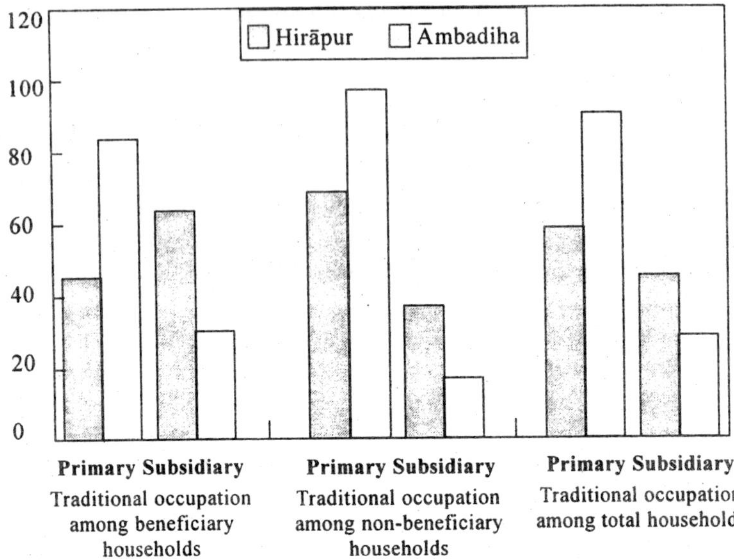

The 'z' value signifies that the difference between the beneficiary households of Hirāpur and Āmbadiha, who have adopted different non-traditional or new occupations, is statistically significant at 5 per cent level of significance. Hence, the second hypothesis which reads as "economic development inputs, i.e., poverty alleviation programmes do not create occupational mobility among the beneficiaries who live in urban fringes", hereby does not come true.

Non-Beneficiary Households

So far as the case of the non-beneficiary households is concerned, like the beneficiary households, these also show a particular pattern. In case of Hirāpur, of the total 53 households it is 28.30 per cent or 15 households as against only 2.90 per cent or 2 out of a total of 69 households of Āmbadiha who have taken to various non-traditional occupations as their primary sources of income. These are followed by 5.66 per cent or 3 households of the former village as against 2.90 per cent or 2 households of Āmbadiha who have adopted various non-traditional occupations as their subsidiary occupations. Hence, in this case the 'z' value also shows a significant difference at 5 per cent level of significance. Consequently, it can be said that "occupational changes also take place among the non-beneficiary households living on the outskirts of urban areas".

Total Households

If one looks at the total figures available in the same table it can be found that of the total 108 households of the village Hirāpur as high a percentage of 41.67 or 45 households have taken to various non-traditional sources of income as their primary occupations as against merely 7.56 per cent or 9 households of the total 119 households of Āmbadiha. Further the said table also speaks that while there are 21.30 per cent or a total number of 23 households in case of Hirāpur who have taken to various non-traditional sources of income as their subsidiary occupations, it is only 5.04 per cent or 6 households in case of the village Āmbadiha. The rest households earn their livelihood out of different traditional occupations.

The 'z' value, which works out to be 6.45 is found to be substantially significant at 5 per cent level of significance.

(ii) Income Expenditure and Indebtedness

(a) Income Level

Beneficiary Households

The income of the Bāuri beneficiary households is shown in Table 4.10. A total number of 9 income groups have been made, starting from the lowest group of below Rs. 4000 per annum to the highest group above of Rs. 11,000. It is found that of the total 55 households of Hirāpur, most households, i.e. 28 accounting for 50.91 per cent have an income above Rs. 11,000 and more per annum followed by as high a percentage of 16.36 or 9 households who earn Rs. 10,001 to Rs. 11,000. Further a cursory look at the same table reveals that more than 10 per cent (12.73) or 7 households have an income between Rs. 8,001 and Rs. 9,000 followed by 7.27 per cent or 4 households with an income in the next lower income group of Rs. 7,001 to Rs. 8,000. About 3.64 per cent or 2 households earn between Rs. 5,001 to Rs. 6,000. But an equal number of households are there who are able to earn between Rs. 9,001 to Rs. 10,000. There is only 1 or 1.82 per cent household which claims that its earning is lowest; remains only within Rs. 4,000. This solitary household is followed by another household, who, however, earns from Rs. 5,000 to Rs. 6,000 and the income of the rest one household comes to be in between Rs. 9,001 to Rs. 10,000 per annum.

So far as the case of the village Āmbadiha is concerned, of the total 50 households, maximum per cent, i.e. 24 or 12 households claim middle income and are concentrated in the income group of Rs. 6,001 to Rs. 7,000 followed by 20 per cent or 10 households who have an income of Rs. 11,001 or more per annum. A total number of 6 or 12 per cent households have an income in between Rs. 8001 to Rs. 9000 but for an equal number of households it comes to be in between Rs. 4001 to Rs. 5000. However, when a total number of 5 or 10 per cent of the households earn between Rs. 5001 to Rs. 6000, a lot of another 5 households are there who are able to earn between Rs. 7001 to Rs. 8000 per annum. Still as high a percentage of 8 or 4 households claim an income of below Rs. 4000. The rest 2 (4%) households earn in between Rs. 9001 to Rs. 10,000 per annum.

TABLE 4.10

Distribution of beneficiary and non-beneficiary households by income groups (per annum)

Income Groups (in Rs.)	Beneficiary		Non-beneficiary		Total	
	H	A	H	A	H	A
(1)	(2)	(3)	(4)	(5)	(6)	(7)
Upto 4000	1 (1.82)	4 (8.00)	1 (1.89)	4 (5.80)	2 (1.85)	8 (6.72)
4001-5000	1 (1.82)	6 (12.00)	3 (5.66)	9 (13.04)	4 (3.70)	15 (12.61)
5001-6000	2 (3.64)	5 (10.00)	1 (1.89)	6 (8.70)	3 (2.78)	11 (9.24)
6001-7000	1 (1.82)	12 (24.00)	1 (1.89)	15 (21.74)	2 (1.85)	27 (22.69)
7001-8000	4 (7.27)	5 (10.00)	9 (16.98)	10 (14.49)	13 (12.04)	15 (12.61)
Sub-Total	9 (16.36)	32 (64.00)	15 (28.30)	44 (63.77)	24 (22.22)	76 (63.87)
8001-9000	7 (12.73)	6 (12.00)	7 (13.21)	6 (8.70)	14 (12.96)	12 (10.08)
9001-10000	2 (3.64)	2 (4.00)	4 (7.55)	4 (5.80)	6 (5.56)	6 (5.04)
10001-11000	9 (16.36)	-	11 (20.75)	9 (13.04)	20 (18.52)	9 (7.56)
11001 & above	28 (50.91)	10 (20.00)	16 (30.19)	6 (8.70)	44 (40.74)	16 (13.45)
Sub-Total	46 (83.64)	18 (36.00)	38 (71.70)	25 (36.23)	84 (77.78)	43 (36.13)
Total	55 (100.00)	50 (100.00)	53 (100.00)	69 (100.00)	108 (100.00)	119 (100.00)

Note: Figures in brackets represent %age
(H=Hirāpur, A=Āmbadiha)

Thus, from the above findings it can be concluded that while as high a percentage of 83.64 or 46 households of Hirāpur earn more than Rs. 8,000 per annum, it is only 36 per cent or 18 households in case of Āmbadiha. What this otherwise means is that for more than 60 per cent (64%) or 32 households of the village Āmbadiha, against merely 16.36 per cent or 9 households of Hirāpur, the earnings remain below Rs. 8,000 per annum.

Non-Beneficiary Households

As in the case of beneficiary households, among the non-beneficiary households of the two study villages also, a similar trend may be noticed. Hence, while the largest number of households, i.e. 16 representing 30.19 per cent of Hirāpur fall in the income range of Rs. 11,001 and more, it is in the initial slab of Rs. 6001 to Rs. 7000 in which maximum household numbering 15 (21.74%) of Āmbadiha fall. The most significant feature that emerges from the above findings is that, even though the households of both the villages are unevenly distributed in the existing 9 income groups, while more than 63 per cent or 44 households of Āmbadiha earn only upto Rs. 8000 per annum, more than 71 per cent or 38 households of Hirāpur earn more than Rs. 8000 per annum.

Hence, when both the beneficiary and non-beneficiary households of each village are added together village-wise, it is found that of the total 108 households of Hirāpur as many as 84 or 77.78 per cent households earn more than Rs. 8000 per annum but in case of Āmbadiha it is only 43 or 36.13 per cent of the total 119 households who have been able to earn more than this, i.e. Rs. 8000 per annum. However, while most of the households, i.e. 44 or 40.74 per cent of Hirāpur are concentrated in the highest income group which is 11,001 and above, it is only 27 or 22.69 per cent households in case of Āmbadiha who are concentrated in lower income slab, i.e. Rs. 6001 to Rs. 7000. When a further cursory look is given at the same table, an opposite trend of income among the households of the study villages is observed. It is found that while minimum percentage of households, i.e. 22.22 or 24 of the village Hirāpur earn below Rs. 8000 per annum, it is maximum, i.e. 63.87 per cent or 76 households in case of Āmbadiha. This otherwise reveals that less than 36 per cent households of the village Āmbadiha earn more than Rs. 8000 annum.

Households Below and Above Poverty Line

To find out the number of Bāuri households living below and above poverty line, five income ranges have been made in Table 4.17

which is based on the classification made by Government of India during the 8th Plan period. The poverty line, which is Rs. 6400 during 7th plan period was raised to Rs. 11,000 in the 8th five year plan. According to this plan period the households earning an income of below Rs. 4000 per annum are termed as destitute. Households with an income between Rs. 4,001 to Rs. 6,000 are termed very very poor, followed by households with an income of Rs. 6,001 to Rs. 8,500 called very poor households and those with an income between 8,501 and Rs. 11,000 as poor. Households with income of Rs. 11,000 or above are considered not being poor and are regarded as households above the poverty line. Hence, basing on this classification, the beneficiary and non-beneficiary households of the above two study villages have been classified and the households above poverty line have been identified.

Beneficiary Households

Table 4.11 reveals that of the total 55 households of Hirāpur, there is only 1 (1.82%) household that may be categorised as destitute, followed by 3 (5.45%) as very very poor, 9 (16.36%) as very poor, and 14 (25.45 %) as poor households. But in the cause of Āmbadiha, out of 50 households there are as many as 4 (8%) destitute households, followed by 11 (22%) very very poor, 18 (36%) very poor, and 7 (14%) as poor households. The rest 28 or 50.91 per cent of the households in Hirāpur are found to have crossed the poverty line as against the rest 10 or 20 per cent households of Āmbadiha. Hence the 'z' value shows a significant difference at 5 per cent level of significance, as a result of which the third hypothesis that reads as "the income level of the beneficiaries living at the outskirts of urban centres is same as their counterparts living in remote areas", is hereby not borne out.

Non-Beneficiary Households

So far as the case of the non-beneficiary households in the two study villages is concerned, it can be said that the total 53 households of Hirāpur, 18 (33.96%) are found to be poor, followed by 14 (26.42%) as very poor, 4 (7.55%) as very very poor and 1 (1.87%) as destitute. But of the total 69 households of Āmbadiha, as many as 23 (33.33%) households are found to be poor, followed by 21 (30.43%) as very poor, 15 (21.74%) as very very poor, and 4 (5.80%) as destitute households. Hence, while there are 16 or 30.19 per cent households in Hirāpur which have crossed the poverty line, in the case of Āmbadiha it is only 6 or 8.7 per cent,

TABLE 4.11

Distribution of beneficiary and non-beneficiary households below poverty line

Poverty Line (in Rs.)	Beneficiary		Non-beneficiary		Total	
	H (N=55)	A (N=50)	H (N=53)	A (N=69)	H (N=108)	A (N=119)
(1)	(2)	(3)	(4)	(5)	(6)	(7)
Upto 4000/-	1 (1.82)	4 (8.00)	1 (1.87)	4 (5.80)	2 (1.85)	8 (6.72)
4001-6000	3 (5.45)	11 (22.00)	4 (7.55)	15 (21.74)	7 (6.48)	26 (21.85)
6001-8500	9 (16.36)	18 (36.00)	14 (26.42)	21 (30.43)	23 (21.30)	39 (32.77)
8501-11000	14 (25.45)	7 (14.00)	18 (33.96)	23 (33.33)	32 (29.63)	30 (25.21)
Sub-Total	25 (49.09)	40 (80.00)	37 (69.81)	63 (91.30)	64 (59.26)	103 (86.55)
11001 & above	28 (50.91)	10 (20.00)	16 (30.19)	6 (8.67)	44 (40.74)	16 (13.45)
'Z' value	3.52		2.97		4.99	

Note: Figures in brackets represent %age
(H=Hirāpur, A=Āmbadiha)

When the figures for both beneficiary and non-beneficiary households of the two villages are put together, it may be noticed that while in Hirāpur there are (1.85%) households as destitute, 7 (6.48%) as very very poor, 23 (21.30%) as very poor, and 32 (29.63%) as poor, the corresponding figures for Āmbadiha are 8 (6.72%), 26 (21.85%), 39 (32.77%), and 30 (25.21%) respectively. Hence, there is a total number of 44 (40.74%) households in the village Hirāpur as against only 16 (13.45%) of the village Āmbadiha. The difference is found to be only 16 (13.45%) of the village Āmbadiha who are found to have crossed the poverty line. The difference is found to be significant at 5 per cent level of significance.

Earning According to Occupation

Beneficiary Households

In the preceding section the occupational profile and income earnings of the beneficiary and non-beneficiary households have been discussed. But when a correlation is made between occupation and income earning, a particular trend emerges. It is found from Table 4.12.1

TABLE 4.12.1

Distribution of beneficiary households according to occupation and different poverty levels

Category of Occupation	Sl. No.	Occupation	Total HHs	Hirāpur Poverty Group / Level (in Rs.)				
				Upto 4000	4001-6000	6001-8500	8501-11000	11001 & above
(1)	(2)	(3)	(4)	(5)	(6)	(7)	(8)	(9)
Traditional	1. a	Agricultural/Wage Labour	14 (100.00)	1 (7.14)	3 (21.43)	8 (57.14)	2 (14.29)	-
	b.	*Haliā/Kothiā*	4 (100.00)	-	-	-	3 (75.00)	1 (25.00)
	2.	Coconut Plucker	1 (100.00)	-	-	-	-	1 (100.00)
	3.	Transport business with bullock & cart	2 (100.00)	-	-	-	-	2 (100.00)
	4.	Stone dressing	2 (100.00)	-	-	-	1 (50.00)	1 (50.00)
	5.	Animal husbandry	2 (100.00)	-	-	1 (50.00)	-	-
		Sub-total	25 (100.00)	1 (4.0)	3 (12.00)	9 (36.00)	6 (24.00)	6 (24.00)

contd.

TABLE 4.12.1 (contd.)

(1)	(2)	(3)	(4)	(5)	(6)	(7)	(8)	(9)
Non-traditional	1.	Rickshaw/Trolley pulling	9 (100.00)	-	-	-	1 (11.11)	8 (88.87)
	2.	Petty business	8 (100.00)	-	-	1 (12.50)	2 (25.00)	5 (62.50)
	3.	Tailoring	1 (100.00)	-	-	-	-	1 (100.00)
	4.	Share cropping	6 (100.00)	-	-	-	4 (66.67)	2 (33.33)
	5.	Horticulture	1 (100.00)	-	-	-	-	1 (100.00)
	6.	Construction work	3 (100.00)	-	-	-	-	3 (100.00)
	7.	Carpenting	1 (100.00)	-	-	-	-	1 (100.00)
	8.	Net Weaving	1 (100.00)	-	-	-	-	1 (100.00)
		Sub-Total	30 (100.00)	-	-	1 (3.33)	7 (23.33)	22 (73.33)
		Total	55 (100.00)	1 (1.82)	3 (5.45)	10 (18.18)	13 (23.64)	26 (50.91)

contd.

TABLE 4.12.1 (contd.)

Category of Occupation	Sl. No.	Occupation	Total HHs	Āmbadiha Poverty Group / Level (in Rs.)				
				Upto 4000	4001-6000	6001-8500	8501-11000	11001 & above
(1)	(2)	(3)	(4)	(5)	(6)	(7)	(8)	(9)
Traditional	1. a	Agricultural/Wage Labour	30 (100.00)	4 (13.33)	9 (30.00)	15 (50.00)	2 (6.67)	-
	b.	*Haliā/Kothiā*	9 (100.00)	-	2 (22.22)	3 (33.33)	3 (33.33)	1 (11.11)
	2.	Coconut Plucker	3 (100.00)	-	-	-	1 (33.33)	2 (65.67)
	3.	Transport business with bullock & cart	1 (100.00)	-	-	-	-	1 (100.00)
	4.	Stone dressing	-	-	-	-	-	-
	5.	Animal husbandary	-	-	-	-	-	-
		Sub-total	43 (100.00)	4 (9.30)	11 (25.58)	18 (41.86)	6 (13.95)	4 (9.30)

contd.

TABLE 4.12.1 (contd.)

(1)	(2)	(3)	(4)	(5)	(6)	(7)	(8)	(9)
Non-traditional	1.	Rickshaw/Trolly pulling	-	-	-	-	-	-
	2.	Petty business	5 (100.00)	-	-	-	-	5 (100.00)
	3.	Tailoring	-	-	-	-	-	-
	4.	Share cropping	2 (100.00)	-	-	-	1 (50.00)	1 (50.00)
	5.	Horticulture	-	-	-	-	-	-
	6.	Construction work	-	-	-	-	-	-
	7.	Carpenting	-	-	-	-	-	-
	8.	Net Weaving	-	-	-	-	-	-
		Sub-Total	7 (100.00)	-	-	-	1 (14.29)	6 (85.71)
		Total	50 (100.00)	4 (8.00)	11 (22.00)	18 (36.00)	7 (14.00)	10 (20.00)

Note: Figures in brackets represent %age.

that, of the total 25 households having different traditional occupations in Hirāpur, 6 or 24 per cent of the households have been able to earn Rs. 11,000 or above per annum, and hence, are found to have crossed the poverty line as against only 4 or 9.3 per cent households of the total 43 in Āmbadiha. So far as the cause of households which have taken to different non-traditional occupations is concerned, of the total 30 households of the former village as many as 22 or 73.33 per cent have crossed the poverty line, as against 6 or 85.71 per cent of the total 7 households of the latter village. Hence, a higher percentage of households of Āmbadiha lives above the poverty line, compared to the village of Hirāpur.

A further look at the same table reveals the fact that there is not a single agricultural or wage-earning household in the village Hirāpur that earns an income of Rs. 11,000 or above per annum. Hence, all 14 such households are found to be below the poverty line. On the contrary all the households of Hirāpur engaged in plucking coconut (1 or 100%), and in transport business with bullocks and carts (2 or 100%) are above the poverty line. Among other households following different traditional occupations, like stone-dressing, and animal husbandry, 50 per cent or 1 household each have been able to cross the poverty line. But all the households who have taken to different non-traditional occupations, like tailoring, horticulture, construction work, carpentry, and net weaving earn more than Rs. 11,000. Hence, they have been able to cross the poverty line. And of the total 9 households who have taken to rickshaw / trolley pulling, 8 households who have taken to different petty business and 6 households who have taken to share-cropping, a total number of 8 or 88.87 per cent, 5 or 62.50 per cent and 2 or 33.33 per cent respectively, are found to have crossed the poverty line.

As in the village of Hirāpur, of the lot of 30 households of Āmbadiha engaged in agricultural or wage-earning, not a single household is found to earn Rs. 11,000 or more. Hence all such households are living below the poverty line. But the only household which is engaged in transport business is observed to have crossed the poverty line as its earning is found to be more than Rs. 11,000 per annum. Of the lot of 9 *Hālia / Kothiā* households, only 1 household accounting for 11.11 per cent has been able to cross the poverty line. But 2 or 66.67 per cent of households engaged in coconut plucking have crossed this line. All the 6 households who practise different petty business are found to have crossed the poverty line. There is only 1 or 50 per cent household practising share-cropping, which has also crossed the poverty line.

Non-Beneficiary Households

So far as the non-beneficiary households of Hirāpur and Āmbadiha are concerned, of the total 38 households in Hirāpur engaged in various traditional occupations, 8 or 11.06 per cent households have crossed the poverty line as against 5 or 7.46 per cent households of Āmbadiha. Likewise, of 15 households in Hirāpur engaged in different non-traditional occupations, 8 or 53.33 per cent have crossed the poverty line, whereas it is 1 or 50 per cent in Āmbadiha. Hence, where there are 15 or 28.30 per cent households who have crossed the poverty line in the former village, it is only 6 or 8.70 per cent in case of Āmbadiha (Table 4.12.2).

The above table also reveals that about 10 per cent or 3 households of Hirāpur depend on agricultural wage-earning and are able to earn Rs. 11,000 or more per annum. In the case of Āmbadiha it is only 1.75 per cent or 1 household. So far as the case of the *Haliā/ Kothiā* households are concerned, 2 or 50 per cent of the households of Hirāpur are found to have crossed the poverty line as against 2 or about 29 per cent of the households in Āmbadiha. Further, both the households of Hirāpur engaged in plucking coconut have been able to cross the poverty line as against 2 or 66.67 per cent of Āmbadiha. The only household of Hirāpur which is engaged in the work of stone-dressing earns Rs. 11,001 or more per annum, and hence, is above the poverty line.

Among the households of Hirāpur which have adopted different non-traditional occupations, it is found that 2 or 66.67 per cent are engaged in rickshaw/trolley pulling and 3 or 60 per cent have taken to different petty business, and have all crossed the poverty line. It only household of Hirāpur, devoted to construction work is found to have been able to cross the poverty line. Likewise, the household which deals in net weaving has also crossed the line. But of the total 5 households of this village living on share cultivation, only 1 or 20 per cent of households have crossed the said line as against 1 or 50 per cent of Āmbadiha.

Per Capita Income

Beneficiary Households

After discussing the distribution of households by income ranges and occupation, it is now important to find out the per capita income. This would give us a fair idea of their status of living.

TABLE 4.12.2

Distribution of non-beneficiary households according to occupation and different poverty levels

Category of Occupation	Sl. No.	Occupation	Total HHs	Hirāpur Poverty Group / Level (in Rs.)				
				Upto 4000	4001-6000	6001-8500	8501-11000	11001 & above
(1)	(2)	(3)	(4)	(5)	(6)	(7)	(8)	(9)
Traditional	1. a	Agricultural/Wage Labour	31 (100.00)	1 (3.23)	4 (12.90)	14 (45.16)	9 (29.03)	3 (9.68)
	b.	*Haliā/Kothiā*	4 (100.00)	-	-	-	2 (50.00)	2 (50.00)
	2.	Coconut Plucking	2 (100.00)	-	-	-	-	2 (100.00)
	3.	Stone dressing	1 (100.00)	-	-	-	-	1 (100.00)
		Sub-total	38 (100.00)	1 (2.63)	4 (10.53)	14 (36.84)	11 (28.95)	8 (11.06)

contd.

TABLE 4.12.2 (contd.)

(1)	(2)	(3)	(4)	(5)	(6)	(7)	(8)	(9)
Non-traditional	1.	Rickshaw/Trolley pulling	3 (100.00)	-	-	-	1 (33.33)	2 (66.67)
	2.	Petty business	5 (100.00)	-	-	-	2 (40.00)	3 (60.00)
	3.	Share cropping	5 (100.00)	-	-	-	4 (80.00)	1 (20.00)
	4.	Construction work	1 (100.00)	-	-	-	-	1 (100.00)
	5.	Net Weaving	1 (100.00)	-	-	-	-	1 (100.00)
		Sub-Total	15 (100.00)	-	-	-	7 (46.67)	8 (53.33)
		Total	53 (100.00)	1 (1.87)	4 (7.55)	14 (26.42)	18 (33.96)	15 (28.30)

contd.

TABLE 4.12.2 (contd.)

Category of Occupation	Sl. No.	Occupation	Total HHs	Āmbadiha Poverty Group / Level (in Rs.)				
				Upto 4000	4001-6000	6001-8500	8501-11000	11001 & above
(1)	(2)	(3)	(4)	(5)	(6)	(7)	(8)	(9)
Traditional	1. a	Agricultural/Wage Labour	57 (100.00)	4 (7.01)	15 (26.32)	24 (42.10)	13 (22.81)	1 (1.75)
	b.	*Haliā/Kothiā*	7 (100.00)	-	-	2 (28.57)	3 (42.86)	2 (28.57)
	2.	Coconut Plucker	3 (100.00)	-	-	-	1 (33.33)	2 (66.67)
	3.	Stone dressing	-	-	-	-	-	-
		Sub-total	67 (100.00)	4 (5.97)	15 (22.39)	26 (38.81)	17 (25.37)	5 (7.46)

contd.

TABLE 4.12.1 (contd.)

(1)	(2)	(3)	(4)	(5)	(6)	(7)	(8)	(9)
Non-traditional	1.	Rickshaw/Trolly pulling	-	-	-	-	-	-
	2.	Petty business	-	-	-	-	-	-
	3.	Share cropping	2 (100.00)	-	-	-	1 (50.00)	1 (50.00)
	4.	Construction work	-	-	-	-	-	-
	5.	Net Weaving	-	-	-	-	-	-
		Sub-Total	2 (100.00)	-	-	-	1 (50.00)	1 (50.00)
		Total	69 (100.00)	4 (5.80)	15 (21.74)	26 (37.68)	18 (26.09)	6 (8.70)

Note: Figures in brackets represent %age.

Table 4.13.1 shows the total income of the beneficiary households of the villages Hirāpur and Āmbadiha in different income groups. A total number of 9 income groups have been made and the total number of households, total number of household members, total income and average house size have been shown against each income group and the per household income and per capita income have been calculated. These figures are self explanatory as available in this table.

It is found that the mean per capita income works out to be Rs. 2936.38 per annum in case of Hirāpur, as against only Rs. 1618.85 of Āmbadiha, whereas the figure for the state as a whole is Rs. 3907 (at 1991-92 price level). Thus, while the per capita income of the village Hirāpur is found to be fairly close to the per caption income of the state with a difference of Rs. 970.62 or 24.85 per cent, the per capita income of Āmbadiha falls short by Rs. 2288.15 or 58.57 per cent of the same at the said price level.

A further look at the data available in the same table shows that the per capita income per month is Rs. 244.70 in case of Hirāpur whereas it is only Rs. 134.91 in Āmbadiha. This means when each person of the former village shares Rs. 8.16 per day, it is about half of that in the case of Āmbadiha which comes to Rs. 4.50.

Non-Beneficiary

The per capita income of the non-beneficiary household is shown in Table 4.13.2.

The average per capita income of Āmbadiha at Rs. 1612.00, is found to be far less than that of Hirāpur which is Rs. 2264.59. Further, the table also indicates that these data in comparison with the per capita income of the state of Orissa show a difference Rs. 1642.41 in the case of Hirāpur, and Rs. 2295.00 in the case of Āmbadiha.

(b) Expenditure Pattern

To find out the expenditure pattern between the beneficiary and the non-beneficiary households of the two study villages, 20 per cent of the households of total beneficiaries as also of total non-beneficiaries in each village were selected on the basis of purposive random sampling. As a result of this, a total number of 11 and 10 beneficiary households of Hirāpur and Āmbadiha followed by 11 or 14 non-beneficiary households of the former and the latter villages were selected respectively and a specific schedule was canvassed for every sample household every evening for a whole year. The total annual income of these households was computed and their expenditure pattern on different food and non-food items was calculated.

TABLE 4.13.1

Distribution of beneficiary households according to per capita income

Income Group (in Rs.)	Hirāpur					Āmbadiha				
	Total HHs covered	Total HH members	Total Income earned	Income per HH	Per-capita	Total HHs covered	Total HH members	Total Income earned	Income per HH	Per-capita
(1)	(2)	(3)	(4)	(5)	(6)	(7)	(8)	(9)	(10)	(11)
Upto 4000	1	1	3600	3600.00	3600.00	4	11	13740	3435.00	1249.09
4001 - 5000	1	3	4680	4680.00	1560.00	6	27	26400	4400.00	977.78
5001 - 6000	2	7	11160	5580.00	1594.29	5	21	27660	5532.00	1317.14
6001 - 7000	1	4	6600	6600.00	1650.00	12	60	78096	6508.00	1301.60
7001 - 8000	4	13	29340	7335.00	2256.92	5	20	37956	7591.20	1897.80
8001 - 9000	7	22	59700	8528.57	2713.64	6	43	52440	8740.00	1219.53
9001 - 10000	2	9	18960	9480.00	2106.67	2	13	19080	9540.00	1467.69
10001 - 11000	9	39	97104	10789.33	2489.85	-	-	-	-	-
11001 & above	28	114	391368	13977.43	3433.05	10	45	133152	13315.20	2958.93
Total	55	212	622512	11318.40	2936.38	50	240	388524	7770.48	1618.85
	SD = 3605.50 CV= 31.86					SD = 3641.36 CV = 46.86				

TABLE 4.13.2

Distribution of non-beneficiary households according to per capita income

Income Group. (in Rs.)	Hirāpur					Āmbadiha				
	Total HHs covered	Total HH members	Total Income earned	Income per HH	Per-capita	Total HHs covered	Total HH members	Total Income earned	Income per HH	Per-capita
(1)	(2)	(3)	(4)	(5)	(6)	(7)	(8)	(9)	(10)	(11)
Up to 4000	1	3	3960	3960.00	1320.00	4	14	14700.00	3675.00	1050.00
4001 - 5000	3	9	13632	4544.00	1514.67	9	35	42780.00	4753.33	1222.29
5001 - 6000	1	1	5760	5760.00	5760.00	6	35	34860.00	5810.00	996.00
6001 - 7000	1	6	6720	6720.00	1120.00	15	68	94788.00	6319.20	1393.94
7001 - 8000	9	30	66024	7336.00	2200.80	10	54	73932.00	7393.20	1369.11
8001 - 9000	7	31	58980	8425.71	1902.58	6	37	52080.00	8680.00	1407.57
9001 - 10000	4	24	39060	9765.00	1627.50	4	14	37980.00	9495.00	2712.86
10001 - 11000	11	48	118200	10745.45	2462.50	9	36	96912.00	10768.00	2692.00
11001 & above	16	80	213048	13315.50	2663.10	6	27	67812.00	11302.00	2511.56
Total	53	232	525384	9912.91	2264.59	69	320	5158.44	7476.00	1612.00
	SD = 3035.64 CV = 30.62					SD = 2335.41 CV = 31.24				

The total annual income of the sample beneficiary and non-beneficiary households of Hirāpur and Āmbadiha comes to Rs. 1,03,920 and Rs. 66,012 and their total annual expenditure works out to be Rs. 1,01,224.05 and Rs. 67,316 respectively. Likewise, the total annual income of the sample non-beneficiary households of the above two villages are found to be Rs. 70,380 in case of Hirāpur and Rs. 72,540 in case of Āmbadiha. These households have spent Rs. 71,835.70 and Rs. 73,630.85 respectively of their total income earned in that year (Table 4.14). But as this income was not sufficient for procuring the daily commodities, both the beneficiary and non-beneficiary households of Āmbadiha have borrowed sums of money, and hence run in deficit. On the other hand, the sample beneficiary households of Hirāpur are found to have saved some money but just as the non-beneficiary households of Āmbadiha, the non-beneficiary households of this village have also run into deficits. This trend of income and expenditure pattern has been shown in Diagram 4.2 depending upon the data available in Table 4.5.

Diagram 4.2

Income and expenditure pattern among beneficiary and non-beneficiary households in Hirāpur and Āmbadiha

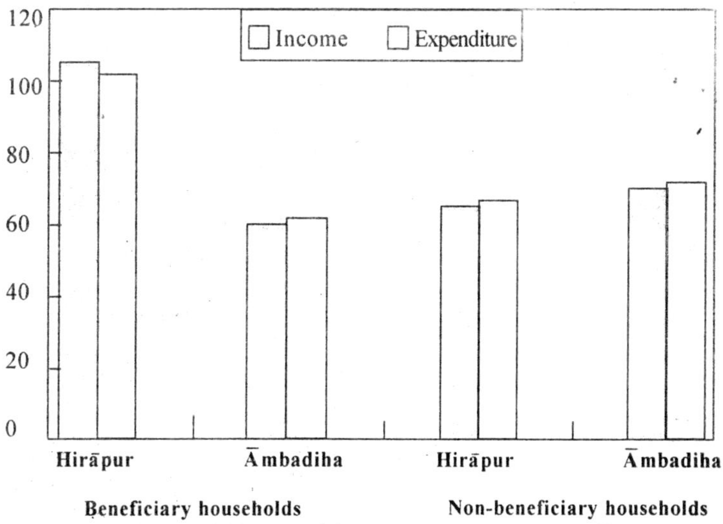

TABLE 4.14

Annual income & expenditure among sample beneficiary and non-beneficiary households (in Rs.)

Income/Expenditure	Beneficiary		Non-Beneficiary	
	Hirāpur (N=11)	Āmbadiha (N=10)	Hirāpur (N=11)	Āmbadiha (N=14)
(1)	(2)	(3)	(4)	(5)
Total Income	103920.00	66012.00	70380.00	72540.00
Total expenditure	101224.05	67316.00	71835.70	73630.85
Difference	2695.95	-1304.00	-1455.70	-1090.00

To find out the expenditure pattern of the sample beneficiary and non-beneficiary households of these two villages, their total annual income has been taken as 100 per cent in each category and the percentage of amount spent on different food and non-food items have been found out.

Beneficiary Households

So far as the expenditure pattern of the sample beneficiary households of both the study villages are concerned, it is observed from Table 4.15 that the beneficiary households of Hirāpur had spent 53.71 per cent of their total annual income on different food items as against 68.31 per cent of those of Āmbadiha. The rest of the income, i.e. 46.29 per cent in the case of Hirāpur and 31.69 per cent of Āmbadiha have been spent on different non-food items.

Among the food items which include cereals, vegetables, meat and fish (both raw and dry) maximum percentage of money has been spent on cereals in case of both the villages. But while the beneficiaries of Hirāpur spent 32.25 per cent of their total income on cereals, it is as high as 46.70 per cent in case of those of Ambadiha. Among the other food items, the beneficiaries of the former village spent 8.29, 8.01 and 5.06 per cent on Kirana, vegetables, and meat/fish, respectively. Like the beneficiaries of Hirāpur, the beneficiaries of Āmbadiha have spent almost an equal (8.03) percentage of their income on vegetables but they had spent only 6.06 per cent of their income on Kirana items. Further, it is observed from the same table that the beneficiaries of Āmbadiha have also spent little more money (7.52%) on meat/fish than those of Hirāpur.

Among the non-food items, both the beneficiaries and non-beneficiaries of Hirāpur as also of Āmbadiha have spent a sizeable

TABLE 4.15
Item-wise expenditure pattern among sample beneficiary and non-beneficiary households

Category of Expenditure	Items	Beneficiary Hirāpur	Beneficiary Āmbadiha	Non-Beneficiary Hirāpur	Non-Beneficiary Āmbadiha
		(N=11)	(N=10)	(N=11)	(N=14)
(1)	(2)	(3)	(4)	(5)	(6)
Food	Cereals	32.35 (32741.85)	46.70 (31437.35)	38.40 (3785.60)	50.54 (37219.75)
	Kirana	8.29 (8395.05)	6.06 (4078.15)	7.78 (5585.60)	3.58 (2636.35)
	Vegetables	8.01 (8112.20)	8.03 (5407.95)	5.58 (4009.05)	5.95 4381.25
	Meat, fish (dry & raw etc.)	5.06 (5121.95)	7.52 (5062.25)	9.58 (6883.90)	10.25 (7550.10)
	Sub-total	53.71 (54371.05)	68.31 (45985.70)	61.34 (44064.15)	70.33 (51787.45)
Non-Food	Drinks/ Alcohol	2.56 (25954.30)	1.21 (812.00)	1.59 (1141.35)	-
	Narcotics	5.29 (5354.25)	7.68 (5169.00)	7.94 (5706.85)	8.96 (6600.15)
	Clothes/ Dress	7.99 (8092.15)	4.66 (3134.55)	6.76 (4858.35)	4.34 (3192.80)
	Medicines	2.07 (2091.20)	0.81 (547.95)	1.88 (1348.25)	0.56 (410.10)
	Sanitation	1.83 (1848.75)	0.88 (595.65)	1.75 (1255.70)	0.98 (724.95)
	Fuel	3.02 (3061.05)	0.91 (613.50)	2.46 (1769.10)	1.60 (1179.05)
	Light	4.09 (4141.95)	2.95 (1989.10)	2.78 (1997.40)	2.02 (1486.60)
	Transport	5.06 (5121.90)	2.56 (1726.65)	2.85 (2047.35)	2.34 (1724.85)
	Education	5.00 (5061.30)	2.19 (1471.20)	3.24 (2325.55)	2.09 (1537.85)
	Fair & Festival etc.	6.04 (6111.95)	5.67 (3817.35)	4.19 (3010.35)	4.86 (3581.00)
	Entertain-ment	2.13 (2151.80)	0.96 (649.25)	1.79 (1284.05)	1.00 (739.65)
	Miscella-neous	1.21 (1222.40)	1.19 (804.10)	1.43 (1027.25)	0.91 (666.40)
	Sub-total	46.29 (46853.00)	31.69 (21330.30)	38.66 (27771.55)	29.67 (21843.90)
	Total	100.00 (101224.05)	100.00 (67316.00)	100.00 (71835.70)	100.00 (73630.85)

Note: Figures in brackets represent absolute value.

amount of their income on alcoholic drinks and narcotics. Expenditure comes to 2.56 per cent on drinks / alcohol and 5.29 per cent on narcotics in case of Hirāpur, as against 1.21 and 7.68 per cent in case of Āmbadiha. Thus, if the money spent on different food items is added up with this, it comes to 61.56 per cent in case of Hirāpur, but it is as high as 77.2 per cent in case of Āmbadiha.

Apart from alcoholic drinks and narcotics, the other non-food items on which the beneficiary households of Hirāpur have spent sizeable amount of their income comes to 7.99 per cent on clothing and dress materials, followed by 6.04 per cent on fairs and festivals and social obligations, 5.06 per cent on transport and 5 per cent on education. Among the other non-food items like medicine, sanitation, fuel, light and entertainment, the people of Hirāpur have spent less than 5 per cent of the total income on each of these items. But on the contrary, the beneficiary of Āmbadiha have spent more than 5 per cent (5.67) of their total income only on fairs and festivals and on social obligations. For the rest of non-food items, they spent less than 5 per cent on each item. Further, a cursory look at the same table also reveals that even though Hirāpur is situated near Bhubaneswar city, they spend more money on transport than the people of Āmbadiha. This is because of the fact that the people of the former village are more mobile as they are more close to the city. Their proximity to Bhubaneswar also accounts for more money being spent on clothing and dress materials in comparison with the people of Āmbadiha. Here, it can also be said that the people of Hirāpur spend more money on alcoholic drinks compared to the villagers of Āmbadiha, because they have easier access to it. However, most of them consume country liquor at brick kilns located in the proximity of their village.

Non-Beneficiary Households

Table 4.15 also reflects the expenditure pattern of the non-beneficiary people of the two study villages. This table shows that the non-beneficiary people of Hirāpur spend 61.34 per cent of their total annual income on different food items. But it is as high as 70.33 per cent in case of Āmbadiha and when for the people of Hirāpur it is only 30.40 per cent of their total income, it is more than 50 per cent (50.54%) in case of Āmbadiha.

Like the beneficiaries, non-beneficiaries of both the villages also spend a sizeable amount of their total income on alcoholic drinks and narcotics. As a result of this, expenditure on the food items together with the expenditure on alcoholic drinks and narcotics constitutes

70.87 per cent for the people of Hirāpur, and about 80 (79.29) per cent for the people of Āmbadiha (Diagram 4.3). Again, like the beneficiaries of Hirāpur, the non-beneficiaries of this village also spend much money on clothing and dress materials which is more than 6 (6.76) per cent of their total income. There is no other non-food item on which the non-beneficiary people of this village spend 5 per cent or more of their total income. But the non-beneficiary people of Āmbadiha do not spend more than 5 per cent of their total income on any non-food item, other than on narcotics.

Diagram 4.3

Expenditure pattern on food and non-food items among sample beneficiary and non-beneficiary households

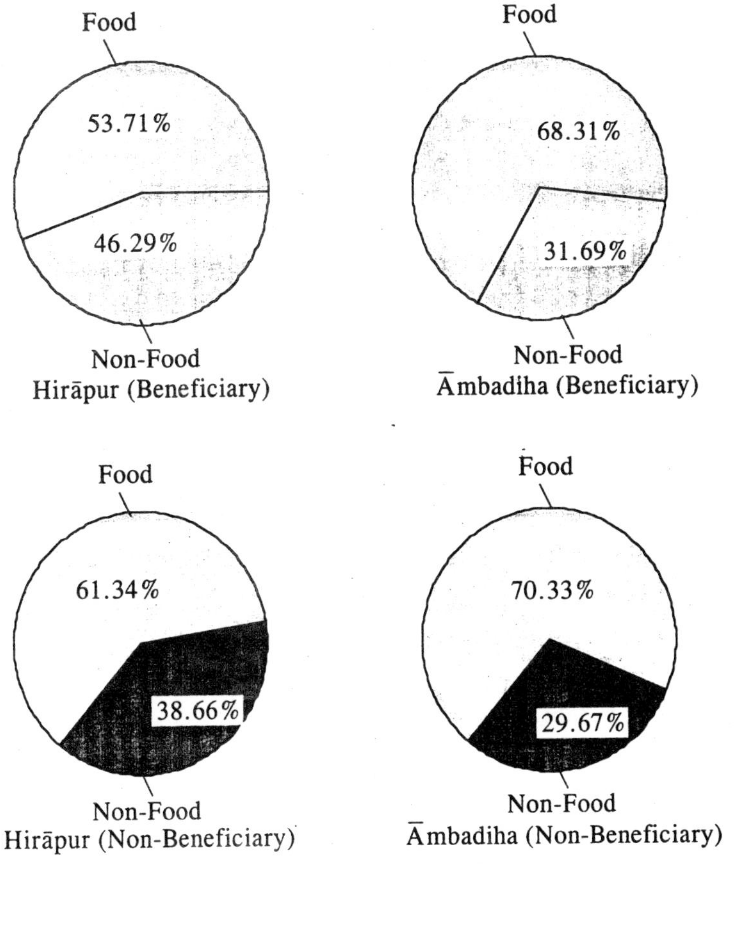

Savings and Indebtedness

The saving and indebtedness pattern of all the beneficiary and non-beneficiary households of both the study villages have been found out and are discussed below:

Beneficiary Households

As shown in Table 4.16, of the 55 households of Hirāpur and 50 households of Āmbadiha, 10 households or 18.18 per cent and 19 or 38 per cent of households, in the two villages respectively have contracted loans, and hence, are under debt. Further, this table also reflects that more households falling in lower income groups, have borrowed money. On the other hand as many as 21 or 38.18 per cent households of the former village as against only 9 or 18 per cent of the latter one have saved some amounts of money. Hence, the rest 24 or 43.64 per cent and 22 or 44 per cent of households in the villages of Hirāpur and Āmbadiha respectively, have spent what they had earned and hence are found to have neither contracted any loan nor to have saved any money for future use. This means that they manage themselves with their income.

Non-Beneficiary Households

So far as the saving and indebtedness pattern of these people is concerned, it is seen from Table 4.17 that in the case of 12 or 22.64 per cent of households of Hirāpur as against 10 or 14.49 per cent in Āmbadiha, the earnings are more than their expenditure, and hence they have saved some amount of their earnings. But in case of 25 or 47.17 per cent of households of the former village as against 31 or 44.93 per cent of the latter one, the expenditure is more than their total earnings. So they have borrowed a loan to meet their extra expenditure, and hence are indebted. The rest 16 or 30.19 per cent households in Hirāpur, as against 16 or 30.19 per cent in Āmbadiha have spent what they had earned and hence neither they have saved nor have borrowed any loan.

Extent of Indebtedness

Beneficiary Households

As regards the extent of indebtedness, it is seen that of the total 10 indebted households of Hirāpur, a large percentage of households,

TABLE 4.16

Nature of consumption, expenditure, saving and indebtedness among beneficiary households

Income Earning Range (in Rs.)	Total Households in Income range		Households under savings		Households under no savings and no debt		Househods under debt	
	Hirāpur	Āmbadiha	Hirāpur	Āmbadiha	Hirāpur	Āmbadiha	Hirāpur	Āmbadiha
(1)	(2)	(3)	(4)	(5)	(6)	(7)	(8)	(9)
Upto 4000	1 (100.00)	4 (100.00)	-	-	-	2 (50.00)	1 (100.00)	2 (50.00)
4001-6000	3 (100.00)	11 (100.00)	-	1 (9.09)	1 (33.33)	6 (54.55)	2 (66.67)	4 (36.36)
6001-8500	10 (100.00)	18 (100.00)	3 (30.00)	3 (16.67)	6 (60.00)	7 (38.89)	1 (10.00)	8 (44.44)
8501-11000	13 (100.00)	7 (100.00)	6 (46.15)	2 (28.57)	4 (30.77)	2 (28.57)	3 (23.08)	3 (42.86)
11001 & above	28 (100.00)	10 (100.00)	12 (42.86)	3 (30.00)	13 (46.43)	5 (50.00)	3 (10.71)	2 (20.00)
Total	55 (100.00)	50 (100.00)	21 (38.18)	9 (18.00)	24 (43.64)	22 (44.40)	10 (18.18)	19 (38.00)

Note: Figures in brackets represent %age.

TABLE 4.17

Nature of consumption, expenditure, saving and indebtedness among non-beneficiary households

Income Earning Range (in Rs.)	Total Households in Income range		Households under savings		Households under no savings and no debt		Househods under debt	
	Hirāpur	Āmbadiha	Hirāpur	Āmbadiha	Hirāpur	Āmbadiha	Hirāpur	Āmbadiha
(1)	(2)	(3)	(4)	(5)	(6)	(7)	(8)	(9)
Upto 4000	1 (100.00)	4 (100.00)	-	-	-	-	1 (100.00)	4 (100.00)
4001-6000	4 (100.00)	15 (100.00)	1 (25.00)	2 (13.33)	1 (25.00)	3 (20.00)	2 (50.00)	10 (66.67)
6001-8500	14 (100.00)	21 (100.00)	3 (21.43)	1 (4.76)	4 (28.57)	12 (57.14)	7 (50.00)	8 (57.14)
8501-11000	18 (100.00)	23 (100.00)	4 (22.22)	3 (13.04)	5 (27.78)	12 (52.17)	9 (50.00)	8 (34.78)
11001 & above	16 (100.00)	6 (100.00)	4 (25.00)	4 (66.67)	6 (37.50)	1 (16.67)	6 (37.50)	1 (16.67)
Total	53 (100.00)	69 (100.00)	12 (22.64)	10 (14.49)	16 (30.19)	28 (40.58)	25 (47.17)	31 (44.93)

Note: Figures in brackets represent %age.

i.e. 30 are under debt burden; above Rs. 801, followed by 20 per cent each in the ranges of Rs. 601 to Rs. 800, Rs. 401 to Rs. 600, and upto Rs. 200. Hence it is manifested that 70 per cent households of Hirāpur are under the debt burden from Rs. 400 to Rs. 800 or more. Likewise, when we compare the data with those of Āmbadiha, it is seen that the highest percentage of households, i.e. 31.58 are found to be under debt burden in the range of Rs. 601 to Rs. 800. An equal percentage of households are also found to be under the debt burden in the range of Rs. 401 to Rs. 600. There are 21.05 per cent or 4 households which have borrowed sums of Rs. 801 or more. Hence about 85 per cent of households of this village are found to be under the debt burden from Rs. 401 to Rs. 801 or more (Table 4.18)

TABLE 4.18

Extent of indebtedness among beneficiary households according to income level

Income Level (in Rs.)	Hirāpur Extent of Indebtedness (in Rs.)						
	Total HHs	Total HHs under debt	Upto 200	201-400	401-600	601-800	801 & more
(1)	(2)	(3)	(4)	(5)	(6)	(7)	(8)
Upto 4000	1	1 (10.00) [100.00]	-	-	-	1 (100.00)	-
4001-6000	3	2 (20.00) [100.00]	1 (50)	-	1 (50)	-	-
6001-8500	10	1 (10.00) [100.00]	-	1 (100)	-	-	-
8501-11000	13	3 (30.00) [100.00]	1 (33.33)	-	-	1 (33.33)	1 (33.33)
11001 & more	28	3 (30.00) [100.00]	-	-	1 (33.33)	-	2 (66.67)
Total	55 (100.00)	10 (100.00)	2 (20.00)	1 (10.00)	2 (20.00)	2 (20.00)	3 (30.00)

contd.

TABLE 4.18 (contd.)

Income Level (in Rs.)	Āmbadiha Extent of Indebtedness (in Rs.)						
	Total HHs	Total HHs under debt	Upto 200	201-400	401-600	601-800	801 & more
(1)	(2)	(3)	(4)	(5)	(6)	(7)	(8)
Upto 4000	4	2 (10.53) [100.00]	-	-	-	2 (100.00)	-
4001-6000	11	4 (21.05) [100.00]	-	-	3 (75.00)	1 (25.00)	-
6001-8500	18	8 (42.11) [100.00]	1 (12.50)	2 (25.00)	-	2 (25.00)	3 (37.50)
8501-11000	7	3 (15.79) [100.00]	-	-	3 (100.00)	-	-
11001 & more	10	2 (10.53) [100.00]	-	-	-	1 (50.00)	1 (50.00)
Total	50 (100.00)	19 (100.00)	1 (5.26)	2 (10.53)	6 (31.58)	6 (31.58)	4 (21.05)

Note: (i) Figures in upper brackets in column number 3 represent %age to total households under debt.

(ii) Figures in other brackets represent %age to total households.

As to the average amount of loan per household, it is Rs. 684.80 in case of Hirāpur, and Rs. 583.42 in case of Āmbadiha (Table 4.20).

Non-Beneficiary Households

Table 4.19 shows that of the total 25 indebted households of Hirāpur, maximum percentage of households, i.e. 24 per cent each are found to be indebted in the range of Rs. 401, Rs. 600, Rs. 601, Rs. 800 and Rs. 801 or more. Thus, a total number of 18 or 72 per cent households are found to be under the debt burden in these three ranges. But when one looks again at the same table, it is revealed that as many as 12 or 38.71 per cent of households of the village Āmbadiha are under the debt burden in the range of Rs. 601 to Rs. 800/- followed by a total number of 8 or 25.81 per cent of households in the range of

Rs. 201 to Rs. 400. The highest range, i.e. Rs. 801 and more is contracted by 9.68 per cent of households with 12.90 per cent household in the range of Rs. 401-600. Thus, a little more than 60 per cent of households in this village are found to be indebted.

A further look at the said table reveals that an amount of Rs. 12,985 has been borrowed by all the 25 indebted households of Hirāpur. The average comes to be Rs. 519.40 per household as against Rs. 462.98 in Āmbadiha as Rs. 14,352 have been contracted as loan by all the 31 indebted household of this village.

TABLE 4.19

Extent of indebtedness among non-beneficiary households according to income level

Income Level (in Rs.)	Hirāpur Extent of Indebtedness (in Rs.)						
	Total HHs	Total HHs under debt	Upto 200	201-400	401-600	601-800	801 & more
(1)	(2)	(3)	(4)	(5)	(6)	(7)	(8)
Upto 4000	1	1 (4.00) [100.00]	-	-	1 (100.00)	-	-
4001-6000	4	2 (8.00) [100.00]	-	-	2 (100.00)	-	-
6001-8500	14	7 (28.00) [100.00]	-	-	3 (42.86)	3 (42.86)	1 (14.29)
8501-11000	18	9 (36.00) [100.00]	3 (33.33)	3 (33.33)	-	2 (22.22)	1 (11.11)
11001 & more	16	6 (24.00) [100.00]	1 (16.67)	-	-	1 (16.67)	4 (66.67)
Total	53 (100.00)	25 (47.17) [100.00]	4 (16.00)	3 (12.00)	6 (24.00)	6 (24.00)	6 (24.00)

contd.

TABLE 4.19 (contd.)

Income Level (in Rs.)	Āmbadiha Extent of Indebtedness (in Rs.)						
	Total HHs	Total HHs under debt	Upto 200	201-400	401-600	601-800	801 & more
(1)	(2)	(3)	(4)	(5)	(6)	(7)	(8)
Upto 4000	4	4 (12.50) [100.00]	-	1 (25.00)	-	3 (75.00)	-
4001-6000	15	10 (32.26) [100.00]	1 (10.00)	-	2 (20.00)	4 (40.00)	3 (30.00)
6001-8500	21	8 (25.81) [100.00]	3 (37.50)	5 (62.50)	-	-	-
8501-11000	23	8 (25.81) [100.00]	-	1 (12.50)	2 (25.00)	5 (62.50)	-
11001 & more	6	1 (3.23) [100.00]	-	1 (100.00)	-	-	-
Total	69 (100.00)	31 (44.93) [100.00]	4 (12.90)	8 (25.81)	4 (12.90)	12 (38.71)	3 (9.68)

Note: (i) Figures in upper brackets in column number 3 represent %age to total households under debt.

(ii) Figures in other brackets represent %age to total house-holds.

TABLE 4.20

Average indebtedness among beneficiary and non-beneficiary households

Category of People	Village	Total indebted households	Total Loan taken (in Rs.)	Average per household (in Rs.)
(1)	(2)	(3)	(4)	(5)
Beneficiary	Hirāpur Āmbadiha	10 19	6848.00 11085.00	684.80 583.42
Non-Beneficiary	Hirāpur Āmbadiha	25 31	12985.00 14352.00	519.40 462.98

Reasons of Indebtedness

Beneficiary Households

As to the reasons for contracting a loan, the most frequent one is for the purpose of improving one's own business establishment in the case of Hirāpur as it is met by 6 or 60 per cent of indebted households of this village. On the other, as many as 15 or about 79 per cent of households in Āmbadiha have contracted loans for sustenance (Table 4.21). But when one looks at Table 4.22, it is found that even though most of the households of the former village have contracted loans for improving their own business/establishment, maximum percentage (36.51) of the total loan money of all the indebted households of this village is spent on subsistence, followed by 29.50 per cent on improving one's own business or establishment. Other reasons for contracting loan in descending order of importance are for meeting life cycle rituals and social obligations (12.05%), fairs and festivals (8.03%), agricultural development (7.01%), treatment of diseases (2.99%), education of children (2.02%) and consumption of liquor and intoxicants (1.90%). Likewise, when the case of Āmbadiha is analysed, it is found that maximum households have contracted loans for the purpose

TABLE 4.21

Causes of indebtedness among beneficiary and non-beneficiary households

Cause/ Purpose	Beneficiary		Non-Beneficiary	
	Hirāpur (N=10)	Āmbadiha (N=19)	Hirāpur (N=25)	Āmbadiha (N=31)
(1)	(2)	(3)	(4)	(5)
Subsistence	4 (40.00)	15 (78.95)	19 (76.00)	28 (90.32)
Consumption of alcoholic drinks and intoxicants	4 (40.00)	-	3 (12.00)	8 (25.81)
Meeting lifecycle rituals and social obligations	3 (30.00)	6 (31.58)	10 (40.00)	9 (29.03)
Improving own business/ establishments	6 (60.00)	2 (10.53)	5 (20.00)	3 (9.68)
Fair & Festival	3 (30.00)	7 (36.84)	15 (60.00)	16 (51.61)
Agricultural development	2 (20.00)	8 (42.11)	13 (52.00)	11 (35.48)
Education of Children	1 (10.00)	3 (5.79)	2 (8.00)	3 (9.68)
Treatment of diseases	1 (10.00)	4 (21.05)	7 (28.00)	4 (12.90)

Note: Figures in brackets represent %age.

TABLE 4.22

Utilisation of loan money on different sectors by the indebted beneficiary and non-beneficiary

Area of utilisation	Beneficiary		Non-Beneficiary	
	Hirāpur	Āmbadiha	Hirāpur	Āmbadiha
(1)	(2)	(3)	(4)	(5)
Subsistence	2500.00 (36.51)	5209.00 (46.99)	5980.00 (46.05)	9352.00 (65.16)
Consumption of alcoholic drinks and intoxicants	130.00 (1.90)	-	-	-
Meeting lifecycle rituals and social obligations	825.00 (12.05)	1887.00 (17.02)	1038.00 (7.99)	1435.00 (10.00)
Improving own business/ establishments	2020.00 (29.50)	332.00 (3.0)	1686.00 (12.98)	285.00 (1.99)
Fair & Festival	550.00 (8.03)	1776.00 (16.02)	2210.00 (17.02)	2485.00 (17.31)
Agricultural development	480.00 (7.01)	1108.00 (10.00)	1680.00 (12.94)	430.00 (3.00)
Education of Children	138.00 (2.02)	55.00 (0.5)	85.00 (0.65)	75.00 (0.52)
Treatment of disease	205.00 (2.99)	718.00 (6.48)	306.00 (2.36)	290.00 (2.02)
Total	6848.00 (100.00)	11085.00 (100.00)	12985.00 (100.00)	14352.00 (100.00)

Note: Figuress in brackets represent %age.

of subsistence and the highest percentage (46.99) of the total loan money is also spent on this sector, followed by meeting of life cycle rituals (17.02%), fairs and festivals (16.02%) agricultural development (10%), treatment of diseases (6.48%), improving one's business/ establishment (3%) and education of children (0.5%).

Non-Beneficiary Household

Among the non-beneficiary households, maximum percentage of households in both the villages, i.e. 76 in Hirāpur as against 90.32 in Āmbadiha have contracted loans for their subsistence purpose (Table 4.21). While 46.05 per cent of the total loan money has been spent on this sector by people of the former village, it is as high as 65.16 per cent in case of Āmbadiha (Table 4.22). Further when one looks at the data available in Table 4.27, it is found that almost an equal percentage (i.e., 17) of the loan money has been spent on fairs and festivals in case of both the villages, but while in Hirāpur people have spent 12.98 and 12.94 per cent of their loan money on improving own business and on agricultural development respectively, it is only 1.99 and 3 per cent in the case of Āmbadiha. In the case of both these villages, more than 7 per cent of the money, i.e. 7.99 in Hirāpur as against 10 per cent in Āmbadiha have been spent on meeting life cycle rituals and social obligations.

Extent of Savings

Beneficiary Households

As mentioned earlier, of the total 55 households in Hirāpur and 50 households in Āmbadiha, 21 or 38.18 per cent and 9 or 18 per cent households respectively, have saved money (Table 4.16). So far as the extent of their savings is concerned it is found from Table 4.23

TABLE 4.23

Extent of savings among beneficiary households according to income level

Income Level (in Rs.)	Hirāpur Extent of Indebtedness (in Rs.)						
	Total HHs	Total HHs under debt	Upto 500	501-1000	1001-1500	1501-2000	2001 & more
(1)	(2)	(3)	(4)	(5)	(6)	(7)	(8)
Upto 4000	1	-	-	-	-	-	-
4001-6000	3	-	-	-	-	-	-
6001-8500	10	3 (14.29) [100.00]	-	2 (66.67)	-	1 (33.33)	-
8501-11000	13	6 (28.57) [100.00]	-	1 (16.67)	-	3 (50.0	2 (33.33)
11001 & above	28	12 (57.14) [100.00]	-	1 (8.33)	1 (8.33)	3 (25.00)	7 (58.33)
Total	55	21 (100.00) [100.00]	-	4 (19.05)	1 (4.76)	7 (33.33)	9 (42.86)

contd.

TABLE 4.23 (contd.)

Income Level (in Rs.)	Āmbadiha Extent of Indebtedness (in Rs.)						
	Total HHs	Total HHs under debt	Upto 500	501-1000	1001-1500	1501-2000	2001 & more
(1)	(2)	(3)	(4)	(5)	(6)	(7)	(8)
Upto 4000	4	-	-	-	-	-	-
4001-6000	11	1 (11.11)	1 (100.00)	-	-	-	-
6001-8500	18	3 (33.33) [100.00]	3 (100.00)	-	-	-	-
8501-11000	7	2 (22.22) [100.00]	1 (50.00)	-	-	-	-
11001 & more	10	3 (33.33) [100.00]	-	1 (50.00)	-	2 (66.67)	1 (33.33)
Total	50	9 (100.00) [100.00]	5 (55.56)	1 (11.11)	-	2 (22.22)	1 (11.11)

Note: (i) Figures in upper brackets in column number 3 represent %age to total household under debt.
(ii) Figures in other brackets represent %age to total household.

that out of the households which have saved money, there are as many as 9 or 42.86 per cent households in Hirāpur which have saved Rs. 2001 or more money as against only 1 or 11.11 per cent household of the village Āmbadiha which saved in this range. Reference to the same table shows that while there is not a single household in Hirāpur which has saved money in the lowest saving range, i.e. within Rs. 500 there are as many as 5 or 55.56 per cent households in Āmbadiha which have saved upto Rs. 500. Thus, it can be concluded that when maximum percentage of households, i.e. 42.86 of Hirāpur have saved Rs. 2001 or more money, minimum percentage household, i.e. 11.11 of Āmbadiha have saved money in this saving range and maximum households accounting for 55.56 per cent of this village have saved money only upto Rs. 500. As a result of this, when the average saving per household comes to be Rs. 820.48 in case of Hirāpur, it is only 232.22 in case of Āmbadiha (Table 4.25).

Non-Beneficiary Households

The case of non-beneficiary households seems to be quite different. As the data available in Table 4.24 shows, of the 12 households of Hirāpur who have saved money, there are as many as 5 cr 41.67 per cent households which are found to have saved money only upto Rs. 500. It is 2 or 20 per cent in the case of Āmbadiha. In case of the latter village, large number of households have saved money in the range of Rs. 1001 to Rs. 1500, and Rs. 1501 to Rs. 2000. Not a single household in the village is found to have saved money in the highest income range, i.e. Rs. 2001 and more, there is only 1 or 8.33 of households in Hirāpur which has saved some money in this range. A further look at the same table suggests that while about 75 per cent of households in the former village has saved money in the lower two ranges, i.e. upto Rs. 1000, it is 60 per cent of households in the case

TABLE 4.24

Extent of savings among non-beneficiary households according to income level

Income Level (in Rs.)	Hirāpur Extent of Indebtedness (in Rs.)						
	Total HHs	Total HHs under debt	Upto 500	501-1000	1001-1500	1501-2000	2001 & more
(1)	(2)	(3)	(4)	(5)	(6)	(7)	(8)
Upto 4000	1	-	-	-	-	-	-
4001-6000	4	1 (8.33) [100.00]	1 (100.00)	-	-	-	-
6001-8500	14	3 (25.00) [100.00]	1 (33.33)	2 (66.67)	-	-	-
8501-11000	18	4 (33.33) [100.00]	3 (78.00)	-	1 (25.00)	-	-
11001 & above	16	4 (33.33) [100.00]	-	2 (50.00)	-	1 (25.00)	1 (25.00)
Total	53	12 (100.00) [100.00]	5 (41.67)	4 (33.33)	1 (8.33)	1 (8.33)	1 (8.33)

contd.

T .BLE 4.24 (.ontd.)

Income Level (in Rs.)	Āmbadiha Extent of Indebtedness (in Rs.)						
	Total HHs	Total HHs under debt	Upto 500	501-1000	1001-1500	1501-2000	2001 & more
(1)	(2)	(3)	(4)	(5)	(6)	(7)	(8)
Upto 4000	4	-	-	-	-	-	-
4001-6000	15	2 (20.00) [100.00]	1 (50.00)	-	-	1 (50.00)	-
6001-8500	21	1 (10.00) [100.00]	-	-	-	1 (100.00)	-
8501-11000	23	3 (30.00) [100.00]	1 (33.33)	2 (66.67)	-	-	-
11001 & above	6	4 (40.00) [100.00]	-	-	3 (75.00)	1 (25.00)	-
Total	69	10 (100.00) [100.00]	2 (20.00)	2 (20.00)	3 (30.00)	3 (30.00)	-

Note: (i) Figures in upper brackets in column number 3 represent %age to total household under debt.

(ii) Figures in other brackets represent %age to total household.

of Āmbadiha. But when the average saving per household is found to be Rs. 372 in case of Hirāpur, it is only Rs. 199.50 in case of Āmbadiha (Table 4.25).

TABLE 4.25

Average savings among beneficiary and non-beneficiary households

Category of People	Village	Total HHs under saving	Total money saved	Average per household
(1)	(2)	(3)	(4)	(5)
Beneficiary	Hirāpur	21	17,230	820.48
	Āmbadiha	9	2,090	232.22
Non-Beneficiary	Hirāpur	12	4,464	372.00
	Āmbadiha	10	1,995	199.50

(iii) Acquisition of Assets

Acquisition of different productive and non-productive or luxurious assets reflects the economic status of a household. Hence, the economic condition of a Bāuri household can well be judged if we look at their asset-possession and find its market value.

Earlier, in the introductory chapter it has been mentioned that since time immemorial the Bāuris had been restrained having and using various assets, and hence, prevent them from raising their economic condition. This was because of the age-old Indian traditional caste system, wherein the orthodox caste Hindus were intensively interfering in the life style of these people. As a result, these people were economically as well as socially depressed and hence were very backward. They were managing their lives with minimum and specific assets as specified by the caste Hindus. But, many of the Bāuri households are now well aware of the situation. With the passage of time some of them have changed and own various assets which they were once restricted from owning or using for the proper imposition of rigid caste norms by caste Hindus.

The assets which the Bāuri households of the two study villages now own can broadly be divided into two categories, such as (i) Immovable, and (ii) Movable.

The immovable assets include land; both homestead and agricultural, house-building and economically important fruit- bearing trees. Of these, agricultural land and economically important fruit-bearing trees are considered as productive assets, and as everywhere else in the world, the house-buildings are used for residential purpose.

The important movable assets which have economic value include domestic animals, agricultural and fishing implements, musical instruments, transport vehicles, audio-visual instruments, furniture, utensils and precious metals, foodgrains and some luxurious goods. However, among these, the most frequent asset found in most households; both among beneficiary, as well as non-beneficiary are agricultural and fishing implements.

Immovable Assets

The position of capital goods against each type of immovable assets, viz. land, house and economically important fruit-bearing trees is presented in Table 4.26.

TABLE 4.26

Possession of capital immovable assets among beneficiary and non-beneficiary households

Types of Assets	Capital Goods/Items	Nature of Goods	Beneficiary					
			Hirāpur (N=55)			Āmbadiha (N=50)		
			Total no. of possession	Total HHs possess	Average	Total no. of possession	Total HHs possess	Average
(1)	(2)	(3)	(4)	(5)	(6)	(7)	(8)	(9)
Land	Homestead (in acre)	M	1.9	46 (83.64)	0.041	2.0	50 (100.00)	0.04
	Agricultural (in acre)	M	2	6 (10.91)	0.33	4.0	11 (22.00)	0.36
House*	Living rooms	U	72	50 (90.91)	1.44	56	50 (100.00)	1.12
Economically important fruit bearing trees	Coconut	M	19	12 (21.82)	1.58	17	13 (26.00)	1.31
	Mango	M	5	4 (7.27)	1.25	2	1 (2.00)	2.00
	Guava	T	5	4 (7.27)	1.25	7	3 (6.00)	2.33
	Drum stick	T	9	7 (12.73)	1.29	13	13 (26.00)	1.00
	Banana	T	67	28 (50.91)	2.39	92	31 (62.00)	2.97
	Bur nut	T	3	3 (5.45)	1.00	3	3 (6.00)	1.00

contd.

TABLE 4.26 (contd.)

Types of Assets	Capital Goods/Items	Nature of Goods	Non-Beneficiary					
			Hirāpur (N=55)			Āmbadiha (N=50)		
			Total no. of possession	Total HHs possess	Average	Total no. of possession	Total HHs possess	Average
(1)	(2)	(3)	(4)	(5)	(6)	(7)	(8)	(9)
Land	Homestead (in acre)	M	2.00	48 (90.57)	0.042	2.8	69 (100.00)	0.041
	Agricultural (in acre)	M	1.5	15 (9.43)	0.30	3	13 (18.84)	0.23
House*	Living rooms	U	59	52 (98.11)	98.11	7.3	69 (100.00)	1.06
Economically important fruit bearing trees	Coconut	M	8	6 (11.32)	1.33	28	19 (27.54)	1.47
	Mango	M	1	1 (1.89)	1.00	-	- -	
	Guava	T	2	2 (3.77)	1.00	3	3 (4.35)	1.00
	Drum stick	T	13	11 (20.75)	1.18	12	11 (9.09)	1.09
	Banana	T	32	12 (22.64)	2.67	85	30 (43.48)	2.66
	Bur nut	T	3	2 (3.77)	1.50	7	7 (10.14)	1.00

Note: (i) T = Traditional, M = Modern, U = Unspecified
(ii) Figures in brackets represent %age.
(iii) *Includes the cost of the whole building of each household.

(a) Land

The table referred above reveals that about 84 per cent of the beneficiary households in Hirāpur have homestead with record of rights, as against 100 per cent in Āmbadiha. But the average size of holding is very small which is more or less same (0.04 acre) in case of both the villages. Likewise, the situation of the non-beneficiary households of these two villages is also exactly the same. Every beneficiary and non-beneficiary household of Hirāpur does not have homestead as they have been staying on the land of local caste Hindu people and some of them have not yet received the *patta* or record of right.

So far as the possession of agricultural land is concerned, it is also ascertained from the same table that among the beneficiary households, there are only 6 or 10.91 per cent households in the village Hirāpur, as against 11 or 22 per cent in Āmbadiha who possess agricultural land but the size of the holdings is only 0.33 and 0.36 acre respectively. Among the non-beneficiary households, while there are 5 or 9.43 per cent households in Hirāpur with an average possession of 0.30 acre per household, it is 13 or 18.84 per cent households in Āmbadiha with an average possession of 0.23 acre per household.

(b) House Building

It may be found from the same table that about 9 per cent of beneficiary households of Hirāpur do not have any living room. These households spend their time in enclosed verandas. On the other hand all households in Āmbadiha own living rooms. Likewise, among the non-beneficiary households of the former village, there are about 2 per cent households which do not possess any living room. Like the beneficiary households of the village Āmbadiha, there is also not a single household which spends time in enclosed veranda.

(c) Economically Important Fruit-bearing Trees

Economically important fruit-bearing trees include coconut, mango, guava, drumstick, banana and bur nut. Of these the last four types of trees are traditionally grown by Bāuri households. But, the most important and economically beneficial tree is coconut, the growing of which was prohibited for them. However, because of the growing awareness among these people, now it is learnt that there are about 12 or 21.82 per cent beneficiary households in Hirāpur as against 18 or 26 per cent in Āmbadiha who grow this.

Among the non-beneficiaries also, while there are about 6 or 11.32 per cent households in the former village who grow coconut, 19 or

27.54 per cent in Āmbadiha also do so. Households possessing other economically important trees are mentioned in the same table, which is self explanatory.

Movable Assets

(a) Livestock

Livestock which the Bāuris generally rear are cattle, both draft and milch, goat, occasionally sheep and poultry. The poultry is usually of native stock. It is commonly reared by almost all Bāuri households for meat. However, sometimes it is also sold to meet unavoidable needs.

The Bāuris consider bullocks as more important bovine assets than cows. Because these animals are more productive than cows, and can be engaged in fields. These animals are used for ploughing agricultural fields or land. Normally, the Bāuris engage the bullocks while share-cropping, and those who do not get any land for share-cropping, hire their bullocks for ploughing and harvesting purposes. The cows which the Bāuris usually own are mostly of native stock. They do not feed the cows with costly cattle-feed but are left free to graze and yield a little milk, if any. The cost of making such cows productive is immense with their limited means, compared with ease of rearing oxen for almost nothing. Thus, the Bāuris normally prefer to rear bullocks. Bāuri households having large holdings of arable land for share-cultivation generally keep some oxen.

Traditionally, these people were not keeping cattle but nowadays they raise these animals as wealth from three main sources, viz. rearing on share basis (*Pālakā*), provision of government scheme, and purchasing these animals from the market. Raising these animals through the traditional system of *Pālakā* is very common among these people. Under this traditional system normally the caste Hindus give their cows to the Bāuris attached to them for rearing, and when a cow gives birth, either the calf is sold and the profit is equally divided between the owner and the share-holder or it is reared until the next calving. In the latter case, the progenies are equally distributed between the two parties; the owner and the rearer.

A look at Table 4.27.1 reveals that there are 26 (45.45%), 12 (23.64%), 12 (21.82%) and 40 (72.73%) beneficiary households in Hirāpur who kept cattle (draught/milch), goat/sheep and poultry, respectively. The corresponding figures for Āmbadiha are 10 (20%), 17 (34%), 6 (12%) and 33 (66.67%).

So far as the case of the non-beneficiary households is concerned, the same table reveals that there are 12 (22.64%), 10 (18.87%), 9

TABLE 4.27.1

Possession of capital movable assets (domestic animals/birds) among beneficiary and non-beneficiary households

Capital Goods/ Items	Nature of Goods	Beneficiary						Non-Beneficiary					
		Hirāpur (N=55)			Āmbadiha (N=50)			Hirāpur (N=53)			Āmbadiha (N=69)		
		Total no. of possession	Total HHs possess	Average	Total no. of possession	Total HHs possess	Average	Total no. of possession.	Total HHs possess	Average	Total no. of possession	Total HHs possess	Average
(1)	(2)	(3)	(4)	(5)	(6)	(7)	(8)	(9)	(10)	(11)	(12)	(13)	(14)
Bullocks	M	36	26 (45.45)	1.38	19	10 (20.00)	1.9	19	12 (22.64)	1.58	18	13 (10.66)	1.38
Cattle	M	34	13 (23.64)	2.62	31	17 (34.00)	1.82	12	10 (18.87)	1.2	25	19 (15.57)	1.32
Goat/ Sheep	T	57	12 (12.82)	4.38	8	6 (12.00)	1.33	23	9 (16.98)	2.56	18	10 (8.20)	18
Poultry	T	177	40 (22.73)	4.43	189	33 (66.67)	5.73	79	34 (64.15)	2.32	103	37 (30.33)	2.78

Note: (i) Figures in brackets represent %age.
(ii) T = Traditional, M = Modern.

(16.98%), 34 (64.35%) households in Hirāpur who have kept cattle (draught/milch), goat/sheep and poultry, respectively. The corresponding figures for Āmbadiha are 12 (10.66%), 19 (15.57%), 10 (8.20%) and 37 (30.37%) households.

(b) Agricultural, Fishing and Musical Instruments

(i) Agricultural Implements

The Bāuri people normally acquire agricultural implements like plough, spade, bullock-cart, sickle, digging-stick, axe, crowbar, etc. But the most common implement which is available in all households is the sickle, followed by billhook which is found in households of more than 85 per cent of beneficiaries and non-beneficiaries in both the villages (Table 4.27.2). However, the most important and valuable implement, the plough, is owned by 54.55 per cent of beneficiary households of Hirāpur, against only 16 per cent of Āmbadiha. Among the non-beneficiary households, while this implement is possessed by 25 per cent of households of the former village it is kept by 18.84 per cent in case of Āmbadiha.

Tarpaulin is used while processing paddy, as also for sheltering it from sudden showers or untimely rain. But because of its high cost, it is owned by a very few households, while 7.27 per cent beneficiary households of Hirāpur possess it, merely 3.77 per cent of the non-beneficiary households in the village have it. But this is not owned by any household in Āmbadiha.

(ii) Fishing Implements

Fishing implements generally include fishing-net, fishing-rod, fishing-traps of various sizes and shapes, etc. But it is a unique feature of Bāuri households that all beneficiary and non-beneficiary households of both the villages own fishing rods. On an average there are 6 rods per household. Comparatively, this implement is cheaper than any other fishing implement. As a result of this, and its suitability to catch fish during leisure, every household has this implement. On the other hand, there are only 4 or 7.27 per cent beneficiary households in Hirāpur as against only one household in Āmbadiha who possess fishing nets. These are normally costly implements.

(iii) Musical Instruments

The musical instruments include only three items, such as conch shell, drum and bell. But the conch shell, which is a traditional asset is possessed by 16 or 29.09 per cent of beneficiary households in

TABLE 4.27.2

Possession of capital immovable assets among beneficiary and non-beneficiary households

Beneficiary

Type of Assets	Capital Goods/Items	Nature of Goods	Hirāpur (N=55)			Āmbadiha (N=50)		
			Total No. No. of Possession	Total HHs possess	Average	Total No. of Possession	Total HHs possess	Average
(1)	(2)	(3)	(4)	(5)	(6)	(7)	(8)	(9)
Agricultural Implements	Plough	T	31	30 (54.55)	1.03	9	8 (16.00)	1.13
	Spade	T	18	18 (32.73)	1.00	32	30 (60.00)	1.10
	Billhook	T	63	52 (94.55)	1.21	50	45 (90.00)	1.11
	Sickle	T	128	55 (100.00)	2.33	171	50 (100.00)	3.42
	Axe	T	15	15 (27.27)	1.00	3	3 (6.00)	1.00
	Crobar	T	9	9 (16.36)	1.00	3	3 (6.00)	1.00
	Digging stick	T	11	11 (20.00)	1.00	7	7 (14.00)	1.00
	Tarpaulin	M	4	4 (7.27)	1.00	-	- -	
Fishing Implements	Fishing Net	M	4	4 (7.27)	1.00	1	1 (2.00)	1.00
	Fishing Food	T	418	55 (100.00)	7.60	391	50 (100.00)	7.82
	Fishing Trap	T	32	30 (54.55)	1.07	59	47 (94.00)	1.26
	Throwing Net		3	3 (5.45)	1.00	3	3 (6.00)	1.00
	Ell trapper	T	7	7 (12.73)	1.00	11	11 (22.00)	1.00
	Poluha	T	36	21 (38.18)	1.71	45	31 (62.00)	1.45
	Conch Shell	T	18	16 (29.09)	1.13	21	17 (34.00)	1.24
Musical Instruments	Beating Drum	M	6	2 (3.64)	3.00	-	-	-
	Beating Bell	M	4	3 (5.45)	1.33	-	-	-

contd.

TABLE 4.27.2 (contd.)

Non-Beneficiary households

Type of Assets	Capital Goods/Items	Nature of Goods	Hirāpur (N=53)			Āmbadiha (N=69)		
			Total No. of Possession	Total HHs possess	Average	Total No. of Possession	Total HHs possess	Average
(1)	(2)	(3)	(4)	(5)	(6)	(7)	(8)	(9)
Agricultural Implements	Plough	T	13	13 (24.53)	1.00	13	13 (18.84)	1.00
	Spade	T	19	19 (35.85)	1.00	21	17 (24.63)	1.24
	Billhook	T	61	50 (94.34)	1.22	62	60 (86.96)	10.03
	Sickle	T	137	53 (100.00)	2.58	180	69 (100.00)	2.61
	Axe	T	9	9 (19.68)	1.00	7	7 (10.14)	1.00
	Crobar	T	7	7 (13.21)	1.00	6	6 (8.70)	1.00
	Digging stick	T	17	17 (32.80)	1.00	2	2 (2.90)	1.00
	Tarpaulin	M	2	2 (3.77)	1.00	-	- -	
Fishing Implements	Fishing Net	M	2	2 (3.77)	1.00	-	- -	
	Fishing Food	T	456	53 (100.00)	8.60	478	69 (100.00)	6.93
	Fishing Trap	T	47	39 (23.58)	1.21	67	60 (86.96)	1.12
	Throwing Net		-	-	-	6	6 (8.67)	1.00
	Ell trapper	T	3	3 (5.66)	1.00	2	2 (2.90)	1.00
	Poluha	T	27	16 (30.19)	1.69	41	34 (49.28)	1.21
	Coonch Shell	T	17	16 (30.19)	1.06	11	11 (15.94)	1.00
Musical Instruments	Beating Drum	M	-	- -	-	-	-	
	Beating Bell	M	-	- -	-	-	-	

Note: (i) Figure in brackets represent %age.
(ii) T = Traditional, M = Modern.

Hirāpur, as against 17 or 34 per cent in Āmbadiha. Similarly, this is also owned by 16 or 30.19 per cent and 11 or 15.94 per cent non-beneficiary households of Hirāpur and Āmbadiha, respectively. The other musical instruments, like *Khanjani* and beating bell, the *gini,* are found in only 2 or 3.64 per cent and 3 or 5.45 per cent of beneficiary households of Hirāpur. These instruments are used for performing devotional songs on the occasions of *Trinath Melā,* i.e. propitiation of three principal Hindu deities viz., *Brahmā,* the creator; *Vishnu*, the saviour; and *Maheswar;* the destroyer.

(c) Luxurious Items

The items of luxury possessed by Bāuri households include various audio and audio-visual instruments like radio, two-in-ones, tape-recorders, and televisions and furniture like sofa, bedsteads, tables, wooden *almirah* (cupboards), dressing tables, chair and some other items for daily or occasional use like lantern, petromax, umbrella, wall clock, wrist watch, fan, fountain pen etc. (Table 4.27.3).

Table 4.27.3 also portrays that among the audio-visual instruments, radio is a common instrument which is owned by 11 or 20 per cent beneficiary households of Hirāpur as against 6 or 12 per cent households of Āmbadiha. So far as the case of non-beneficiary households is concerned, it is observed that while this instrument is owned by 7 or 13.21 per cent of households in the former village, it is 6 or 8.7 per cent in the latter village. Two-in-one, tape-recorder and television are found with very few beneficiary households of Hirāpur.

Among items of furniture, chair is the main item which is owned by 13 or 14.55 per cent of the beneficiary households of Hirāpur against only 2 or 4 per cent of households of Āmbadiha. The other items of furniture are found only in 1 or 2 beneficiary households of Hirāpur. These items are not found either among the non-beneficiary households of Hirāpur or in any beneficiary and non-beneficiary household of Āmbadiha.

Among other luxurious items lanterns, umbrellas, flash-lights, wrist watches and fountain pens are found respectively in 17 or 30.91 per cent, 27 or 49.09 per cent, 21 or 38.18 per cent, 27 or 49.09 per cent and 41 or 74.51 per cent of beneficiary households of Hirāpur as against 8 or 16 per cent, 21 or 42 per cent, 13 or 26 per cent, 18 or 36 per cent and 31 or 62 per cent of households in Āmbadiha. Petromax lights and wall clocks are owned by only 3.64 per cent or 2 and 1.81 per cent or 1 beneficiary household in Hirāpur. These items are not found in large numbers in any of the beneficiary households of Āmbadiha. However, while electric fan is found in 10.91 per cent or

6 households of Hirāpur, it is found in only 2 per cent or 1 household in Āmbadiha.

As far as non-beneficiary households are concerned, lanterns and umbrellas are owned by 21 or 39.62 per cent households, flashlight

TABLE 4.27.3

Possession of capital movable assets (luxurious items) among beneficiary and non-beneficiary households

Beneficiary

Type of Assets	Capital Goods/ Items	Hirāpur (N=55)			Āmbadiha (N=50)		
		Total No. of Possession	Total HHs possess	Average	Total No. of Possession	Total HHs possess	Average
(1)	(2)	(3)	(4)	(5)	(6)	(7)	(8)
Audio & Audio-visual Instruments	Radio	11	11 (20.00)	1	6	6 (12.00)	1.00
	Two-in-one	1	1 (1.81)	1.00	-	-	-
	Tape-recorder	1	1 (1.81)	1.00	-	-	-
	T.V.	2	2 (3.64)	1.00	1	1 (2.00)	1.00
Furniture	Sofa	1	1 (1.81)	1.00	-	-	-
	Cot	1	1 (1.81)	1.00	-	-	-
	Table	2	2 (3.64)	1.00	-	-	-
	Almirah (wooden)	1	1 (1.81)	1.00	-	-	-
	Dressing table	1	1 (1.81)	1.00	-	-	-
	Chair	13	8 (14.55)	1.63	6	2 (4.00)	3.00
Other luxury goods	Lantern	17	17 (30.91)	1.00	8	8 (16.00)	1.00
	Petromax	2	2 (3.64)	1.00	-	-	-
	Umbrella	29	27 (49.02)	1.07	21	21 (42.00)	1.00
	Torch	22	21 (38.18)	1.05	13	13 (26,00)	1.00
	Wall clock	1	1 (1.81)	1.00	-	-	-
	Wrist Watch	28	27 (49.09)	1.04	18	18 (36.00)	1.00
	Fan	6	6 (10.91)	1.00	1	1 (2.0)	1.00
	Fountain Pen	47	4 (74.55)	1.16	50	31 (62.00)	1.61

contd.

TABLE 4.27.3 (Contd.)

Non-Beneficiary households

Type of Assets	Capital Goods/ Items	Hirāpur (N=53)			Āmbadiha (N=50)		
		Total No. of Posse-ssion	Total HHs po-ssess	Ave-rage	Total No. of Posse-ssion	Total HHs po-ssess	Ave-rage
(1)	(2)	(3)	(4)	(5)	(6)	(7)	(8)
Audio & Audio-Visual Instru-ments	Radio	7	7 (13.21)	1.00	6	6 (8.70)	1.00
	Two-in-one	-	-	-	1	1 (1.45)	1.00
	Tape-recorder	-	-	-	-	-	-
	T.V.	1	1 (1.89)	1.00	-	- -	
Furni-ture	Sofa	-	- -	-	-	-	
	Cot	-	- -	-	-	-	
	Table	-	- -	-	-	-	
	Almirah (wooden)	-	- -	-	-	-	
	Dressing table	-	- -	-	-	-	
	Chair	4	2 (3.77)	2.00	-	- -	
Other luxury goods	Lantern	21	21 (39.62)	1.00	14	13 (18.84)	1.08
	Petromax	3	3 (5.66)	1.00	1	1 (1.45)	1.00
	Umbrella	21	21 (39.62)	1.00	19	19 (27.54)	1.00
	Torch	19	17 (32.08)	1.12	7	6 (8.70)	1.17
	Wall clock	2	2 (3.77)	1.00	-	- -	
	Wrist Watch	26	25 (47.17)	1.04	9	9 (13.04)	1.00
	Fan	2	2 (3.77)	1.00	1	1 (1.45)	1.00
	Fountain Pen	28	28 (52.83)	1.00	37	31 (44.93)	1.19

Note: Figures in brackets represent %age.

by 17 or 32.68 per cent, wrist watch by 25 or 47.17 per cent, and fountain pen by 28 or 52.83 per cent of Hirāpur. But on the other hand lanterns and umbrellas are found in 13 or 18.84 per cent and 19 or 27.54 per cent households of Āmbadiha. Flashlights and wrist watches are found in very few households as these items are owned by only 6 or 8.70 per cent and 9 or 13.04 per cent of households of this village. However, fountain pen is found in 31 or 44.93 per cent households.

(d) Utensils and Precious Metals

Generally utensils which the Bāuri people use include plates, *lotas*, tumblers, bowls, skimmer etc. made of either aluminium or brass.

Data relating to these items are available in Table 4.27.4. This table shows that 30 beneficiaries or 60 per cent of Hirāpur own about 67 kgs. of brass utensils that account for possessing an average of 2.03 kgs. per household. But in Āmbadiha, it is 18 or 36 per cent households who possess only 16.5 kgs. of utensils made of this metal with an average ownership of only 0.92 kg. per household.

The utensils made of aluminium is possessed by all the households of each category of both the villages. But while the average possession of aluminium utensils comes to be 1.62 kg. per beneficiary household in Hirāpur, it is 1.06 kg. per household in Āmbadiha. Likewise, among the non-beneficiary households of Hirāpur and Āmbadiha, the average possession of aluminium utensils comes to be 1.26 kg. and 1.01 kg. per household, respectively.

So far as the ownership of gold ornaments is concerned, it is reflected from the table referred to above that only 2 or 3.64 per cent of beneficiary households in Hirāpur own 15 gm. of gold that comes to an average of 7.5 gm. per household, and there is neither any beneficiary nor any non-beneficiary household in Āmbadiha which possesses any ornament made of gold. However, 12 or 21.82 per cent of beneficiary households of Hirāpur own about 60 gm. silver ornaments that comes to an average of 5 gm, per household, as against 2 or 4 per cent households of Āmbadiha who own 15 gms. In case of non-beneficiary households, while there are only 6 or 11.32 per cent households in Hirāpur who own 70 gm. of silver ornaments on an average of 11.67 gm. per household, there is not a single household in Āmbadiha who possesses any ornament made out of it (Table 4.27.4).

(e) Transport Vehicles

The transport vehicles which are owned by Bāuri households include bullock carts, rickshaws/trolleys, bicycle and moped. But bicycle is the most important vehicle as it is owned by most beneficiary, as well as non-beneficiary households. It is found from Table 4.27.5 that a total number of 37 or 67.27 per cent beneficiary households of Hirāpur own this vehicle as against 21 or 42 per cent households of Āmbadiha. But in the case of non-beneficiary households, while a total number of 25 or 45 per cent of households in the former village who own these vehicles, it is 24 or 34.28 per cent in case of the latter one.

TABLE 4.27.4

Possession of capital movable assets (utensils & precious metal) among beneficiary and non-beneficiary households

Beneficiary

Type of Assets	Capital Goods/Items	Nature of Goods	Hiṛāpur (N=55)			Āmbadiha (N=50)		
			Total No. of Posse-ssion	Total HHs possess	Average	Total No. of Posse-ssion	Total HHs possess	Average
(1)	(2)	(3)	(4)	(5)	(6)	(7)	(8)	(9)
Utensils	Bucket	T	9	7 (12.73)	1.86	2	2 (4.00)	1.00
	Plate, Lota, Glass, Bowl, Skimmer etc. (in kg.) [Brass]	M	67	33 (60.00)	2.03	16.50	18 (36.00)	0.92
	Plate, Lota, Glass, Bowl, Skimmer etc. (Aluminium)	T	89.50	55 (100.00)	1.62	45.30	50(100.00)	1.06
Precious metal	Gold (in gms.)	M	15	2 (3.64)	7.5	-	- -	
	Silver (in gms.)	M	60	12 (21.82)	5.0	15	2 (4.00)	7.5

contd.

TABLE 4.27.4 (contd.)

Non-Beneficiary

Type of Assets	Capital Goods/Items	Nature of Goods	Hirāpur (N=53)			Āmbadiha (N=69)		
			Total No. of Posse-ssion	Total HHs possess	Average	Total No. of Posse-ssion	Total HHs possess	Average
(1)	(2)	(3)	(4)	(5)	(6)	(7)	(8)	(9)
Utensils	Bucket	T	3	3 (5.66)	1.00	3	3 (4.35)	1.00
	Plate, Lota, Glass, Bowl, Skimmer etc. (in Kg) [Brass]	M	31.5	23 (43.40)	1.32	10.50	7 (10.14)	1.50
	Plate, Lota, Glass, Bowl, Skimmer etc. (Aluminium)	T	67	53 (100.00)	1.26	70.00	69(100.00)	1.01
Precious metal	Gold (in gms.)	M	5	1 (1.89)	5.00	-	-	-
	Silver (in gms.)	M	70	6 (11.32)	11.67	-	-	-

Note: Figures in brackets represent %age.

TABLE 4.27.5

Possession of capital movable assets (transport) among beneficiary and non-beneficiary households

Beneficiary

Capital Goods/ Items	Nature of Goods	Hirāpur (N=55)			Āmbadiha (N=50)		
		Total No. of Posse-ssion	Total HHs possess	Ave-rage	Total No. of Posse-ssion	Total HHs possess	Ave-rage
(1)	(2)	(3)	(4)	(5)	(6)	(7)	(8)
Cart	T	4	4 (7.27)	1.00	2	2 (4.00)	1.00
Rickshaw/ Trolley	M	14	14 (25.45)	1.00	3	3 (6.00)	1 00
Bi-cycle	M	37	37 (67.27)	1.00	21	21 (42.00)	1.00
Moped	M	1	1 (1.82)	1.00	-	-	-

Non-Beneficiary

Capital Goods/ Items	Nature of Goods	Hirāpur (N=53)			Āmbadiha (N=69)		
		Total No. of Posse-ssion	Total HHs possess	Ave-rage	Total No. of Posse-ssion	Total HHs possess	Ave-rage
(1)	(2)	(3)	(4)	(5)	(6)	(7)	(8)
Cart	T	2	2 (3.77)	1.00	2	2 (2.90)	1.00
Rickshaw Trolley	M	4	4 (7.55)	1.00	1	1 (1.45)	1.00
Bi-cycle	M	25	24 (45.28)	1.00	24	24 (34.78)	1.00
Moped	M	-	-	-	-	-	-

Note: (i) Figure in brackets represent %age.
(ii) T=Traditional, M=Modern.

Just as bicycles are owned by a very large number of beneficiary households of Hirāpur, Rickshaws/Trolleys are also owned by these households (14 or 25.45 per cent) of this village, as they utilise this vehicle for their business in Bhubaneswar city. In case of non-beneficiary households, possession of this vehicle is limited to only 4 or 7.55 per cent in Hirāpur, as against only 1 or 1.45 per cent in Āmbadiha. So far as the ownership of bullock cart is concerned, it is found from the same table that 4 or 7.27 per cent of beneficiary house-

TABLE 4.27.6

Possession of capital movable assets (food grains/oil seeds etc.) among beneficiary & non-beneficiary households

Beneficiary

Capital Goods/ Items (in kg.)	Nature of Goods	Hirāpur (N=55)			Āmbadiha (N=50)		
		Total No. of Posse-ssion	Total HHs possess	Ave-rage	Total No. of Posse-ssion	Total HHs possess	Ave-rage
(1)	(2)	(3)	(4)	(5)	(6)	(7)	(8)
Paddy	T	1950	18 (32.73)	108.33	2000	31 (62.00)	64.52
Par Boil-ed Rice	T	375	21 (38.18)	17.86	350.00	17 (34.00)	14.71
Groundnut	M	100	2 (3.64)	50.00	-	-	-
Arum	T	120	3 (5.45)	40.00	250	9 (18.00)	29.41
Horse-gram	T	6	1 (1.82)	6.00	-	-	-
Coconut (in no.)	M	1303	7 (12.73)	186.14	503	19 (38.00)	26.47

Non-Beneficiary

Capital Goods/ Items (in Kg.)	Nature of Goods	Hirāpur (N=53)			Āmbadiha (N=69)		
		Total No. of Posse-ssion	Total HHs possess	Ave-rage	Total No. of Posse-ssion	Total HHs possess	Ave-rage
(1)	(2)	(3)	(4)	(5)	(6)	(7)	(8)
Paddy	T	2800	27 (50.94)	103.73	6000	8 (11.59)	75.00
Par Boil-ed Rice	T	150	12 (22.64)	12.50	330.00	20 (28.99)	16.50
Groundnut	M	-	-	-	-	-	-
Arum	T	235	18 (33.96)	13.06	115	13 (18.84)	10.12
Horse-gram	T	-	-	-	-	-	-
Coconut (in no.)	M	910	12 (22.64)	75.83	800	22 (31.88)	36.36

Note: (i) Figure in brackets represent %age.
(ii) T=Traditional, M=Modern.

TABLE 4.28

Value of capital immovable assets among beneficiary and non-beneficiary households

Type of Assets	Capital Goods/ Items	Beneficiary					
		Hirāpur (N=55) Total Value			Āmbadiha (N=50) Total Value		
		Total HHs Poss.	(a)	(b)	Total HHs Poss.	(a)	(b)
(1)	(2)	(3)	(4)	(5)	(6)	(7)	(8)
Land	Homestead	46	42750 (929.35)	42750 (929.35)	50	40000 (800.00)	40000 (800.00)
	Agricultural	6	41250 (687.50)	41250 (687.50)	11	82000 (7454.55)	82000 (7454.55)
House	Building (Kutcha/Pucca)	50	227000 (4540.00)	227000 (4540.00)	50	82500 (1650.00)	82500 (1650.00)
Economically important fruit bearing trees	Coconut	12	2100 (175.00)	2100 (175.00)	13	2450 (188.46)	2450 (188.46)
	Mango	4	750 (187.50)	750 (187.50)	1	125 (125.00)	125 (125.00)
	Guava	4	200 (50.00)	200 (50.00)	3	150 (50.00)	150 (50.00)
	Drum stick	7	1125 (160.71)	1125 (160.71)	13	1300 (100.00)	1300 (100.00)
	Banana	28	635 (22.68)	635 (22.68)	31	590 (19.03)	590 (19.03)
	Bur nut	3	340 (120.89)	340 (120.89)	3	350 (116.67)	350 (116.67)
	Total	55	316150 (5748.18)	316150 (5748.18)	50	209465 (4189.30)	209465 (4189.30)

contd.

TABLE 4.28 (contd.)

Type of Assets	Capital Goods/ Items	Non-Beneficiary					
		Hirāpur (N=53) Total Value			Āmbadiha (N=69) Total Value		
		Total HHs Poss.	(a)	(b)	Total HHs Poss.	(a)	(b)
(1)	(2)	(3)	(4)	(5)	(6)	(7)	(8)
Land	Homestead	48	45000 (937.5)	45000 (937.5)	69	40000 (529.71)	40000 (529.71)
	Agricultural	5	30937 (6187.4)	30937 (6187.4)	13	61500 (4730.77)	61500 (4730.77)
House	Building (Kutcha/Pucca)	52	82500 (1650.00)	82500 (1650.00)	69	136500 (1978.26)	136500 (1978.26)
Economically important fruit bearing trees	Coconut	6	1418 (236.33)	1418 (236.33)	19	2370 (124.74)	2370 (124.74)
	Mango	1	150 (150.00)	150 (150.00)	-	-	-
	Guava	2	100 (50.00)	100 (50.00)	3	210 (70.00)	210 (70.00)
	Drum stick	11	1450 (131.82)	1450 (131.82)	11	1250 (113.64)	1250 (113.64)
	Banana	12	260 (21.67)	260 (21.67)	30	500 (16.67)	500 (16.67)
	Bur nut	2	300 (150.00)	300 (150.00)	7	225 (32.14)	225 (32.14)
	Total	53	211415 (3988.96)	211415 (3988.96)	69	242555 (3515.19)	242555 (3515.19)

Note: (i) a = as per the own estimation of the informants, b = as per the straight line method
(ii) Figures in brackets represent average value per household.

TABLE 4.29.1

Value of capital movable assets (domestic animals) among beneficiary and non-beneficiary households

Capital Goods/ Items	Beneficiary					
	Hirāpur (N=55) Total Value			Āmbadiha (N=50) Total Value		
	Total HHs Poss.	(a)	(b)	Total HHs Poss.	(a)	(b)
(1)	(2)	(3)	(4)	(5)	(6)	(7)
Bullocks	26	8350 (321.15)	8350 (321.15)	10	4350 (435.00)	4350 (435.00)
Cattle	13	3950 (303.85)	3950 (303.85)	17	4200 (247.06)	4200 (247.06)
Goat/ Sheep	12	7330 (610.83)	7330 (610.83)	6	1950 (325.00)	1950 (325.00)
Poultry	40	1750 (43.75)	1750 (43.75)	33	1395 (42.27)	1395 (42.27)
Total	55	21380 (388.73)	21380 (388.73)	50	11895 (237.90)	11895 (237.90)

Capital Goods Items	Non-Beneficiary					
	Hirāpur (N=53) Total Value			Āmbadiha (N=69) Total Value		
	Total HHs Poss.	(a)	(b)	Total HHs Poss.	(a)	(b)
(1)	(2)	(3)	(4)	(5)	(6)	(7)
Bullocks	12	4020 (335.00)	4020 (335.00)	13	3010 (231.54)	3010 (231.54)
Cattle	10	2375 (237.50)	2375 (237.50)	19	5080 (267.37)	5080 (267.37)
Goat/ Sheep	9	2000 (222.22)	2000 (222.22)	10	2750 (275.00)	2750 (275.00)
Poultry	34	550 (16.18)	550 (16.18)	37	721 (19.49)	721 (19.49)
Total	53	8945 (168.77)	8945 (168.77)	69	11561 (167.55)	11561 (167.55)

Note: As per Table No. 4.28

holds of Hirāpur own this vehicle, as against only 2 or 4 per cent of Āmbadiha. There are only 2 households each among non-beneficiary households who have this vehicle. As these people seem to be very poor, only one beneficiary household of Hirāpur possesses a moped, utilised mostly for doing business in Bhubaneswar city.

(f) Food grains/Oil seeds etc.

These items normally include paddy, parboiled rice, groundnut, arum, horsegram and coconut. These items are conserved either for consumption in lean seasons or for sale in the peak seasons.

It is seen from the Table 4.27.6 that among the above items, paddy and rice are the most important and common assets. These items are preserved by about 25 per cent households of both the beneficiary and non-beneficiary households in the two study villages. But the quantity held is very little as the majority of Bāuris do not own agricultural fields.

Value of Assets

The value of immovable assets like land, house-building and economically important fruit-bearing trees has been mentioned in Table 4.28. Likewise, the value of movable assets such as different domestic animals, different implements/instruments, items of luxury, various utensils, precious metals, transport vehicles and foodgrains, oilseeds etc. have been mentioned in Tables 4.29.1, 4.29.2, 4.29.3, 4.29.4, 4.29.5, and 4.29.6 respectively. The average values of the assets are presented in the Table 4.30.

To calculate the values of the above capital assets two different methods have been adopted. In the first method, the informants were asked to value their own assets and the result is presented in the 'a' column of each of the above tables. But to avoid ambiguities and to overcome the disadvantages of this method, a different method called 'straight line method' which is more scientific has been adopted and the result is presented in 'b' column of the above tables.

While computing the second method, first, the year of purchase and purchase price of each asset of every household was found out. (Excluding land, trees and bovine assets as the value of these assets do not depreciate. Also excluded are utensils made of brass, aluminium and ornaments made of gold, silver etc. as these have fixed selling values in the local market for old assets of these metals). And then the purchase price was inflected on the basis of the general price index (all commodities) to 1991-92 (which was the year of survey) prices. After conversion of the purchase price of the assets into the present price (June 1991), depreciation charge was made under the straight line method. The formula for computing the amount of depreciation charge is compounded for each year at the rate of 10 per cent per year subject to a maximum period of 10 years for the assets aged 10 or more. The value that comes after depreciation for 10 years is known as 'Scrap' value.

TABLE 4.29.2

Value of capital immovable assets (different implements/instruments) among beneficiary and non-beneficiary households

Type of Assets	Capital Goods/ Items	Beneficiary					
		Hirāpur (N=55), Total Value			Āmbadiha (N=50), Total Value		
		Total HHs Poss.	(a)	(b)	Total HHs Poss.	(a)	(b)
(1)	(2)	(3)	(4)	(5)	(6)	(7)	(8)
Agricultural implements material	Plough	30	2700 (90.00)	3833.75 (127.76)	8	1200 (150.00)	1115.93
	Spade	18	310 (17.22)	412.36 (22.91)	30	660 (22.00)	477.65
	Billhook	52	620 (11.92)	707.92	45	505 (11.22)	481.51
	Sickle	55	315 (5.73)	378.99	50	400 (8.00)	615.00
	Axe	15	260 (17.33)	318.00	3	80 (26.67)	112.00
	Crowbar	9	200 (12.22)	136.04	3	60 (20.00)	152.70
	Digging Stick	11	120 (10.91)	98.00	7	75 (10.71)	1.70
	Tarpouline	4	1200 (300.00)	1040.90	-	-	-
Fishing implements	Fishing net	4	1700 (425.00)	1315.80	1	400 (400.00)	328.95
	Fishing rod	55	515 (9.36)	618.30	50	390 (7.80)	410.00
	Fishing trap	30	256 (8.53)	479.51	47	515 (10.96)	671.89
	Throwing net	3	710 (236.67)	571.24	3	445 (148.33)	315.88
	Ell traper	7	150 (21.43)	93.86	11	230 (20.91)	141.87
	Poluha	21	1730 (82.38)	3907.64	31	1685 (54.35)	3559.27
Musical instruments	Conch shell	16	360 (22.50)	370.68	17	400 (23.53)	450.31
	Beating drum	2	1270 (635.00)	1398.11	-	-	-
	Beating bell	3	215 (71.67)	307.93	-	-	-
	Total	55	12631 (229.65)	16187.62	50	7045 (140.90)	8802.66

contd.

TABLE 4.29.2 (contd.)

Type of Assets	Capital Goods/ Items	Non-Beneficiary					
		Hirāpur (N=53), Total Value			Āmbadiha (N=69), Total Value		
		Total HHs Poss.	(a)	(b)	Total HHs Poss.	(a)	(b)
(1)	(2)	(3)	(4)	(5)	(6)	(7)	(8)
Agricultural implements material	Plough	13	800 (61.54)	1306.00	13	750 (57.69)	1218.33
	Spade	19	315 (16.58)	416.00	17	300 (17.65)	277.00
	Billhook	50	595 (11.90)	433.30	60	480 (8.00)	455.49
	Sickle	53	370 (6.98)	390.00	69	580 (8.41)	576.00
	Axe	9	250 (27.78)	330.00	7	150 (21.43)	212.80
	Crowbar	7	130 (18.57)	398.44	6	100 (16.67)	277.61
	Digging Stick	17	165 (9.71)	201.00	2	20 (10.00)	41.70
	Tarpouline	2	600 (300.00)	520.25	-	-	-
Fishing implements	Fishing net	2	560 (280.00)	657.90	-	-	-
	Fishing rod	53	650 (12.26)	778.03	69	500 (7.25)	618.33
	Fishing trap	39	615 (15.77)	530.77	60	715 (11.92)	368.38
	Throwing net	-	-	-	6	1300 (216.67)	630.00
	Ell traper	3	55 (18.33)	65.38	2	400 (20.00)	68.56
	Poluha	16	1100 (68.75)	2041.90	34	1450 (42.65)	4293.67
Musical instruments	Conch shell	16	375 (23.44)	525.60	11	250 (22.73)	305.83
	Beating drum	-	-	-	-	-	-
	Beating bell	-	-	-	-	-	-
	Total	53	6580 (124.15)	8114.63	69	6635 (96.16)	9348.70

Note: Figures as per Table No. 4.28

TABLE 4.29.3

Value of capital movable assets (luxurious items) among beneficiary and non-beneficiary households

Type of Assets	Capital Goods/ Items	Beneficiary					
		Hirāpur (N=55), Total Value			Āmbadiha (N=50), Total Value		
		Total HHs Poss.	(a)	(b)	Total HHs Poss.	(a)	(b)
(1)	(2)	(3)	(4)	(5)	(6)	(7)	(8)
Audio & Audiovisual instruments	Radio	11	1830 (166.36)	1872.82	6	1500 (250.00)	1529.28
	Two-in-one	1	400 (400.00)	562.20	-	-	-
	Tape recorder	1	400 (400.00)	562.20	-	-	-
	T.V.	2	2850 (1425.00)	5531.52	1	2630 (2630.00)	3633.67
Furniture	Sofa	1	1800 (1800.00)	577.45	-	-	-
	Cot	1	800 (800.00)	800.00	-	-	-
	Table	2	100 (50.00)	115.48	-	-	-
	Almirah	1	350 (350.00)	336.84	-	-	-
	Dressing table	1	615 (615.00)	837.30	-	-	-
	Chair	8	700 (87.50)	1069.60	2	300 (150.00)	249.82
Other Luxury goods	Lantern	17	220 (12.94)	256.52	8	200 (25.00)	142.78
	Petromax	2	375 (187.50)	514.95	-	-	-
	Umbrella	27	410 (15.19)	589.72	21	390 (18.57)	379.59
	Torch	21	305 (14.52)	425.35	13	380 (29.23)	199.14
	Wall clock	1	80 (80.00)	76.81	-	-	-
	Wrist watch	27	4600 (170.30)	5940.63	18	4110 (28.33)	3780.39
	Fan	6	1150 (191.67)	2185.82	1	275 (275.00)	305.39
	Fountain pen	41	92 (1.96)	178.29	31	215 (6.94)	253.74
	Total	55	17077.00 (310.49)	22433.50 (407.88)	50	10000 (200.00)	10473.80 (209.48)

contd.

TABLE 4.29.3 (contd.)

Type of Assets	Capital Goods/ Items	Non-Beneficiary					
		Hirāpur (N=53), Total Value			Āmbadiha (N=69), Total Value		
		Total HHs Poss.	(a)	(b)	Total HHs Poss.	(a)	(b)
(1)	(2)	(3)	(4)	(5)	(6)	(7)	(8)
Audio & Audiovisual instruments	Radio	7	1920 (274.29)	1503.90	6	1600 (266.67)	2337.69
	Two-in-one	-	-	-	1	800 (800.00)	446.81
	Tape recorder	-	-	-	-	-	-
	T.V.	1	1500 (1500.00)	2520.42	-	-	-
Furniture	Sofa	-	-	-	-	-	-
	Cot	-	-	-	-		-
	Table	-	-	-	-	-	-
	Almirah	-	-	-	-	-	-
	Dressing table	-	-	-	-	-	-
	Chair	2	460 (230.00)	372.30	-	-	-
Other luxury goods	Lantern	21	405 (19.29)	576.72	13	285 (21.92)	212.40
	Petromax	3	310 (103.33)	549.90	1	120 (120.00)	274.96
	Umbrella	21	400 (19.05)	452.34	19	490 (25.79)	542.91
	Torch	17	460 (27.06)	380.26	6	218 (36.33)	154.16
	Wall clock	2	160 (80.00)	257.48	-	-	-
	Wrist watch	25	4300 (172.00)	5710.96	9	1680 (186.67)	1457.08
	Fan	2	570 (285.00)	687.86	1	390 (390.00)	297.86
	Fountain pen	28	90 (3.21)	81.78	31	192 (6.19)	380.77
	Total	53	10575 (199.53)	13093.92 (247.05)	69	5775 (83.70)	6104.64 (88.47)

Note: Figures as per Table No. 4.28

TABLE 4.29.4

Value of capital movable assets (utensils and precious metals) among beneficiary and non-beneficiary households

Type of Assets	Capital Goods/ Items	Beneficiary						Non-Beneficiary					
		Hirāpur (N=55)			Āmbadiha (N=50)			Hirāpur (N=53)			Āmbadiha (N=69)		
		Total HHs Poss.	Total Value (a)	(b)	Total HHs Poss.	Total Value (a)	(b)	Total HHs Poss.	Total Value (a)	(b)	Total HHs Poss.	Total Value (a)	(b)
(1)	(2)	(3)	(4)	(5)	(6)	(7)	(8)	(9)	(10)	(11)	(12)	(13)	(14)
Utensils (in nos.)	Bucket	7	104 (14.86)	230 (32.86)	2	40 (20.00)	44.50 (22.25)	3	60 (20.00)	92.79 (30.93)	3	30 (10.00)	98.70 (32.91)
	Brass items	33	3015 (91.36)	3015 (91.36)	18	743 (41.28)	743.00 (41.28)	23	1260 (54.78)	1260.00 (54.78)	7	472.00 (67.43)	472.00 (67.43)
	Allu. items	55	2685 (48.82)	2685 (48.82)	50	1230 (24.60)	1230.00 (24.60)	53	1800 (33.96)	1800.00 (33.96)	69	1890 (27.39)	1890.00 (27.39)
Precious Metal	Gold (in gm)	2	4575 (2287.50)	4575 (2287.50)	-	-	-	1	1525 (1525.00)	1525.00 (1525.00)	-	-	-
	Silver (in gm)	12	1230 (10.83)	1230 (10.83)	2	80 (40.00)	80.00 (40.00)	6	150 (25.00)	150.00 (25.00)	-	-	-
	Total		10509 (191.07)	11735 (213.36)	-	2093 (41.86)	2097.50 (41.95)	-	4795 (90.47)	4287.79 (91.09)	-	2392 (34.67)	2460.74 (35.66)

Note: As per Table No. 4.28

TABLE 4.29.5

Value of capital movable assets (transport) among beneficiary and non-beneficiary households

Beneficiary

Capital Goods/ Items	Hirāpur (N=55) Total Value			Āmbadiha (N=50) Total Value		
	Total HHs Poss.	(a)	(b)	Total HHs Poss.	(a)	(b)
(1)	(2)	(3)	(4)	(5)	(6)	(7)
Cart	4	2070 (517.50)	3531.71	2	1300 (650.00)	1620.31
Rickshaw/ Trolley	14	12300 (878.57)	13629.60	3	2750 (916.67)	2854.60
Bicycle	37	7770 (210.00)	7992.69	21	5900 (280.95)	5916.29
Moped	1	3000 (3000.00)	3373.20	-	-	-
Total	55	25140 (457.09)	28527.20 (518.67)	50	9950 (199.00)	10391.20 (207.82)

Non-Beneficiary

Capital Goods/ Items	Hirāpur (N=53) Total Value			Āmbadiha (N=69) Total Value		
	Total HHs Poss.	(a)	(b)	Total HHs Poss.	(a)	(b)
(1)	(2)	(3)	(4)	(5)	(6)	(7)
Cart	2	1150 (575.00)	2701.93	2	1390 (695.00)	2249.68
Rickshaw/ Trolley	4	4100 (1025.00)	4265.48	1	1480 (1480.00)	1635.20
Bicycle	25	6000 (240.00)	4754.65	24	5060 (210.83)	7566.29
Moped	-	-	-	-	-	-
Total	53	11250 (212.26)	11722.06 (221.17)	69	7930 (114.93)	11451.17 (165.59)

Note: As per Table No. 4.28

Beneficiary Households

When one looks at Table 4.30 it may be seen that in the first method, the average value of all assets irrespective of any category comes to Rs. 7434.45 per household in case of Hirāpur as against

TABLE 4.29.6

Value of capital movable assets (food grains, oil seeds etc.) among beneficiary and non-beneficiary households

Beneficiary

Capital Goods/ Items	Hirāpur (N=55) Total Value			Āmbadiha (N=50) Total Value		
	Total HHs Poss.	(a)	(b)	Total HHs Poss.	(a)	(b)
(1)	(2)	(3)	(4)	(5)	(6)	(7)
Paddy	18	2437.50 (135.42)	2437.50 (135.42)	31	2200 (70.97)	2200 (70.97)
Par boiled rice	21	1312.50 (62.50)	1312.50 (62.50)	17	1140 (67.06)	1140 (67.06)
Ground-nut	2	600.00 (300.00)	600.00 (300.00)	-	-	-
Arum	3	180 (60.00)	180 (60.00)	9	375 (41.67)	375 (41.67)
Horse gram	1	45.00 (45.00)	45.00 (45.00)	-	-	-
Coconut (in nos.)	7	1433.00 (204.71)	1433.00 (204.71)	19	630 (33.16)	630 (33.16)
Total	55	6008 (109.24)	-	50	4345 (86.90)	-

Non-Beneficiary

Capital Goods/ Items	Hirāpur (N=53) Total Value			Āmbadiha (N=69) Total Value		
	Total HHs Poss.	(a)	(b)	Total HHs Poss.	(a)	(b)
(1)	(2)	(3)	(4)	(5)	(6)	(7)
Paddy	27	3500 (129.63)	3500 (129.63)	8	7500 (937.50)	7500 (937.50)
Par boiled rice	12	525 (43.75)	525 (43.75)	20	1072 (53.60)	1072 (53.60)
Ground-nut	-	-	-	-	-	-
Arum	18	352.50 (19.58)	352.50 (19.58)	13	144 (11.08)	144 (11.08)
Horsegram	-	-	-	-	-	-
Coconut (in nos.)	12	1000 (83.33)	1000 (83.33)	22	1150 (52.57)	1150 (52.57)
Total	53	5377.50 (101.46)	-	69	9866 (142.99)	-

Note: As per Table No. 4.28

TABLE 4.30
Average value of capital assets among beneficiary and non-beneficiary households

Type of Assets	Beneficiary				Non-beneficiary			
	Hirāpur (N=55)		Āmbadiha (N=50)		Hirāpur (N=53)		Āmbadiha (N=69)	
	(a)	(b)	(a)	(b)	(a)	(b)	(a)	(b)
(1)	(2)	(3)	(4)	(5)	(6)	(7)	(8)	(9)
Land, house & economically important fruit bearing trees	316150.00 (5748.18)	316150.00 (5748.18)	209465.00 (4189.50)	209465.00 (4189.50)	211415.00 (3988.96)	211415.00 (3988.96)	24255.50 (3515.29)	24255.50 (3515.29)
Domestic Animals	21380.00 (388.73)	21380.00 (388.73)	11895.00 (237.90)	11895.00 (237.90)	8945.00 (168.77)	8945.00 (168.77)	11561.00 (167.55)	11561.00 (167.55)
Agricultural, hunting & Birding, fishing, musical instruments	12631.00 (229.65)	16187.62 (294.32)	7045.00 (140.90)	8802.66 (176.05)	6580.00 (124.15)	8114.63 (153.11)	6635.00 (96.16)	9348.70 (135.49)
Luxurious items	17077.00 (310.49)	22433.50 (407.88)	10000.00 (200.00)	10473.80 (209.48)	10575.00 (199.53)	13093.92 (247.08)	5775.00 (83.70)	6104.64 (88.47)
Utensils & precious metals	10509.00 (191.07)	11735.00 (213.36)	2093.00 (41.86)	2097.50 (41.95)	4795.00 (90.47)	4827.79 (91.09)	2392.00 (34.67)	2460.74 (35.66)
Transport vehicles	25140.00 (557.09)	28527.20 (518.68)	9950.00 (199.00)	10391.20 (207.82)	11250.00 (212.26)	11722.00 (221.17)	7930.00 (114.93)	11451.17 (165.96)
Food grains, oil seed etc.	6008.00 (109.24)	6008.00 (109.24)	4345.00 (86.90)	4345.00 (86.90)	5377.50 (101.46)	5377.50 (101.46)	9866.00 (142.99)	9866.00 (142.99)
Total	408895 (7434.45)	422421.32 (7680.39)	254793.00 (5095.86)	257470.16 (5149.00)	258937.50 (4885.61)	263495.90 (4971.62)	286714.00 (4155.28)	287853.25 (4171.79)

Note:- As per Table No. 4.28

Rs. 5095.86 of Āmbadiha. According to the second or 'straight line' method it works out to Rs. 7680.39 in case of the former village as against Rs. 5149.40 of Āmbadiha.

Non-Beneficiary Households

So far as the case of the non-beneficiary households is concerned, it is found from the same table that in the first method, the average asset value in case of Hirāpur is Rs. 4885.61 per household, as against Rs. 4155.28 of Āmbadiha. But valued by the straight line method Rs. 4971.79 is the value derived for Hirāpur and Rs. 4171.79 for Āmbadiha.

Hence, the above findings suggest that the asset values of both the beneficiary and non-beneficiary households of Hirāpur is higher than those of the village Āmbadiha.

Chapter V

CONSEQUENTIAL CHANGES

Development planning brings forth occupational and economic mobility. Simultaneously, it also influences various social behaviour of the people. Some of the major effects of the development process may be improvement of political awareness and participation in the modern political processes, awareness of the need of family planning and adoption of new family planning measures, treatment of diseases through utilization of modern resources like consultation with professional medical practitioners and thereby availing medicines, awareness of maternal and child care including availing modern immunization facilities from Government and its various agencies etc.

5.1 POLITICAL PARTICIPATION AND POLITICAL AWARENESS

Political Participation

Both the Bāuri beneficiaries and the non-beneficiaries of Hirāpur and Āmbadiha participate in modern political processes to a large extent (Table 5.1). But the level of their political awareness is poor (Table 5.2). This is described below:

Beneficiary Households

Table 5.1 reveals that the overall average participation rate in casting votes in the last election for M.P., M.L.A., *Sarpanch* and Ward members is 90.31 per cent in case of Hirāpur as against 91.56 per cent in Āmbadiha. Hence, the participation rate of the people of Āmbadiha in modern politics is found to be marginally higher than those of Hirāpur. But the difference, which is a little more than 1 per cent, is very slight. Hence, the 'z' value shows an insignificant variation at 5 per cent level of significance. This means that there is no significant difference in the voting behaviour between the people of Hirāpur and Āmbadiha.

Non-Beneficiary Households

As in the case of beneficiaries, the case of the non-beneficiaries is also almost the same. Where a little less than 90 per cent (88.44) of the non-beneficiaries of Hirāpur have cast their votes in the above elections, it is slightly higher than 90 per cent (90.31) in case of Āmbadiha. In this case the 'z' value also shows an insignificant variation at 5 per cent level of significance.

TABLE 5.1

Political Participation among beneficiary and non-beneficiary people

Level of elections	Beneficiary		Non-Beneficiary	
	Hirāpur (N=80)	Āmbadiha (N=80)	Hirāpur (N=80)	Āmbadiha (N=80)
(1)	(2)	(3)	(4)	(5)
Member of Parliament	64 (80.00)	69 (86.25)	71 (88.75)	70 (87.00)
M.L.A.	77 (96.25)	72 (90.00)	74 (92.50)	75 (93.75)
Sarpanch	74 (92.50)	76 (95.00)	69 (86.25)	72 (90.00)
Ward-Member	74 (92.50)	76 (95.00)	69 (86.25)	72 (90.00)
Overall average	72.25 (90.31)	73.25 (91.56)	70.75 (88.44)	72.25 (90.31)
Z	0.44		0.41	

Thus, from the above analysis it can be concluded that the rate of political participation of the people of Hirāpur and Āmbadiha in modern democratic processes is more or less the same, and there is no significant difference either between the beneficiaries or between the non-beneficiaries. However, fewer beneficiaries as well as non-beneficiaries of Hirāpur than those of Āmbadiha participate in such elections to cast their votes. This is because of the fact that the Bāuri people of Hirāpur, who are engaged in various business activities, one way or the other, in Bhubaneswar, leave the village early in the morning. They do not like to waste their time by standing in long queues to cast their votes at the local voting booths.

Level of Political Awareness

In order to find out the level of political awareness among the beneficiaries and non-beneficiaries, three specific types of questions were put to a sample group of Bāuris. The first type of question constituted names of five different political leaders, viz. the names of the Prime Minister, the Chief Minister, the Local M.P., the local M.L.A. and the local *Sarpanch*. The second type of question included the political parties which have formed the Union Government and that in their own state. The last type of question included the political symbol of two important and leading parties of the country. These parties are the Indian National Congress (INC) and the Janata Dal (JD).

Beneficiary Households

Table 5.2 portrays that a majority of these people, i.e. 70 per cent of Hirāpur are able to identify the symbol of INC and the JD followed by 44.25 per cent people who could correctly name different political leaders. But only about 30 per cent (29.38) could name the parties which formed the Union Government at the Centre and in the state.

The pattern of political participation among the beneficiaries of Āmbadiha, though, more or less same with those of Hirāpur, their level of awareness is much lower than the beneficiary people of the village Hirāpur. In this regard, as findings show, while there are 55 per cent people in this village who could rightly identify the political symbols of the said parties, only one-fifth (20%) could name the parties forming the Union Government and that in the state. Relating to the names of different political leaders, there are 36 per cent people on an average, who are able to name such persons. Hence, the overall average awareness level comes to 46.39 per cent in case of Hirāpur as against 36.53 per cent of Āmbadiha. In other words, it can be said that even if the level of political participation of the people of Hirāpur in modern elections is a little less than that of Āmbadiha, their political awareness of modern politics is more than the people of Āmbadiha. But when the 'z' value is calculated, the result shows an insignificant variation at 5 per cent level of significance on the level of political awareness between the people of Hirāpur and that of Āmbadiha.

Non-beneficiary Households

Among the non-beneficiary households of Hirāpur, a little less than 50 per cent (49.38) people know the political symbols of the INC and the JD parties, but 70 per cent of the people do not know the name of the parties which have formed the Union Government and that in the state. However, 30 per cent of people know the names of different political leaders. On the contrary when the case of the non-beneficiaries of Āmbadiha is taken into consideration, it is found that while 57.5 per cent people know the political symbols of the said parties, only 15 per cent people know the names of the parties which have formed the Union Government and the State Government, followed by 34 per cent, who are able to name different political leaders. Hence, the overall average awareness level comes to 41.11 per cent in case of Hirāpur as against 34.86 per cent of Āmbadiha. However, in this case the 'z' value also indicates an insignificant difference at 5 per cent level of significance.

TABLE 5.2

Political Awareness among beneficiary and non-beneficiary people

Areas of Political Awareness/Questions	Beneficiary		Non-Beneficiary	
	Hirāpur (N=80)	Āmbadiha (N=80)	Hirāpur (N=80)	Āmbadiha (N=80)
(1)	(2)	(3)	(4)	(5)
Name of the Prime Minister	45 (56.75)	37 (46.25)	42 (52.50)	40 (50.00)
Name of the Chief Minister	83 (41.25)	26 (32.50)	36 (45.00)	23 (28.25)
Name of the local MP	2 (2.50)	-	-	-
Name of the local MLA	46 (57.50)	30 (37.50)	39 (48.75)	30 (37.50)
Name of the local Sarpanch	47 (58.75)	50 (62.50)	52 (65.00)	42 (52.50)
Sub-Total	173-	143-	169-	135-
Overall average	34.6 (43.75)	28.6 (35.75)	33.8 (42.25)	27 (33.75)
Name of the Party formed Govt. at Centre	30 (37.5)	11 (13.75)	19 (23.75)	12 (15.00)
Name of the Party formed Govt. at State	17 (21.25)	21 (26.25)	29 (36.25)	12 (15.00)
Sub-Total	47-	32-	48-	24-
Overall average	23.5 (29.38)	16 (20.00)	24 (30.00)	12 (15.00)
Political symbol of Congress Party	51 (63.75)	43 (53.75)	43 (53.75)	45 (56.25)
Political symbol of Janta Party	61 (76.25)	45 (56.25)	36 (45.00)	47 (58.75)
Sub-Total	112-	88-	79-	92-
Overall average	56 (70.00)	44 (55.00)	39.5 (49.38)	46 (57.50)
Total	334-	263-	296-	251-
Overall average	37.6 (46.39)	29.22 (36.53)	32.89 (41.11)	27.89 (34.86)
Z	1.27		0.94	

Note: Figures in brackets represent %age.

5.2 FAMILY PLANNING, TREATMENT OF DISEASE AND HEALTH STATUS OF THE BĀURIS

Family Planning

In a diversified cultural base, the Indian rural people differ much from one another in adopting family planning measures. The Bāuris, being mainly rural-based, illiterate and agricultural labourers, have very little knowledge of different modern family planning methods and are also very hesitant to adopt any modern family planning measure. This is because they believe that children born to them are blessings of God in terms of becoming economic assets. As a result, one must not go against the will of God.

ATTITUDE OF MARRIED WOMEN TOWARDS FAMILY PLANNING

Beneficiary Households

A look at Table 5.3 shows that among the beneficiaries, out of 41 couples in Hirāpur, 18 or 43.90 per cent disapprove of any family planning measure, as against 40 out of 60 couples or 66.67 per cent in Āmbadiha. But while 9.76 per cent of couples in Hirāpur approve of family planning, in case of Āmbadiha it is 8.33 per cent.

TABLE 5.3

Attitude of married women towards family planning

Attitudes	Beneficiary		Non-Beneficiary	
	Hirāpur (N = 41)	Āmbadiha (N = 60)	Hirāpur (N = 40)	Āmbadiha (N = 63)
(1)	(2)	(3)	(4)	(5)
Husband disapproves but wife approves	2 (4.88)	2 (3.33)	-	1 (1.59)
Wife disapproves but husband approves	5 (12.20)	-	6 (15.0)	5 (7.94)
Both disapprove	18 (43.90)	40 (66.67)	20 (50.00)	41 (67.21)
Both spouses approve	4 (9.76)	5 (8.33)	2 (5.00)	4 (6.35)
Husband approves but wife unsure	7 (17.00)	4 (6.67)	7 (17.5)	6 (9.84)
Wife unsure but husband disapproves	4 (9.76)	9 (15.00)	5 (12.50)	6 (9.84)

Note: Figures in brackets represent %age.

Non-Beneficiary Households

As findings in the above table show, a majority of couples (50%) of Hirāpur disapprove adopting any family planning measure as against 67.21 per cent of Āmbadiha. On the contrary, only 5 per cent couples approve family planning in Hirāpur, and 6.35 per cent in Āmbadiha.

ADOPTION OF FAMILY PLANNING MEASURES

Beneficiary Households

Despite negative attitudes of a majority of couples in the beneficiary category of both the villages, as many as 18 or 43.90 per cent of couples in Hirāpur have adopted various family planning measures, against only 11 or 18.33 per'cent in Āmbadiha (Table 5.4). Further scrutiny of the same table reveals that, out of 41 couples of Hirāpur, only 1 couple (2.44%) has opted for vasectomy, followed by 2 (4.88%) couples using condoms. But 6 or 14.63 per cent couples have undergone various intra-uterine contraceptive devices (IUCD). The rest 3 or 7.32 per cent couples take oral pills for contraception Likewise, of 60 couples in Āmbadiha, 6 or 10 per cent have chosen tubectomy, while 3 or 5 per cent couples have favoured intra-uterine contraceptive devices (IUCD). They are followed by the rest 2 or 3.33 per cent who take oral pills in planning their family. In case of both the villages, among those who have adopted family planning measures, either the male spouse has taken the initiative and persuaded the female partner, or the female partners have voluntarily taken the risks of tubectomy, intra-uterine devices or of using oral pills. This is because they think that undergoing vasectomy means emasculation, resulting in loss of manly vigour and health. Since, the males are head of the family and the chief bread-winner of the family, they do not like to risk the health of their male partners.

Here the 'z' value shows a significant difference between the beneficiaries of Hirāpur and those of Āmbadiha at 5 per cent level of significance.

Non-Beneficiary Households

So far as the case of non-beneficiary couples is concerned, it is observed from the same table that of the total 40 couples in Hirāpur, 15 constituting 37.5 per cent, have taken to different family planning measures. Here in this case, not a single male partner has undergone vasectomy. No male spouse is found to use condom either. In the case of all the 15 couples who have adopted different family planning

TABLE 5.4

Adoption of family planning measures among beneficiary and non-beneficiary married couples

Beneficiary

Family Planning Methods	Hirāpur				Āmbadiha			
	< 20 (N=2)	21-35 (N=23)	36-45 (N=16)	Total (N=41)	<20 (N=17)	21-35 (N=32)	36-45 (N=11)	Total (N=60)
(1)	(2)	(3)	(4)	(5)	(6)	(7)	(8)	(9)
Vasectomy	-	-	1 (6.25)	1 (2.44)	-	-	-	-
Condom	-	2 (8.70)	-	2 (4.88)	-	-	-	-
Tubectomy	-	2 (8.70)	4 (25.00)	6 (14.67)	-	3 (9.38)	3 (27.27)	6 (10.00)
Intra-Uterine-Device (IUD)	-	4 (17.39)	2 (12.50)	6 (14.67)	-	3 (9.38)	-	3 (5.00)
Oral Pill	1 (50.00)	1 (4.35)	1 (6.25)	3 (7.32)	-	2 (6.25)	-	2 (3.33)
Total	1 (50.00)	9 (39.13)	8 (50.00)	18 (43.90)	-	8 (25.00)	3 (27.27)	11 (18.33)

Non-Beneficiary

Family Planning Methods	Hirāpur				Āmbadiha			
	< 20 (N=31)	21-35 (N=25)	36-45 (N=12)	Total (N=40)	< 20 (N=18)	21-35 (N=34)	36-45 (N=11)	Total (N=63)
(1)	(2)	(3)	(4)	(5)	(6)	(7)	(8)	(9)
Vasectomy	-	-	-	-	-	-	1 (9.09)	1 (1.59)
Condom	-	-	-	-	-	-	-	-
Tubectomy	-	1 (4.00)	4 (33.33)	5 (12.50)	-	2 (5.90)	1 (9.09)	3 (4.76)
Intra-Uterine-Device (IUD)	-	5 (20.00)	3 (25.00)	8 (20.00)	-	6 (17.65)	5 (45.45)	11 (17.46)
Oral Pill	-	2 (8.00)	-	2 (5.00)	1 (5.60)	2 (5.88)	-	3 (4.76)
Total	-	8 (32.00)	7 (58.33)	15 (37.50)	1 (5.60)	10 (29.41)	7 (63.64)	17 (26.98)

Note: Figures in brackets represent %age.

measures, the initiative and burden of adoption lies with the female partners. About 12.5 per cent have undergone tubectomy, followed by 20 per cent couples who have accepted intra-uterine devices and 5 per cent use oral pills. On the contrary of the 63 couples in Āmbadiha, altogether 17 couples constituting 26.98 per cent have adopted family planning. Interestingly, here one male partner is found to have undergone vasectomy, and in the rest 16 cases the burden lies with the wives. Here, as in Hirāpur, the largest percentage (17.46) of female partners have taken to intra-uterine contraceptive devices (IUCD), followed by 4.76 per cent female partners who have undergone tubectomy, and the same percentage of female partners use oral pills.

It suggests that the people of Hirāpur are more conscious of family planning as a result of which more couples of this village have adopted family planning methods than their counterparts in Āmbadiha. But the 'z' value shows an insignificant variation at 5 per cent level of significance.

HEALTH STATUS AND TREATMENT OF DISEASES

The health status of the Bāuri people has been highlighted in Table 5.5. This table illustrates the minor and major diseases (as per the opinion of the Bāuri people) from which they have suffered during the survey year. The minor diseases include common headache, infestation of hookworm, itching, scabies and sores. The diseases which are considered as major include bronchitis, colic, diarrhoea, earache, jaundice, malaria, paralysis, piles, toothache, tuberculosis and viral or common fever.

Beneficiary Households

From the said table it may be seen that, of the total 212 people of Hirāpur as many as 43 persons accounting for 20.28 per cent have suffered from various minor diseases as against 65 persons or 27.08 per cent of the total people of 240 in Āmbadiha. In both these villages, scabies is found to be the most widely prevalent of minor diseases which afflicted 8.49 per cent of people of Hirāpur and 12.92 per cent of Āmbadiha.

Similarly, of the total population of Hirāpur and Āmbadiha, 15.57 and 11.25 per cent respectively have suffered from various major diseases, but in the case of both the villages the incidence of viral or common fever is found to be very high as compared with other ailments. It is 6.13 per cent in Hirāpur as against 6.67 per cent in Āmbadiha.

TABLE 5.5

General diseases occurred among the beneficiary and non-beneficiary

Type of disease	Disease	Beneficiary		Non-beneficiary	
		Hirāpur (N=212)	Āmbadiha (N=240)	Hirāpur (N=232)	Āmbadiha (N=320)
(1)	(2)	(3)	(4)	(5)	(6)
Minor	Common Headache	3 (3.95) (1.42)	-	3 (3.57) (1.29)	-
	Hook-worm	2 (2.63) (0.94)	6 (6.57) (2.50)	-	6 (7.14) (1.88)
	Itching	7 (9.21) (3.30)	13 (14.13) (5.42)	11 (13.10) (4.74)	16 (19.05) (5.0)
	Scabbies	18 (23.68) (8.49)	31 (33.70) (12.92)	20 (23.81) (8.62)	20 (23.81) (6.25)
	Wounds	13 (17.11) (6.17)	15 (16.30) (6.25)	23 (23.81) (8.62)	13 (15.48) (4.06)
	Sub-total	43 (56.58) (20.28)	65 (70.65) (27.08)	57 (67.86) (24.57)	55 (65.48) (17.19)
Major	Bronchitis	-	2 (2.17) (0.83)	-	-
	Collic	1 (1.32) (0.47)	-	-	-
	Diarrhoea	6 (7.89) (2.83)	6 (6.52) (2.5)	3 (3.57) (1.29)	8 (9.52) (2.5)
	Earache	2 (2.63) (0.94)	-	2 (2.38) (0.86)	-
	Jaundice	1 (1.32) (0.47)	-	-	-
	Malaria	-	-	-	3 (3.57) (0.94)
	Paralysis	-	-	1 (1.19) (0.43)	-
	Piles	2 (2.67) (0.94)	-	1 (1.19) (0.43)	-
	Toothache	8 (10.53) (3.71)	3 (3.26) (1.25)	2 (2.38) (0.86)	1 (1.19) (0.31)
	Tuberculosis	-	-	-	2 (2.36) (0.63)
	Viral fever	13 (17.11) (6.13)	16 (17.39) (6.67)	18 (21.43) (7.76)	15 (17.86) (4.69)
	Sub-total	33 (43.42) (15.57)	27 (29.35) (11.25)	27 (32.14) (11.64)	29 (34.52) (9.06)
	Total	76 (100.00) (35.85)	92 (100.00) (38.33)	84 (100.00) (36.21)	84 (100.00) (26.75)
	Z	0.44		2.50	

Note: Figures in brackets represents %age.

A look at the total figures shows that while 76 or 35.85 per cent people of Hirāpur have suffered from various minor ailments and major diseases, in Āmbadiha it is 92 or 38.33 per cent. So, the 'z' value does not indicate any significant difference at 5 per cent level of significance.

Non-Beneficiary

So far as the non-beneficiaries are concerned, from the same table, it can be seen that, of 332 persons in Hirāpur, 57 persons accounting for 24.57 per cent have suffered from various minor ailments against 55 out of 320 or 17.19 per cent in Āmbadiha. Like the beneficiaries in both the study villages, among the non-beneficiaries there is also a large number of people who suffered from scabies.

In Hirāpur, 27 persons or 11.64 per cent suffered from various major diseases, as against 29 or 9.06 per cent in Āmbadiha.

In case of both the villages, a fair number of people suffered from viral or common fever, which comes to 7.76 and 4.69 per cent in the case of Hirāpur and Āmbadiha respectively. When the total figures for both the villages are compared, it shows that while in Hirāpur 84 or 36.21 per cent people have suffered from various minor and major diseases, in Āmbadiha it is 84 or 26.25 per cent. So, in this case the 'z' value is found significant at 5 per cent level of significance.

Treatment of Diseases

The Bāuri do not have their own traditional healers for curing ailments. As a result a sizable number of people consult the local medicine-men who normally belong to the backward castes. Apart from this, they also consult the local quacks. They also very often visit the local public health centres or hospitals to benefit from modern medical facilities. However, because of their poverty and limited time during the day, i.e. during working hours, either they take the advice of the local medicine-men or the local quacks or the registered medical practitioners or both these two groups of consultants depending upon their suitability and the availability of time. They also have strong faith in the local traditional healers but most often, they consult the local quacks when they are not cured with the medicine prescribed by such persons. After they fail to be cured with the medicine of the local quacks, they consult the registered medical practitioners available at the local public health centres or hospitals. However, there are some people who do not believe in the prescription of the traditional medicine-men at all. Such people take the help of the registered medical practitioners. Still some are compelled to consult the local medicine-men because of their poverty. In this context the data available in Table 5.6 represent the following type of consultations for treatment of diseases:

1. those who consulted the local medicine-men/traditional healers only;
2. those who consulted the local quacks only;
3. those who consulted both the local medicine-men and the quacks;
4. those who consulted the local medicine-men, quacks and the registered medical practitioners or doctors; and
5. those who consulted the doctors available at the local PHCs or hospitals or in private clinics.

The 'z' value is calculated on the data presented in the code 5, i.e. those who have consulted only the registered medical practitioners or doctors.

TABLE 5.6

Type of treatment of disease

Type of treatment	Beneficiary		Non-beneficiary	
	Hirāpur (N=76)	Āmbadiha (N=92)	Hirāpur (N=84)	Āmbadiha (N=84)
(1)	(2)	(3)	(4)	(5)
Only consulted the local medicineman/ traditional healer	9 (11.84)	15 (16.30)	5 (5.95)	6 (7.17)
Only consulted the local quacks	8 (10.53)	17 (18.48)	15 (17.86)	23 (27.38)
Consulted both the local medicinemen and quacks	11 (14.47)	18 (19.57)	17 (20.24)	22 (26.19)
Consulted the local medicinemen, quack and the doctors	12 (15.79)	17 (18.48)	6 (7.14)	11 (13.10)
Only consulted the doctors	36 (47.37)	25 (27.27)	41 (48.81)	22 (26.19)

Note: Figures in brackets represent %age.

Beneficiary Households

Of 76 patients, who have suffered from various diseases in Hirāpur, 36 or 47.37 per cent have consulted the doctors available at the local PHCs or hospitals or in private clinics as against 25 or 27.17

per cent of the total number of 92 patients in Āmbadiha. Of the rest, while there are 9 or 11.84 per cent patients in the former village who have consulted only the local traditional medicine-men, 16.30 per cent or 15 patients have done so in Āmbadiha. Hence, there is a big gap between the patients of Hirāpur and Āmbadiha who have consulted registered medical practitioners available at the local PHCs, hospitals or private clinics. As a result the 'z' value is found to be significant at 5 per cent level of significance.

Non-Beneficiary

There is a total number of 84 beneficiary patients in the village Hirāpur. Of these, a total number of 41 or 48.81 per cent patients have taken the consultancy of registered medical practitioners as against 22 or 26.19 per cent patients of the total number of 84 patients of the village Āmbadiha. There are about 6 per cent (5.95) patients in the former village who have gone to take the help of the traditional medicine-men, but it is 7.14 per cent in case of the village Āmbadiha. Hence, as the gap is 22.62 per cent between the patient of the former and the latter village who have only taken the help of the registered medical practitioners, the 'z' value shows a significant difference at 5 per cent level of significance.

EXPECTANT MOTHERS, NEW-BORN BABIES AND IMMUNIZATION PROCESS

Nature of Delivery of Offsprings

Taking care of expectant mothers and new-born babies, and immunizing both, is an important aspect in bringing up a healthy family. But the Bāuris do not give this much importance. They follow their own age-old traditional modes of immunization and treatment of expectant mothers and the new-born babies. Even now, most of them do not prefer to have expectant mothers medically checked up, and prefer to have the babies delivered at their own home with the help of the local traditional midwives rather than in the local PHC or hospital. It happens because of their illiteracy, superstitious beliefs, ignorance of modern medical facilities and also because of their poor economic condition.

Beneficiary Households

In the above context when one looks at Table 5.7, it is manifested that amongst the beneficiaries of Hirāpur, there are 21 living children in the age group of 0-5 years. Of these, 38.1 per cent or 8 were born at home, whereas in Āmbadiha as many as 60 per cent or 21 babies were born at home. On the contrary, when 47.62 per cent or 10 babies of the former village were born at the local PHCs or hospitals, 34.29 per cent or 12 babies were so born in Āmbadiha. Hence, the 'z' value, calculated on the related data, shows an insignificant difference at 5 per cent level of significance.

TABLE 5.7

Place of Delivery of Children

Place of Delivery	Beneficiary		Non-beneficiary	
	Hirāpur (N=21)	Āmbadiha (N=35)	Hirāpur (N=29)	Āmbadiha (N=52)
(1)	(2)	(3)	(4)	(5)
At home	8 (38.1)	21 (60.00)	14 (48.28)	35 (61.40)
On the way to the local PHC/Hospital	3 (14.29)	2 (5.71)	2 (6.9)	3 (5.26)
At local PHC/ Hospital	10 (47.62)	12 (34.29)	13 (44.83)	19 (33.33)
Z	1.0		1.08	

Note: (i) N includes the children in the age group of 0-5.
(ii) Z value is calculated out of the data relating to the deliveries taken place at local PHCs or Hospitals.
(iii) Figures in brackets represent %age.

Non-Beneficiary Households

Like the beneficiaries, the case of the non-beneficiaries is also more or less same. Hence, in this case 48.28 per cent or 14 babies of Hirāpur as against 61.40 per cent or 35 babies of Āmbadiha were born at home. And while there are 44.83 per cent or 13 cases in Hirāpur who were born at the local PHC or hospital, 33.33 per cent or 19 babies were born so in Āmbadiha. The rest babies were born on the road while the expectant mothers were on their way to the local PHCs or hospitals to deliver. The 'z' value shows an insignificant variation at 5 per cent level of significance.

IMMUNIZATION OF EXPECTANT MOTHERS

Beneficiary Households

For pregnant women, two doses of tetanus vaccine viz., tetanus-I and tetanus-II are given at a month's interval, any time during pregnancy, but before the beginning of the ninth month of conception. Apart from this, expectant mothers are also required to take a full course of iron supplement for the benefit of both themselves and the growing foetus. But it is observed that the Bāuri people are not so conscious about this. From the data available in Table 5.8, it is seen that an overall average of 50 per cent expectant mothers of Hirāpur have taken the vaccine along with the full course of iron supplement as against only 29.19 per cent of Āmbadiha. Still the 'z' value is found to be insignificant at 5 per cent level of significance.

TABLE 5.8

Immunization of Expectant Mothers

Immunity	Beneficiary		Non-beneficiary	
	Hirāpur (N=12)	Āmbadiha (N=16)	Hirāpur (N=11)	Āmbadiha (N=24)
(1)	(2)	(3)	(4)	(5)
Titanus I	9 (75.00)	7 (43.75)	7 (63.64)	9 (37.50)
Titanus II	6 (50.00)	6 (37.50)	7 (63.64)	8 (33.33)
Full course of iron tablets	3 (25.00)	1 (6.25)	2 (18.18)	-
Overall	6 (50.00)	4.67 (29.19)	5.33 (48.46)	5.66 (23.58)
Z	1.15		1.38	

Note: (i) N includes expectant mothers during last years.
(ii) Figures in brackets represent %age.

Non-Beneficiary Households

Like the expectant mothers of the beneficiary households, the case of the expectant mothers of non-beneficiary household is also almost same. When there are 48.46 per cent expectant mothers on an average in the village Hirāpur who have taken the above vaccine along with the full course of iron tablets, only 23.58 per cent in case of Āmbadiha have done so. In this case the 'z' value is also found to be insignificant at 5 per cent level of significance.

IMMUNIZATION OF NEWLY BORN BABIES

Beneficiary Households

For a newly born baby, the first year immunization doses include BCG, DPT-I, DPT-II, Polio-I, Polio-II, Polio-III, one vaccine against measles and a course of vitamin-A. The second year immunization doses include a booster dose of each of polio and DPT viz. DPT-B, Polio-B and Vitamin-A. The third year immunization constitutes doses of vitamins A_3, A_4, and A_5.

In the above context, Table 5.9 reveals that of 15 cases in Hirāpur, 5 or 33.33 per cent babies have been fully immunized. They are followed by the same percentage babies who are partly immunized. But in Āmbadiha 5 babies or 21.74 per cent are fully immunized, followed by 7 or 30.43 per cent of 23 cases who are partly immunized. The rest 5 or 33 per cent babies of Hirāpur, as against 11 or 47.87 per cent of Āmbadiha have not been immunized. Hence, the 'z' value calculated on the data pertaining to the babies who are fully immunized shows a significant difference at 5 per cent level of significance.

Non-Beneficiary

Where the immunization of the newly born babies of the non-beneficiary households is concerned, the same table shows that of 18 cases in Hirāpur, 44.44 per cent or 8 have been fully immunized, whereas in Āmbadiha 38.46 per cent of 15 or the total of 39 cases are fully immunized. Only 16.33 per cent or 3 babies in case of Hirāpur have been partially immunized, as against 20.51 per cent or 8 babies of Āmbadiha. The rest 16.67 per cent or 6 babies of Hirāpur as against 41.03 per cent or 16 babies or Āmbadiha are found not to have been immunized. In this case the 'z' value also shows an insignificant variation at 5 per cent level of significance.

5.3 RITUAL BELIEF PATTERN AND PRACTICES: PERSISTENCE AND CHANGE

As discussed in the introductory chapter, the Bāuris connect their origin with Hindu mythology, and believe in a wide range of Gods, spirits, demi-gods supernatural beings and propitiate them following elaborate magico-religious and shamanistic practices. They believe that any mishap including natural calamity, drought, ill-health, poverty, wealth etc. which befall them are because of such elements. Some of these elements, they believe, are malevolent and some benevolent in nature. The benevolent spirits or deities have to be propitiated with prayers, fasts and observances, and offerings; whereas the malevolent ones have to be controlled, averted by spells, threats and other means of black magic. Some of the benevolent ones require offerings while some others require only casual offerings, which may include animal or bird sacrifices.

There are some Bāuris in Hirāpur, as also in Āmbadiha who do not believe in these elements. On the contrary there are others who have developed strong faith in the Hindu deities, and hence have placed some Hindu idols in their pantheon and also observe many Hindu

TABLE 5.9

Immunization of newly born babies among beneficiary and non-beneficiary

Beneficiary

Year of Immunization	Hirāpur				Āmbadiha			
	N	P1	F1	N1	N	P1	F1	N1
(1)	(2)	(3)	(4)	(5)	(6)	(7)	(8)	(9)
1st year Immunization doses (B.C.G, DPT-I, DPT-II, DPT-III, Polio-I, Polio-II, Polio-III, Measles and Vitamin A)	6 (100.00)	3 (50.00)	1 (16.67)	2 (33.33)	13 (100.00)	4 (30.72)	2 (15.00)	7 (53.85)
2nd year Immunization doses (DPT-B, Polio-B and Vitamin A-5)	4 (100.00)	1 (25.00)	2 (50.00)	1 (25.00)	6 (100.00)	2 (33.33)	3 (50.00)	1 (16.67)
3rd year Immunization doses (Vitamin A-3, Vitamin A-4 and Vitamin A-5)	5 (100.00)	1 (20.00)	2 (40.00)	2 (40.00)	4 (100.00)	1 (25.00)	-	3 (75.00)
Total	15 (100.00)	5 (33.33)	5 (33.33)	5 (33.33)	23 (100.00)	7 (30.47)	5 (21.74)	11 (47.89)
Z								

(contd.)

Non-Beneficiaries

Year of Immunization	Hirāpur				Āmbadiha			
	N	P1	F1	N1	N	P1	F1	N1
(1)	(2)	(3)	(4)	(5)	(6)	(7)	(8)	(9)
1st year Immunization doses (B.C.G, DPT-I, DPT-II, DPT-III, Polio-I, Polio-II, Polio-III, Measles and Vitamin A)	7 (100.00)	1 (14.29)	4 (57.14)	2 (28.57)	18 (100.00)	4 (22.23)	6 (33.33)	8 (44.44)
2nd year Immunization doses (DPT-B, Polio-B and Vitamin A-5)	6 (100.00)	3 (50.00)	2 (33.33)	1 (16.67)	9 (100.00)	2 (22.22)	4 (44.44)	3 (33.33)
3rd year Immunization doses (Vitamin A-3, Vitamin A-4 and Vitamin A-5	5 (100.00)	-	2 (40.00)	3 (60.00)	12 (100.00)	2 (16.67)	5 (41.67)	5 (41.67)
Total	18 (100.00)	3 (16.33)	8 (44.44)	6 (16.67)	39 (100.00)	8 (20.51)	15 (38.46)	16 (41.03)
Z								

Note: (i) N includes children with 3 years of age.

(ii) P1 = Partly Immunized, F1 = Fully Immunized, N1 = Not Immunized

(iii) Z is calculated out of the data relating to children who are fully immunized.

(iv) Figures in brackets represent %age.

fairs and festivals. The nature and type of benevolent and malevolent deities and spirits are discussed below, based on which the changing attitude and the belief pattern of the Bāuris in the two study villages are discussed.

The benevolent deities or spirits worshipped by the Bāuri people are generally of three types such as (i) household deities (ii) village or communal deities and (iii) natural deities. The malevolent deities or supernatural beings include different types of ghosts like *Chandi, Khandiā Bhuta* and *preta.*

BENEVOLENT DEITIES

(i) Household Deities

The household deities include *Esāna, Chaurā, Trināth* and *Gomātā.*

(a) Esānā

This is an earthen platform daubed with cow dung at the *aisānya* (north-east) corner of the kitchen where the souls or the spirit of the ancestors are believed to reside. These spirits are propitiated on festive occasions and rituals. The annual death anniversary rite of the recent forefathers called *Srāddha* is also performed here and at this place the sacramental food is offered to the ancestral spirits. This place is also used for keeping the daily cooked food prepared for the household members.

(b) Chaurā

This is a non-traditional deity for the Bāuris. The mythological deity *Brundabati* is worshipped in the form of a holy plant called *Tulasi* (*basil plant*), which has great medicinal value. This plant is planted in a sacred pot and is placed on a pedestal called *Chaurā,* in front of the main entrance or in the courtyard of the house. In the caste Hindu households, daily-worshipping of this deity is a very common feature. In such households, generally the women water the plant and worship the deity with some offerings which may be sweet or fruits, daily after bath early in the morning. At evening, shortly after sunset, *sanja,* a lighted wick is offered. But, as planting *Tulasi* and worshipping of this deity among the Bāuris in both the study villages is a new trend, most of them do not follow the Hindu ways of propitiation. They just water the plant depending upon their suitability, even without taking bath. Neither material offerings are made nor the lighted wick (*sanja*) is offered to the deity as is done by the caste

Hindu people. They water the plant not out of reverence but as the water is required by the plant for its survival.

(c) Trinath Melā

Propitiating the three supreme deities, *Brahma*, the creator; *Vishnu*, the preserver; and *Maheswar*, the destroyer, is a new trend among the Bāuris. The three deities are represented by three areca-nuts kept on three betel leaves. When these three deities are worshipped together, it is called *Trināth mela*. Generally the mela is held in the evening in the midst of a large gathering of family members, relations, friends, well-wishers and even neighbours. A holy book meant for propitiating *Trinath* is read out by the traditional priest or by any one who is able to do so. After the book is read, material offerings are made and the sacred smoke of *Ganjā* is passed round among the male members and the betel leaves are distributed among the devotees as *prasad*. These three deities are kept in the form of idols or photographs and worshipped individually by the households.

(d) Gomātā

Cows are worshipped by caste Hindus on the day of *Gamhā Purnimā*. As the Bāuris were all landless agricultural labourers, they did not have any cattle, and hence, never observed this Hindu festival. But as mentioned in the earlier chapter, many of them now own cattle and so they imitate the rituals of this festival from the caste Hindus. As among the caste Hindus, the killing of a cow is equated with that of killing a *Brāhman*, and any one having done so has to expiate by performing elaborate rite. So also among the Bāuris who follow this purificatory rite in case they unwittingly cause the death of a cow.

(ii) Village Communal Deity

The Bāuris of Hirāpur believe in five different deities, namely *Sabākhāi, Duladei, Geladei, Kāluni* and *Chhoti*. These five goddesses are considered as the daughters of the mother goddess *Mahāmāyee*, the chief deity of *Chousathi-Yogini* temple, managed by caste Hindus of Hirāpur. All the five sister-deities reside together in a temple.

It is generally believed that when the deities are not satisfied, they may cause diarrhoea, fever, and even epidemic etc. among the villagers, causing large-scale deaths. They may also cause devastating floods, storms and other natural calamities. In such cases the villagers arrange to sacrifice animals like goats or sheep and birds like cocks to appease the deity. These sacrifices are arranged with the *Kālasi-*

shaman, who sits in a trance to know the cause of her dissatisfaction and prescribes remedies accordingly.

The village deities are worshipped daily by a man belonging to the family of the shaman-priests.

(iii) Natural Deities

The natural deities include mother-earth, sun, moon and water. Mother earth is known as *Thāna,* sun as *Surya Debata,* moon as *Janha* and water as *Gangāmatā. Thana* is worshipped by the *Pada-Beherā* (village head) on particular occasions like birth and marriage ceremonies. It is generally believed that unless the deity is contented with due propitiation, a child lacks physical growth. He may suffer from various deadly diseases and eventually die. To propitiate this deity one is to inform her about the newcomer, whom she may bear on her lap. The priest prays to the deity in the following words, "Oh earth goddess, a new member has come; please look after him/her, offer your lap for the baby, do not let the baby suffer from any disease". In a similar vein when a new bride comes into the village, the deity is also approached to recognise the newcomer as her child or *Santāna.* This worship is known as *Thāna-Pujā.*

Propitiation of water goddess is as important as the propitiation of mother-earth. It is believed that unless she is propitiated, the soul of the dead may roam around and cause mishaps or misfortunes.

Malevolent Deities

The Bāuri people believe in two types of she-ghosts such as (i) *Entudi Chandi* and (ii) *Bāta Chandi.*

(i) Entudi Chandi

Entudi Chandi is believed to reside on the outskirts of the village. She always tries to cause harm to the new-born babies. As a result, soon after the birth of a child, some mustard seeds are scattered around the outer courtyard of the household. The *Chandi* tries to enter the *entudisāla* (the room where the baby is born and confined for 12 or 21 days). But as she is also scared of iron, some pieces of iron are kept at different places of the *entudisāla.* Generally, an iron plate is kept at the main entrance of the room to prevent the *Chandi* from entering it. A sickle or *kohl* container is ordinarily placed below the mat on which the baby sleeps. Immediately after the birth, both the mother and child use talisman (*Deunriāh*) to prevent entry of the *chandi* into the body of the baby. Thus, to keep the *Chandi* away from the baby and the mother, a four-stage preventive measure is adopted, viz. scattering of mustard seeds around the outer courtyard, which prevents her entry into the outer boundary, secondly keeping an iron piece at the entrance of the room means to check the entry of the *chandi* into the room in which the baby sleeps, thirdly keeping a sickle or kohl container under the bedding of the baby prevents the *chandi* from approaching the bed of the baby, and fourthly using talisman prevents the *chandi* from entering the body of the baby and to do any harm.

(ii) Bāta Chandi

Bāta Chandi is that evil spirit which resides in any dense tree located on the outskirts of the village. She has to be propitiated with incense sticks and lighted wicks on the day of *Panā Sankrānti*. Otherwise she enters into the body of the girls and causes untold misery.

(iii) Khandia Bhuta

When an unmarried man dies he is believed to become a ghost called *Khandiābhuta*. He always feels thirsty but the popular belief holds that whenever he goes to any water body, it suddenly dries up and the anger of the *khandiābhuta* increases.

(iv) Preta

Pretas are the spirits of the forefathers. Normally, they do not cause any harm unless annual ancestral worship (*Srāddha*) is improperly done.

ATTITUDES TOWARDS ENTERING CASTE HINDU TEMPLES AND WORSHIPPING HINDU DEITIES

In the introductory chapter, it has been discussed that the Bāuris were suppressed and deprived in religious matters. They were neither allowed to enter caste Hindu temples nor allowed to worship caste Hindu deities. They were not even allowed to read Hindu religious scriptures. On the other hand, most of the Bāuris thought that these set practices have been set up by God and they must not deviate from this set practice in order to avoid misfortunes and evil effects of God. But with the passage of time, many Bāuris have become aware and go against these practices, and try to break the restrictions made by the caste Hindus. In this context when one looks at Tables 5.10, 5.11, 5.12, 5.13 and 5.14 some interesting facts come to light.

TABLE 5.10

Do you think that there should be any restriction to enter into the caste Hindu temples?

Villages	Category of Population			
	Total HHs	Beneficiary	Total HHs	Non-Beneficiary
(1)	(2)	(3)	(4)	(5)
Hirāpur	55 (100.00)	14 (25.45)	53 (100.00)	13 (24.53)
Āmbadiha	50 (100.00)	6 (12.00)	69 (100.00)	6 (8.70)
Z	1.79		1.91	

Note: Figures in brackets represent %age.

TABLE 5.11

Number of households of which at least one member has entered into a caste Hindu temple

Villages	Category of Population			
	Total HHs	Beneficiary	Total HHs	Non-Beneficiary
(1)	(2)	(3)	(4)	(5)
Hirāpur	55 (100.00)	22 (40.00)	53 (100.00)	18 (33.96)
Āmbadiha	50 (100.00)	9 (18.00)	69 (100.00)	11 (15.94)
Z	2.64		2.78	

Note: Figures in brackets represent %age.

TABLE 5.12

Households who have purchased idols of Hindu deitiies

Villages	Category of Population			
	Total HHs	Beneficiary	Total HHs	Non-Beneficiary
(1)	(2)	(3)	(4)	(5)
Hirāpur	55 (100.00)	25 (45.45)	53 (100.00)	20 (37.73)
Āmbadiha	50 (100.00)	4 (8.00)	69 (100.00)	6 (8.7)
Z	4.86		3.78	

Note: Figures in brackets represent %age.

TABLE 5.13

Households worshipping basil plant at their courtyards

Villages		Category of Population			
		Total HHs	Beneficiary	Total HHs	Non-Beneficiary
(1)	(2)	(3)	(4)	(5)	
Hirāpur		55 (100.00)	17 (21.82)	53 (100.00)	14 (26.42)
Āmbadiha		50 (100.00)	3 (6.00)	69 (100.00)	6 (8.70)
Z		3.52		3.52	

Note: Figures in brackets represent %age.

TABLE 5.14

Households adopting caste Hindu festivals

Festive occasions	Beneficiary		Non-Beneficiary	
	Hirāpur (N=55)	Āmbadiha (N=50)	Hirāpur (N=53)	Āmbadiha (N=69)
(1)	(2)	(3)	(4)	(5)
Badaosā	8 (14.55)	-	4 (7.55)	-
Gamhā Purnimā	26 (47.27)	17 (34.00)	12 (22.64)	19 (27.54)
Pimpeyi Amābashyā	55 (100.00)	50 (100.00)	53 (100.00)	69 (100.00)
Raja	17 (30.91)	2 (4.00)	6 (11.32)	3 (4.35)
Sankrānti	3 (5.45)	-	2 (3.77)	-
Sudasābrata	55 (100.00)	50 (100.00)	53 (100.00)	69 (100.00)
Overall	29 (52.73)	19.83 (39.66)	21.67 (40.89)	26.67 (38.58)
Z	1.34		0.22	

Note: Figures in brackets represent %age.

Beneficiary Households

Table 5.10 clearly shows that one-fourth (25.48%) of the households of Hirāpur, as against only about one-eighth (12%) of Āmbadiha think that there should not be any restriction to enter into caste Hindu temples. But while there are about 40 per cent households in Hirāpur, of which at least one member has entered into a caste Hindu temple not belonging to one's own village, merely 18 per cent have done so in Āmbadiha (Table 5.11). But in all cases they have done so without the knowledge of the caste Hindu people. In case of both villages, not a single Bāuri has yet been able to enter into the village caste Hindu temple, i.e. the temple of goddess *Mahamayee* in Hirāpur and the temple of Lord *Siva* in Āmbadiha. Likewise, it is interesting to note that there are 25 households accounting for 45.45 per cent of the total 55 households of Hirāpur, as against only 4 or 8 per cent of the 50 households in Āmbadiha, who have purchased various idols of Hindu deities (Table 5.12). The number of households which have planted *tulasi* (basil plant) is 17 or 21.82 per cent in Hirāpur and 3 or 6 per cent in Āmbadiha (Table 5.13). But even though these religious practices are borrowed from the local caste Hindus, the set practices and the rites associated with these deities are not rigidly observed. Most of the idols are just hung on the walls as decorative items. Even though the sacred basil plant is planted in the courtyards, they do not offer prayers or water regularly, as is done by the caste Hindus. They water the plants now and then depending upon the need of the plant and their suitability.

Non-beneficiary households

Among the non-beneficiary households more or less the same picture is found. It can be seen from Table 5.10 that 13 or 24.53 per cent household heads of Hirāpur, as against 6 or 8.7 per cent of Āmbadiha, think that there should not be any restriction for the Bāuris to enter caste Hindu temples. However, of a total of 18 or 33.45 per cent households of Hirāpur and 11 or 15.94 per cent of Āmbadiha, at least one member has entered at least one caste Hindu temple, without the knowledge of local caste Hindu people (Table 5.11). Likewise, 20 or 37.73 per cent households of Hirāpur as against 6 or 8.7 per cent of Āmbadiha have kept different idols of Hindu deities (Table 5.12). Similarly while there are 14 or 26.42 per cent households in Hirāpur which have planted basil plant in their courtyards, 6 or 8.7 per cent have done so in Āmbadiha (Table 5.13).

OBSERVANCE OF HINDU FESTIVALS

Beneficiary Households

The Bāuris have not only adopted worshipping of caste Hindu deities but have also started observing of various festive occasions and attending fairs associated with these of the caste Hindu people. So far, the Bāuris of Hirāpur have adopted such festivals, viz. *Badaosā, Gamhā Purnimā, Pimpei Amābāsyā, Raja, Sankrānti* and *Sudasābrata.* The Bāuris of Āmbadiha have adopted 4 of these occasions excluding *Badaosā* and *Sankrānti.* But they just try to imitate the elaborate procedures and rites of each of these ceremonies from the local caste Hindus and try to observe it as exactly as the caste Hindu people observe, but fail to do so due to various factors, the main being the economic constraints.

Table 5.14 shows that all the households of both the villages observe *Pimpeyi Ambāsayā* and *Sudasābrata.* But while there are 8 or 14.85 per cent and 3 or 5.45 per cent households in Hirāpur which observe *Badaosā* and the monthly *Sankrānti,* respectively, there is nobody in Āmbadiha doing so. However, while there are 22 or 47.27 per cent and 17 or 30.91 per cent households in Hirāpur which observe *Gamhāpurnimā* and *Raja* respectively, 17 or 34 per cent and 2 or 4 per cent do so in Āmbadiha. On the whole it may be said that, while there are 29 or 52.73 per cent households in Hirāpur which have adopted various caste Hindu festive occasions, in Āmbadiha 20 or 39.66 per cent households have done so.

Non-Beneficiary Households

Like the beneficiary households, all the non-beneficiary households of both the villages also observe *Pimpeyi Amābāsyā* and *Sudasābrata.* But while there are 4 or 7.55 per cent and 2 or 3.77 per cent households in Hirāpur who observe *Badaosā* and monthly *Sankrānti,* no one in Āmbadiha observes these two occasions. But *Gamhā Purnima* is observed by 12 or 22.64 per cent households in Hirāpur and 19 or 27.54 per cent households in Āmbadiha. This festival is more popular in Āmbadiha because there are more cattle-owners, who celebrate this occasion dedicated to cattle. But *Raja* is observed by 6 or 11.32 per cent of households in Hirāpur and by 3 or 4.35 per cent in Āmbadiha. While there are 21.67 or 40.89 per cent of households in Hirāpur who have adopted these occasions of the local caste Hindu people, it is 27 or 38.58 per cent households in Āmbadiha.

Chapter VI

QUALITY OF LIFE

Quality of life refers to various multi-dimensional factors relating to basic necessities and amenities of life. Some of the important factors are settlement locality and housing facility, economic condition and food habit, education, health services and hygienic behaviour, political participation in modern democratic processes, ability for self management etc. Factors like economic condition, political participation in democratic process among the Bāuris have been discussed in earlier chapters. Rest of the factors are discussed below:

6.1 SETTLEMENT AND HOUSE PATTERN

Since time immemorial the Bāuris have been deprived of settling inside the caste Hindu villages. Hence, all Bāuri hamlets in both the study villages are found segregated and are located on the outskirts.

Generally, the Bāuri hamlets are surrounded by paddy fields, and hence are nucleated in nature. As a result of this, almost all the Bāuri hamlets are disconnected from the main roads of the caste Hindu villages. Not a single Bāuri hamlet in either of the study villages is approachable by jeep, either in rainy on the dry season. During rainy season, their hamlets are cut off from the main caste Hindu villages and it becomes very difficult and inconvenient to approach their hamlets on foot.

In case of both the study villages, straight streets have been provided in between two parallel rows of linear clusters or assemblages of caste Hindu houses. But the settlement pattern of the Bāuri people does not follow any particular order.

In case of both the study villages more than 50 per cent Bāuri houses are nucleated. Around 33 per cent of houses of Hirāpur are found to be clustered having a continuous roof and central courtyard. This type of houses account for little more than 20 per cent in case of Āmbadiha. The rest of the houses in the above two villages are arranged in linear clusters having a continuous roof, but without a central courtyard.

House Pattern

Poor housing facility leads to ill health of the family members. When the house is not provided with basic hygienic requirements like window, proper height of the roof, required plinth area etc., it affects the health of the inmates.

The houses of the Bāuris can be categorised into two groups, such as traditional and modern. The traditional houses are normally made of wattle and clay. The houses are mostly provided with single rooms and do not possess any window for ventilation. It is primarily because of two important reasons. The first being that these people were not allowed to have windows, as having windows was considered a status symbol among local caste Hindus, and the second factor is that this type of houses help them to keep their rooms warm during winter.

Most of the Bāuri houses lack veranda facility at the front. But in some cases a house that possesses a front veranda does not provide enough space to seat seven for two persons. On an average, its height from the ground remains within a foot and its width varies from 1 to 2 feet. In some cases the verandas are very rough in nature and are found unsuitable for daily use.

The height of the front wall of a house is about 5 to 6 feet. But the height of the door is normally 3.5 to 4 feet. As a result of this, one has to bend down to enter into the room. In some cases the roofs slope down about 2 to 2.5 feet above the ground.

The houses are rectangular in shape. For the foundation, earth is dug for about a foot deep and the walls are erected piling clods clay layer on layer. Sometimes bamboo splits are used as a frame for the wall in order to reinforce the soft clay till it hardens. The front and back walls are comparatively thicker than the side walls. This is so as the roof is mainly borne on these two walls.

For the construction of thatch roofs, five different types of wooden beams are used. Among the caste Hindu people, straight wooden beams of *Kendu (diospyromelouoxylon), Tāla (Borassus flabellifer)* and *Jāmu (syzygium cumini)* are extensively used for the cross-beam that holds the sloping roofs of the house. But as the market value of the wood of these trees is very costly, it is not generally affordable by the Bāuris. So they use two to three bamboo beams tied together for making the cross-beam. Hence, any Bāuri household who manages to use the cross-beam of either *Kendu,* or *Tāla* or *Jāmu* tree, becomes a matter of talk among the villagers and in that case the owner feels very proud of it. So every Bāuri household has a craze to have it and in some cases they also borrow loan from the local moneylenders to buy a cross-beam of the wood of the above trees. Interestingly in one case a Bāuri of Hirāpur namely Maga Bhoi borrowed Rs. 150 from a local caste Hindu moneylender in 1985 to buy a *Jāmu* log for this purpose but later on ultimately he became a bonded labour at the creditor's house to repay the loan.

The roof of the house is thatched with straw of the paddy plant (Oryza Sativa). Generally the fibre of palm tree is used for making a strong binder while tying the beams, ribs etc., in setting the frame for the thatch. But as the Bāuris do not generally own this tree, they use the fibres of *Kiā* plant (*Pandanus tectorious*), abundantly available free of cost all around the village, or the fibre of the fronds of coconut tree (cocous sativa) which are considered as inferior thatching accessories.

The door panels of many houses are made of bamboo strips. In some cases the doors are also made from planks of wood. In a few cases the entrance of the house is without a worthwhile door. Such houses, however, use sack screens set in bamboo frames.

Households with panel door facility

Earlier in chapter IV, it has been discussed that of the total 55 beneficiary households in Hirāpur, as many as 46 or 83.64 per cent possess homesteads with records of right. But 50 households accounting for 90.91 per cent have living rooms and the rest 5 households reside in enclosed veranda. On the other hand, all the beneficiary households of Āmbadiha have homesteads with record of right, and all of them possess living rooms.

Among the non-beneficiary households of Hirāpur, out of 53 households, 48 accounting for 90.57 per cent have homesteads with records of right and 52 have living rooms. The members of the rest one household reside in an enclosed veranda. On the other hand all the non-beneficiary households of Āmbadiha have homesteads with records of right and have living rooms.

Beneficiary Households

Data available in Table 6.1 shows that out of 50 households with living rooms in Hirāpur, 5 or 10 per cent households do not have any door panel facility. These households use sack screens set in bamboo frames for ensuring privacy and the meagre safety it provides. An equal percentage of such households is also found in Āmbadiha.

Non-beneficiary Households

Among the 52 non-beneficiary households of Hirāpur who have living rooms, 9 accounting for 17.31 per cent lack door panel facility. These households use sack screens set in bamboo frames. But of the total 59 households of Āmbadiha who have living rooms, 14 or 20.29 per cent sue sack screens set in bamboo frames. But the z value is observed to be insignificant at 5 per cent level of significance (Table 6.1).

TABLE 6.1

Distribution of beneficiary and non-beneficiary households according to door panel facility

Village	Beneficiary HHs			Non-beneficiary HHs		
	Total HHs with Living Rooms	HHs with Door Panel	HHs without Door Panel	Total HHs with Living Rooms	HHs with Door Panel	HHs without Door Panel
(1)	(2)	(3)	(4)	(5)	(6)	(7)
Hirāpur	50 (100.00)	45 (90.00)	5 (10.00)	52 (100.00)	43 (82.69)	9 (17.31)
Āmbadiha	50 (100.00)	45 (90.00)	5 (10.00)	69 (100.00)	55 (79.71)	14 (20.29)
'Z' value	0.00			0.042		

Note: (i) Households without door panel includes those who use sack screens.
(ii) Figures in brackets represent %age.
(iii) 'Z' value is calculated out of data relating to households having door panel.

HOUSEHOLDS WITH WINDOW FACILITY

Beneficiary Households

Table 6.3 reflects that of the total 50 beneficiary households of Hirāpur having living rooms, as many as 16 households accounting for 32 per cent have windows, as against only 2 or 4 per cent of those in Āmbadiha. So the difference is found to be quite significant.

This means that the beneficiary households of Hirāpur have become status-conscious by upgrading their houses by providing windows.

TABLE 6.2

Distribution of beneficiary and non-beneficiary households according type of door panels

Village	Beneficiary HHs			Non-beneficiary HHs		
	HHs with Door Panel facility	Plank	Flattened bamboo	HHs with Door Panel	Plank	Flattened bamboo
(1)	(2)	(3)	(4)	(5)	(6)	(7)
Hirāpur	45 (100.00)	19 (42.22)	26 (57.78)	43 (100.00)	9 (20.93)	34 (79.07)
Āmbadiha	45 (100.00)	9 (20.00)	36 (20.00)	55 (100.00)	12 (21.82)	43 (78.18)
Z value	2.32				0.12	

Note: (i) Figures in brackets represent %age.

(ii) 'Z' value is calculated out of data relating to households having door panel made of planks.

TABLE 6.3

Distribution of beneficiary and non-beneficiary households according to window facility

Village	Beneficiary HHs			Non-beneficiary HHs		
	Total HHs with Living Rooms	HHs with window facility	HHs without window facility	Total HHs with Living Rooms	HHs with window facility	HHs without window facility
(1)	(2)	(3)	(4)	(5)	(6)	(7)
Hirāpur	50 (100.00)	16 (32.00)	34 (78.00)	52 (100.00)	7 (13.46)	45 (86.54)
Āmbadiha	50 (100.00)	2 (4.00)	48 (96.00)	69 (100.00)	3 (4.35)	66 (95.65)
'Z' value	3.91			1.65		

Note: (i) Figures in brackets represent %age.

(ii) 'Z' value is calculated out of the data relating to households having window facility.

Non-Beneficiary Households

The above table also shows that of the total 52 non-beneficiary households of Hirāpur who have living rooms, 7 or 13.46 per cent have window facility as against only 3 or 4.35 per cent of the total 69 non-beneficiary households of Āmbadiha. So, in this case the 'z' value is also found significant at 5 per cent level of significance.

TYPE OF DOORS

Beneficiary Households

So far as the type of doors used is concerned, of the total 45 households of Hirāpur having door panels, 42.22 per cent or 19 households have doors made of planks and the rest 57.78 per cent or 26 households have inferior quality of doors made of flat bamboo splits. But out of 45 households in Āmbadiha who have door facility, while 20 per cent or 9 households have door panels made of planks, as high a percentage as 80 or 36 households possess doors made of flat bamboo splits. But the z value is found insignificant at 5 per cent level of significance (Table 6.2).

Non-Beneficiary Households

The said table also shows the position of type of door panels among the non-beneficiary households. While 20.45 per cent or 9 households in Hirāpur have door panels made of planks, 21.82 per cent or 12 households have these in Āmbadiha. Hence so far as the door panels made of planks are concerned there is no significant difference between the above two villages. Rest of the households in both the villages have door panels made of flat bamboo splits.

HOUSEHOLDS USING VALUABLE CROSS-BEAMS FOR CONSTRUCTION OF ROOF

Beneficiary Households

As regards the use of valuable wood of trees like *Kendu*, *Tāla* and *Jāmu* for the use of cross-beam in roofing the house, it is observed from Table 6.4 that, of the total 49 households of Hirāpur who have thatched roofs, 30.61 per cent or 15 households have used wooden crossbeams made from trees of the above species. The rest 69.38 per cent or 34 households have used simply bamboos, which lack both strength and durability. But in case of Āmbadiha, of the total 50 households having thatched roofs, only 14 per cent or 7 households are found to have used valuable wooden cross-beams in roofing their houses. The rest 86 per cent or 43 households have simply used bamboos. But, so far as the use of valuable cross-beams for construction of the roof is concerned, there is no significant difference between the households of these two villages at 5 per cent level of significance.

TABLE 6.4

Distribution of beneficiary and non-beneficiary households according to use of costly wooden cross-bars for construction of roofs

Village	Total thatched houses		Beneficiary HHs		Non-beneficiary HHs	
	Benefi-ciary	Non-Bene-ficiary	Costly Wooden cross-bars	Bamboo cross-bars	Costly wooden cross-bars	Bamboo cross-bars
(1)	(2)	(3)	(4)	(5)	(6)	(7)
Hirāpur	49 (100.00)	52 (100.00)	15 (30.61)	34 (69.39)	11 (21.15)	41 (78.85)
Āmbadiha	50 (100.00)	69 (100.00)	7 (14.00)	43 (86.00)	11 (15.96)	58 (84.06)
'Z' value	-	-	2.07	-	0.70	-

Note: (i) Figures in brackets represent %age.
(ii) 'Z' value is calculated out of the data relating to the households used costly wooden cross-bars.

Non-Beneficiary Households

Regarding the use of valuable wooden crossbeams for construction of roofs among the non-beneficiary households, it is found from the same table that of 52 households in Hirāpur having thatched roofs, 21.15 per cent or 11 households have superior roofs as these have used wooden crossbeams made from valuable trees. The percentage of such type of households is 15.46 or 11 households in Āmbadiha. Hence, among these people also, there is no significant difference. The rest of the households in both the villages have simply used bamboos for the roofs of their houses.

TYPE OF HOUSE

Beneficiary Households

Data available in Table 6.5.1 reveals that in case of either villages the percentage of *kutcha* houses is very high, i.e. 74 per cent in the case of Hirāpur, as against 88 per cent of Āmbadiha. There is only one household in the former village which has a *pucca* house, i.e.

brick and cement construction with steel reinforced cement concrete roof. This type of house is not found in the village Āmbadiha. However, mixed variety of houses are more (24%) in Hirāpur than in (12%) Āmbadiha.

TABLE 6.5.1

Distribution of house types among beneficiary and non-beneficiary households

Category of Households	Village	Total HHs with living rooms	Type of House		
			Pucca	Kutcha	Mixed
(1)	(2)	(3)	(4)	(5)	(6)
Beneficiary	Hirāpur	50 (100.00)	1 (2.0)	37 (74.0)	12 (24.0)
	Āmbadiha	50 (100.00)	-	44 (88.00)	6 (12.00)
Non-Beneficiary	Hirāpur	52 (100.00)	-	44 (84.62)	8 (15.38)
	Āmbadiha	69 (100.00)	-	62 (89.86)	7 (10.14)

Note: Figures in brackets represent %age.

So far as building materials used in *kutcha* and mixed type of houses are concerned, it is observed that of 37 *kutcha* houses of Hirāpur, as high a percentage as 72.97 houses have mud walls and floor, with a thatched roof. This type of house is found to be more than 90 per cent (90.91) in cases of Āmbadiha. The rest 27.03 per cent households of Hirāpur as against 9.09 per cent of the village Āmbadiha have walls made of either burnt or unburnt bricks with mud plaster and thatched roof.

Of the total 12 mixed type of houses of Hirāpur, while 33.33 per cent houses have mud walls having cemented floor and thatched roof, all the 6 houses of this type in Āmbadiha have mud walls having cement floor and thatched roof. The rest 66.67 per cent of mixed type of houses of Hirāpur are made of laterite rock walls but without cement plaster, with mud floor and thatched roof (Table 6.5.2).

Non-Beneficiary Households

The house type of the non-beneficiary households is more or less same as those of the beneficiaries. But in this case, there is not a single *pucca* house in any of the village.

TABLE 6.5.2

Category of house building among beneficiary households according to building materials used

Village	Total Houses			Kutcha		Mixed		Pucca
	Kutcha	Mixed	Pucca	A1	A2	B1	B2	
(1)	(2)	(3)	(4)	(5)	(6)	(7)	(8)	(9)
Hirāpur	37 (100.00)	12 (100.00)	1 (100.00)	27 (72.97)	10 (27.03)	4 (33.33)	8 (66.67)	1 (100.00)
Āmbadiha	44 (100.00)	6 (100.00)	-	40 (90.91)	4 (9.09)	6 (100.00)	-	-

Note: (i) A1 - Mud wall and floor having thatched roof.
A2 - Wall made of burnt and unburnt bricks with mud paste and thatched roof.
B1 - Mud wall having cemented floor and thatched roof.
B2 - Ignious rock wall without cement plaster with mud floor and thatched roof.

(ii) Figures in brackets represent %age.

In case of the village Hirāpur, there are 84.62 per cent of *kutcha* houses, but it is about 90 per cent in case of Āmbadiha. The mixed type of houses constitute 15.38 per cent in case of the former village as against 10.14 per cent of the latter one (Table 6.5.2).

Considering the building materials used in the above houses, it is found that among all the *kutcha* houses of Hirāpur, 75 per cent of houses have mud walls and floor having thatched roofs. But in Āmbadiha 88.71 per cent of the houses are such. The rest 25 per cent houses of Hirāpur and 11.29 per cent of Āmbadiha are made of either burnt or unburnt brick walls with mud plaster and thatched roofs.

Among the mixed type of houses, while there are 37.5 per cent houses in Hirāpur which have mud walls, cement floor and thatched roofs, 85.71 per cent of the houses in Āmbadiha are such. The rest 62.5 per cent houses of the former village, as against 14.29 per cent of the latter one have houses with walls of laterite rock pieces but without cement plaster, with mud floor and thatched roofs (Table 6.5.2).

BUILT-UP AREA OF HOUSES

Merely possessing a house does not make any sense unless it provides sufficient space for each of its inmates. If the built-up-space of a house is not sufficient, living is inconvenient, unhygienic and unhealthy. It has very bad consequences in psychological and physical development of the children and even of adults.

TABLE 6.5.3

Category of house buildings among non-beneficiary households according to building materials used

Village	Total Houses		Kutcha		Mixed	
	Kutcha	Mixed	A1	A2	A1	A2
(1)	(2)	(3)	(4)	(5)	(6)	(7)
Hirāpur	44 (100.00)	8 (100.00)	33 (75.00)	11 (25.00)	3 (37.50)	5 (62.50)
Āmbadiha	62 (100.00)	7 (100.00)	55 (88.71)	7 (11.29)	6 (25.71)	1 (14.29)

Note: As per Table 6.5.2

In order to find out the average built-up area per household and per person, 20 per cent of each of the beneficiary and non-beneficiary households of both the study villages were measured on the basis of purposive random sampling giving weightage to a coverage of 50 per cent of traditional and modern houses of the total sample of each category of beneficiary and non-beneficiary households of the two study villages.

Beneficiary Households

Data available in Table 6.6 explains that when the average built-up area of the beneficiary households of Hirāpur comes to 153.5 and 43.29 sq. feet per household and per person respectively, it is 120.8 and 27.45 sq. feet in case of Āmbadiha. Hence, if we consider the average built-up area available per person, there is a significant difference between the two villages. But even though more space is available for a person of Hirāpur, this little area is not sufficient for leading a healthy and happy life.

TABLE 6.6

Distribution of average built-in area per household and per person among beneficiary and non-beneficiary households

Category of House-holds	Village	Sample House-holds	Total House-hold members	Total Built-in-area	Average Built-in-area per HH	Average Built-in area per person	Z-value
(1)	(2)	(3)	(4)	(5)	(6)	(7)	(8)
Benefi-ciary	Hirāpur	11	39	1688.5	153.5	43.29	2.87
	Āmbadiha	10	44	1208.0	120.8	28.43	
Non-Be-neficiary	Hirāpur	11	47	1336.5	121.5	28.43	2.70
	Āmbadiha	14	66	1586.2	133.3	23.33	

Note: Sample households include 20% households of each category.

On one hand, the Bāuris mostly own single living rooms. But this room is also used for storing of various household materials including unprocessed foodgrains. As a result of this, it becomes very congested to accommodate each member of the household. In many cases during night, married couples lack privacy and their sexual act is unwittingly witnessed by the children. Hence children fall under harmful influences at a vulnerable age. Later on, their personality and individuality are shaped in this mould, developing strong inclination towards sex from early adolescence. This problem is age-old and inherent among these people.

Non-Beneficiary Households

So far as the case of the non-beneficiary households is concerned, the said table shows that while the average built-up area available for a household in Hirāpur is 121.5 sq. ft., it is 133.3 sq. feet in Āmbadiha. On the other hand when a person of the former village shares 28.43 sq. feet on the average, it is 23.33 in case of the latter village. Thus, even though the average built-up area per household is found to be more in case of Āmbadiha than Hirāpur, the latter village enjoys more built-up area on an average than Āmbadiha. The 'z' value is found to be significant at 5 per cent level of significance.

6.2 ENVIRONMENT, SANITARY HABITS AND CHANGING CONCEPT OF HEALTH AND HYGIENE

Environmental sanitation and personal hygiene are very essential for healthy living.

Environmental sanitation refers to clean surroundings by safe and hygienic disposal of various waste products as improper disposal adversely affects the environment. It has serious consequences on health. Spread of infections and various diseases may be attributed to unhygienic environmental sanitation caused through improper disposal and management of various waste products, like kitchen wastes (including garbage, left-over food, rotten fruits and vegetables etc.) dry refuses (like paper, straw, ash, polythene etc.) garden refuses, waste water of kitchen and bathrooms, excreta of both human as well as of various domestic animals and birds etc.

The waste heaps or gatherings in the neighbourhood, besides being a suitable breeding place for mosquitoes, flies and other vermins like rodents and noxious insects, parasitic worms generated from these heaps cause air pollution. Various disease-causing germs rapidly grow in these waste product heaps and are carried by flies and related insects, poultry and other birds as well as through air and cause serious infectious diseases in human beings. Further, improper disposal of waste also causes contamination to drinking or cooking water available in wells and ponds etc.

In rural areas, proper maintenance of environmental sanitation is very poor among the people belonging to the lower caste Hindu communities. More particularly, the knowledge of environmental sanitation is very poor among the *Dalits*. As a result of this combined with their poor personal hygiene are most often attributed as major factors for treating them as untouchables.

The environmental sanitary habit of the Bāuri people is very poor as compared to the local caste Hindu people. However, the sanitary habits of these people may be discussed under the following broad headings:

i) channelling of street water during rainy season;
ii) maintenance of cow sheds and poultry on *veranda* or courtyards;
iii) use of dung-pit/waste heap;
iv) use of open field for defecation;
v) cleaning of utensils at dug-well and tube-well points; and
vi) use of ponds for various domestic as well as non-domestic purposes.

The Bāuri people of both the study villages have maximum opportunity to get clean air as their hamlets are mostly located amidst the paddy fields. But the people do not keep their surroundings clean because of their illiteracy, lack of awareness, and unwillingness to render voluntary service in the case of common interest.

The Bāuri hamlets do not have any drainage system that causes stagnation of water during rainy season. It facilitates the breeding of mosquitoes, flies etc. There insects spread many diseases like malaria, diarrhoea etc.

The most important unhygienic practice that creates unclean surrounding is their strange habit of keeping poultry on veranda and in some cases even inside the living rooms. Most often these birds pollute the veranda, courtyards and also the living rooms.

The cowsheds are generally found inside the courtyards and very often attached to the home. The dung and urine of the cattle are treated as auspicious and are cleaned in open hand and bare foot without any hesitation either by the children or adult members.

The Bāuri hamlets do not possess any dung-pit in common where the dung and waste food materials of the cattle of all the households of the village may be gathered. Because the cattle are mostly owned by individual households and hence the dung is sold as manure and the money comes to the hand of the owner-household.

So far as the location of the dung-pits is concerned, these are mostly located at the house sites. These pits cause foul smell throughout the year and a very strong pungent smell occurs from these pits during rainy season. The Bāuri households owning cattle dispose of their kitchen and other waste products in the dung-pit but others have garbage or waste heaps very near to their house sites within their courtyards as no household is permitted to use the dung-pit of other households.

Another important adverse sanitary habit of these people is using of open fields near the village sites for defecation. It causes the surrounding very unclean and unhygienic throughout the year as not a single Bāuri household in any of the two study villages is having lavatory facility. Children often use house sites for defecation. Interestingly the Bāuri people are very hesitant to use lavatory as they think that it would cause very unsatisfactory bowel cleaning because of the bad smell within. It also involves the difficult task of carrying water to the lavatory. In this context when some people were asked if they would be interested in using lavatory if provided free of cost by the Government, an amazing revelation came out into the picture. Among the beneficiary households of Hirāpur 68.33 per cent people do not like to use a lavatory, as against as many as 88.33 per cent of Āmbadiha. Among the non-beneficiary households, 65 per cent in Hirāpur, and 86.67 per cent in Āmbadiha are not interested in using lavatories. Interestingly, there is not a single woman in Āmbadiha who is interested in availing this facility. However, about 23 per cent women in each category of Hirāpur who opined that they would use a lavatory if made available to them free of cost.

By and large the Bāuri people of the study villages depend on three sources of water for both domestic as well as non-domestic purpose. These sources are pond, dug-well and tube-well. However, some people also use canal water as this source of water is not available close to each Bāuri settlement.

There are two tube-wells and two dug-wells available inside the Bāuri hamlets of Hirāpur. An equal number of tube-wells and three dug-wells are there for the Bāuri people of the village Āmbadiha. While the tube-wells are owned communally in both the villages, the dug-wells are owned by individual households.

The surroundings of dug and tube-wells always remain very unclean as most of the people clean utensils, clean teeth and throw the used teeth cleaning sticks at the spot; some people bathe and also clean clothes. The waste water mixed with various impurities is soaked into the soil as drains are not provided for. So the unclean water is recycled and the infected water enters the body as potable water. The surroundings of these water points look unsighty as teeth cleaning sticks are heaped up day by day and no voluntary action is taken by any of them to clean the surroundings.

The bathing ghats of the local ponds are frequently used for both domestic as well as non-domestic purposes. The same bathing ghat is used for a number of non-domestic purpose, like bathing a human beings as well as domestic animals, cleaning of utensils, washing of clothes, cleaning of teeth, washing of body after defecation etc. Water from the same ghat is also collected for various domestic purposes like cooking and drinking. But some people of both the villages have become aware and conscious of the adverse effects of using a common ghat for all purposes. This will be discussed in detail later on in a separate section in this chapter.

Changing Concept of Health and Hygiene

Personal hygiene should be a matter of daily routine as it is essential for leading a healthy life. Personal cleanliness keeps one mentally healthy, physically fit and it ensures development of working ability and personality.

Personal hygiene refers to the following personal cleanliness:

(a) keeping different parts of the body clean like;
(i) washing face early in the morning;
(ii) clearing of bowels regularly in the morning;
(iii) use of soap for washing hand after defecation;
(iv) cleaning teeth and
(v) taking bath daily;
(b) paring nails and keeping these clean;
(c) washing hair regularly, at least once a week,
(d) washing hands before taking food;
(e) using water of tube-wells for drinking and cooking purpose, or boiling the water if collected from other sources like well or pond.

In these respects, the Bāuris neglect themselves as because they are mostly illiterate, and hence not aware and conscious of the adverse consequences of remaining unclean and unhygienic. Now, let us discuss each of the above issues in great detail.

Washing Face after Leaving Bed every Morning

Eyes are precious organs of the body. So sufficient care should be given to keep eyes clean and these should be protected from being infected. At least eyes should be washed with clean water every morning in order to remove the dirty secretions gathered at the corners of the eyelids. Apart from this, a clean face in the morning makes a positive feeling on other members of the society. But while 60 per cent of the beneficiaries of Hirāpur are habituated to this hygienic practice regularly, there are about 52 (51.67) per cent in Āmbadiha who do so.

So far as the non-beneficiary people are concerned, while 63.33 per cent of people in Hirāpur go through the morning ablutions like washing face and cleaning eyes every morning after leaving bed, 45 per cent in case Āmbadiha do so regularly. The rest people are either irregular in doing so or do not follow the practice at all (Table 6.7).

Passing of Motion Regularly in the Morning

Regular passing of stool early in the morning is believed to be a very important and crucial factor for good health. It helps in carrying out daily work efficiently.

Quite a large percentage of people belonging to each of the beneficiary and non-beneficiary category people in both the study villages are habituated to passing stool early every morning and in the evening. But while among the beneficiary people, 90 per cent in Hirāpur, as against 86.67 per cent in Āmbadiha are habituated to passing stool every morning, among the non-beneficiaries, the corresponding figures are 88.33 and 96.67 per cent respectively (Table 6.8).

Habit of Using Soap after Defecation

Development of the habit of using soap for cleaning hands after defecating is an important measure of preventing infectious diseases. But it is found that the majority of the Bāuri people regularly use clay instead of soap or any other such antiseptic material for the purpose. Interestingly, there is not a single person either among the beneficiary or among the non-beneficiary people in Āmbadiha who is found to use soap or any other antiseptic material regularly for cleaning hand after defecation. However, even though there are some persons among both the beneficiary and non-beneficiary category of people in Hirāpur who use shop or other such materials regularly for cleaning hand after defecation, their percentage is very negligible which comes to 5 and 6.67 respectively in Āmbadiha (Table 6.9).

Habit of Using Lavatory

So far as the place of passing stool is concerned, all from the beneficiary and non-beneficiary groups in both the villages use village sites or open fields for the purpose as none of the households in any of the study villages has lavatory facility. However, in comparison with the people of Āmbadiha, a larger number of people of Hirāpur are willing to use lavatories, if provided free of cost. In this context Table 6.10 explains that while among the beneficiary households 31.67

TABLE 6.7

Habit of washing face daily after leaving bed in morning

Habit	Beneficiary HHs						Non-Beneficiary HHs					
	Hirāpur			Āmbadiha			Hirāpur			Āmbadiha		
	M	F	T	M	F	T	M	F	T	M	F	T
(1)	(2)	(3)	(4)	(5)	(6)	(7)	(8)	(9)	(10)	(11)	(12)	(13)
Regular	15 (50.00)	21 (70.00)	36 (60.00)	13 (43.33)	18 (60.00)	31 (51.67)	18 (60.00)	20 (66.67)	38 (63.33)	13 (43.33)	14 (46.67)	27 (45.00)
Irregular	6 (20.00)	5 (16.67)	11 (18.33)	8 (26.67)	3 (10.00)	11 (18.33)	4 (13.33)	4 (13.33)	8 (13.33)	11 (36.67)	10 (33.33)	21 (35.00)
Do not wash	9 (30.00)	4 (13.33)	13 (21.16)	9 (30.00)	9 (30.00)	18 (30.00)	8 (26.67)	6 (20.00)	14 (23.33)	6 (20.00)	6 (20.00)	12 (20.00)
Z value	1.0						1.94					

Note: (i) Sample include 30 men (15 adult and 15 minor) and 30 women (15 adult and 15 minor) of each category of each village.

(ii) M = Male, F = Female, T = Total

(iii) Figures in brackets represent %age.

(iv) 'Z' is calculated out of the data relating to those who regularly wash their face.

TABLE 6.8

Habit of passing motions regularly early in morning

Habit	Beneficiary HHs						Non-Beneficiary HHs					
	Hirāpur			Āmbadiha			Hirāpur			Āmbadiha		
	M	F	T	M	F	T	M	F	T	M	F	T
(1)	(2)	(3)	(4)	(5)	(6)	(7)	(8)	(9)	(10)	(11)	(12)	(13)
Regular	26 (86.87)	28 (93.33)	54 (90.00)	25 (83.33)	27 (90.00)	52 (86.67)	29 (96.67)	27 (90.00)	56 (93.33)	30 (100.00)	28 (93.33)	58 (96.67)
Only when feel so	4 (13.33)	2 (6.67)	6 (10.00)	5 (16.67)	3 (10.00)	8 (13.33)	1 (3.33)	3 (10.00)	4 (6.67)	-	2 (6.67)	2 (3.33)
Z value	0.52						- 0.32					

Note: (i) to (iii) As per Table 6.7

(iv) 'Z' is calculated out of the data relating to those who regularly pass motions.

TABLE 6.9

Habit of using soap after defecation

Habit	Beneficiary HHs						Non-Beneficiary HHs					
	Hirāpur			Āmbadiha			Hirāpur			Āmbadiha		
	M	F	T	M	F	T	M	F	T	M	F	T
(1)	(2)	(3)	(4)	(5)	(6)	(7)	(8)	(9)	(10)	(11)	(12)	(13)
Regular use of soil	17 (56.67)	22 (73.33)	39 (65.00)	25 (83.33)	27 (90.00)	52 (86.69)	23 (76.67)	21 (70.00)	44 (73.33)	27 (90.00)	26 (86.67)	53 (88.33)
Regular use of soap	1 (3.33)	2 (6.67)	3 (5.00)	-	-	-	1 (3.33)	3 (10.00)	4 (6.67)	-	-	-
At times soil and at times soap	12 (40.00)	6 (20.00)	18 (30.00)	5 (16.67)	3 (10.00)	8 (13.33)	6 (20.00)	6 (20.00)	12 (20.00)	3 (10.00)	4 (13.33)	7 (11.67)

Note: As per Table 6.7

TABLE 6.10

Choice of place for cleaning after defecation

Choice of Place	Beneficiary HHs						Non-Beneficiary HHs					
	Hirāpur			Āmbadiha			Hirāpur			Āmbadiha		
	M	F	T	M	F	T	M	F	T	M	F	T
(1)	(2)	(3)	(4)	(5)	(6)	(7)	(8)	(9)	(10)	(11)	(12)	(13)
Open Field	20 (66.67)	21 (70.00)	41 (68.33)	23 (76.67)	30 (100.00)	53 (88.33)	16 (53.33)	23 (76.67)	39 (65.00)	22 (73.33)	30 (100.00)	52 (86.67)
Lavatory	10 (33.33)	9 (30.00)	19 (31.67)	7 (23.33)	-	7 (1.67)	14 (46.67)	7 (23.33)	21 (35.00)	8 (26.67)	-	8 (13.33)
Z value	2.73						2.92					

Note: (i) to (iii) As per Table 6.7

(iv) 'Z' is calculated out of the data relating to those who opt to use lavatory.

TABLE 6.11
Habit of cleaning teeth daily morning

Habit	Beneficiary HHs						Non-Beneficiary HHs					
	Hirāpur			Āmbadiha			Hirāpur			Āmbadiha		
	M	F	T	M	F	T	M	F	T	M	F	T
(1)	(2)	(3)	(4)	(5)	(6)	(7)	(8)	(9)	(10)	(11)	(12)	(13)
Regular	25 (33.33)	27 (90.00)	52 (86.67)	23 (76.67)	25 (83.33)	48 (80.00)	26 (86.67)	25 (83.33)	51 (85.00)	27 (90.00)	27 (90.00)	54 (93.33)
Irregular	5 (16.67)	3 (10.00)	8 (13.33)	7 (23.33)	3 (10.00)	10 (16.67)	3 (10.00)	5 (16.67)	8 (13.33)	3 (10.00)	3 (10.00)	6 (10.00)
Do not clean	-	-	-	-	2 (6.67)	2 (3.33)	1 (3.33)	-	1 (1.67)	-	-	-
Z value	1.04						- 0.83					

Note: (i) to (iii) As per Table 6.7

(iv) 'Z' is calculated out of the data relating to those who are regular in cleaning teeth daily morning.

per cent people in Hirāpur, as against 11.67 per cent in Āmbadiha, are willing to use lavatories if provided free of cost. The corresponding figures for non-beneficiary households is 35 per cent in Hirāpur and 13.33 per cent in Āmbadiha.

Habit of Cleaning Teeth Regularly in the Morning

Taking proper care of teeth is very essential. One should rinse the mouth and brush teeth regularly every morning, and if possible again before going to bed at night. It helps to remove food particles lodged between teeth. Otherwise it creates bad smell in the mouth, decays teeth, creates cavities in teeth and also causes numerous problems of the oral cavity, resulting in other associated complications and may even lead to oral cancer.

Even though oral hygiene is so essential among the beneficiary people, 13.33 per cent people in Hirāpur as against 16.67 per cent in Āmbadiha do not brush their teeth regularly in the morning. But surprisingly there are 3.33 per cent people in the latter village who do not brush their teeth at all. So far as the case of the non-beneficiary people is concerned, 13.33 per cent in Hirāpur and 10 per cent in Āmbadiha are irregular in cleaning their teeth.

Use of Commercial Tooth Brush and Tooth Paste

The Bāuris mostly clean their teeth with twigs of various trees and plants. Many of them use dung ash, red-soil etc. as dentifrice. A majority people also use a tobacco paste called *Gudakhu* for this purpose. On the contrary, there are very few people who use tooth brush and tooth paste to clean their teeth. In this context Table 6.12 shows that among the beneficiaries, 11.67 per cent people in Hirāpur as against only 3.33 per cent in Āmbadiha use commercial tooth brush and tooth paste. Among the non-beneficiaries, use of these materials is found among 3.33 per cent people in Āmbadiha, and 8.33 per cent in Hirāpur.

Habit of Cleaning Hair among Women

Hair should always be kept clean. It should be washed at least four times a month. The frequency should be more in case of those who carry headloads and work as wage or agricultural labourers. This is because they are supposed to collect more dust particles than others. If not washed regularly with soap or other such materials, the hair becomes dirty, matted and infested with lice, dandruff, resulting in hair loss, or premature greying.

TABLE 6.12

Habit of using commercial tooth brush and tooth paste

Use of	Beneficiary HHs						Non-Beneficiary HHs					
	Hirāpur			Āmbadiha			Hirāpur			Āmbadiha		
	M	F	T	M	F	T	M	F	T	M	F	T
(1)	(2)	(3)	(4)	(5)	(6)	(7)	(8)	(9)	(10)	(11)	(12)	(13)
Commercial Tooth Brush and Tooth Paste	5 (16.67)	2 (6.67)	7 (11.67)	2 (6.67)	-	2 (3.33)	3 (10.00)	2 (6.67)	5 (8.33)	2 (6.67)	-	2 (3.33)
Others	25 (83.33)	28 (93.33)	53 (88.33)	28 (93.33)	30 (100.00)	58 (96.67)	27 (90.00)	28 (93.33)	55 (91.67)	28 (93.33)	30 (100.00)	58 (96.67)
Z value	1.90						1.21					

Note: (i) to (iii) As per Table 6.7

(iv) 'Z' is calculated out of the data relating to those who use commercial tooth brush and tooth paste.

TABLE 6.13

Habit of taking bath daily (in the month of October)

Frequency of times (in days)	Beneficiary HHs						Non-Beneficiary HHs					
	Hirāpur			Āmbadiha			Hirāpur			Āmbadiha		
	M	F	T	M	F	T	M	F	T	M	F	T
(1)	(2)	(3)	(4)	(5)	(6)	(7)	(8)	(9)	(10)	(11)	(12)	(13)
1-10	-	-	-	-	-	-	1 (33.33)	-	1 (1.67)	-	-	-
11-20	1 (33.33)	1 (33.33)	2 (3.33)	2 (6.67)	1 (33.33)	3 (5.00)	2 (6.67)	2 (6.67)	4 (6.67)	1 (33.33)	-	1 (1.67)
21-30	6 (20.00)	3 (10.00)	9 (15.00)	4 (13.33)	3 (10.00)	7 (11.67)	2 (6.67)	3 (10.00)	5 (8.33)	5 (83.33)	7 (23.33)	12 (20.00)
31	23 (76.67)	26 (86.67)	49 (81.67)	24 (80.00)	26 (86.67)	50 (83.33)	25 (83.33)	25 (83.33)	50 (83.33)	24 (80.00)	23 (76.67)	47 (78.53)
Z value	0.94						0.69					

Note: (i) to (iii) As per Table 6.7

(iv) 'Z' is calculated out of the data relating to those who taken bath for all the 31 days.

The Bāuri women being wage and agricultural labourers often carry headloads of various materials including soil, manure, compost, paddy seedlings etc. and their hair gets dirty. But they do not take proper care to clean their head regularly.

Normally the Bāuri women do use soap, but those who are unable to buy soap manage to wash their hair with red-soil, and juice of some local twigs. But the frequency of washing head is not satisfactory either among the beneficiary or among the non-beneficiary people.

A total number of 30 sample women of each category in each village were interviewed to know the frequency of washing their hair in the month of October. It is found that among the beneficiary people, there is only one woman each in Hirāpur and Āmbadiha who has washed her hair for three or more times in that month, followed by 3 or 10 per cent women in each village who have washed their hair twice. Those who have washed their hair only once constitute 40 per cent in case of Hirāpur but only 23.33 per cent in case of Āmbadiha. The rest 46.68 per cent women of the former village as against as many as 63.33 per cent of the latter one have not washed their hair even once in the concerned month (Table 6.14).

TABLE 6.14

Habit of cleaning hair among women (in the month of October)

Frequency (in times)	Beneficiary HHs		Non-Beneficiary HHs	
	Hirāpur	Āmbadiha	Hirāpur	Āmbadiha
(1)	(2)	(3)	(4)	(5)
Nil	14 (14.67)	19 (63.33)	13 (43.33)	20 (66.67)
Once	12 (40.00)	7 (23.33)	14 (46.67)	8 (26.67)
Twice	3 (10.00)	3 (10.00)	3 (10.00)	2 (6.67)
Thrice & More	1 (3.33)	1 (3.33)	-	-

Note: As per Table 6.7.

The case of the non-beneficiary people is more or less same. But a little more than 45 per cent women of Hirāpur have washed their hair at least once in the month, as against 26.27 per cent of Āmbadiha. The women who have not washed their hair even once in the month account for 43.33 per cent in the former village and as many as 66.67 per cent in case of the latter one.

Habit of taking Regular Bath

Our body collects a lot of dust particles daily while working outdoors. So a person must wash the body everyday, otherwise the skin harbours germs and it causes various infections like scabies, sores, boils and many other related diseases.

The Bāuris are mostly wage and agricultural labourers. As a result their body is soiled by sweat, grime and dust during the day's work. So, most of them are habituated to bathing daily after their work is over. But taking bath daily is not a habitual practice among the Bāuri children.

In order to have a better understanding of this aspect, 60 persons from each category of people in each of the village were interviewed in the month of October. From the data compiled, it is seen that among the beneficiary households 81.67 per cent people in Hirāpur have taken bath on all the 31 days of the concerned month, followed by 15 per cent who have taken bath for 21-30 days, and 3.33 per cent for 11-20 days. The corresponding figures for Āmbadiha are 83.33, 11.97 and 5 per cent, respectively.

Among the non-beneficiary people, the trend is more or less same. But while there are 8.33 per cent people in Hirāpur, it is 20 per cent in case of Āmbadiha who have taken bath for 21-30 days in the said month. On the contrary there are quite a fewer people (1.67%) in Āmbadiha than in Hirāpur (6.67%) who are found to have taken bath for 11-20 days. The rest 78.53 per cent of Āmbadiha as against 83.33 per cent of Hirāpur are found to have taken bath on all the 31 days.

Habit of paring and cleaning Nails

Keeping nails short and clean is essential as long nails retain dirt and harbour germs. It causes various diseases like diarrhoea and other diseases.

The Bāuri people collect a lot of dirty materials daily in their nails because of their nature of work. But most of them do not pare their nails and keep them clean.

It is seen from Table 6.15 that among the beneficiary households 25 per cent people in the village Hirāpur who are observed to have short and clean nails as against only 10 per cent people of the village Āmbadiha. Among the non-beneficiary households the case is almost same as when there are 23.33 per cent people in the former village who have kept short and clean nails, it is 11.67 per cent in case of the village Āmbadiha.

TABLE 6.15

Habit of keeping nails short and clean (observation made in the month of October)

Frequency in times (in days)	Beneficiary HHs						Non-Beneficiary HHs					
	Hirāpur			Āmbadiha			Hirāpur			Āmbadiha		
	M	F	T	M	F	T	M	F	T	M	F	T
(1)	(2)	(3)	(4)	(5)	(6)	(7)	(8)	(9)	(10)	(11)	(12)	(13)
Short & Clean	2 (6.67)	13 (43.33)	15 (25.00)	2 (6.67)	4 (13.33)	6 (10.00)	6 (20.00)	8 (26.67)	14 (23.33)	4 (13.33)	3 (10.00)	7 (11.67)
Long & clean	-	3 (10.00)	3 (5.00)	-	1 (3.33)	1 (1.67)	2 (6.67)	5 (16.67)	7 (11.67)	1 (3.33)	3 (10.00)	4 (16.67)
Short & unclean	16 (53.33)	7 (23.33)	23 (38.33)	18 (60.00)	7 (23.33)	25 (41.67)	8 (26.67)	11 (36.67)	19 (31.67)	10 (33.33)	2 (6.67)	12 (20.00)
Long & unclean	12 (40.00)	7 (23.33)	19 (31.67)	10 (33.33)	18 (60.00)	28 (46.67)	16 (53.33)	6 (20.00)	22 (36.67)	15 (50.00)	22 (73.33)	37 (61.67)
Z value	2.21						1.60					

Note: (i) As per Table 6.7
(iv) 'Z' is calculated out of the data relating to those who have short and clean nails.

Habit of Washing Hands before Taking Food

A fairly large number of people belonging to the beneficiary and non-beneficiary households in both the study villages are found to be very unhygienic in maintaining their nails short and clean. Still quite a large number of people neglect to wash their hands before taking food. As a result of this germs pass into the food items and cause diseases. Data available in Table 6.16 reveals that among the beneficiary households people who do not wash and occasionally wash their hands before eating food together constitute about 37 per cent in Hirāpur as against as many as about 67 per cent in Āmbadiha. The rest, however, wash their hands before eating food.

Among the non-beneficiary there are 35 per cent in Hirāpur who do not wash or occasionally wash their hands before taking food. For Āmbadiha the figure is about 58 per cent. The rest are habituated to wash their hands regularly before eating food.

Use of Drinking and Cooking Water

Water of tube-well is considered potable. But even though this source of water is available in both the study villages, not a single Bāuri household of either village is found to use its water either for drinking or for cooking purpose. This is because the people experience that using this water blackens the teeth and is not tasty if used for cooking. Hence, the people of these villages use either the water of dug-wells or ponds depending upon the availability and ownership of such water sources. As in other rural areas, the owners of dug-wells do not open their dug-wells for the public, among the Bāuri people even though all of them consider the water of dug-wells safe and sweet for drinking and cooking purpose, each and every Bāuri household does not have access to dug-wells as these are owned individually. Hence among the beneficiary households there are 21.82 per cent households in Hirāpur who use only pond water for both drinking and cooking purpose. In Āmbadiha 34 per cent do so. Likewise in the former village, when 25.45 per cent households use water from either dug-wells or ponds depending upon their choice, it is 24 per cent who do so in the latter village. The rest 52.73 per cent households of Hirāpur as against 42 per cent of Āmbadiha use water from dug-wells only.

So far as the case of the non-beneficiary households is concerned, 41.22 per cent households in Hirāpur use water from dug-wells only, whereas 40.58 per cent do so in Āmbadiha. But when 18.87 per cent households in the former village use water from ponds, in the latter

TABLE 6.16
Habit of cleaning hands before taking food

Frequency	Beneficiary HHs						Non-Beneficiary HHs					
	Hirāpur			Āmbadiha			Hirāpur			Āmbadiha		
	M	F	T	M	F	T	M	F	T	M	F	T
(1)	(2)	(3)	(4)	(5)	(6)	(7)	(8)	(9)	(10)	(11)	(12)	(13)
Regularly clean	22 (73.33)	16 (53.33)	38 (63.33)	13 (43.33)	13 (43.33)	26 (43.33)	22 (73.33)	17 (56.67)	39 (65.00)	14 (46.67)	11 (36.67)	25 (41.70)
Occasionally clean	4 (13.30)	7 (23.33)	11 (18.33)	8 (26.67)	7 (23.33)	15 (25.00)	3 (10.00)	6 (20.00)	9 (15.00)	8 (26.67)	12 (40.00)	20 (33.33)
Do not clean	4 (13.30)	7 (23.33)	11 (18.33)	9 (30.00)	10 (33.33)	19 (31.67)	5 (66.67)	7 (23.33)	12 (20.00)	8 (26.67)	7 (23.33)	15 (25.00)
Z value	2.24						2.60					

Note: (i) to (iii) As per Table 6.7

(iv) 'Z' is calculated out of the data relating to those who regularly clean hands before taking food.

village the percentage is as high as 37.68. Likewise, while 33.96 per cent households of Hirāpur use either water from dug-wells or ponds depending upon their choice, in Āmbadiha it is 21.74 per cent.

Expenditure Pattern on Sanitation and Health and Hygiene

From the above discussion, it can be concluded that in matters of health and hygiene, the beneficiaries of Hirāpur are more aware and conscious than those of Āmbadiha and they also spend more money in this area. In this respect as already discussed in Chapter IV, where the beneficiaries of Hirāpur spend 1.83 per cent of their total income on sanitation, health and hygiene, in Āmbadiha 0.88 per cent is spent. Likewise, while the non-beneficiary households of Hirāpur spend 1.75 per cent of their total income on this area, it is 0.98 per cent in Āmbadiha.

6.3 DRESS PATTERN

Clothing is considered as one of the three most important basic requirements of human life. But among the *Dalits*, clothing has been a great problem closely interlinked with the traditional Indian social system.

The problem of clothing is considered as both a social and economic proposition (Parvathamma, 1984, 269). From the social point of view caste Hindus had their absolute supremacy over the *Dalits* in regulating their mode of living. As a result, the *Dalits* had to follow the directives of caste Hindus as to which dress to wear and how to wear. These people were not allowed to wear good dresses. On the contrary, the poor economic condition of these people did not permit them to buy good and costly dress materials and dress up as caste Hindus did. Hence, a *Dalit* person was easily indentified in public by the quality and manner of dress. Hence, because of the age-old traditional Indian social system combined with poor economic condition, the *Dalits* had been tied to a particular dress pattern.

Today even though there is nobody in any of the study village who imposes restrictions on the dress pattern of these people in general and the Bāuri in particular, these people still seem to be very backward insofar as their clothing and dress materials are concerned. This is mainly because of their poor economic condition combined with their unwillingness to spend much of their income like as the caste Hindus. However, now a significant difference is marked in the acquisition of various modern and costly and stylish clothing materials among the beneficiary and non-beneficiary people of the two study villages.

TABLE 6.17

Habit of using tube-well water for cooking and drinking purpose

Sources of water	Beneficiary HHs		Non-Beneficiary HHs	
	Hirāpur (N=55)	Āmbadiha (N=50)	Hirāpur (N=53)	Āmbadiha (N=69)
(1)	(2)	(3)	(4)	(5)
Only Tube-well	-	-	-	-
Only Dug-well	29 (52.73)	21 (42.00)	22 (41.51)	28 (40.58)
Only pond	12 (21.82)	17 (34.00)	10 (18.87)	26 (37.68)
Either Dug-well or pond	14 (25.45)	12 (24.00)	18 (33.96)	15 (21.74)
Z value	1.13		1.22	

Note: (i) As per Table 6.7

(ii) Z is calculated out of the data relating to those who use water of tube-well.

Beneficiary Households

The dress pattern of the Bāuri people is quite distinct. The adult Bāuri men generally wear a piece of napkin and the upper part of their body remains bare while they are within the village and often even when they go out of it. However, some use *lungi* and very few use *dhoti,* in their day-to-day life. Use of modern dress like full pants, shirt, T-Shirt, and footwear like slippers and shoes is found in some cases. But comparatively, use of these materials is found more among the beneficiary households in Hirāpur rather than those of Āmbadiha. In this context Table 6.18 reveals that, while 70.91 per cent households in Hirāpur have 88 pieces of full pants (trousers) at an average of 2.26 per household, there are only 36 pieces at an average of 1.55 per household in Āmbadiha. Likewise, while 76.36 per cent households in Hirāpur have an average of 3.11 pieces of shirts/T-shirts per household, in Āmbadiha merely 38 per cent households have an average of 2.26 pieces of shirt/T-Shirts per household. This difference of possession of full pants and Shirt/T-Shirt between the beneficiary households of these two villages is because of the fact that the people of Hirāpur visit city areas like Bhubaneswar, Cuttack etc. more frequently than those of Āmbadiha.

So far as the use of footwear like slippers, shoes etc. is concerned, the people of Hirāpur are found to be more fancy to use these materials

TABLE 6.18

Posession of clothing assets among beneficiary and non-beneficiary households

Beneficiary Households

Capital Assets	Hirāpur			Āmbadiha			z
	Total No. of posse-ssion (a)	Total HHs po-ssession (b)	Ave-rage (c)	a	b	c	
(1)	(2)	(3)	(4)	(5)	(6)	(7)	(8)
Full pants	88	39 (70.91)	2.26	28	18 (36.00)	1.55	3.83
Shirt/ T-shirt	131	42 (76.36)	3.11	43	19 (38.00)	2.66	4.24
Slipper*	49	35 (63.64)	1.4	19	13 (26.00)	1.46	4.24
Shoes*	11	11 (20.00)	1.00	-	-	-	3.71
Wrist-watch	27	27 (49.09)	1.00	18	16 (32.00)	1.23	1.80
Petti-coat	12	9 (9.09)	1.33	3	2 (4.00)	1.50	2.12
Blouse	34	24 (3.6)	1.12	7	3 (6.00)	2.33	5.07
Blanket	7	5 (16.36)	1.40	-	-	-	2.31
Cushion	8	2 (43.64)	4.00	-	-	-	1.43

Non-Beneficiary Households

Full pants	46	30 (56.60)	1.53	24	20 (28.99)	1.2	3.22
Shirt/ T-shirt	50	35 (66.04)	1.42	45	25 (36.23)	1.8	3.45
Slipper*	36	25 (47.17)	1.44	16	15 (21.74)	1.07	3.10
Shoes*	4	3 (5.66)	1.33	1	1 (1.45)	1.00	3.73
Wrist-watch	18	17 (33.96)	1.06	9	9 (13.04)	1.00	2.50
Petti-coat	13	7 (13.71)	1.86	4	2 (2.99)	2.00	2.02
Blouse	36	22 (41.51)	1.64	12	8 (11.59)	1.50	3.72
Blanket	3	2 (3.77)	1.5	-	-	-	1.46
Cushion	-	-	-	-	-	-	-

Note: (i) '*' represents in pairs, (ii) Figures in brackets represent %age, (iii) 'z' is calculated out of the data relating to the total households.

more than those of Āmbadiha. In this context, the said table represents that when members of a little more than 60 per cent households in Hirāpur use slippers, on an average possessing 1.4 pair per household, only 26 per cent households in Āmbadiha own 1.46 pairs per household on an average. Interestingly, while 20 per cent households of the former village also own shoes averaging just a pair per household, there is not a single household in the latter village that possesses a pair.

Use of a wrist watch is not merely to consult it, rather it is also used as a status symbol. It is used by the members of about 50 per cent (49.09) households of Hirāpur as against only 32 per cent in Āmbadiha.

So far as the dress of the women is concerned, sarees are worn mostly without any undergarments such as petticoats, brassieres and blouses. But the data available in the said table shows that 16.36 and 43.64 per cent households of Hirāpur use petticoats and blouses respectively, as against merely 4 and 6 per cent of Āmbadiha.

The Bāuri people use handmade winter clothes and pillows. But about 9.09 and 3.6 per cent households in Hirāpur use modern blankets and pillows respectively. On the contrary, there is not a single household in Āmbadiha that owns any of these.

Thus, from the above discussion, it is evident that more people of Hirāpur than those of Āmbadiha use modern dresses. The 'z' value on the use of full pants, shirt/T-shirt, slipper, shoes, blouse, blanket and pillows, respectively shows a significant variation at 5 per cent level of significance.

Non-Beneficiary Households

Among the non-beneficiaries, 55.6 and 66.04 per cent of households of Hirāpur use full pants and Shirt/T. Shirt respectively as against only 28.99 and 36.23 per cent of Āmbadiha. So the 'z' values show significant variations between these two villages on the use of these materials at 5 per cent level of significance.

So far as the use of footwear is concerned, 47.17 and 5.66 per cent of the households in Hirāpur have slippers and shoes, respectively, with an average holding of 1.44 and 1.33 pairs per household. It is as less as 21.74 and 1.45 per cent in Āmbadiha with an average possession of 1.07 and 1 pair per household. Hence, the 'z' value is also significant for both these assets at 5 per cent level of significance.

Wrist watch is found among 33.96 per cent households of Hirāpur and 13.04 per cent of Āmbadiha. The average holding comes to 1.06

and 1 pair per household on an average in the former and latter village respectively.

Women of 13.71 and 41.45 per cent households of Hirāpur use petticoats and blouses respectively as against merely 2.99 and 11.59 per cent of Āmbadiha.

So far as the use of winter clothes is concerned, 3.77 per cent households of Hirāpur use modern blankets but on the other hand there is not a single household in Āmbadiha which possesses any such article. Further, not a single household is found, either in the former or in the latter village in which a modern pillow is available for comfort and sound sleep.

6.4 FOOD HABIT AND DIETARY PATTERN

Poor food habit and dietary pattern lead to ill-health. To maintain good health, whether one is a vegetarian or a non-vegetarian or consume both vegetarian and non-vegetarian food depending upon his/her interest and economic condition, nutritious food is important. In order to have a balanced diet, expenses are high, be it vegetarian or non-vegetarian.

Almost all the Bāuris are non-vegetarian. For a common Bāuri man, it becomes expensive to be a vegetarian rather than a non-vegetarian. They consume meat, pork, chicken and fish but they do not spend much of their income on these commodities. Rather they are habituated to catch fish free of cost from the local public water bodies during leisure. Apart from this, they are also very fond of snail, frog, turtle, crab, and a snake-like creature called *kochiā.* In addition to the consumption of these creatures, the Bāuris also consume different rodents like mongoose, rats and birds like sparrow and pigeons. For consumption of adequate flesh they hunt wild cats and a cat-like animal living in trees called *Sāliā pātni.* They also consume flesh of the bat with keen interest. But consumption of snails, frog, *kochiā* wild cat and rodents makes them polluted in the eyes of society, and hence they are regarded as untouchables. As a result, many Bāuri households of Hirāpur have become conscious of their inferior social position in the society and have given up these food habits. But the Bāuris of Āmbadiha still consume all these items without any hesitation. In this context the data available in Table 6.19 shows that among the beneficiary households, 21.82, 20.0, 18.18, 29.09 and 5.45 per cent households of Hirāpur have given up consumption of snail, *kochiā,* frog, rat and wild cats respectively, but all households of Āmbadiha still continue consuming the flesh of these creatures, except

TABLE 6.19
Household given-up traditional food habit

Consumption of	Beneficiary HHs				Non-Beneficiary HHs			
	Hirāpur (N=57)		Āmbadiha (N=50)		Hirāpur (N=53)		Āmbadiha (N=69)	
	Continuing	Given up	Continuing	Given up	Continuing	Given up	Continuing	Given up
(1)	(2)	(3)	(4)	(5)	(6)	(7)	(8)	(9)
Snail	43 (78.18)	12 (21.82)	50 (100.00)	-	47 (26.68)	6 (11.32)	69 (100.00)	-
Kotchia	44 (80.00)	11 (20.00)	50 (100.00)	-	42 (79.25)	11 (20.75)	69 (100.00)	-
Frog	45 (81.82)	10 (18.18)	50 (100.00)	-	50 (93.34)	3 (5.66)	69 (100.00)	-
Crab	55 (100.00)	-	50 (100.00)	-	53 (100.00)	-	69 (100.00)	-
Turtle	55 (100.00)	-	50 (100.00)	-	53 (100.00)	-	69 (100.00)	-
Mongoose	55 (100.00)	-	50 (100.00)	-	53 (100.00)	-	69 (100.00)	-
Sparrow	55 (100.00)	-	50 (100.00)	-	53 (100.00)	-	69 (100.00)	-
Rat	39 (70.91)	16 (29.09)	37 (74.00)	13 (26.00)	41 (76.36)	12 (22.00)	55 (79.71)	14 (20.29)
Wild cat	52 (94.55)	3 (5.45)	50 (100.00)	-	53 (100.00)	-	69 (100.00)	-
Salia Pathi	55 (100.00)	-	50 (100.00)	-	53 (100.00)	-	69 (100.00)	-

Note: Figures in brackets represent %age.

26 per cent households who have given up consuming the meat of rats. Likewise while there are 11.32, 20.75, 5.69 and 22.64 per cent non-beneficiary households in Hirāpur who have given up consuming the meat of snail, *kochiā,* frog and rat respectively, there is not a single non-beneficiary household in Āmbadiha, members of which are found to have given up consumption of the meat of these creatures, except 20.29 per cent households which have given up consumption of the meat of rats.

Normally, a Bāuri takes rice-in-water at about 8 am and leaves home for the day's work at about 9 am. But many of them manage with tea prepared especially with molasses (a variety of sweetener cheaper than sugar) and salt. They do not use milk as it is costly. An adult Bāuri man takes about half to one litre of tea or even more with puffed rice (Plate: C. 4). They come back by 4 pm and take their supper at about 7 pm. They never take rice-in-water in the evening as it renders one lazy.

Vegetable curry is mainly prepared with arun, potato and locally available leafy vegetables. Often in most households only leafy vegetables and *dal* are prepared and consumed with hot rice. They also prepare curry out of various costly vegetables but the frequency and quantity consumed of such curries are minimised to reduce expenditure. Sometimes, the poorer households manage with *khechudi*, a combination of rice, *dal*, salt, leafy vegetables and sometimes sugar to avoid expenses in preparing a vegetable curry.

Expenditure Pattern on Food Items

The expenditure pattern on various food items like cereals, kirana, vegetables, meat, fish and non-food items has been discussed earlier in Chapter IV. It is found that among the beneficiary households in Hirāpur, 53.71 per cent of the total income of the sample households has been spent on food items, whereas in Āmbadiha it was 68.31 per cent. Among the non-beneficiary households, the expenditure figures are 61.34 per cent of the total income for Hirāpur but it was rather high at 70.33 per cent of the total income in Āmbadiha (Table 4.16). Further, data in the same table reveals that the beneficiary households of both the villages spend more money on vegetables rather than on meat or fish. A reverse trend is observed among the non-beneficiary households in both the study villages.

When the total amount spent on different food items is considered as 100 per cent, and percentage of amount spent on various broad food items like cereals, kirana, vegetables and meat, fish is calculated, a clear picture of expenditure on food emerges. These are discussed below:

Beneficiary Households

Table 6.20 explains that of the total amount of Rs. 54371.05 spent on food items among the sample beneficiary households of Hirāpur, 60.22 per cent is exclusively spent on cereals, as against 68.36 per cent of Rs. 45985.70 spent by the households of Āmbadiha. The cereals mainly include rice as the principal foodgrain. In very few cases it includes wheat flour and flattened rice. But expenditure on these items is found to be very negligible in both the villages. So far as *Kirana* items are concerned, the people of the former village have spent 15.44 per cent of total expenditure on food items, whereas only 8.87 per cent was spent by the latter one. Pulses like *Arhar* and *Mung* constitute the principal items of purchase among a limited variety of associated kirana items like red chilli, oil, turmeric powder and spices.

The people of Hirāpur spend more money on vegetables than those of Āmbadiha. But potato remains the most important of vegetables for the people of both the villages as it constitutes 40.19 per cent of the total money spent on vegetables in case of Hirāpur, as against 55.47 per cent of Āmbadiha. The rest 9.42 per cent of Hirāpur as against 11.01 per cent of Āmbadiha is spent on meat and fish. Interestingly even though expenditure on dried fish is more than on other non-vegetarian commodities in case of both the villages, the people of Hirāpur have spent quite a significant amount of their income on meat and fresh fish. This is attributed to the fact that when the people return home from Bhubaneswar city in the evening, many fish vendors line the roadsides and in that case they fall to the temptation to purchase. This situational scope is very rare for the people of Āmbadiha and hence the difference. Another factor responsible for this is that non-beneficiary people generally spend some time in fishing from the local public ponds and other such water bodies which the beneficiary people do not normally get as they spend most of their time in business activities in Bhubaneswar. A look at the total figures shows that when the people of the former village spend 75.82 per cent of their income on rice, dal, potato, dried fish, etc. it is as high as 85.66 per cent in case of Āmbadiha.

Non-Beneficiary Households

The total expenditure on food items of the non-beneficiary households of Hirāpur is Rs. 44064.15 as against Rs. 51787.45 of

Āmbadiha. But the people of Hirāpur have spent 62.60 per cent of the total income on cereals as against as much as 71.87 per cent by those of Āmbadiha.

TABLE 6.20

Expenditure pattern on different food items

Broad category of Items	Specific Items	Beneficiary		Non-Beneficiary	
		Hirāpur	Āmbadiha	Hirāpur	Āmbadiha
(1)	(2)	(3)	(4)	(5)	(6)
Cereals	Rice	31176.85 (92.22)	30820.75 (98.04)	26882.50 (97.45)	36604.75 (98.35)
	Others	1565.00 (11.78)	616.60 (1.96)	703.10 (2.55)	6115.00 (1.65)
	Total	32741.85 (100.00) [60.25]	31437.35 (100.00) [68.36]	27585.60 (100.00) [62.60]	37219.75 (100.00) [71.87]
Kirana	Pulses	5006.00 (59.63)	2336.80 (57.30)	3462.70 (61.99)	1630.00 (61.83)
	Others	3389.05 (40.37)	1741.35 (47.70)	21229.90 (38.01)	1006.35 (38.17)
	Total	8395.05 (100.00) [15.44]	40785.15 (100.00) [8.87]	5585.60 (100.00) [12.65]	2636.35 (100.00) [5.09]
Vegetables	Potato	3260.00 (40.19)	3000.00 (55.47)	1985.00 (49.51)	2115.00 (48.27)
	Others	4857.20 (59.81)	2407.95 (44.53)	2024.05 (50.49)	2266.25 (51.75)
	Total	8112.20 (100.00) [14.92]	5407.95 (100.00) [11.76]	4009.05 (100.00) [9.10]	4381.25 (100.00) [8.46]
Meat, Fish etc.	Dry-fish	17.80 (34.75)	3234.50 (63.89)	3880.00 (56.36)	3630.00 (48.08)
	Others	3341.95 (65.25)	1827.75 (36.11)	3003.90 (43.64)	3920.10 (51.92)
	Total	5121.95 (100.00) [9.42]	5062.25 (100.00) [11.01]	6883.90 (100.00) [15.60]	7550.10 (100.00) [14.58]
Grand Total	Rice, Pulses Pot., D.F.	4122.85 (75.92)	39392.05 (85.66)	36710.20 (82.18)	43979.75 (84.92)
	Others	13148.20 (24.18)	6593.65 (14.34)	7853.85 (17.82)	7807.75 (15.08)
	Total	54371.05 (100.00) [100.00]	45985.70 (100.00) [100.00]	44064.15 (100.00) [100.00]	51787.45 (100.00) [100.00]

Note: (i) Figures in brackets represent %age.

(ii) Figures in upper-brackets represent %age to the grand total figures.

As regards the expenditure on different *kirana* commodities the people of the former village are found to have spent more money (12.68%) than those of Āmbadiha (5.09%). Likewise, the people of Hirāpur spent more money (9.10%) on different vegetables than those of Āmbadiha (8.46%). Regarding the expenditure on meat, fish etc., while 15.62 per cent of the total income has been spent on these commodities by the people of Hirāpur, it is 14.58 per cent in the case of Āmbadiha.

Like the beneficiary households of both the villages, in this case also, rice, pulses like dal, potato and dried fish are found to be the principal commodities among cereals, *kirana*, vegetables and meat and fish items respectively.

Data in the same table also reveals that when the people of Hirāpur spent 82.18 per cent of their total income exclusively on cereals like rice, pulses like *dal*, vegetables like potato and on dried fish, it is 84.92 per cent in case of the village Aímbadiha.

6.5 DEVELOPMENT OF ABILITY FOR SELF-MANAGEMENT

Development of ability for self-management here refers to the management of home from various viewpoints.

Traditionally, the role of men and women has been quite specific and distinct for the smooth management of home. Normally the men function in the public sphere but the private or domestic sphere remains in the hands of women (cf. Jayawardena, 1986: 8).

As a result of this, women's participation in decision-making at home and managing it is directly linked with women in Indian society. It is usual that their supremacy over men is recognised in matriarchal societies, but their active participation in decision-making and managing the family is also given due importance in patriarchal societies, even though they do not head families in such societies.

Among the backward caste Hindu communities in general and *Dalit* communities in particular, a different picture is prevalent as the women of these communities are economically important almost at par with their male counterparts. They are not only concerned with the management of their homes at the domestic level, but are also equally able to earn money outside the home for themselves, as well as for their whole family. Thus, even though most of the *Dalit* communities are patriarchal and patrilocal in nature, absolute male supremacy in decision-making and managing the home is not tolerated by women. As a result, most often both men and women take important decisions in managing themselves and their families with mutual understanding and co-operation.

Against the above background, development of ability for self-management or management of home among the Bāuri people under study, 8 broad specific areas have been discussed below. These areas are: management of daily employment of family members, especially the women as wage-earner; participation of women in decision-making on daily expenditure; management of distribution of food among boy and girl children during scarcity of food; management of educating boy and girl children; decision-making on borrowing loan, management of family planning among married men and women; and management of participation of family members in political processes.

Management of Women as Labour Force Wage-Earner

Like caste Hindus, when a Bāuri becomes rich, he becomes conscious of his social prestige. For such a Bāuri, not allowing his wife to take up employment as a wage-earner is a matter of his status symbol. He feels very proud when he is able to do so. While interrogating on this a Bāuri very proudly replied "No, no, sir our women do not go for wage-earning". In another case a lady of a household also replied, "*Āme Kana Āau Ebe Kāmaku Jabu Bābu?*" meaning, "should we sir, go for wage-earning any more?" This reply signifies that she has become rich enough not to work for a living. But women of rich households may work in their own fields and even in the field of others while share-cropping.

When a bride is searched for a boy, great stress is laid on her capacity for work. But she is not sent for wage-earning immediately after marriage. Initially she is kept at home, at least for 3 days, and then sent for wage-earning. However, in many cases this period may vary from 7 days to 1 to 2 years depending upon the economic condition of the household. But at the same time she finds it difficult to take an independent decision in this regard even if there is intense need for it. Thus, whether to employ women or not remains the prerogative of the male members. In this context, the difference between the beneficiary households and the non-beneficiary households of the two study villages are described below:

Beneficiary Households

It is quite evident from Table 6.21 that the men of a large number of households (15%) in Hirāpur are much more prestige conscious than those of Āmbadiha (4.17%). These people do not send their women-folk for wage-earning any more.

TABLE 6.21

Management of employing women as wage-earners

Frequency	Beneficiary HHs		Non-Beneficiary HHs	
	Hirāpur (N=50)	Āmbadiha (N=48)	Hirāpur (N=49)	Āmbadiha (N=66)
(1)	(2)	(3)	(4)	(5)
Always	36 (37.00)	44 (91.67)	42 (85.71)	62 (93.94)
Occasionally	6 (12.00)	2 (4.17)	4 (8.16)	1 (1.52)
Not at all	8 (16.00)	2 (4.17)	3 (6.12)	3 (4.55)
Z value	2.12		0.37	

Note: (i) Z is calculated out of the data relating to those households from which the women are not employed as wage-earners at all.

(ii) N includes only those households having married/adult women.

(iii) Figures in brackets represent %age.

Non-beneficiary Households

A perusal of the said table also makes it clear that the people of 6.12 per cent households of Hirāpur as against 4.55 per cent of Āmbadiha do not like to engage their women folk in wage-earning work. This apparently shows that more people of Hirāpur have become prestige conscious than those of Āmbadiha.

Decision-Making on Daily Expenditure

The bulk of the Bāuri live from day-to-day earnings. They earn every day and spend every day. Daily expenditure normally includes purchase of rice, grocery and other commodities.

Generally the wife hands over her day's income to her husband after she returns from work in the evening. But neither the husband nor the wife takes any independent decision on how to utilise the money. In most cases both the wife and husband decide on matters of managing family affairs with the limited means.

Beneficiary Households

In the above context a perusal of Table 6.22 makes it quite evident that among the beneficiary households, on an average, women of Hirāpur have independently decided on daily expenditure for about 50 per cent (49.32), i.e. 180 days in a year, against only 19.18 per cent or 70 days in case of Āmbadiha. On the other hand, on a majority of days, i.e. 256 days in a year or 70.14 per cent, both the wife and husband of Āmbadiha have decided together. Hence, so far as the rate of participation of women in decision-making on daily expenditure is concerned, there is a significant difference at 5 per cent level of significance between these two villages. The rate of participation of females in case of Hirāpur is found more because the beneficiary people are busy in their business activities in Bhubaneswar and come home late in the evening. They have the necessity of entrusted decision-making of their wives.

TABLE 6.22

Average participation of women and men in decision-making on daily expenditure

Persons	Beneficiary HHs		Non-Beneficiary HHs	
	Hirāpur	Āmbadiha	Hirāpur	Āmbadiha
(1)	(2)	(3)	(4)	(5)
Women	180 (49.32)	70 (19.18)	113 (30.96)	54 (14.79)
Men	85 (23.29)	39 (10.68)	55 (15.07)	24 (6.62)
Both	100 (27.40)	256 (70.14)	197 (53.97)	287 (78.63)
Z value	9.02		5.23	

Note: (i) Z is calculated out of the data relating to the women who have taken decision independently.

(ii) Figures in brackets represent %age.

Non-Beneficiary Households

Among the non-beneficiary households of Hirāpur women have taken independent decision on 30.96 per cent or 113 days in a year, whereas women of Āmbadiha have decided on 14.79 per cent or 54 days.

A further cursory look at the same table also reveals that for about 54 per cent or 197 days in a year both the spouses of Hirāpur have decided together and in case of Āmbadiha it is as high as 78.63 per cent or 287 days.

Among the non-beneficiary households, the people have more scope to remain at home than those of the beneficiary households. Hence, both the wife and husband decide which commodities are to be purchased on priority and its quantity depending upon their daily income.

Management of Food among Family Members during Food Scarcity

It is very important to note that the Bāuri people are very discriminatory towards a girl child. A girl child is in various ways neglected at different stages of her life. She is not only exploited in favour of the well-being of a boy child even while both depend on the breast of their mother, but a girl child is also neglected and under-fed as compared to a boy child in scarcity conditions. When a women has two breast-fed babies; a boy and the other a girl, the girl is generally breast-fed for a shorter period even if she is younger to the boy baby.

Beneficiary Households

In the above context Table 6.23 makes it clear that among the beneficiary households of both the villages, quite a large number of women opine that they prefer to give more food to their boy child rather than the girl child during scarcity of food. Not a single woman in any of the villages prefers to give more food to their girl child during such period of food scarcity.

TABLE 6.23

Management of distribution of among boy and girl children during scarcity

Preference	Beneficiary HHs		Non-Beneficiary HHs	
	Hirāpur (N=50)	Āmbadiha (N=48)	Hirāpur (N=49)	Āmbadiha (N=66)
(1)	(2)	(3)	(4)	(5)
More to son	38 (76.00)	41 (85.42)	38 (77.55)	58 (87.88)
More to daughters	-	-	-	-
Equal to both the children	12 (24.00)	7 (14.58)	11 (22.44)	8 (12.12)
Z value	- 63.50		1.75	

Note: (i) Z is calculated out of the data relating to those who give equal importance for both children.

(ii) Figures in brackets represent %age.

While in Hirāpur 76 per cent of women opine that they would prefer to give more food to their boy child during scarcity of food, in Āmbadiha more than 85 per cent people do so. The rest 24 per cent of women of the former villages as against 14.58 per cent of the latter village opine that they would distribute the available food equally between the two children. Hence more people of Hirāpur have become conscious about the equal status of girl and boy children than those of Āmbadiha.

Non-Beneficiary Households

The attitude of the non-beneficiaries is similar to that of the beneficiaries. The said table shows that while 22.44 per cent in Hirāpur give equal importance to both boys and girls in the matter of sharing food during scarcity, only 12.12 per cent do so in Āmbadiha. The rest of the people seem to discriminate.

Management of Educating Boy and Girl Children

Not only the girl children are discriminated in the matters of nourishment but in the field of education also. Preference is generally given on the education of boys rather than those of the girls. They view girls as the wealth or asset of some other unknown household, into which they would get married, and that they are primarily meant for the kitchen. There is, therefore, no need of spending much money on their education. In this context a question regarding the choosing of two children from amongst two sons and two daughters for getting free education at a school was posed, and the following picture emerged.

Beneficiary Households

Table 6.24 indicates the clear-cut attitude of the people in both the study villages in their preferences on educating sons and daughters. Whereas in Āmbadiha as many as 83.33 per cent persons chose both the sons, in Hirāpur 70 per cent did so. About 16.7 per cent in the former and 30 per cent in the latter village chose one boy and one girl for the purpose. Hence, it is clear that more people of Hirāpur than Āmbadiha give equal importance to the education of both boys and girls.

Non-Beneficiary Households

Among the non-beneficiary people also, a similar view prevails as is indicated in the said table. While 24.49 per cent people in Hirāpur give equal importance on educating both sons and daughters as against only 13.64 per cent in Āmbadiha, there is not a single person who prefers educating only daughters.

TABLE 6.24

Management of educating boy and girl children

Preference	Beneficiary HHs		Non-Beneficiary HHs	
	Hirāpur (N=50)	Āmbadiha (N=48)	Hirāpur (N=49)	Āmbadiha (N=66)
(1)	(2)	(3)	(4)	(5)
Both sons	35 (70.00)	40 (83.33)	37 (75.51)	57 (86.36)
Both daughters	-	-	-	-
One son and one daughter	15 (30.00)	8 (16.67)	12 (24.49)	9 (13.64)
Z value	1.54		1.35	

Note: (i) Z is calculated out of the data relating to those who give importance on the education of both children.

(ii) Figures in brackets represent %age.

Decision-Making on Borrowing Loan

The Bāuris borrow loan frequently from local money-lenders during lean seasons. But some interesting revelations come to light from Table 6.25 on decision-making on borrowing of loan during such lean patches.

TABLE 6.25

Decision making on contracting loan

Persons	Beneficiary HHs		Non-Beneficiary HHs	
	Hirāpur (N=10)	Āmbadiha (N=19)	Hirāpur (N=25)	Āmbadiha (N=31)
(1)	(2)	(3)	(4)	(5)
Women	-	-	1 (4.00)	-
Men	6 (60.00)	3 (15.79)	12 (48.00)	4 (12.90)
Both	4 (40.00)	16 (84.21)	13 (52.00)	27 (87.10)
Z value	- 2.50		- 3.00	

Note: (i) N includes only indebted households.

(ii) Z is calculated out of the data relating to decision taken by both.

(ii) Figures in brackets represent %age.

Beneficiary Households

Among the 10 households of Hirāpur and 19 of Āmbadiha, who have taken loans, there is not a single household in either of the villages in which the female members have exclusively decided to borrow.

But surprisingly when in maximum households, i.e. 16 or 84.21 per cent in Āmbadiha both the wife and husband have decided together to contract a loan to meet unavoidable expenses, in Hirāpur men alone have taken decisions independently in case of 60 per cent of households. However, in case of the rest 40 per cent households of this village, both the wife and husband are found to have taken a decision together to borrow loan.

Non-Beneficiary Households

The said table focuses that in case of a majority of households in both the villages, both wife and husband are found to have decided together to borrow loan during emergencies. But when in Hirāpur such cases are 52 per cent, in Hirāpur these are as high as 87.10 per cent. On the contrary, in case of 48 per cent of loanee households of Hirāpur men have independently decided as against 21.90 per cent households in Āmbadiha. Surprisingly there is only one household in the former village in which women have taken independent decision to borrow the loan.

Management of Family Planning among Married Men and Women

Management of family planning is a crucial issue among the *Dalit*, as most of them consider that children born to couples are the gifts of God, and they view them as economic assets. Hence, most people show a negative attitude towards family planning and do not like to limit their family size. This is mainly so because of their illiteracy and lack of awareness. But with the passage of time many of them have become conscious of the problems which large family size create. To a question relating to the desired number of children per couple, both beneficiary and non-beneficiary households of the two study villages have made some interesting revelations as follows.

Beneficiary Households

A perusal of Table 6.26 reveals that in case of both the villages, majority of the people, i.e. more than 50 per cent desire having 3-4 children. But 21.95 per cent in Hirāpur want only 1-2 children, thereby limiting the family to 4 persons, whereas merely 3.33 per cent do so in Āmbadiha.

Non-Beneficiary Households

Like the beneficiary people, in this case also, most people desire to have 3-4 children. Where 65 per cent in the former village desire so, it is 68.25 per cent in Āmbadiha. Interestingly when there are 4 persons accounting for 10 per cent in the village Hirāpur who want only 1-2 children, there is not a single person in Āmbadiha desiring so (Table 6.26).

TABLE 6.26

Management of family planning among married men and women

Desired size of family (in no. of children)	Beneficiary HHs		Non-Beneficiary HHs	
	Hirāpur (N=41)	Āmbadiha (N=40)	Hirāpur (N=40)	Āmbadiha (N=63)
(1)	(2)	(3)	(4)	(5)
1-2	9 (21.95)	2 (3.33)	4 (10.00)	-
3-4	24 (58.54)	41 (68.33)	26 (65.00)	43 (68.25)
5 or more	8 (19.51)	17 (28.33)	10 (20.00)	20 (31.75)
Z value	2.72		2.11	

Note: (i) Z is calculated out of the data relating to those who like to have 1-2 children.

(ii) Figures in brackets represent %age.

Management of Decision-Making for Casting of Votes in General Elections

Even though a majority of Bāuris participate in modern political processes, especially in casting votes in various elections, their political awareness is very limited in both the villages (Tables 5.1 and 5.2). These people are motivated by the local political brokers and they vote against those from whom they get little immediate incentives like cash or clothes. But it seems that in many cases they take their own decision and cast their votes accordingly. But as the political awareness is very low among the womenfolk, they find themselves unable to decide as to which party they should support. As a result they mostly depend upon their husbands for advice.

Beneficiary Households

Table 6.27 shows that in case of 80 per cent households of Hirāpur the men decide the party in favour of which their wives and other family members should cast their votes. But this is so only in 62.5 per cent of cases in Āmbadiha. Interestingly, in a number of 37 per cent households of Āmbadiha both the wife and husband together decide the party they would support, but in Hirāpur such cases are only 16 per cent. This happens because the people of Hirāpur have greater awareness of political realities by coming in contact with various people in Bhubaneswar. On the other hand the people of Āmbadiha remain indecisive, and hence take one another's help in deciding the party to elect.

TABLE 6.27

Management of casting votes in general elections

Persons taking decision	Beneficiary HHs		Non-Beneficiary HHs	
	Hirāpur (N=50)	Āmbadiha (N=48)	Hirāpur (N=49)	Āmbadiha (N=66)
(1)	(2)	(3)	(4)	(5)
Women	2 (4.00)	-	-	-
Men	40 (80.00)	30 (62.50)	35 (71.43)	42 (63.64)
Both	8 (16.00)	18 (37.50)	14 (28.57)	24 (36.36)
Z value	- 1.52		- 0.80	

Note: (i) Z is calculated out of the data relating to both persons.
(ii) Figures in brackets represent %age.

Non-Beneficiary Households

The said table shows that the people of non-beneficiary households in both the villages have decided independently the party in favour of which their wives and other family members should cast their votes. But whereas in Hirāpur it is 71.43 per cent, it is 63.64 per cent in Āmbadiha. So far as the decision made by both the wife and husband jointly is concerned, when it is 28.57 per cent in case of the former village, it is 36.36 per cent in the latter village.

Chapter VII

SUMMARY AND CONCLUSION

Indian social order is characterized by four-fold *Varna* organisation, i.e. *Brahman,* the priest; *Kshyatriya,* the warrior; *Vaishya*; the trader and *Shudra*, the artisan and cultivator. This system is known as *Chaturvarna* doctrine in which a large chunk of the population do not find their place. They are, therefore, called as A-*verna* or non-*varna*, *Panchama* or fifth born, *Antyaja* or last born, *Achhuan* or untouchable etc. Nowadays they are generally referred to as *Dalits* meaning the ex-untouchables.

Since time immemorial these people were discriminated against by the caste Hindus. They were forced to lead a miserable life by way of being forced to do menial jobs. They were segregated from caste Hindus villages through implementation of rigid caste norms of purity and pollution. Hence, they were denied their basic human rights and thus they had to lead a wretched life in a sub-human condition.

During the later part of the British regime in India, some social reformers attempted to integrate these people within the fold of Hinduism by shortening the discrepancies persisted between them and the caste Hindus. But they could not succeed in their goals. After independence, concerted efforts were made to bring them into the mainstream. Special constitutional safeguards were formulated and subsequently implemented for the well-being of these people.

The Constitution of India laid down a protective action plan under Article 46. It reads as "...that the state shall promote with special care the educational and economic interest of the weaker sections of the people, and shall protect them from social injustice and all forms of exploitation". Subsequently Articles 14, 15, 16, 17, 19, 23, 330, 335, 337, 340, 341, 366 etc. were also formulated to protect and safeguard various common interests of these people. In order to execute all these in proper manner Article 398 was also formulated by which the Constitution empowers the President of India to appoint a commission to study the socio-economic conditions of Scheduled Castes and Scheduled Tribes and submit an annual report to the President. These are altogether known as "Protective Discrimination" by which means the Scheduled Castes and other such groups are provided with special care in various ways. Similarly, during different Five Year Plans, due importance was also given to fulfil the requirements of the Article 46 and thereby to bring them into the mainstream.

As high illiteracy among these people seems to have been very much responsible for their woeful conditions and miserable plight, reservation of seats in educational institutions and other fora has been made. They are exempted from tuition fees, and are provided with reading and writing materials and scholarships. In order to enable them to enter into private and public sector organisations, provision of job-reservation has also been ensured. Apart from all these, right from the time of independence, much efforts have been put forth to provide them gainful employment through the provision of various anti-poverty programmes in different Five Year Plan periods, especially during sixth and seventh plan periods. People below the poverty line were identified and economic assistance was rendered to them with the provision of subsidy facility from 33 to 75 per cent under various economically gainful income generating schemes like dairy, goatery, poultry, petty business, rickshaw and trolley pulling, bullock-cart etc. under various national and state level programmes.

A large chunk of money has been diverted through these programmes for the welfare and economic upliftment of the *Dalits* but it is generally agreed upon by the planners that the outcome of the efforts put into has not yet been satisfactory. They are still lagging behind economically and are leading a pitiable life even after five decades of independence of our country.

So, keeping this background image in mind, in the present study an attempt has been made to explore the magnitude of change that has occurred among the Bāuris, a *Dalit* caste of Khurdha district in the state of Orissa.

For the practical reasons, two caste Hindu villages having sizeable Bāuri population in two different localities, i.e. one (Hirāpur); on the outskirts of Bhubaneswar city, the state capital of Orissa and another (Āmbadiha); away from this have been studied for the present work. The people of the former village are 'more exposed' to different forces of modernization, like transport, market, mass media, bureaucratic administration, formal education, developed communication facility etc., than those of the latter one. It is because of their proximal existence to the capital city.

Under the process of high pressure of modernization, over the years, some peculiar social situations have emerged in the village

Hirāpur which have considerably disintegrated the social structure of the village and hence weakened the traditional role of castes and also of the people of different castes. What are more particularly visible here, under which situations the Bāuris of this village have become very cunning and tactful to come out of the grip of the orthodox caste Hindus and to take advantage of any opportunity, be it social or economic, may be noted as follows.

Traditionally the Bāuris and the local caste Hindus are economically inter-dependent. The caste Hindus require the labour force of the Bāuris and the Bāuris in turn depend on them for their livelihood. Still then the Bāuris are socially discriminated and economically exploited by the caste Hindus in various ways. They are considered as untouchables and hence are segregated from the village. But when after the establishment of the state capital of Orissa in Bhubaneswar in 1948, ample wage-earning and other job opportunities were available for the poors or the Bāuris, and also when conditions were created for self-employment of these people with the financial assistance from various poverty alleviation programmes of the Government, the equation of economic inter-dependence between the Bāuris and the local caste Hindus started changing very fast and finally it took a new turn in the village. Under this emerging situation, the bargaining power of the Bāuris has tremendously increased over the last few decades and consequently the local caste Hindus have now become more dependent of these people than they were previously.

Interestingly since the establishment of the state capital in Bhubaneswar, the Bāuris of Hirāpur have been demanding treatment at par with the caste Hindus. This ultimately creates sustained social tension between the two. But whenever there is a rigid implication of untouchability and the Bāuris protest or revolt against it, the caste Hindus restrict the Bāuris to enter into the village and purchase their daily commodities from the village shops. In such a situation the Bāuris convene a regional level meeting of their caste and decline to work in the fields of the caste Hindus and come over to Bhubaneswar city to work as daily wage-labour. The caste Hindus on the other hand fail to procure the required labour force from the locality as there is no other wage-earning people who could substitute the Bāuris. So, as the caste Hindus cannot afford to lose their crops, they wait for some time but ultimately they are compelled to go to the doors of the Bāuri leaders to settle down the disputes. And in that situation the voice of the Bāuris prevail. Hence, from many such instances the Bāuris of this village have now very rightly realised the nature of dependence of the caste

Hindus on them and very tactfully try to exploit the situation to their advantage. Surprisingly this situation has even accelerated the process of sanskritic model of social change whereby the Bāuris try to adopt the caste Hindu rituals and festive occasions and even try to adopt various implications of cultural ways of observing such occasions. What is more conspicuous here is that the Bāuris of Hirāpur not only try to adopt the caste Hindu culture in order to raise their social status but also argue that one's social position should be judged according to its caste occupation. And since they do not have any unclean occupation as their caste identity, they must not be treated as untouchables. What is more phenomenal here is that interestingly many of the Bāuri households of Hirāpur have also started giving up their traditional food habit that relegates them to an inferior position in the society. This sort of social bent of mind of the Bāuris of Hirāpur has in other ways also developed an economic zeal in the minds of these people. The Bāuris of this village have understood that simply acculturating some of the caste Hindu cultural traits or by giving up some socially harmful cultural practices of their own culture like consumption of unclean food which is parasitical to their social status does not help them to raise their social status. They have also become very careful as how to raise their economic condition. Most of them have become more conscious about the value of money and hence its utility. They try to utilise their hard earned money in proper manner rather than simply spending it either for consumption or for life cycle rituals. It has become more evident among the people of Hirāpur who have been provided with various assistance under different poverty alleviation programmes of the Government and hence taken to various non-traditional occupations in Bhubaneswar city and work hard to earn accordingly.

So, in order to have a comparative picture of the impact of the development planning and modernization, the whole Bāuri population of each village has been divided into two groups such as beneficiary[1] and non-beneficiary and then comparison is made between the beneficiary of the village Hirāpur with those of Āmbadiha. Likewise a comparison is also made between the non-beneficiaries of these two villages.

The broad objectives of the study may be noted as follows:

(i) to ascertain the extent of educational development between the family members of beneficiary households and also between the family members of the non-beneficiary households of the village Hirāpur and Āmbadiha;

(ii) to ascertain occupational mobility and changes pertaining to economic condition between the beneficiary households and also between the non-beneficiary households of the village Hirāpur and Āmbadiha; and

(iii) to ascertain consequential changes pertaining to political awareness and participation in modern politics, family planning and treatment of diseases, ritual belief pattern and practices, sanitation, dress pattern, food habit, and development of ability for self-management between the beneficiary households and also between the non-beneficiary households of the village Hirāpur and Āmbadiha.

The summary findings which have been obtained are discussed under the following broad headings. The summary conclusion discussed in the first part, i.e. (i) of each heading is for the beneficiary households and the second part, i.e. (ii) for the non-beneficiary households.

(A) CHANGES IN EDUCATIONAL STATUS

That the overall literacy of the Bāuri people of the village Hirāpur is higher (28.68%) than those of Āmbadiha (26.71%). But surprisingly the family members of the beneficiary households of the former village record less literacy than those of the latter one.

(i) Out of the total of 191 family members of the beneficiary households of Hirāpur, only 47 or 24.61 per cent are found to be literate as against 56 or 27.32 per cent of the total 205 of those of the village Āmbadiha. But the difference is found to be insignificant at 5 per cent level of significance. As a result, the first hypothesis which reads as "that the economic development inputs, i.e. poverty alleviation programmes, cause educational advancement among the family members of the beneficiary living at the proximal villages of urban centres" is hereby not borne out. So, it can be said that economic development inputs, i.e. poverty alleviation programmes may not necessarily cause educational development among the family members of *Dalit* beneficiaries living on the outskirts of urban centres.

(ii) So far as the level of literacy among the family members of non-beneficiary households of the study villages is concerned, in case of the villages Hirāpur it is found to be 32.5 per cent as against 26.24 per cent of Āmbadiha. In this case the difference is also observed to be insignificant at 5 per cent level of significance.

From the above findings it can be tentatively said that literacy among the family members of beneficiary households of Hirāpur is lower than those of Āmbadiha. Conversely the literacy among the family members of the non-beneficiary households of the former village is higher than those of the latter one. But if the literacy of the family members of both the beneficiary and non-beneficiary households is added together village-wise, the literacy of the Bāuri people of the Hirāpur as a whole is found to be slightly higher than that of Āmbadiha.

However, the low level of literacy among the family members of beneficiary households of Hirāpur is observed to be primarily because of the persistence of high illiteracy (71.43%) among the children who fall in the school going age. But it is as less 33.33 per cent in case of the village Āmbadiha.

As regards the reasons responsible for non-enrolment, dropout or in other words low level of literacy among the Bāuris of these two villages, as many as 7 inter-related factors are attributed by these people. But the most important reason which is found to be responsible in reducing literacy to a great extent among the family members of the beneficiary households of Hirāpur is that the poor economic condition of parents combinedly with easy and better availability of job opportunities for both the adult and young people in Bhubaneswar city. It is borne out by highest percentage of people (77.5) and the intensity of this reason is also rated with highest score (87.94 points) in a three point scale. The next important reason which is focused by 61.25 per cent people and rated with 77.78 score points is that negligence of parents towards the education of their children as they mostly spend their time in different economic pursuits in Bhubaneswar city. Thus, those intending to educate their children are helpless as adult males or sometimes both the parents come over to Bhubaneswar city in the morning and go back home late in the evening. This pattern of engagement of adult family members or the guardians in the above city apparently creates a negative impact on the education of their children. On the contrary, women who do not come over to Bhubaneswar city to work also do not take much interest and care in the education of their children either because of their illiteracy or poverty. Consequently the children become wayward and most often try to remain away from the school even if they are sent to school.

(B) OCCUPATIONAL MOBILITY

(i) Out of the total of 55 beneficiary households of Hirāpur, more than 50 per cent (54.55) or 30 households have taken to various profitable non-traditional occupations (Rickshaw/ Trolley pulling 9 or 16.36 per cent, petty business 8 or 14.55 per cent, Tailoring 1 or 1.82 per cent, share-cropping 6 or 10.91 per cent, horticulture 1 or 1.82 per cent, construction work 3 or 5.45 per cent, carpentry 1 or 1.82 per cent and weaving of fishing nets for sale 1 or 1.82 per cent households) as their primary source of income as against a mere 14 per cent or 7 households of Āmbadiha (petty business 5 or 10 per cent and share-cropping 2 or 4 per cent households).

The remaining beneficiary households of Hirāpur earn their livelihood from various traditional occupations like daily/annual labour (18 or 32.73 per cent), coconut plucking (1 or 1.82 per cent), transport business with bullock-cart (2 or 3.69 per cent), stone dressing (2 or 3.64 per cent) and animal husbandry (2 or 3.64 per cent) as their primary occupation. On the contrary the remaining beneficiary households of Āmbadiha earn their livelihood primarily from daily/ annual labour (30 or 78 per cent), Coconut plucking (3 or 6 per cent) and transport operation with bullock-cart (3 or 6 per cent).

There are 36.36 per cent or 20 households in Hirāpur as against merely 7 per cent or 4 households in case of Āmbadiha who earn their livelihood subsidiarily out of various non-traditional occupations. Thus, from the above findings it is observed that the occupational mobility among the beneficiary households of Hirāpur is found to be much higher than those of Āmbadiha. And the 'z' value signifies that the difference obtained between the beneficiary households of Hirāpur and Āmbadiha who have adopted various non-traditional or new occupations as their primary source of income, is statistically significant at 5 per cent level of significance. Hence, the second hypothesis that reads as "that economic developments inputs, i.e. poverty alleviation programmes do not create occupational mobility among the beneficiaries who live in urban fringes" is hereby not borne out (cf. pp. 229-230). As a result, it can be said that the economic development inputs, i.e. poverty alleviation programmes create occupational mobility among the beneficiary households who live in urban fringes.

(ii) As regards the non-beneficiary households, of the total 53 households in Hirāpur, 28.30 per cent or 15 households have taken to various non-traditional occupations like rickshaw/ trolley pulling (5.66 per cent or 3 households), petty business (9.43 per cent or 5 households) share-cropping (9.43 per cent or 5 households) construction work (1.89 per cent or 1 household), weaving of fishing (net for sale) 1.89 per cent or 1 household) as their primary source of income as against only 2.90 per cent or 2 households of the total 69 such households of Āmbadiha. These two households have taken to share-cropping.

Regarding subsidiary occupations, it is found that only 5.66 per cent or 3 households of Hirāpur as against 2.90 per cent or 2 households of Āmbadiha have taken to some non-traditional occupations as their secondary sources of income. However, so far as adoption of non-traditional occupations as primary source of occupations among the non-beneficiary households is concerned, the difference comes to be significant at 5 per cent level of significance.

(iii) Irrespective of beneficiary and non-beneficiary households, among the total 108 households in Hirāpur as high a percentage of 41.67 or 45 households have taken to different non-traditional sources of income as their primary occupational as against merely 7.56 per cent or 9 households of the total 119 households in Āmbadiha.

(C) INCOME, EXPENDITURE AND INDEBTEDNESS

(i) It is natural that when people adopt new or non-traditional occupations, these are normally more income generating than their traditional ones. Accordingly their income level is also changed.

As a significant number of Bāuri beneficiary households of Hirāpur have taken to different non-traditional occupations which are more profitable in nature than their traditional ones, their income level is also observed to have been increased. It is found that as high a percentage of 50.91 or 28 beneficiary households of this village are found to have crossed the poverty line which is fixed at Rs. 11,000 per annum as against only 20 per cent or 10 households of Āmbadiha. So, the 'z' value shows a significant variation at 5 per cent level of significance, as a result of which the third hypothesis that reads as "that the income level of the beneficiaries living at the outskirts of urban centres is same as their counterparts living in remote areas" is hereby not borne out (cf. p. 272). As a result of this, it can be said that the income level of the beneficiary households living on the periphery of the urban centres is not same as those who live in remote areas. Rather it is much higher than the income level of the beneficiaries of the remote villages.

Among the rest of the households of Hirāpur, 25.45 per cent or 14 households are found to be poor, followed by 16.36 per cent or 9 households is very poor, 5.4 per cent or 3 households as very very poor and the rest 1.82 per cent or 1 household as destitute. There are 14 per cent or 7 households, 36 per cent or 18 households, 22 per cent or 11 households and 8 per cent or 4 households respectively in case of the village Āmbadiha.

(ii) So far as the case of non-beneficiary households is concerned while, of the total of 53 households of Hirāpur, 30.19 per cent or 16 households have crossed the poverty line, it is only 8.7 per cent or 6 households in the village Āmbadiha.

(iii) Irrespective of the beneficiary and non-beneficiary households, when a total number of 40.74 per cent or 44 households in Hirāpur have crossed the poverty line, it is merely 13.45 per cent or 16 households in the village Āmbadiha.

(D) PER CAPITA INCOME

(i) The mean per capita income works out to be Rs. 2936.38 per annum in case of the village Hirāpur, as against only Rs. 1618.85 of Āmbadiha, whereas the figure for the state as a whole is Rs. 3907. Thus, while the per capita income of the village Hirāpur is found to be fairly close to the per capita income of the state with a difference of Rs. 970.62 or 24.85 per cent, the per capita income of Āmbadiha falls short by Rs. 2288.15 or 58.57 per cent of the same.

(ii) Amongst the non-beneficiary households the per capita income of Hirāpur comes to be Rs. 2264.59 as against Rs. 1612 in Āmbadiha.

(E) EXPENDITURE PATTERN

(i) In order to find out the expenditure pattern 20 per cent of the total beneficiary and non-beneficiary households of each study village were selected and a specific schedule was canvassed for every sample household every evening for a whole year. And it is found that the beneficiary households of Hirāpur have spent 53.71 per cent of the total annual income on different food items (32.35 per cent on cereal, 8.29 per cent on grocery, 8.01 per cent on vegetables and 5.06 per cent on meat, fish etc.) as against 68.31 per cent of those of Āmbadiha (46.70 per cent on cereals, 6.06 per cent on grocery, 8.03 per cent on vegetables and 7.25 per cent on meat, fish etc.). The rest of the income i.e. 46.29 per cent in case of Hirāpur and 31.69 per cent of Āmbadiha have been spent on different non-food items.

Amongst a varieties of non-food items, like drinks/alcohol, narcotics, clothing, dress materials, medicine, sanitation, fuel, light, transport, education, fair and festival and social obligation, entertainment and miscellaneous, clothes / dress materials account for maximum percentage (7.99) of money of Hirāpur but it is narcotics in the village Āmbadiha (7.68). Thus, the expenditure on the food items together with the expenditure in alcoholic drinks and narcotics constitutes 61.56 per cent in Hirāpur, but it is as high as 77.2 per cent in Āmbadiha.

(ii) So far as the expenditure pattern of non-beneficiary households is concerned these people of Hirāpur have spent 61.34 per cent of their total income on different food items (38.40 per cent on cereals, 7.7 per cent on grocery, 5.58 per cent on vegetables and 9.58 per cent on meat, fish etc.) as against 70.33 per cent in Āmbadiha (50.54 per cent on cereals, 3.58 per cent on grocery, 5.95 per cent on vegetables and 10.25% on meat, fish etc.). Amongst the non-food items these people of either study villages have spent highest percentage of their income on narcotics and alcoholic drinks but when it is 9.53 per cent in case of Hirāpur, it is 8.96 per cent in Āmbadiha. So, the expenditure on food items together with narcotics and alcoholic drinks comes to be 70.87 per cent in the former villages as against a percentage of 79.29 in Āmbadiha.

(F) SAVINGS AND INDEBTEDNESS

(i) (a) Among the 55 beneficiary households of Hirāpur 18.15 per cent or 10 households have contracted loans and hence are under debt as against 38 per cent or 19 households of Āmbadiha.

(b) About 38.18 per cent or 21 households of Hirāpur as against only 18 per cent or 9 households of Āmbadiha have saved some amount of money. The rest 43.64 per cent or 24 households of the former village as against 44 per cent or 22 households of the latter one have spent what they had earned. They have neither contracted any loan nor have saved any money for further use.

(c) As regards the extent of indebtedness when 30 per cent or 3 households of Hirāpur are in the debt burden of above Rs. 800, it is 21 per cent or 4 households in Āmbadiha.

(d) As regards savings, when there are 42.80 per cent or 9 households in the village Hirāpur who have saved money in the highest range, i.e. Rs. 2000 or more, it is merely 11.11% or 1 household in Āmbadiha.

(ii) (a) Among the non-beneficiary households, in case of 47.17 per cent or 25 households in Hirāpur, the expenditure is more than their earnings as against 44.93 per cent or 31 households in Āmbadiha. So, they have incurred loans to meet their extra expenditure and hence are in debt.

(b) The earning is more than expenditure in case of 22.64 per cent or 12 households in Hirāpur as against 14.49 per cent or 10 households in Āmbadiha. Hence they have saved some amount of their earnings for future use. The rest 30.19 per cent or 16 households of the former village as against 30.19 per cent or 16 households of the latter one have managed themselves with the money they had earned. But, neither they have saved any money for the use in future nor have incurred any loan.

(c) So far as the extent of indebtedness is concerned, when 24 per cent households of Hirāpur are found to be under the debt burden in the highest debt range of Rs. 801 and more, it is 9.65 per cent or 3 households in Āmbadiha.

(d) As regards the extent of savings, 1 or 33 per cent of household in Hirāpur has saved money in the highest range of savings i.e. Rs. 2000 or more, there is none in Āmbadiha.

(G) Reasons of Indebtedness

(i) As to the reasons of incurring a loan by the beneficiary households in Hirāpur, the most frequent reason is for the purpose of improving one's own business as it is met by 6 or 60 per cent of the total 10 indebted households of this village. On the contrary, there are as many as 79 per cent or 15 households of the total 19 indebted households in Āmbadiha who have incurred loan for subsistence.

The other reasons for contracting a loan are subsistence (40 per cent), consumption of alcoholic drinks and intoxicants (40 per cent), meeting life cycle rituals and social obligations (30 per cent), fair and festival (30 per cent), agricultural development (20 per cent), education of children (10 per cent) and treatment of disease (10 per cent) in Hirāpur. But it is 42.11 per cent for agricultural development, 36.64 per cent for fairs and festivals, 31.58 per cent for meeting life cycle rituals and social obligations, 10.53 per cent for improving own business establishment and 5.79 per cent for the education of children in Āmbadiha.

(ii) Among the beneficiary households, maximum percentage of households of both the study villages, i.e. 76 in Hirāpur as against 90.32 in Āmbadiha, have borrowed loan for their subsistence purpose. The other reasons for contracting a loan are found to be fairs and festivals (60 per cent), agricultural development (52 per cent), meeting of life cycle rituals and social obligations (40 per cent), treatment of disease (28 per cent), improving own business establishment (20 per cent), consumption of alcoholic drinks (12 per cent) and education of children (8 per cent) in Hirāpur. These figures come to be 51.65 per cent, 35.48 per cent, 29.03 per cent, 12.90 per cent, 9.68 per cent, 25.81 per cent, 9.68 per cent respectively for the village Āmbadiha.

(H) ACQUISITION OF ASSETS

Acquisition of various productive and non-productive assets often indicates the status of a household.

In the past, the Bāuris were not allowed to use or own various luxurious assets rather they were to manage themselves with the minimum and specific assets as specified by the caste Hindus. But nowadays many of them are quite aware of their rights and now own various assets. The assets which these people now own, can broadly be divided into two categories, viz. (i) Immovable and (ii) Movable.

The immovable assets include land; both homestead and agricultural, house buildings and economically important fruit bearing trees. Among the movable assets which have economic value include domestic animals, agricultural and fishing implements, musical instruments, vehicles, audio-visual gadgets, furniture, utensils, and precious metals, foodgrains, and some luxurious goods. However, among all these, the most popular assets which are found in almost all Bāuri households include agricultural and fishing implements.

In order to find out the value of different immovable and movable assets, two different methods have been adopted. In the first method, the informants were asked to value their own assets. But to avoid the ambiguities of this method, a different scientific method called 'straight line method' has also been used. The results obtained in these methods are presented below:

(i) Among the beneficiary households, the average value of all assets irrespective of any category of assets, comes to Rs. 7434.45 per household in Hirāpur as against Rs. 5095.86 in Āmbadiha. As per the second or the straight line method, it works out to be Rs. 7680.39 in Hirāpur village as against Rs. 5149.40 in Āmbadiha.

(ii) Among the non-beneficiary households, according to the first method, the average value of assets irrespective of any category comes to Rs. 4885.61 per household in Hirāpur as against Rs. 4155.28 in Ambadiha. But as valued by the straight line method, it is Rs. 4971.79 in Hirāpur as against Rs. 4171.79 in Āmbadiha.

Development planning not only brings forth occupational and economic mobility but also influences various social behaviour of the people. Some of the major effects of this are improvement of political awareness and political participation in democratic processes, development of awareness on family planning and adoption of family planning measures, development of awareness on mother and child health care, etc. It also influences the ritual belief pattern and ritual practices of the people. The summary results may be discussed as follows:

(i) Political Participation

(i) The Bāuri people of both the study villages participate in modern political processes to a great extent but the level of their political awareness is very poor. As regards the political participation in modern democratic process, on an average, an equal percentage of beneficiary people in both the villages have cast their votes in the last elections for M.P., M.L.A., *Sarpanch* and Ward members. It comes to be 90.31 per cent in case of the village Hirāpur as against 91.56 per cent of Āmbadiha. This marginal difference does not show any significance. But the level of political awareness of the people in Hirāpur is much higher than those in Āmbadiha. On an average, the level of political awareness among the people of the former villages comes to 46.39 per cent but it is only 36.43 per cent in case of the latter one. Now it comes to the mind that when the level of political awareness of the Bāuris in Āmbadiha is much less than that in Hirāpur, how could it be possible on the part of such a high percentage of people of this village to participate in the above elections? This is of course not surprising. As elsewhere in rural India, the role of the grassroots level petty political brokers becomes very important in motivating the people during elections, here in Āmbadiha, such brokers also play an important role in motivating the Bāuri people to cast their votes for particular parties. They provide marginal incentives like rice, cloth etc. and this results in their participation in political elections.

(ii) As among the beneficiary households, the level of political participation of non-beneficiary households is also more or less the same. But the overall level of awareness comes to 41.11 per cent in case of the village Hirāpur as against 34.86 per cent in Āmbadiha.

(J) Family Planning

In a country like India, where population is growing very fast and the people are facing its negative consequences, the need of family planning has been a major objective of the nation. But the level of awareness on family planning is very poor among majority of Indian people as most are rural-based and are illiterate. The Bāuris being mainly rural poor, illiterate and agricultural labourers do have very little knowledge on the use of family planning. They hesitate to adopt any modern family planning measure as they believe that the children born to them are the gifts of God and hence they must not go against it. They consider children as economic assets and hence try to procreate more rather than reducing the size by adoption of any family planning method.

(i) As regards the attitude towards family planning, among the beneficiary households, when 43.90 per cent of married women in Hirāpur disapprove the need of family planning, it is as high a percentage as 66.67 in Āmbadiha. Similarly among the beneficiary households when it is 50 per cent in case of the former village who opine against the need of planning their family, it is 67.21 per cent in case of the latter one. However, despite negative attitude of a majority of people in beneficiary category of both the villages, as many as 18 or 43.90 per cent couples in Hirāpur have adopted various family planning measures as against only 11 or 18.33 per cent in Āmbadiha.

In case of both the villages, among those who have adopted various family planning measures, either the male spouses have taken the initiative and persuaded their female partners or the female partners themselves have voluntarily taken the risks of tubectomy, intra-uterine devices or of using oral pills. This is because they think that undergoing vasectomy means emasculation that results in the loss of manly vigour and health. Since the males are the head of the family and are the chief bread-earners, they do not like to risk the health of their male partners.

(ii) Among the non-beneficiary households, there are 15 couples or 37.5 per cent in Hirāpur who have adopted different family planning measures but it is 17 or 26.98 per cent in case of Āmbadiha.

Thus from the above findings, it comes to the notice that the people in Hirāpur have become more conscious about the necessity of family planning than their counterparts in Āmbadiha.

(K) Health Status and Treatment of Diseases

The Bāuri people suffer from various diseases. Some of these are minor and some are major. As per the perception of these people, the minor ailments include headache, hookworm, itching, scabies and sores. The major diseases as considered by them are bronchitis, colic, diarrhoea, earache, jaundice, malaria, paralysis, piles, toothache, tuberculosis and viral or common fever. However, the most common diseases from which many of the Bāuri suffer, are scabies and common or viral fever in both the villages.

(i) Treatment of disease is an important matter. As a result one must consult a medical practitioner in order to avoid risks of life. But, even though many Bāuris suffer from various diseases, they do not give much importance on this either because of their illiteracy or because of their poverty. Most often they consult the local traditional healers or the local quacks. Some of them who do not believe on the prescription of these practitioners and have money go to the local public health centres or consult the private doctors depending upon their suitability. However, among the beneficiary households, of the total 76 patients in Hirāpur who had suffered from various diseases during the survey year 36 or 47.37 per cent patients had consulted the doctors available at the local PHCs or hospitals or private clinics as against only 25 or 27.17 per cent of the total number of 92 patients in Āmbadiha. The rest patients had either taken the help of the local medicine-men or the local quacks or both of them.

(ii) So far as the case of the family members of non-beneficiary households is concerned, of the total 84 patients in Hirāpur, 41 or 78.81 per cent patients have taken the consultancy of registered medical practitioners as against 22 or 26.91 per cent of the total 84 patients in Āmbadiha. The rest patients, however, have consulted the local traditional healers and quacks.

(L) Expectant Mothers, New-born Babies and Immunization Process

Taking proper care of the expectant mothers and the new-born babies and immunizing both of them is very much essential in bringing about a healthy family. But the Bāuris normally do not give much importance on this. They follow their own traditional modes of immunization and accordingly treat the expectant mothers and the new-born babies. Even they do not like to check-up the expectant mothers medically and prefer to deliver at the local PHCs or hospitals. Rather they like to deliver at home with the help of the traditional midwives. However, many of them have become aware of the modern medical facilities and prefer to check-up the expectant mothers medically and deliver at PHCs or hospitals.

(i) Among the beneficiary households, of the total 21 living children in the age group of 0-5 years in Hirāpur, as many as 10 or 47.62 per cent babies were born at the local PHCs or hospitals as against 12 or 34.29 per cent babies of Āmbadiha. These babies were born with the help of the midwives.

(ii) Among the non-beneficiary households, while 44.83 per cent or 13 babies of Hirāpur were born at the local PHCs or Hospitals, it is 33.33 per cent or 19 babies in case of the village Āmbadiha.

Immunization of Expectant Mothers

(i) Among the beneficiary households, about 50 per cent expectant mothers of the village Hirāpur have taken the required number of vaccines, i.e. Titanus-I and Titanus-II along with full course of iron tablets. But it is merely 29.19 per cent in the village Āmbadiha.

(ii) Among the non-beneficiary households, when about 48 per cent expectant mothers of the village Hirāpur have taken the above vaccines along with the full course of iron tablets, it is 23.58 per cent in case of Āmbadiha.

Immunization of Newly-born Babies

(i) Immunization of newly-born babies are very important. For a newly-born baby, the first year immunization doses include BCG, DPT-I, DPT-II, Polio-I, Polio-II, Polio-III, one injection of measles vaccine and a course of Vitamin-A. The second year immunization doses include one booster dose of Polio and DPT. The third year immunization constitutes doses of Vitamin A-3, Vitamin A-4, and Vitamin A-5. But the Bāuri parents do not immunize their children properly. Among the beneficiary households in Hirāpur, 33.33 per cent babies have been fully immunized followed by same percentage babies who are partly immunized. But it is 21.74 per cent babies followed by 30.43 per cent in case of Āmbadiha who are fully and partly immunized respectively. The rest babies have not been immunized.

(ii) As regards the immunization of the babies in non-beneficiary households concerned, 44.44 per cent babies of the village Hirāpur have been fully immunized as against 38.46 per cent of the village Āmbadiha. It is only 16.33 per cent in the former village as against 20.51 per cent in the latter one who are partially immunized. The rest babies of each village are not been immunized.

(M) Ritual Belief Pattern and Practices

The Bāuris were suppressed and deprived in various religious matters. They were neither allowed to enter into the caste Hindu temples nor were allowed to worship caste Hindu deities. Even, there were much restrictions on them to read religious scriptures. On the other hand most of them were thinking that these set practices had been set up by the God and they must not break up the tradition by deviating the norms. But by the passage of time, many Bāuri have become aware and have started worshipping of such deities.

(i) Among the beneficiaries, 25.45 per cent people of Hirāpur as against 12 per cent of Āmbadiha think that there should not be any restriction to enter into the caste Hindu temples. But surprisingly while there are about 40 per cent households in Hirāpur of which at least one member has entered into a caste Hindu temple, though, not of course of their own village, it is only 18 per cent households in case of the village Āmbadiha who have done so. Likewise, it is interesting to note that while there are 45.45 per cent or 25 households in Hirāpur who have purchased various idols of Hindu deities from the market and have kept these at home, it is merely 8 per cent or 4 households in Āmbadiha who have kept such idols at home. Further, the number of households which have planted basil plants at their courtyards is 17 or 21.82 per cent in Hirāpur as against only 3 or 6 per cent households in Āmbadiha. But even though these religious traits have been borrowed from the local caste Hindu culture with a hope of improving the status, the Bāuris do not practise the rituals and the set practices associated with these deities. Most of the idols are just hung on the walls as decorative items. Even though the Bāuris plant basil plants in their courtyards, they do not offer prayer or water the plant regularly as is done by the caste Hindus. Apart from all these, while there are 29 or 52.75 per cent households in Hirāpur which have adopted various caste Hindu festive occasions, like *Badaosā, Gamhā-Purnimā, Raja Sankrāti* and *Sudasā-brata,* it is 20 or 36.66 per cent in case of Āmbadiha who have adopted these occasions.

(ii) Regarding the non-beneficiary households, it can be said that while 13 or 24.53 per cent households heads of Hirāpur think that there should not be any restriction for the Bāuris to enter into the caste Hindu temples, it is 6 or 8.7 per cent in Āmbadiha. However, of a total number of 18 or 33.46 per cent households in Hirāpur as against 11 or 15.94 per cent of Āmbadiha, at least one member has entered at least one caste Hindu temple without the knowledge of the local caste Hindus. But 20 or 37.73 per cent households of Hirāpur as against 6 or 8.7 per cent of Āmbadiha have kept different idols of caste Hindu deities. Similarly, while there are 14 or 26.42 per cent households in Hirāpur which have planted basil plants in their courtyard, it is 6 or 8.2 per cent in Āmbadiha. Apart from all these when there are 22 or 40.89 per cent households in Hirāpur who have adopted various fairs and festive occasions of the local caste Hindus, it is 27 or 38.58 per cent households in case of Āmbadiha.

(N) House Pattern

House is one of the three basic necessities of life. It protects people from sun, rain and cold and also from the animals. For healthy living, a house should have some basic hygienic facilities, like window, proper height of the roof, proper plinth area etc.

Traditionally the Bāuri houses are provided with single rooms and do not possess window for ventilation. This is normally because of the fact that these people were not allowed to keep windows as keeping windows was considered as a status symbol among the caste Hindus and on the other hand houses without window facility was helping them to keep rooms warm during winter.

Normally the Bāuri houses do not possess outer veranda. The height of the front wall of a house is normally about 5 to 6 feet. But the height of a door is normally 3.5 to 4 feet. Some houses lack door panel facility and some use inferior quality of door panels because of their poverty.

Households with Door Panel Facility

(i) Among the beneficiary households, 10 per cent households of Hirāpur do not have any door panel facility. These households, however, use sack screens set in bamboo frames for ensuring the primary safety it provides. An equal percentage of such households is also found in Āmbadiha. The rest households, however, have door panel facility. But so far as the type of door panels used is concerned in Hirāpur, 42.72 per cent or 19 households have doors made of planks and the rest 57.78 per cent or 26 households have inferior quality of doors made of flat bamboo splits. On the other hand, only 20 per cent or 7 households of Āmbadiha have doors made of planks and the rest 36 or 80 per cent households possess doors made of flat bamboo splits.

(ii) Among the non-beneficiary households, when 17.31 per cent or 9 households do not have any door facility, it is 20.89 per cent or 14 households in case of the village Āmbadiha. These households, however, use sack screens set in bamboo frames. The rest households have door panels but among these households 9 or 20.45 per cent in Hirāpur as against 12 or 21.82 per cent in Āmbadiha have door panels made of planks.

Households with Window Facility

(i) Window is an essential part of a house as it provides lighted ventilation but among the beneficiary households, while 16 or 32 per cent households in the village Hirāpur have this facility it is only 2 per cent households in the village Āmbadiha.

(ii) So far as the possession of window facility among the non-beneficiary households is concerned, in Hirāpur 13.46 per cent or 7 households possess this facility as against only 4.35 per cent or 3 households in the village Āmbadiha.

Type of house

(i) Among the beneficiary households, 75 per cent houses in Hirāpur as against 88 per cent are of *Kutcha* variety, i.e. either having mud wall and floor having thatched roof or wall made of burnt or unburnt bricks with mud paste and thatched roof. There is only one household in Hirāpur which is a *pucca* one, i.e. bricks and cement construction with steel reinforced cement concrete roof. This type of house is not found in the village Āmbadiha. The rest households are of mixed variety, i.e. either having mud wall, cemented floor and thatched roof or having igneous rock wall without cement plaster with mud floor and thatched roof. This type of houses are found in 24 per cent houses in Hirāpur as against 12 per cent in Āmbadiha.

(ii) So far as the house type of the non-beneficiary households is concerned, in case of the village Hirāpur, there are 84.62 per cent of *kutcha* houses, but it is about 90 per cent in case of Āmbadiha. All the rest houses are of mixed type of both the villages.

Built-in Area of House

As discussed earlier, merely possessing a house does not make any sense unless it provides sufficient built-in area for each of its inmates. Otherwise its negative impact is reflected among the children and also among the adult persons.

(i) The average built-in area per household and per person comes to 153.5 and 43.29 sq. feet. respectively in case of the beneficiary households of Hirāpur but it is 120.08 and 27.45, 19 sq. feet in case of the village Āmbadiha. But even though little more built-in area is available for a person of the village Hirāpur, this meagre space is not adequate for leading a healthy life.

It is a matter of concern that on one hand, the Bāuri people mostly own single living rooms but on the other hand it is also used for storing of household materials including food grains. As a result, it becomes very congested to accommodate each member of the house and most often the married couples do not get any privacy. In that case, their sexual act is witnessed by the children and hence they learn the sexual act and utter vulgar languages from the very beginning of their childhood. Hence, their personality and individuality go on in this way and they develop an inclination towards sex from early adolescent and most often they also indulge in sex much before they attain adulthood. This problem is age-old and inherent in them.

(ii) As regards the non-beneficiary households, the average built-in area available for a household in Hirāpur is 121.5 sq. feet as against 133.3 in Āmbadiha. But when the average built-in area per person comes to 28.43 sq. feet. in case of the former village, it is only 23.33 sq. feet in case of the latter one.

(O) Environment, Sanitary Habit and Changing Concept of Health and Hygiene

Knowledge of environmental sanitation and personal hygiene among the Bāuri people is very poor. All the Bāuri hamlets are located amidst the paddy fields. So, they have maximum opportunity to have clean air but they do not keep their surroundings clean because of their illiteracy, lack of awareness and unwillingness to render voluntary service in the cause of the common interest.

No Bāuri hamlet has drainage system. It causes stagnation of water during rainy season that facilitates breeding of mosquitoes, flies etc. and diseases, like diarrhoea, malaria etc. are spread by these insects. The more important unhygienic practice among the Bāuris that creates the surrounding unclean is that their strange habit of keeping poultry on veranda and in some case inside the bedroom also.

The cow sheds are generally attached to the household and dung and urine of the cattle are gathered in the dung pit located very near to the households or within the courtyard. The dung and urine of the cattle are considered as auspicious and are cleaned in open hand and bare foot.

One of the adverse sanitary habits of these people is using of open fields and the village sites for defecation. It renders the surrounding very unclean throughout the year. Most often the children use the house sites for the purpose.

These people do not like to use lavatory. On the contrary not a single Bāuri household in any of the study villages possesses a lavatory. They point out that using lavatory involves unsatisfactory bowel cleaning because of its bad smell within. It also involves the difficult task of carrying water to the lavatory. In this regard, when the people were asked if they would be interested to use lavatory if provided free of cost by the Government, among the beneficiary households, 68.33 per cent people of Hirāpur as against 88.33 per cent of Āmbadiha did not like to use it. Among the non-beneficiary households, these figures come to 65 per cent in Hirāpur as against 86.67 per cent in Āmbadiha.

By and large the Bāuri people of the study villages depend on three sources of water for domestic as well as non-domestic purposes. These are ponds, dug-wells and tube-wells in both the villages. But the surrounding of these water points always remain very unclean. Generally the people clean utensils, clean teeth and throw the used teeth cleaning sticks at the spot. Some people take bath and also wash clothes. The water mixed with various impure particles is soaked into the soil since drains are not provided for. So the unclean water is recycled and the infected water enters the body as potable water. Likewise, the bathing ghats of the local ponds are also used for both the domestic as well as non-domestic purposes. However, some people of the either villages have become aware of the adverse effects of using common bathing ghats for all purposes.

On the matter of personal hygiene, it can be said that the Bāuri people are not aware and conscious of the adverse effects of remaining unclean and unhygienic. It is mainly because of their illiteracy and lack of proper awareness. However, the personal hygiene that refers to keeping different parts of the body clean, like (i) washing face daily early in the morning, cleaning of bowels regularly in the morning, using of soaps for washing hand after defecation, cleaning of teeth and taking bath daily; (ii) paring nails and keeping these clean; (iii) washing hand before taking food; and (iv) using water of tube-wells for drinking and cooking purpose and using boiled water if collected from the other sources like dug-wells or ponds.

Washing Face after leaving Bed Every Morning

Washing face and cleaning eyes regularly every morning after leaving bed is the foremost important personal hygienic care of every person. But the percentage of the beneficiary people who are habituated to this habit is found to be 60 in the village Hirāpur as against 51.67 per cent in Āmbadiha. So far as the case of the people of non-beneficiary households is concerned, while it comes to be 63.33 per cent in case of the former village, it is only 45 per cent for the latter one.

Habit of Using Soap after Defecation

The Bāuri people are not habituated to wash hands with soap or any other such antiseptic material after defecation. Rather most of them use clay for this purpose. However, when 5 per cent beneficiary people of Hirāpur regularly use soap for this purpose there is nobody in Āmbadiha. Likewise, among the non-beneficiary households, 6.67 per cent people of the former village regularly use soap but there is none in the village Āmbadiha who is found to use this.

Habit of Cleaning Teeth Regularly in the Morning

One must be very careful to take proper care of teeth by rinsing mouth and brushing teeth every morning in order to arrest mouth ulcer, tooth decay or any other such complications. But even though oral hygiene is so essential and important, among the beneficiary households, when there are 13.33 per cent people in Hirāpur who do not brush their teeth regularly, it is 16.67 per cent in Āmbadiha. Among the non-beneficiary households, 13.33 per cent people of Hirāpur are also there as against 10 per cent in Āmbadiha who are irregular in cleaning their mouth and teeth regularly every morning.

Use of Commercial Tooth Brush and Tooth Paste

The Bāuri use twigs and leaves of various plants and trees for cleaning their teeth. Most of them also use tobacco paste (*Tamakhu*), dung-ash, red-soil etc. for this purpose. Use of commercial tooth brush and tooth paste of powder is very rare among them. However, among the beneficiary households, 11.67 per cent people in Hirāpur use commercial tooth brush and tooth paste or powder as against only 3.33 per cent in Āmbadiha. Similarly among the non-beneficiary households, more (8.33%) people of the former village use tooth brush and tooth paste than those of Āmbadiha (3.33%).

Habit of Cleaning Hair among Women

Hair should be washed at least four times a month. The frequency should be more in case of those women who work as wage-earners and carry headloads of agricultural materials. But being such labourers, the Bāuri women do not give due importance on this personal hygienic care. As a result their hair seems to be very dirty, matted and infected with lice.

Normally the Bāuri women use soap for cleaning their head but most of them also use red-soil and juice of leaves of some local plants for this purpose. However, among the beneficiary households, 46.68 per cent women of the village Hirāpur as against 63.33 per cent of the latter village have not washed their hair even for once in the month of October of the study year. On the contrary, about 43 per cent women of non-beneficiary households of Hirāpur as against as many as 66.67 per cent women of these households of Āmbadiha have not washed their head on any day in the said month.

Habit of taking Bath Regularly

In order to know the habit of taking bath regularly among the Bāuris, 60 persons of each group of each village were interviewed in the month of October. Among the beneficiary households, 81.67 per cent people of Hirāpur have taken bath of all the 31 days of the said month as against 83.33 per cent people of Āmbadiha. They are followed by 15 per cent and 3.33 per cent in Hirāpur who have taken bath for 21-30 days and 11-20 days respectively. The corresponding figures for Āmbadiha come to be 11.97 per cent and 5 per cent respectively. Among the non-beneficiary people, the trend is more or less same in both the villages.

Habit of Paring and Cleaning Nails

Habit of keeping nails short and clean is essential as long nails retain dirt and harbour germs. It causes various diseases by coming in contact with food materials. The Bāuris collect a lot of dirty materials in their nails while working in the fields but they neglect to pare their nails in time and keep these clean.

Among the beneficiary households, 25 per cent people in Hirāpur are observed to have short and clean nails as against only 10 per cent people in Āmbadiha. But among the family members of the non-beneficiary households, when it is 23.33 per cent in the former village, the latter village records 11.67 per cent people who have kept short and clean nails.

Habit of Washing Hand before Taking Food

Fairly a large number of people of both the villages are observed to be very irregular in maintaining their nails short and clean. Still quite a large number of people neglect to wash their hands before taking food. Among the beneficiary households the people who do not wash or occasionally wash their hands before taking food together constitute about 37 per cent in Hirāpur as against as many as 67 per cent persons in Āmbadiha. The case of the non-beneficiary people of both the villages is more or less same.

Use of Potable Water

Water of tube-well is considered clean and pure for drinking and cooking purposes. But even though this source of water is available in both the villages, not a single Bāuri household is witnessed to use this water either for drinking or for cooking purpose as using of this water blackens the teeth. The people also opine that this water is not tasty for cooking compared to the water of the dug-well. Hence most of the beneficiary as well as non-beneficiary people use the water of dug-wells for drinking and cooking purposes. However, among the beneficiary households when about 53 per cent people in Hirāpur use the water of dug wells, it is 42 per cent in case of Āmbadiha. The case of the non-beneficiary households is almost the same in both the villages. But certainly they do not use the water of dug-wells after boiling either because of their illiteracy or lack of fuel. As a result, most of them fall ill and suffer from various diseases.

(P) Dress Pattern

The dress pattern of the Bāuris was quite unique as the Bāuris were not permitted to use good dress materials as per their own choices. But, nowadays, even though there is nobody in any of the study villages who imposes restriction on the dress pattern of these people, the Bāuris are still observed to be very backward insofar as their dress materials and clothings are concerned.

Comparatively larger percentage of beneficiary people in Hirāpur use various modern dress materials, like full pants (70.91 per cent), shirt or T-shirt (76.36 per cent), footwear like slipper (63.46 per cent) than those of Āmbadiha. The corresponding figures are found to be 35 per cent, 38 per cent and 26 per cent for the people in Āmbadiha. So far as the dress pattern of the women folk is concerned, a high percentage of women in Hirāpur use petticoats and blouses as compared to those of the village Āmbadiha. The case of the non-beneficiary households of both the villages is more or less similar with the above trend, but there are less people who are found to have possessed these materials.

(Q) Development of ability for self-management

Development of ability for self-management is a crucial aspect of judging the quality of life. It refers to various facets of life that differs from society to society and even culture to culture. But in the present context some specific aspects of life concerning to the local culture were chosen to evaluate the ability of Bāuri people for self-management. These aspects included management of women as labour force, decision-making on daily expenditure, management of food among family members during food scarcity, management of education of boy and girl children, decision-making on casting votes in general elections etc. The conclusion of some of the important and specific subjects is summarized below:

Management of Employing Women as Labour Force or wage-earners

When a Bāuri man becomes rich as per his own perspectives, he becomes very prestige conscious and in that case he does not like to employ his wife as a wage-earner. However, the wives of such men may work in their own agricultural fields. Among the beneficiary households, there are 60 per cent households in Hirāpur of which the women do not go for wage-earning as against merely 4.17 per cent in Āmbadiha. However, the decision of employing the women remains the prerogative of the male members. Even if there is food shortage, women cannot take any independent decision and hence can work as wage-earners without the permission of their husbands. Among the non-beneficiary households these figures come to 6.12 per cent in Hirāpur as against 4.55 per cent in Āmbadiha.

Management of Food among Family Members During Food Scarcity

In the Bāuri society, traditionally the status of a girl child is sub-ordinate. She is not only exploited for the well-being of a boy child but also underfed beginning from her birth. Surprisingly if a woman has two breast-fed babies; one boy and the other girl, the girl baby is normally breast-fed for a shorter period of time even if she is younger to the boy baby. The Bāuris point out various reasons for this. But ultimately it indicates the superior status of the male in their society.

Quite a large number of women of both the study villages opine that they would prefer to give more food to boy children rather than the girl children during scarcity of food. Not a single woman in any village prefers to give more food to a girl child during such a crucial period. However, the people of Hirāpur differ much with the opinion of the women of Āmbadiha as among the beneficiaries, when about 24 per cent women in Hirāpur opine that they would certainly distribute the available food between the both, in Āmbadiha only 14.58 per cent people prefer so and the rest opine that they would give more food to the boy children during such a period. The case of the non-beneficiary households is more or less the same.

Management of Educating Boy and Girl Children

The girl children are not only discriminated in the matter of nourishment but on the matter of education also. The Bāuris consider the girl as the wealth of some other households where they would get married. Hence there is no need of spending such money on the education of the girl children. In order to find out the attitude of the Bāuri men and women when a hypothetical question regarding choosing of two children from two sons and two daughters for getting free education at a school was asked, among the beneficiary households, more people of Hirāpur than Āmbadiha are found to give equal importance on the education of both the children. It comes to 30 per cent in Hirāpur as against only 16.67 per cent in Āmbadiha. The trend is almost the same among the non-beneficiary households of both the study villages.

Management of Family Planning among Married Men and Women

The Bāuris consider the children as the gifts of God and as economic assets. Hence, they do not normally like to reduce their family size and stick to have the ideal number of one or two children per couple. However, among the beneficiary households, as many as 21.95 per cent people in Hirāpur opine that one should have only 1-2 children thereby limiting the family size to 4 members only. But it is nearly 3.33 per cent in Āmbadiha who desire so. The rest persons, however, opine to have 3-4 or more children. Among the non-beneficiary households, more people also want 3-4 children but interestingly when there are 10 per cent people in Hirāpur who argue that it is better to have 1-2 children per couple there is none in Āmbadiha who supports this view.

Thus, from the above findings it can be concluded that the people of both the beneficiary as well as non-beneficiary households of the village Hirāpur have become more advanced in various facets of life than those of the village Āmbadiha. Occupational mobility has occurred among more number of these people. Accordingly their income level has also increased and consequently the per-capita income per household and per person is found to be comparatively higher. This has certainly helped them to acquire various new or non-beneficiary assets to lead life more comfortably than previously. Similarly, they have become more aware and conscious of the human rights and hence try to revolt against the local caste Hindus whenever they impose social discrimination and untouchability which are not acceptable to the Bāuris. Surprisingly, they also Sanskritize themselves by adopting various cultural and religious traits of the local caste Hindus and demand treatment at par with them.

The political awareness of the Bāuris of Hirāpur has considerably increased over the past few decades and the ability for self-management relating to various aspects of life has also been developed. Hence, the overall quality of life of these people is also found to be better than their counterparts in Āmbadiha. However, these have certainly been possible because of the high pressure of modernization or the influence of the Bhubaneswar city and so also because of the development planning of the Government by which various direct or indirect financial assistance was provided to these people. However, the changes which have come out as the consequences of these plans, are not satisfactory as most of the Bāuris in both the villages are still found to be illiterate and are below the poverty line. So, they are still to go miles ahead in order to come up into the mainstream. For, this, both the Government functionaries as well as the Bāuri beneficiaries be very careful. On the one hand the Government have to implement the development plans and programmes more appropriately with implications of sufficient follow-up and awareness building programmes on various Government plans and policies and also on various ways of self-employment possibilities. On the other hand, the Bāuris themselves are to be very careful as regards utilisation of the assistance they get from the Government and also their own hard earned money in proper ways, like in productive units rather than simply spending it either for consumption or for life cycle rituals, if at all they are to be educationally advanced and economically well-to-do.

REFERENCE

1. The Bāuris as a whole have been assisted under various poverty alleviation programme of the Government in different parts of the state but the beneficiary Bāuri households of the two study villages have been assisted under different sectoral schemes of the programmes like Integrated Rural Development Programme (IRDP), Economic Rehabilitation of Rural Poor (ERRP), Bonded Labour Rehabilitation Programme (BLRP), and Orissa State Scheduled Caste Scheduled Tribe Development Finance Co-operative Ltd. (OSSCSTDFCL). The Sectoral Schemes irrespective of these programmes includes rickshaw/trolley pulling, diary farming, goat and sheep rearing, paddy and rice business, transport business with the help of bullocks and cart, vegetable vending, grocery and stationery shop and betel leaf business.

BIBLIOGRAPHY

A. BOOKS

Abbasayulu, Y.B., 1978, *Scheduled Castes,* Hyderabad: Book Links Crop.

Agarwal, P.C. et al, 1976, *Equality Through Privilege: A study of special privileges in Haryana,* New Delhi: Sri Ram Centre for Industrial Relations and Human Resources.

Agarwal, S.P. et al, 1991, *Education and Social Upliftment and Backward Classes,* New Delhi: Concept.

Ahuja Ram, 1992, *Social problems in India,* Jaipur: Rawat.

Aiyappan, A., 1965, *Social Revolution in a Kerala Village,* Bombay: Asia

Alexander, K.C., 1968, *Social Mobility in Kerala,* Poona: Decan P.G. College and Research Institute.

Alladi, V., 1972, *Income Earning Trends and Social Status of Harijan Community in Tamil Nadu,* Madras: Sangam.

Ambedkar, B.R. , 1943, *Mr. Gandhi and the Emancipation of the Untouchables*, Bombay: Thacker & Co.

__________ , 1945, *Annihilation of Caste with a Reply to Mahatma Gandhi,* Bombay: Bharat Bhusan Press.

__________ , 1946, *What Congress and Gandhi had done to the Untouchables,* New Delhi: Amrit Book Co.

__________ , 1948, *The Untouchables: Who were they & Why they Became Untouchables,* New Delhi: Amrit Book Co.

Anant, S.S., 1972, *Changing Concept of Caste in India,* New Delhi: Vikas

Apasthamba, 1879, *Dharmasutra* (Buhler's trans. in Sacred Book of the East, 1879) cited in G.S. Ghurey, *Caste and Race in India,* 1969, Bombay: Popular Prakashan.

Atal, Y., 1968, *The Changing Frontiers of Caste,* New Delhi: National.

Aziz, A., 1989, *Developmental Programmes for Weaker Sections,* Jaipur: Printwell.

Babb, L., 1975, *The Divine Hierarchy: Popular Hinduism in Central India,* New York: Columbia University Press.

Bailey, F.G., 1957, *Caste & Economic Frontier—A Village Highland,* Manchester: Manchester University press.

__________ , 1960, *Politics and Social Change in Orissa*, Barkeley & Los Angles: University of California.

Basu, N.N., 1931, *Modern Budhism and It's Followers in Orissa,* Calcutta.

Beals, A.R., 1954, *Cultural Change and Social Conflict in a South Indian Village,* Barkeley: University of California.

__________ , 1962, *Gopalpur—A South Indian Village,* New York: Halt Rinehart and Winston Inc.

Behura, N.K., 1978, *Peasant Potters of Orissa,* New Delhi: Sterling.

Bernard, H.R. et al, (eds.) 1972, *Technology and Social Change,* New York: The Macmillan Company.

Betelle, A., 1965, *Caste, Class and Power,* Barkeley and Los Angles: University of California.

__________ , 1966(a), *Caste, Class and Power: Changing Power of Stratification in a Tanjore Village,* Bombay: Oxford University Press.

__________ , 1966(b), *Inequality Among Men,* Bombay: Oxford University Press.

__________ , 1969, *Caste: Old and New,* Bombay: Asia

Betelle, A. (ed), 1981, *The Backward Classes and New Social Order,* New Delhi: Oxford University Press.

Bhardwaj, A.N., 1979, *Problems of Scheduled Castes and Scheduled Tribes in India,* New Delhi: Light & Life.

Bhatta, V.R., 1941, *The Harijans of Maharashtra,* New Delhi: All India Harijan Sevak Sangha.

Bhowmick, P.K., 1961, *Socio-Cultural Profile of Frontier Bengal,* Calcutta: Punthi Pustak.

Black, C.E., 1966, *The Dynamics of Modernisation: A Study in Comparative History,* New Delhi: Harper and Row.

Bose, N.K., 1975, *The Structure of Hindu Society,* New Delhi: Orient Longman.

Boudhyayan, 1882, *Dharmasastra* (Buhler's trans. in Sacred Book of the East, 1882) cited in G.S. Ghurye, *Caste and Race in India,* 1969, Bomnbay: Popular Prakashan.

Buhler, G., 1886, *The Laws of Manu,* Vol. XXV of Sacred Book of the East, ed. by F. Maxmuller, Printed in 1964, Oxford.

Brings, G.W., 1920, *The Chamars,* Calcutta: Association Press.

Bhusan, V. and Sachdeva, 1989, *An Introduction to Sociology,* Allahabad: Kitab Mahal.

Centre for Regional Studies (CRS), 1982, *Strategy for Development of SCs and STs,* Bhubaneswar: Utkal University.

Chandra, D., 1993, *Rural Credit Role of Informal Sector,* New Delhi: Segment Books.

Chandana, R.C., 1989, *Spatial Dimensions of Scheduled Castes,* New Delhi: Intellectual.

Chauhan, N., 1968, *The Autobiography of an Unknown Indian,* Barkeley: University of California Press.

Chetty, V.B.K., 1991, *Scheduled Castes and Development Programmes in India,* Allahabad: Vohra.

Coser, L.A., 1956, *The Functions of Social Conflict,* Glencoe: Free Press.

Crooke, W., 1896, *Tribes and Castes of North-Western Provinces and Oudh.* Calcutta: Office of the Superintendent of Govt. Printing, India, (Reprint, 1974, New Delhi: Cosmo)

Dahiwale, S.M., 1989, *Emerging Entrepreneurship Among Scheduled Castes of Contemporary India—A Study of Kolhapur City,* New Delhi: Concept.

Das, K.B., 1990, *Rural Development Through Decentralisation,* New Delhi: Discovery.

Damble, V.B. et al, 1963, *Note on the Position of Scheduled Castes and Their Position in the Villages in Group Relations in a Village Community,* Poona: Deccan P.G. College and Research.

Day, F., 1863, *The Law of the Permauls Cochin, Its past and present,* Madras.

Dayanand, S., 1933, *Dayananda Commemoration Volume—A Tribute,* Ajmer: The Vedic Tantralaya.

Desai, I.P., 1976, *Untouchability in Rural Gujrat,* Bombay: Popular.

Desai, A.R., 1988, *Rural Sociology in India,* Bombay: Popular.

__________ , 1990, *Changing Profile of Rural India and Human Rights of Agrarian Poor,* Chandigarh : CRRID

Desai, V., 1988, *Rural Development Programmes and Strategies,* Bombay: Himalaya.

D'Souza, V.S., 1980, *Educational Inequalities Among Scheduled Castes,* Chandigarh: Punjab University Press.

Dubey, S.C., 1955, *Indian Village,* London: Routledge and Kegan Paul.

__________, 1988(a), *Modernization and Development,* New Delhi: Vistar.

__________, 1988, *India's Changing Village,* London Rutledge and Kegan Paul.

Dubey, S.N., 1973, *Administration of Social Welfare Programmes in India.* Bombay: Somaliya.

Dubey, K.N. (ed.), 1990, *Planning & Development in India*, New Delhi : Ashish.

Dubey, S.N., 1973, *Administration of Social Welfare Programmes in India,* Bombay : Somaliya.

Dutta, N.K., 1931, *Origin and Growth of Caste in India,* Calcutta: The Book Co.

__________ , 1968, *Origin and Growth of Caste in India,* Vol. I, Calcutta: Firma K.L. Mukhapadhyay.

Epstein, T.S., 1962, *Economic Development and Social Change in South India, Manchester:* Manchester University Press.

Falendra, K.S. & N.K. Gupta, 1990, *Women at Work in Developing Economy,* New Delhi: Anmol.

Fisherman., A.T., 1941, *Cultural Change and Under Priviledged: A Study of Madigas in South India,* Madras: Christian Guidance.

Foster, G.M., 1962, *Traditional Cultures and the Impact of Technical Change,* New York: Harper & Brothers.

Frazer, J.T., 1968, *Cultural Change in India—The Barpali Experience,* Amnerst: University of Massachussetts Press.

Freeman, J.M., 1979, *Untouchables—An Indian History,* London: George Allen and Unwin.

Fuchs, S., 1951, *The Children of Hari,* New York: F.A. Prager.

__________ , 1965, *Rebellious Prophets,* Bombay: Asia.

Gandhi, M.K., 1954*The Removal of Untouchability,* Ahmedabad: Navjivan.

__________ , 1964, *Caste Must Go, the Sin of Untouchability,* Ahmedabad: Navjivan.

Gaur, K.D., 1992, *Dynamics of Rural Development,* New Delhi: Mittal.

Gautama, 1882, *Dharmasastra* (Buhler's trans. in Sacred Book of the East, 1882) cited in G.S. Ghurye, *Caste and Race in India,* Bombay: Popular.

Ghosh, Arun, 1992, *Planning in India Through Decentralization,* New Delhi: Sage.

Ghosh, S.K., 1980, *Protection of Minorities and Scheduled Castes,* New Delhi: Ashish.

Ghurey, G.S., 1961, *Caste, Class and Occupation,* Bombay: Popular.

__________ , 1968, *Caste and Race in India,* Bombay: Popular.

Gobal, B.R., 1981, *Educating Harijans,* Haryana: The Academic Press.

Gorwaney, N., 1977, *Self Image and Social Change,* New Delhi: Sterling.

Govindankutty, S., 1975, "SCs of Kerala" (Mimeographed)

Hadimani, R.N., 1984, *Politics of Poverty,* New Delhi: Ashish

Hall, R.H., 1975, *Occupation and the Social Structure,* New Jersey: Prentice Hall.

Hocart, A.M., 1950, *Caste: A Comparative Study,* London.

Hockings, P., 1965, *Cultural Change Among the Bagada: A Community in South India,* Barkeley: California University, Press.

Hooja, R. and B.Y. Raju, 1993, *Decentralisation Planning in Multilevel Framework,* New Delhi: Rawat.

Hunter, G., 1970, *Modernity in Peasant Societies,* London: Oxford University Press.

Hutton, J.H., 1951, *Caste in India—its Nature, Function and Origin,* Bombay: Oxford University Press (Reprinted in 1986)

Issacs, Haq, 1965, *India's Ex-Untouchables,* Bombay: Asia.

Jarry, D. and J. Jarry, 1995, *Collins Dictionary of Sociology,* Glassgow: Collins Publishers.

Jatova, D.R., 1965, *The Political Philosophy of Ambedkar,* Agra: Phoenix.

Jayawardana, K., 1986, *Feminism and Nationalism in Third World,* London: Zed Books.

Jha, H., 1991, *Social Structure of Indian Villages,* New Delhi: Sage.

Kamble, N.D., 1982, *The Scheduled Castes,* New Delhi: Ashish.

Karve, I., 1961(a), *Changing India—Aspects of Caste Society,* Bombay.

__________, 1961(b), *Hindu Society: An Introduction,* Poona: Sangam.

Keer, D., 1982, *Dr. Ambedkar, Life and Mission,* Bombay: Popular.

Khan, M.A., 1980, *Scheduled Castes and their Status in India,* New Delhi: Uppal.

Kluckhorn, C., 1950, *Mirror for Man,* London: George G. Harper.

Kodetotad, N.K., 1977, *Religion and Society Among the Harijans,* New Delhi: B.R. Pub. Corpn.

Kolenda, P., 1984, *Caste in Contemporary India: Beyond Organic Solidarity,* Jaipur: Rawat.

Kshirsagar, V.P., 1989, *Untouchability in India,* New Delhi: Deep and Deep.

Kumari, V.P., 1991, *Poverty Alleviation and Rural Harijans,* New Delhi: Discovery.

Kuppuswamy, B., 1972, *Social Change in India,* New Delhi: Vikas.

__________, 1986, *Social Change in India,* New Delhi, Vani Educational Books.

Lakshana, C., S.P. Srivastav & R.C. Sarikwal (eds), 1990, *Social Action and Social Change,* New Delhi: Ajanta.

Lakshmana, C., 1973, *Caste Dynamics in Village India,* Bombay: Nachiketa.

Lal, A.K., et al, 1980, *The Educated Harijan Elite and Development,* New Delhi: Concept.

Lynch, O.M., 1969, *The Politics of Untouchability,* New Delhi: National

Madan, G.R., 1990, *India's Developing Villages,* New Delhi: Allied.

Maffat, M., 1979, *An Untouchable Community in South India: Structure and Consensus,* Princeton: Princeton University Press.

Mahar, J.M., 1972, *The Untouchables in Contemporary India,* Arizona: University of Arizona Press.

Maheswari, S.R., 1985, *Rural Development in India,* New Delhi: Sage.

Mathur, H.M., 1989, *Anthropology and Development in Traditional Societies,* New Delhi: Vikas.

Mathur, I., 1987, *Change in Agrarian Society,* Jaipore: Printwell.

Mathur, K.S., 1964, *Caste and Ritual in Malwa Village,* Bombay: Asia.

Mayer, A.C., 1956, *Caste and Kinship in Central India,* Barkeley: University of California.

Mehta, S., 1971, *Social Conflict in a Village Community,* New Delhi: S. Chand & Co.

Mehta, S.R. (ed), 1997, *Poverty, Population & Sustainable Development,* New Delhi: Rawat.

Mishra, P.K., 1992, *Harijan in Hindu and Tribal Social Structures,* New Delhi: Discovery.

Mohammad, N., 1988, *Caste and Primary Occupations,* New Delhi: Concept.

Mohapatra, M., 1978, *Bauri of Bhubaneswar,* Bhubaneswar: THRTI.

Montagu. P.D., 1977, *Occupation and Society,* New York: John Willey and Sons.

Mulay, S., et al, 1973, *Towards Modernisation,* New Delhi: National.

Murphy, G., 1953, *In the Minds of Men. The Study of Human Behaviour and Social Tensions in India,* New York: Basic Books.

Nandekar, 1991, *District Planning—Proxis and Perspective,* New Delhi: Rawat.

O'Malley, L.S.S., 1932, *Indian Caste Customs,* Cambridge: University Press.

O'renstein, M., 1965, *Gaon Conflict and Cohesion in an Indian Village,* New Jersey: Princeton University Press.

Paramjit, S.J. & S.K. Sharma (eds), 1997, *Dimensions of Social Changes,* New Delhi: Rawat.

Paranjpee, A.C., 1970, *Caste Prejudice and the Individual,* New Delhi: Lalwani.

Parmer, S., 1990, *Development and Backwardness, Coexistence of Leather Workers of Karnataka,* New Delhi: Reliance.

Parvathama, C., 1978, *Under the Directed Change,* New Delhi: National.

__________, 1984, *Scheduled Castes and Tribes—A Socio-Economic Survey,* New Delhi: Ashish.

__________, 1989, *Scheduled Caste of Cross Road,* New Delhi: Ashish.

Parvathama, C. & Satyanarayan, 1984, *New Horizons and Scheduled Castes,* New Delhi: Ashish.

Patnaik, N. & B. Choudhury, 1989, *Sapuakela,* Bhubaneswar: THRTI

Patnaik, N. & S.C. Mohanty, 1988, *The Ganda—A Scheduled Caste Weaver Community of Western Orissa,* Bhubaneswar: THRTI.

Patwardhan, S., 1973, *Change Among India's Harijans—A Case Study,* Bombay: Orient Longman.

Pimpley, N., 1980, *A Profile of Scheduled Caste Students—The Case of Punjab,* Punjab University Press.

Purohit, B.R., 1965, *Hindu Revivalism and Indian Nationalism,* Sakti Prakashan.

Prabhu, P.N., 1963, *Hindu Social Organisation,* Bombay: Popular Prakashan.

Praharaj, G.C., 1934, *Purnachandra Odia Bhasakosa,* Cuttack: Utkal Sahitya Press.

Prakash, N., 1989, *Scheduled Castes—Socio-Economic Changes,* Allahabad: Chugh.

Radhakrishnan, S. et al, 1989, *Impact of Education on Scheduled Caste Youths in India,* New Delhi: Radiant.

Ram, J., 1980, *Caste Challenge in India,* Bombay: Vision.

Rangarao, K., 1980, *Village Politics,* Bombay: Popular.

Rangari, D., 1984, *Indian Caste System and Education,* New Delhi: Deep & Deep.

Ranjana, K. (ed), 1992, *Women in Decision Making,* New Delhi: Vikas.

Rao, D.V., 1981, *Dimensions of Backwardness—A Study of Taluk, Village and Household Level in Karnataka,* New Delhi: Concept.

Rao, Y.V., 1994, *Administration of IRDP,* New Delhi: Delta Publishing House.

Rao, M.S.A., 1972, *Tradition, Rationality and Change,* Bombay: Popular.

Rath, R., 1975, *Study of Educational Profile of Scheduled Caste and Scheduled Tribe Students (College) in Orissa,* Bhubaneswar: Utkal University.

Rayappa, P.H. & R. Mutharayappa, 1986, *Backwardness and Welfare of Scheduled Castes and Scheduled Tribes in India,* New Delhi: Ashish.

Rishley, H.H., 1951, *The People of India, New Edition of Tribes and Castes of Bengal.*

Robertson, A., 1938, *The Mahars,* Calcutta: Oxford University Press.

Russel, R.V. & H. Lal, 1891, *The Tribes and Castes of Bengal, Ethnographic Glossary,* Calcutta.

Sachidananda, 1979, *Harijan Elite,* Faridabad: Thomson Press.

Samal, K.C., 1990, *Urban Informal Sector,* New Delhi: Manak.

Sarkar, J., 1984, *Caste, Occupation and Change,* B.K. Publishing Corpn.

Satpathy, K.M., 1992, *A Handbook of IRDP, (Planning, Monitoring and Co-ordination),* Bhubaneswar: Satpathy and Partner.

Selvanathan, S., 1989, *Status of Scheduled Castes,* New Delhi: Ashish.

Senapati, N., 1977, *Gezetteer of India, Orissa, Puri,* Bhubaneswar: Dept. of Revenue, G.O.O.

Senjano, J.E., 1946, *Caste and Outcastes,* Bombay. Thacker & Co.

Sharma, B.D., 1994, *Dalits Betrayed,* New Delhi: Har Anand.

Sharma, P.N. & R.K. Verma, 1989, *Project Planning for IRDP,* Lucknow: Print House (India).

Sharma, M.L. et al, 1985, *Caste and Class in Agrarian Society—Elite Politics in Rural India,* New Delhi: Ajanta.

Shamkunwar, M.R., 1985, *Scheduled Castes—Socio Economic Survey,* Allahabad: Kitab Mahal.

Showeb, M., 1986, *Education and Mobility Among Harijans,* Varanasi: Gandhian Institute of Studies.

Singh, I., 1984, *Rural Development in India,* New Delhi: N.C.E.R.T.

Singh, K., 1988, *Rural Development—Principles, Policies and Management,* New Delhi: Sage.

Singh, K.K., 1967, *Pattern of Caste Tension,* Bombay: Asia.

Singh, K.S., 1995, *The Scheduled Castes,* Delhi: Oxford University Press.

Singh, M., 1947, *The Depressed Classes,* Bombay: Hind Kitab.

Singh, S., 1987, *Scheduled Castes of India—Dimensions of Social Change,* New Delhi: Gian.

Singh, S., 1995, *IRDP & District Development: Role and Implementation of DRDA Schemes,* New Delhi: Deep & Deep.

Singh, S.S. et al, 1987, *Emerging Harijan Elite,* Varanasi: Gandhian Institute of Studies.

Singh, Y., 1986, *Modernization of Indian Tradition,* Jaipur: Rawat.

__________, 1989, *Essays on Modernization in India,* New Delhi: Manohar.

Sivarama, P., 1990, *Social Mobility—A Sociological Study,* New Delhi: Discovery.

Sreenivasan, K., 1964, *Poverty and Social Environment*, New Delhi: Asia.

Srinivas, M.N., 1964, *Caste of Modern India,* Bombay: Allied.

__________, 1962, *Caste In India and other Essays,* Bombay: Asia.

__________, 1966, *Social Change in Modern India,* Bombay: Allied.

__________, 1952, *Religion and Society Among Coorgs of South India,* Oxford: Oxford University Press.

Stanley, M. (ed), 1972, *Social Development: Critical Perspective,* New York: Basic Book Inc.

Subramanyan, S., 1975, *Social Change in Village India—Andra Case Study,* New Delhi: Prithviraj.

Sundarananda, S., 1945, *Hinduism and Untouchability,* New Delhi: Harijan Sevak Sangha.

Thurston, E., 1909, *Caste and Tribes of Southern India,* New Delhi: Cosmo.

Tiwari, R.T. et al, 1988, *Development and Change in India,* New Delhi: Ashish.

Tripathy, R.B., 1994, *Dalits: A Sub-Human Society,* New Delhi: Ashish.

Upadhyay, H.C., 1991, *Scheduled Castes and Scheduled Tribes in India,* New Delhi: Anmol.

Usha Rao, N.T., 1981, *Deprived Caste in India.* Allahabad: Chugh.

Vakil, A.K., 1985, *Reservation Policy and Scheduled Castes in India,* New Delhi: Ashish.

Vasistha, 1882, *Dharmasutra* (Buhler's trans. in Sacred Book of the East, 1882) cited in G.S. Ghurye. *Caste & Race in India.* 1969, Bombay: Popular.

Vatsyayan, 1987, *Anthropology, Social and Cultural,* Meerut: Kadar Nath Ram Nath.

Venkataswarulu, D., 1990, *Harijan Upper Class Conflicts,* New Delhi: Discovery.

Vidyarthi, L.P., 1967, *Leadership in India,* New Delhi: Asia.

__________, 1969, *Conflict, Tension and Cultural Trend in India,* Calcutta: Punthi Pustak.

__________, 1977, *Harijan To-day,* New Delhi: Classical.

Zaltman, G. (ed.), 1973, *Progress and Phenomena of Social Change,* New York: John Wiley & Sons.

B. JOURNALS/ARTICLES

Bhatia, H.S., 1970, "Inter-Caste Relations and Aspirational Levels", *Indian Journal of Social Work,* Vol. XXXI, No.1.

Bhowmick, K.L., 1968, "Sex Initiation in a Dule Bauri Village", *Adivasi,* Vol. X.

Bhowmic, P.K., 1963, "Change and Services in a Bengal Village", *Man in India.*

Bose, N.K., 1954, "Who are the Backward Castes" *Man in India,* Vol. 34.

Chandney, J.C., 1978, "Caste and Class in India, Principle and Resources" *Man in India,* Vol. 58.

Chandidas, R., 1969, "How Close to Equality are Scheduled Castes", *Economic and Political Weekly,* June 10.

Channa, S.M., 1991, "Caste, 'Jati' and Ethnicity—Some Reflections based on a Case Study of Dhobis", *Indian Anthropologists,* Vol. 21, No. 2.

Chitnis, S., 1972, "Education for Equality—Case of Scheduled Castes", *Economic and Political Weekly,* Vol. VII, Nos. 31-33.

Cohn, B.S., 1961, "The Changing Status of a Depressed Caste", in M. Marriot (ed), *Village India,* Chicago: University Press of Chicago.

__________, 1958, "Changing Tradition of a Low Caste", *Journal of American Folklore,* Vol. 21.

Coleman, J.S., 1968, "Modernisation: Political Aspects", *International Encyclopaedia of Social Sciences,* Vol. 10, New York: Collier and Macmillan, Inc.

Coser, L., 1957, "Social Conflict and Social Change", *British Journal of Sociology.* Vol. 7, No. 3.

Das, K.K., et al, 1971, "Study of Utilisation of Government Resources by Scheduled Caste Community", *Indian Journal of Social Research,* Vol. 12.

Dande, A.K., 1987, "Statutory Provisions Safeguarding Interests of Scheduled Tribes and Scheduled Castes" in L.P. Vidyarthi (ed), *Applied Anthropology in India,* Allahabad: Kitab Mahal.

Devi, B., 1966, "Sweepers and Scavangers in Bhubaneswar", *Adivasi,* Vol. VIII, No. 3.

__________, 1973, "Conflict Between Brāhmin Patrons and Bāuri Clients in a Shasan Village in Orissa—A Preliminary Survey" *Man in Society.* Inaugral Volume.

Doshi, H., 1980, "Occupational Diversification and Removal of Untouchability" in V.P. Shah (ed.), *Removal of Untouchability,* Allahabad.

D'Souza, V., 1962, "Changing Status of Scheduled Castes", *Economic and Political Weekly,* Vol. 16, No. 48.

Dube, S.C., 1949, "Ritual Friendship in Chhatisgarh", *Man in India,* Vol. XX, No. 12.

Dushkin, L., 1972, "Scheduled Caste Politics" in J.M. Mahar (ed), *The Untouchables in Contemporary India,* Tucson: University of Arizona Press.

Galanter, M., 1964, "Temple Entry and the Untouchability (Offences) Act", *Jornal of Law Institute,* Vol. 7.

__________ , 1969, "Untouchability and the Law", *Economic and Political Weekly,* Vol. IV, No. 1.

__________ , 1972, "The Abolition of Disabilities on Untouchability and the Law", in J.M. Mahar (ed), *The Untouchables in Contemporary India,* Tucson: University of Arizona.

Gough, K., 1973, "Harijan in Tanjavur" *Imperialism and Revolution in South Asia,* New York: Monthly Review Press.

Govindkutty, K., 1975, "Contours of Change: Harijan Development in Kerala", *Social Welfare,* Vol. 21.

Gusfield, J.R., 1967, "Tradition and Modernity, Misplaced Polarities", *American Journal of Sociology,* Vol. 12, No. 4.

Jat, J.N., 1979, "Modernization: Concept, Characteristics and Criticisms", *Special Article for Correspondence Course of Master Degree,* University of Rajsthan.

Kshirsagar, R.K., 1991, "Constitutional Safeguards for the Scheduled Castes" in H.C. Upadhyay (ed), *Scheduled Castes and Scheduled Tribes in India—A Socio-Economic Profile,* New Delhi: Anmol.

Lakshmana, C., 1968, "Abolition of Untouchability in Andhra Pradesh", *Social Welfare,* Vol. 15, No. 2.

Lapoint, E.C. & D.N. Lapoint, 1985, "Socio-Economic Mobility Among Village Harijans", *The Eastern Anthropologists,* Vol. 38, No. 1.

Mahapatra, L.K., 1973, "Ritual Kinship in Peasant Societies", *Man in Society,* Inaugural Volume.

Mahapatra, K., 1958, "The Changing Status of Harijans in a village of Cuttack District", *Adivasi,* No. 3.

__________ , 1972, "Status of Kuli Caste in the District of Bolangir and Sambalpur", *Adivasi,* Vol. XIV.

Mahapatra, L.K., 1973, "Ritual Kinship in Peasant Societies", *Man in Society,* Inaugural Volume.

Mohapatra, M., 1964, "Changing Status of a Scheduled Caste", *Adivasi,* No. 1.

__________, 1966, "Organisation of Caste Among the Bāuris of Bhubaneswar", *Adivasi,* Vol. VIII, No. 3.

__________, 1973, "Voting Behaviour of a Scheduled Caste", *Man in Society,* Vol. I.

Maharana, A.K., 1986, "Untouchability and Its Eradication for Social Development", *Adivasi,* Vol. XXVI, No. 2.

Makwana, M.H., 1990, "The Untouchables—An Overview", Unpublished Article.

Mandal, B.B., 1975, "Social Mobility: An Approach in Indian Context", *Journal of Social Research,* Vol. 18, No. 1.

Mehra, S., et al, 1984, "Changing Correspondence Between Caste and Occupation—A Socio-Economic Essay", *Anthropologists,* Vol. 37, No. 4.

__________, 1985, "Social Mobility—Trends in Rural Haryana in the Context of Regional Advancement", *The Indian Journal of Social Work,* Vol. 46, No. 1.

Mishra, P.K., 1983, "Persistence of Untouchability in a Multi Ethnic Area of Orissa", *Manav,* Vol. I, No. 1.

__________, 1990, "Degree of Persistence of Untouchability in the Caste and Tribal Societies of Orissa" *Adivasi,* Vol. XXX, No. 4.

Mishra, S.N., 1987, "Development of Scheduled Castes After Independence", *Adivasi,* Vol. XXVII, No. 4.

Mohanty, U.C., 1973, "Bond Friendship Among the Godaba", *Man in Society,* Inaugural Volume.

Mukherjee, A., 1985, "Removal of Untouchability", *News Magazine,* Bhubaneswar: Directorate of Harijan & Tribal Welfare, Govt. of Orissa.

Mukherjee, P., 1993, "Participatory Planning, Democratic Decentralisation and Development", in R. Hooja and B.Y. Raju (eds), *Decentralised Planning in Multilevel Framework,* New Delhi: Rawat.

Nandi, S.B., 1988, "Forms of Indian Village" in A.R. Desai (ed), *Rural Sociology,* Bombay: Popular.

Nath, U., 1993, "Decentralised and District Planning under Economic Liberalisation", in R. Hooja and B.Y. Raju (eds), *Decentralised Planning in Multilevel Framework,* New Delhi: Rawat.

Nijhawan, N.K., 1971, "Occupational Mobility and Political Development", *Economic and Political Weekly* Vol. VI, Annual Number.

Panda, R.K., 1985, "Impact of Gottery Scheme on Income and Indebtedness of Scheduled Tribes—A Case Study", *Orissa Economic Journals,* Vol. XVIII, No. 1 & 2.

__________, 1987, "Asset Debt Position Among Rural Households", *Indian Journal of Agricultural Economics,* Vol. XIII, No. 3.

Panda, R.K. et al, 1984(a), "A Micro level Study of Rural Credit in Puri District", Utkal Economic Papers, Vol. III.

__________, 1984(b), "Economic Gains from ERRP—A Case Study in Nimapara Block", *Utkal Economic Papers,* Vol. I.

Parmar, Y.A., 1978, "Occupational Change Among Mandhavanshis—A Scheduled Caste", *The Indian Journal of Social Work,* Vol. 39.

Patnaik, N., 1960(a), "Dhoba of Diminia Village of Puri District", *Data on Caste Orissa,* No. 7.

__________, 1960(b), "Bhoi or Bāuri of Puri District", *Data on Caste Orissa,* No. 7.

Ramu, G.N., 1968, "Untouchability in Rural Areas", *Indian Journal of Social Work,* No. 24 (2).

Sarkar, R.M., 1964, "The Religious Activities of Bāuris and Its Modern Trend", *Vanyajati.*

Singh, S., 1976, "Occupational Mobility Among Scheduled Castes", *Indian Journal of Social Work,* Vol. 37, No. 3.

__________, 1977, "The Scheduled Caste and New Dimensions of Social Change", *Indian Journal of Comparative Sociology,* Vol. 3.

Sinha, A., 1993, "State Level Planning System" in R. Hooja and B.Y. Raju (eds), *Decentralised Planning in Multilevel Framework,* New Delhi: Rawat.

Srinivas, M.N., 1955, "Caste, Can They Exist in India of Tomorrow", in *The Report of the Seminar in Casteism for the Removal of Untouchability,* Bombay.

Tripathy, K.C., 1968, "A Genetic Survey Among the Bhois (Bauris) of Bhubaneswar" *Adivasi,* Vol. X.

Upadyay, H.C., 1991, "Constitutional Safeguards for Scheduled Castes and Scheduled Tribes in India" in H.C. Upadhyay (ed), *Scheduled Castes and Scheduled Tribes in India—A Socio-Economic Profile,* New Delhi: Anmol.

Venkataswarulu, D., 1991, "Eradication of Untouchability—A Case for a Radical Approach" in H.C. Upadhyay (ed), *Scheduled Castes and Scheduled Tribes in India—A Socio-Economic Profile*, New Delhi: Anmol.

Zelliot, E., 1966, "Buddhism and Politics in Maharastra", *Religion and Politics in South Asia,* Princeton University Press.

C. REPORTS/DISSERTATIONS

Allen, B.C., 1901, *Census of India Report Assam,* Part-I, Shillong.

Blunt, E.A.H., 1912, *Report of the Census of United Provinces of Agra and Oudh,* Allahabad.

Chakrabarti, S., 1972, *Planning Process in India—An Appraisal and Framework,* New Delhi: Planning Commission, Govt. of India.

Devi, B., 1969, *Domb—The Neighbour of Khondhs,* Dissertation in Anthropology, Utkal University.

Giat, E.A., 1903, *Report on the Census of Bengal, Bihar and Orissa and Sikhism,* Vol. VI of Census of India, Calcutta.

G.O.I., 1935, *Govt. of India Act, 1935, Section 279, Para 26, Schedule-I,* New Delhi.

__________, 1952, *The First Five Year Plan,* Planning Commission, New Delhi.

__________, 1956, *The Second Five Year Plan,* Planning Commission, New Delhi.

__________, 1961, *The Third Five Year Plan,* Planning Commission, New Delhi.

__________, 1969, *Report of the Commissioner for Scheduled Castes and Scheduled Tribes,* Vol.II, New Delhi.

__________, 1971, *The Fourth Five Year Plan,* Planning Commission, New Delhi.

__________, 1974, *The Fifth Five Year Plan,* Planning Commission, New Delhi.

__________, 1980, *The Sixth Five Year Plan,* Planning Commission, New Delhi.

__________, 1985, *The Seventh Five Year Plan,* Planning Commission, New Delhi.

__________, 1992, *The Eighth Five Year Plan,* Planning Commission, New Delhi.

__________, 1964, *Annual Administrative report,* 1963-64 and 1965-66, Tribal and Rural Welfare Department, Bhubaneswar.

__________, 1965, *Living Conditions of Scheduled Tribes and Scheduled Castes in Orissa,* Planning and Co-ordination Department, Bhubaneswar.

__________, 1982, *Socio-Economic Conditions of SCs and STs of Orissa (Eighth Assembly),* Orissa Legislative Assembly Secretariat, Bhubaneswar.

__________, 1983, *Third report of the Committee on the Welfare of SCs and STs (Eighth Assembly),* Orissa Legislative Assembly Secretariat, Bhubaneswar.

__________, 1984(a), *Seventh Plan (1985-90) Orissa, and Annual Plan (1985-86),* Orissa, (Draft) Vol. I, Bhubaneswar.

__________, 1984(b), *Seventh Plan (1985-90),* Orissa, (Draft) Vol. III Bhubaneswar.

__________, 1985, *Third Report of the Committee on the Welfare of SCs and STs* (Eighth Assembly), Orissa Legislative Assembly Secretariat, Bhubaneswar.

__________, 1987(a), *Sixth Report of the Committee on the Welfare of SCs and STs* (Ninth Assembly), Orissa Legislative Assembly Secretariat, Bhubaneswar.

__________, 1987(b), *Seventh Report of the Committee on the Welfare of SCs and STs* (Ninth Assembly) Orissa Legislative Assembly Secretariat, Bhubaneswar.

__________, *1988, Ninth Report of the Committee on the Welfare of SCs and STs* (Ninth Assembly) Orissa Legislative Assembly Secretariat, Bhubaneswar.

__________, 1990, *Annual Plan (1989-90)* Orissa, Bhubaneswar.

__________, 1991(a), *Final Population Tables,* Census of Tables, Directorate of Census Operations, Orissa.

__________, 1991(b), *Annual Report on the working of ORV in Posts and Services,* Department of Tribal Welfare, Bhubaneswar.

__________, 1991(c), *Sixteenth Report of the Committee on Welfare of SCs and STs* (Tenth Assembly), Orissa Legislative Assembly Secretariat, Bhubaneswar.

__________, 1992, *Eighteenth Report of the Committee on the Welfare of SCs and STs (Tenth Assembly),* Orissa Legislative Assembly Secretariat, Bhubaneswar.

__________, 1993, *Twenty third Report of the Committee on the Welfare of SCs and STs,* Orissa Legislative Assembly Secretariat, Bhubaneswar.

__________, 1994-95, *The Study of Scheduled Caste Students of College in East U.P.* Research Project passed by ICSSR, New Delhi.

Goyal, S.K., 1973-74, A Survey of Research in Social Anthropology, New Delhi.

ICSSR, 1974, Report of the Commission for SCs and STs, 1978-79, Dept. of Social Welfare, Govt. of India.

Shishir Kumar, 1980, Report of the Commission for SCs and STs, 1978-79, Department of Social Welfare, Government of India.

Index